D1568256

Andrew D. White—
Educator, Historian, Diplomat

Andrew D. White in 1865, when he assumed the presidency of Cornell University

Andrew D. White—
Educator, Historian, Diplomat

BY GLENN C. ALTSCHULER

CORNELL UNIVERSITY PRESS   Ithaca and London

Cornell University Press gratefully acknowledges a grant from the
Andrew W. Mellon Foundation that aided in bringing this book to
publication.

First published 1979 by Cornell University Press.
Published in the United Kingdom by Cornell University Press Ltd.,
2–4 Brook Street, London W1Y 1AA.

International Standard Book Number 0–8014–1156–4
Library of Congress Catalog Card Number 78–58065

Printed in the United States of America

*Librarians: Library of Congress cataloging information
appears on the last page of the book.*

*To Mom and Dad
    with love and respect*

Contents

Illustrations

Abbreviations

AC	Alonzo Cornell
ADW	Andrew Dickson White
Autobiography	*Autobiography of Andrew D. White*, 2 vols., New York, 1905
CDW	Clara Dickson White
DAG	Dispatches from United States Ambassadors to Germany, 1897–1902, Record Group 59, General Records of the Department of State, National Archives
DMG	Dispatches from United States Ministers to the German States and Germany, 1879–1881, Record Group 59, General Records of the Department of State, National Archives
DMR	Dispatches from United States Ministers to Russia, 1892–1894, Record Group 59, General Records of the Department of State, National Archives
EC	Ezra Cornell
HW	Horace White
WMC	Andrew D. White Microfilm Collection, Cornell University

Preface

The doctrine of progress—the belief seemed particularly applicable to the United States in the nineteenth century.[1] The American republic, unfettered by monarchy and aristocracy and blessed with abundant resources, appeared to have been chosen by God to fulfill a glorious destiny. Even the Civil War could be taken as proof of the inevitability of progress. The triumph of the Union and the destruction of slavery, Bruce Catton has observed, convinced most Americans of their ability to triumph over any challenge.[2] As the United States industrialized in the years after the war, optimism continued to be the reigning mood. Asked where he would prefer to spend a second life, the journalist and diplomat Walter Hines Page unhesitatingly responded: in the United States in the future.[3] Foreign observers usually agreed that Americans looked confidently to the future. Johan Huizinga suggested that the grapefruit should be adopted as the symbol of the United States: always fresh, it was served in the still hopeful hours of the morning. "America was promises"—promises certain to be fulfilled.

Not surprisingly, historians have cited this optimistic rhetoric in characterizing the last half of the nineteenth century as an era of complacency. Van Wyck Brooks entitled his volume on the history of American literature between 1885 and 1915 *The Confident Years*. Several years ago, the American Heritage Publishing Company used the same title for its pictorial history of the United States between the Civil War and World War I.[4] Daniel Aaron found the same period peopled by "men of good hope,"

1. See, for example, Arthur Ekirch, *The Idea of Progress in America, 1815–1860* (New York, 1944).
2. Cited in Michael G. Kammen, "Personae as Pastime: The Sense of Self in Time Past," *New York History* 14 (October 1973): 452–53.
3. Cited in Johan Huizinga, *America: A Dutch Historian's Vision from Afar and Near*, trans. Herbert Rowen (New York, 1972), p. 311.
4. Ralph Andrist, ed., *The Confident Years* (New York, 1969). Although aware of the tension and anxiety in this period, Martin Marty has recently called it "a complacent era" for Protestant elites. See *Righteous Empire: The Protestant Experience in America* (New York, 1970), pp. 133–76, 189, 195.

energetic progressives who were more creative and confident than their "pseudo-progressive" counterparts of the twentieth century. The Victorian Age, William McLaughlin has concluded, moved from "anxiety to assurance."[5]

In the last ten years, however, a number of historians have attacked the thesis that Americans, and elites in particular, were optimistic in the last half of the nineteenth century. John Sproat's "best men" had once fancied themselves capable of persuading their fellow Americans to defer to their judgment and adopt their values. When this goal proved impossible to achieve, "they concluded that they and their age were incompatible." Always suspicious of democracy, they came to dread it; "each rumble of discontent from the people sent [them] into virtual panic." Shunted to the sidelines, these "querulous aristocrats" lived out their days in pessimistic bitterness.[6] John Tomsich's analysis of genteel culture produced similar conclusions. Lack of confidence, he argued, had produced the genteel endeavor. "The charge of smugness so often leveled against genteel culture is a fair indictment only of its public face. Its private face was fear."[7] For several recent historians of the later nineteenth century, then, "crisis" has replaced "confidence" as the proper characterization of the period. For Paul Carter, "spiritual crisis" pervaded the Gilded Age; for Robert Wiebe, there was "crisis in the communities."[8] Indeed, the confident rhetoric of the period receives little treatment in these volumes; these authors concern themselves primarily with what they see as the "dominant" emotion, anxiety.

For Andrew Dickson White, optimism and pessimism existed in dynamic tension. The rhetoric of progress was his device—in public and private—to convince himself and others of the primacy of optimism. An earnest young abolitionist from the "Burned-Over District"—that area of western New York which nourished a luxuriant growth of religious sects after it had repeatedly been swept by spiritual fires, presumably kindled

5. Daniel Aaron, *Men of Good Hope: A Story of American Progressives* (New York, 1951); William McLaughlin, *The Meaning of Henry Ward Beecher* (New York, 1970), pp. 3–7. For a recent view at variance with McLaughlin's, see Daniel Walker Howe, "American Victorianism as a Culture," *American Quarterly* 27 (December 1975): 507–532.

6. John Sproat, *The Best Men: Liberal Reformers in the Gilded Age* (New York and London, 1968), esp. pp. 273–81. For a similar analysis of some of the same men, see Robert Beisner, *Twelve against Empire: The Anti-Imperialists, 1898–1900* (New York, 1968). See also Stow Persons, *The Decline of American Gentility* (New York, 1973).

7. John Tomsich, *A Genteel Endeavor* (Stanford, Calif., 1971), pp. 23, 187.

8. Paul Carter, *The Spiritual Crisis of the Gilded Age* (De Kalb, Ill., 1971); Robert Wiebe, *The Search for Order* (New York, 1967). While Wiebe is less concerned with Genteel America than are Sproat, Tomsich, and Beisner, he describes the pervasive mood of America similarly: "A pall of thwarted opportunity, of frustrated dreams, hung over large parts of the nation" (p. 3).

by the Holy Spirit—he imbibed much of the hopeful millennialist rhetoric of the antislavery crusade. Of equal significance, his parents instilled in him a profound sense of *noblesse oblige*. Family wealth disposed him to decry materialism and to dedicate himself to public service. Like Sproat's best men, he was convinced that deference to paternalists like himself ensured a great future for America. White did not believe that the great future he envisioned necessitated fundamental alterations in American society. As Rush Welter has recently suggested, most Americans believed that their country was already uniquely free and progressive. Therefore progress could take the form of only incidental improvement rather than substantive change.[9] For White, America's future would be secure if it became a more thoroughgoing meritocracy. If everyone had fair access to an education and if government offices were reserved for talented men, no further changes would be necessary. Thus, although he was a social and political conservative, White regarded himself as a reformer. As president of Cornell University, he helped to democratize higher education and to train enlightened public servants. Education was his panacea, to be used to persuade advocates of massive social change that their efforts were unnecessary and destructive.

Events in the late nineteenth century often seemed to threaten White's belief in the inevitability of progress. It was difficult to remain sanguine in the face of major political setbacks. And industrial unrest, increased crime, and the vitality of political bosses reminded him that Americans were unwilling to accept rule by an educated elite. But again and again White found "objective" evidence that the nation's difficulties were minor when compared with breathtaking gains in civil service reform and burgeoning opportunities for education at all levels. White's faith enabled him to pursue his reform activities. Although he often asserted that progress was inevitable, White simultaneously believed that individuals could shape and hasten its arrival. Like many determinists, he always acted as though the outcome were in doubt. One may quarrel with the specifics of his reform proposals, but one must admit that White's theory of progress did not preclude action.[10]

Faith in the future became the medium White used to overcome personal tragedies and a recurrent sense that disaster might really be the fate of America. Although he was convinced that he had divined the great lines of historical evolution, his vision of the future did not seem appreciably

9. Rush Welter, *The Mind of America, 1820–1860* (New York, 1975), esp. chaps. 1 and 2.
10. In *Social Darwinism in American Thought* (Philadelphia, 1944), Richard Hofstadter points out that Social Darwinism easily accommodated programs of both activity and passivity.

nearer to realization at the end of his life than at the beginning. Immigrants flooded America's shores, mocking attempts to create an informed electorate. White observed with dismay, moreover, that all too often, university graduates leagued themselves with the forces of corruption. Often on the verge of despair, White used the doctrine of progress to sustain his frail constitution and mercurial psyche.

At times White responded to perceived threats to the United States by championing measures such as suffrage restriction and harsh punishment of criminals. He recognized that such policies were retrogressive but argued that progress could sometimes best be served by "revolutions that went backward." Placed in such a context, progress became an increasingly meaningless term. When there seemed little cause for optimism, White steadfastly proclaimed that the very thought, the very hope of progress was the most certain omen of progress. Although he proudly regarded himself as a rationalist, faith was at the bottom of White's creed.

While the doctrine of progress guarded White against disillusionment and facilitated the limited reform activity he regarded as beneficial, history inexorably grated against his protective covering. World War I, especially, exposed deep-seated fears. The Cornell president loved Germany as a second fatherland, the home of free thought and free inquiry. He was stunned, therefore, when the Kaiser's troops violated the neutrality of Belgium. Here was a graphic demonstration of the innate human penchant for evil. For years a bewildered White would refuse to comment on international relations. Yet with American participation on the side of the Allies in 1917, his optimism surfaced once again. The terrible conflagration would facilitate world progress by preserving stability, democracy, and the rule of law through international arbitration, which White had long championed. If the best men had given up on America in disgust before 1900, White continued to insist that a greater good would come out of great evil.

Don Quixote, after twice mending and testing his ancestral helmet, found that it fell apart after the first blow received in combat. Undaunted, he mended it a third time, this time with a ribbon of green—the color of hope—and without testing it pronounced it to be a trusty and perfect helmet. Progress was Andrew D. White's helmet. Without it, he could not make sense of a chaotic, changing world or establish his place in the cosmos. Perhaps sensing his vulnerability, White rarely ventured forth without his armor.

One of the compensations for the often exasperating task of researching and writing a book is the opportunity when it is finished to thank colleagues and friends. Michael Kammen suggested the topic and provided aid and encouragement when it was sorely needed; he also furnished an example of what it is to be a professional teacher and scholar. Michael Colacurcio, Walter LaFeber, and R. Laurence Moore enriched the manuscript with their vast knowledge of nineteenth-century American history. Abraham S. Eisenstadt, an earlier mentor, brought me to the field of history and helped shape my understanding of it. More, he has been a friend of incalculable value.

The staff of the Cornell University Libraries patiently listened to my every request and served my needs far beyond the call of duty. Scholarship at Cornell is immeasurably enhanced by their presence. The Department of Manuscripts and University Archives graciously permitted me to reproduce the photographs contained in this book. That department also houses the White Papers and other White material, both as manuscripts and as part of the White Microfilm Collection. Mrs. Andrew S. White graciously granted permission to quote from the White Papers. An earlier version of Chapter 12 appeared in *Church History* and is printed here with that journal's kind permission. The staff of Cornell University Press, especially Bernhard Kendler and my talented manuscript editor, Barbara Salazar, have been most professional and patient with a neurotic first-time author. Dottie Owens, my typist (and sometimes instructor in grammar), was most helpful and most delightful, and Marlene Dressner improved my often stodgy prose. Todd Bernstein and Mark Lamphier, superb Ithaca College undergraduates, helped prepare the index.

Finally, there are my friends—David and Phyllis Crew, Richard Dressner, Zillah Eisenstein, Beau Grosscup, Jim Hijiya, Eric Himmel, Hilmar Jensen, Diane and Ken Jones, and Randy Model. Some of them helped to shape the book; others were a positive detriment. But I could not have done it without them, nor would I have wanted to, for Lord Byron was right when he said: "All who joy would win must share it. Happiness was born a twin."

GLENN C. ALTSCHULER

Part I

A RADICAL OF SORTS

Making a vocational choice proved to be extremely difficult for Andrew D. White. Son of a self-made man who urged him to a life of public service, White turned his back on mere moneymaking. He ultimately chose a career as an educator, subsuming all other interests within an educational framework. Education became for him the reform of reforms, and allowed him to deemphasize or ignore other proposals for change.

White liked to think of himself as a radical, but in reality his radicalism was severely limited. Most of his fire was rhetorical. Beneath that rhetoric was the bedrock conservatism common to men of wealth. The sense of *noblesse oblige* that prompted White's involvement in public causes ensured that he would not countenance change that toppled men of his class and education from power. White was, at bottom, an elitist, and his attitude shines clearly through all of his attacks on the status quo.

The issue that won White the label of "radical" was slavery. Although he boasted that he risked the ostracism of fellow Syracusans and Yale classmates, White's abolitionism was socially acceptable in the Burned-Over District. Significantly, both parents shared his antislavery views. Abolition was, in a curious way, socially conservative. It deflected concerns from pressing problems, such as prison reform, that were much closer to home. And, as Eric Foner and David Brion Davis have observed, abolition was the means by which many hoped to preserve and extend the social order of the North. White's social conscience was seldom aroused by inequality in the North, and although his "radical" views on slavery required courage, he did not go much beyond declarations. He applauded his fellow Syracusans for the rescue of the runaway slave known as Jerry, and agreed that violence was justified in the freeing of slaves, but his advice came from the security of New Haven. When opposition to his views threatened his election as editor of Yale's literary magazine, he prudently agreed to stop printing antislavery essays.

In the late 1850s White published several abolitionist tracts, and he enthusiastically greeted the outbreak of the Civil War. By then a professor at Michigan, he organized and drilled companies, while agonizing over his own role in the conflict. Ultimately he refused to volunteer for the army, and even made preparations to hire a substitute if he were called. White rationalized his actions by insisting that he was more valuable as an organizer and propagandist than as a soldier at the front. Ever the elitist, he convinced himself that those he trained "represented" him in battle.

As a state senator in New York during Reconstruction, White had an opportunity to help transform promises into reality. He strenuously supported the 13th, 14th, and 15th Amendments to the United States Constitution. White also led a lonely struggle to integrate New York's public schools, and persisted despite charges that he was thereby promoting miscegenation. The overwhelming defeat that greeted his efforts indicates that he was more enlightened than many of his Radical Republican colleagues. Beyond education White did not envision a continuing role for either the state or the federal government in promoting black rights. He did not realize that the federal government might have to enforce the rights acknowledged in the amendments to the Constitution. Most conspicuously, the wealthy White, like many other abolitionists, feared that the confiscation and redistribution of land, which might have given blacks a chance to prosper, would set a dangerous precedent. Increased education, he convinced himself, was the only means of black self-improvement, and the only legitimate activity of government toward that end. Emancipation and education, then, were the essence of White's program. It is not surprising that White called for an early end to Reconstruction, or that his interest in blacks ebbed dramatically in the years after Appomattox.

If White's attitude toward black rights extended little beyond a call for the abolition of slavery, his criticism of Christianity was more thoroughgoing. Even before he became familiar with biblical higher criticism or Darwinian theory, he rejected the "immoral" aspects of orthodox religion. He simply could not accept his minister's statement that infants who died before they were baptized fried in eternal hellfire, or that his kindly old grandmother was doomed to damnation because she had joined the "wrong" denomination. Orthodox Christianity offended White, and he refused confirmation in the Protestant Episcopal church, despite repeated pleas from his mother.

Although his religious idol was Theodore Parker, White did not join the abolitionist minister on the fringes of Christianity; nor did he shift allegiance to the Unitarian church. Impressed with the dignified service of the Episcopal church and unwilling to antagonize his parents further, White refused to make a clean break with Episcopalianism. He continued to attack orthodoxy, but he believed that change could best be achieved by working from within the church. Thus his radical critique of orthodoxy was translated into a mild reformist stance. White was among the rarest of hyphenates, a Parkerite-Episcopalian.

The radical label is perhaps most appropriate to White's educational philosophy. In an era when coeducation and racially mixed schools were revolutionary concepts, White insisted that they would be central in the university he hoped someday to found. He believed, moreover, that the university could be nondenominational without destroying its essentially religious character. Henry Tappan, who had opposed coeducation and had been unenthusiastic about integration, was deposed at Michigan during White's tenure there, primarily because he had championed non-denominationalism. Thus White knew that the changes he advocated would not be easily instituted. The test of his radical educational philosophy would come during his presidency at Cornell.

Before he was thirty, White had settled upon the career of university educator. Once the Civil War began, he was certain that slavery would be abolished. Hence he felt he could help blacks best by improving opportunities for learning and by agitating for integrated universities. Similarly, White's religious concerns could be furthered within the university. He hoped that his institution would be a force for liberal Christianity rather than dogmatic theology; he was convinced that an alliance between truth-seeking and religion would benefit both. The university was, White believed, the vehicle of change for all areas of human activity. He therefore put his hopes for progress in the training of an army of young men and women who would ultimately rationalize society. Even if his vision of education as the primary mechanism of change was correct, it necessitated an admission that the new society lay in the distant future.

Chapter 1   *In Search of an Education and a Career*

Horace and Clara Dickson White eagerly anticipated Henry Ward Beecher's visit to Syracuse. Although pillars of St. Paul's Episcopal Church in that city, they welcomed an opportunity to hear the great Congregationalist minister. Had Horace White known that Beecher would examine the characteristics of the sons of rich men, he would have been even more eager to attend the lecture. Decades before Ragged Dick shined shoes on the streets of New York, the Horatio Alger myth was already firmly established in the American consciousness. Poverty, many argued, was the greatest incentive to achievement. But the myth provided no motivation for the inheritors of wealth, whose role in society remained undefined.[1] White, a wealthy banker and railroad man, feared that his own prosperity would hinder the development of ambition and virtue in his two sons. He was often troubled by his friends' admonitions that he was "laying up money to ruin [his] boys."[2]

Beecher's sermon relieved White, Clara Dickson reported to her son Andrew, who was then hard at work at Yale. Wealth, the Brooklyn minister had argued, was not inconsistent with intellect. Nor would wealth necessarily be squandered because it had been inherited. The son was apt to inherit the same intellectual energy possessed by the father, although he might not always use it to accumulate money.

While the coincidence of Beecher's conclusions with his own views momentarily reassured Horace White, a definitive solution to the dilemma of a wealthy father continued to elude him. How was a father to provide his son with the best things in life and at the same time build a virtuous, self-sufficient man? Horace White's own father lost money when his uninsured mills burned to the ground, forcing Horace to leave school to help meet the emergency, and eventually to become one of the leading

1. See Irvin Wyllie, *The Self-Made Man in America* (New Brunswick, N.J., 1954); John Cawelti, *Apostles of the Self-Made Man* (Chicago, 1965).
2. CDW to ADW, December 5, 1851, WMC.

businessmen in central New York.[3] White recognized that the task of building character would be more difficult for Andrew.

Adolescence can be psychically trying for sons of self-made men. When the accumulation of wealth is unnecessary, vocational choice can become a problem. If law, medicine, or the ministry proved unattractive, young men of the mid–nineteenth century, especially those imbued with a sense of *noblesse oblige*, faced a paucity of alternatives. Confusion and frustration often resulted, sometimes, as with Andrew White, supplemented by youthful rebelliousness. Hemmed in by his father's success, Andrew turned to the abolition of slavery and refusal to join the Episcopal church to express his anxiety at his failure to be "called," to God or a career. Yet early in life, and even more strikingly in his mature years, he had a firm sense of the socially acceptable boundaries of protest. If Andrew was exuberant and at times rhetorically rash in his "radicalism," he hardly constituted a threat to the society that offered him elite status.

Andrew Dickson White was born in the little town of Homer, New York, on November 7, 1832. He was a delicate child, and for a time his hold on life was tenuous. Though ever solicitous about his health, the Whites strove not to spoil the boy. They probably concealed from him his $100,000 inheritance from Grandfather Dickson, who died when Andrew was three.[4] The boy remembered a solidly middle-class upbringing that emphasized frugality. Horace White would permit neither waste nor extravagance.[5]

Horace White did not neglect the formal education of his son; he enrolled Andrew at Syracuse Academy in 1839, five years after the family had relocated in that city. Joseph Allen, teacher of English at the academy, preferred moral suasion to the use of the rawhide, and spurred by his enthusiasm, Andrew was inspired by the treasures of English and American literature. He memorized passages from Shakespeare, Milton, Bryant, Whittier, and Longfellow; even spelling did not seem boring. Allen left Syracuse while White was still at the academy, but he had made his mark on the young adolescent, who began to view himself as a nascent litteratteur.[6]

With Allen's departure from Syracuse Academy, the Whites decided to place their son in the more advanced Syracuse Classical High School. Andrew's classmates at this new school quickly recognized his literary

---

3. *Autobiography*, vol. 1, p. 5.
4. *Western Christian Advocate*, July 15, 1903; ADW to HW, April 13, 1864; WMC.
5. *Autobiography*, vol. 1, p. 5.
6. Ibid., p. 9.

White's birthplace, Homer, New York

bent and chose him to be editor of *The Bee*, one of the school's student magazines. The young editor used his column to exhort his fellow students to do their duty, a theme with which he was thoroughly familiar. "Go To It While You're Young," he told them.[7]

Although quick to acknowledge Andrew's energy and ability, the students at the high school did not hesitate to mock his self-assurance. *The Bee*'s competitor, *The Frolic Manual*, charged that Andrew had purchased a pair of shoulder braces to ensure that the world would look up to him. Andrew replied: "Why, most superhuman friend, it is our candid opinion that if you resided in some parts of our country and set forth such claims, you would wear not the shoulder brace, but the strait jacket of the lunatic."[8] In the rough-and-tumble of the public school, White never doubted that he was a leader.

In the formation of character, the church was at least as important as the school. The Whites agreed that a firm foundation of religious principles would prepare Andrew for life and eternity. Horace, a vestryman and

7. *The Bee* Extra, November 1848; *The Bee*, March 19, 1849; both in WMC.
8. *The Bee*, February 25 and March 10, 1848, WMC.

senior warden at St. Paul's, had expected his six-year-old son to read the Psalter and join in the chants. When the boy faltered, a gentle rap with the knuckles on the side of the head reminded him of his duty.[9] To Clara Dickson White, the church was second only to her own family in importance. Born a Congregationalist, she embraced Episcopalianism because she found the theology of her family crude and harsh. Above all, she felt that church membership with full participation in religious thought and activities was essential for all. Even a child less alert than Andrew could hardly have been unaffected by her unceasing call to Christian communion.[10]

Imagine the dismay of the parents, then, when the otherwise obedient child refused to join the flock. He could not accept Minister Henry Gregory's insistence that a recently deceased unbaptized child would burn in hell. Nor could he comprehend Gregory's sentence of eternal punishment for those who did not join the Episcopal church. Kindly, pious Grandma Dickson had remained a Congregationalist, and Andrew knew that a just God would not condemn her.[11]

Like many of their generation, Horace and Clara Dickson White managed to reject Gregory's strident theology and yet remain in the church, but their young son thought such a stance hypocritical. Andrew began to recite only those parts of the creed in which he believed and refused to accept confirmation. Religion was a serious and solemn matter to Andrew, and confirmation, though stripped of much of its meaning by the 1840s, implied to him complete agreement with Gregory's theology. Andrew insisted that he had not been "called," thus giving confirmation an orthodox definition that his parents had abandoned. Throughout her life, Clara entreated her son to enter the church. When Horace died and Andrew was a thirty-year-old professor of history, she reopened the subject: "When you see your last hour approaching, and indeed it would be the last excuse you would think of making at such a time—you may say you have no time to attend to religious things. Is this not the same old excuse which has been urged year after year, and are you any nearer to having time? Do make up your mind *at once* and endeavor to live a Christian life." In all other respects a devoted son, Andrew ignored her request.[12]

Andrew's refusal to be confirmed did not indicate diminished interest in

9. *Autobiography*, vol. 2, p. 515.
10. CDW to ADW, April 30, 1853; Notes on the Death of ADW's Mother, August 26, 1882, both in WMC.
11. *Autobiography*, vol. 2, p. 534.
12. CDW to ADW, March 11, 1850, and CDW to ADW, February 12, 1861, WMC.

religious affairs. He pleased his parents by continuing to attend church. Andrew's quarrel was, and would continue to be, less with religion than with dogmatic theology and sectarianism. Each denomination and its representative in the pulpit reminded him of rival sarsaparilla salesmen in Syracuse: each glorified himself as the possessor of the original recipe and denounced the others as pretenders.[13] Andrew's appetite for righteousness, however, allowed him to disregard differences in seasoning.

Though stalemated in their attempts to bring their son into full religious communion, the Whites were successful in transmitting their passionate hatred of slavery. Religious principles, in fact, seemed to dictate no other course, and Mrs. White constantly reminded her son of the connection. "I am glad to see that the fugitive slave law does not receive any quarter from you," she wrote, "as it seems at variance with every principle of love or mercy taught by our Savior."[14] Andrew needed little prodding and soon became more militant than his parents. In 1851 a number of prominent Syracusans aided the escape of a supposed runaway captured under the fugitive slave law. The "Jerry Rescue" became a *cause célèbre* in New York State. Clara hoped the affair would contribute to repeal of the law, but despite her strong feelings, she was relieved that her son was not in Syracuse at the time of the rescue. "I do most earnestly hope," he advised, "that in case an arrest is attempted those men who have means will not be sparing in aiding the troops of freedom which may be necessary to aid the fugitive. . . . [T]ill the hour of my death I shall hold to my hatred of slavery and those who make it their business to hold it up."[15]

Ironically, Andrew's abolitionism contributed to his dissatisfaction with the Episcopal church. If her ministers shared Mrs. White's belief that slavery was odious in the eyes of God, they failed to acquaint their congregations with this vision.[16] Amid the deafening silence of the Episcopal clergy, one could hear the thunder of righteous indignation from Unitarian ministers Theodore Parker and Samuel J. May. Here were men to whom the fine points of theology meant little; May had helped engineer the Jerry Rescue, while the Episcopal divines quivered in their pulpits. The church of his mother and father, it seemed to Andrew, was unable to discriminate between the transient and permanent in Christianity.

In choosing a college for their son, the Whites renewed their crusade to

13. *Autobiography*, vol. 2, p. 534.
14. CDW to ADW, April 8, 1851, WMC.
15. CDW to ADW, October 7, 1850, and October 8, October 16, and November 3, 1851; ADW to CDW, October 10, 1852, all in WMC.
16. Leonard Richards, *Gentlemen of Property and Standing* (New York, 1970). Richards finds that, of all denominations, Episcopalianism contained the fewest abolitionists.

draw him into the Episcopal church. Geneva College, later known as Hobart, was a modest denominational school not far from Syracuse to which Horace White occasionally contributed money. The school promised strict discipline and a firm tutelage in religious principles. Although Andrew would have preferred Yale University, Horace dispatched him to Geneva in the fall of 1849.

Geneva's president, Benjamin Hale, promised parents that the development of disciplined young men was one of the college's primary aims, but Andrew discovered that pandemonium reigned. Like many small denominational schools, Geneva suffered from perennial financial difficulties, and students soon realized that Hale simply could not afford to expel them. They threw shoes at professors, rolled cannon balls down the corridors at night, led horses into the chapel, and on one occasion forced the president to flee the lecture room by way of a ladder propped under a window.[17]

Andrew took his studies far too seriously to be more than momentarily amused by these antics. If the college would not enforce discipline, he would discipline himself. He arose every day at five A.M. and walked three to five miles before classes began. Andrew assured his parents that he had made no exceptions to his pledge of abstinence from coffee, tea, and tobacco. Nor had he imbibed any alcoholic beverages, except for one glass of spruce beer with pepper sauce for a sore throat. Andrew devoted so much of his energy to study that his parents constantly admonished him to spare his eyes and read less.[18]

Andrew ultimately informed his parents of the sterility of the education available at Geneva. The meager resources of the school did not permit the purchase of books or laboratory equipment. Moreover, Andrew could not complete his assignments when his roommate constantly interrupted him by shuffling his newly purchased deck of playing cards. No matter what the complaint, parental guidance never varied. He was obliged, Clara told her son, to bring his wayward roommate "into the right path," and to preserve himself from "yielding to the allurements of vice." Horace agreed, alerting his son to the opportunities offered by an unruly group of students: "You will be able to some extent at least to exercise an influence on your school mates for good." Preoccupied with the need to inculcate disinterested virtue, the Whites remained insensitive to the boredom of their son.[19]

There seemed to be no escape from Geneva, but Andrew's growing

17. *Autobiography*, vol. 1, pp. 18–20.
18. HW to ADW, March 9, 1849, and ADW to CDW, March 16, 1849, WMC.
19. CDW to ADW, November 16, 1849, and HW to ADW, March 9, 1849, WMC.

dissatisfaction reinforced his determination to leave. He resolved to attend Yale, despite its reputation as the seat of Congregationalist orthodoxy.[20] Unfortunately, Horace was not so easily persuaded. Discussion soon became a battle of wills, with Clara assuaging harsh feelings on both sides. The power of the purse was crucial, Andrew realized, and he decided that he must disobey his father before stalemate turned to defeat.

In the early autumn of 1850, with his sophomore year barely begun, Andrew left Geneva and journeyed to the village of Moravia. William Paret, a former teacher at Syracuse Academy and at that time principal of the Academy of Moravia, agreed to take in his former student. For three months Andrew vigorously applied himself to his studies and reminded his parents that the search for knowledge was the only reason for his desire to attend Yale. Mrs. White was convinced, and at last she persuaded her husband to relent.[21]

Determined to demonstrate to his parents the wisdom of his choice, Andrew set an exhausting pace for himself at Yale. On at least two occasions his health broke, forcing him to take short leaves of absence.[22] It was not merely to please his parents, however, that Andrew worked as he did. Friends and acquaintances noted an intense ambition in the young man. A family friend likened Andrew to a "large engine on a small boat— . . . it worked with so much power that it would very soon break the boat all to pieces." Intimates thought Andrew's humility a rather transparent pose. "I don't believe a word of your modest expectations for yourself in the future," a classmate told him.[23] Andrew's diligence served the dual purpose of satisfying his parents and fulfilling his ambition.

With the advantage of hindsight, Andrew White later criticized the quality of education at Yale in the middle of the nineteenth century, but there is no evidence of dissatisfaction at the time. The Yale faculty boasted many of the foremost scholars in the nation, and Andrew seemed content to sit at Professor James Hadley's feet, even if his course consisted merely of memorizing dates in Pitz's *Ancient History*. Even rote memorization was palatable when Theodore Dwight Woolsey, the president of Yale and a renowned expert on international law, led the class.

Ever competitive, White won the De Forest Prize for the best original oration in 1853. The subject of the oration, "The Diplomatic History of Modern Times," indicated that President Theodore Dwight Woolsey's

20. ADW to the Reverend Benjamin Bacon, May 22, 1913, WMC.

21. *Autobiography*, vol. 1, p. 23.

22. ADW to Burt Wilder, March 17, 1903, WMC.

23. CDW to ADW, March 11, 1852; Theodore Bacon to ADW, October 27, 1855, both in WMC.

talks on international law had opened up a new field of interest for him. Europeans, White declared, were motivated by such negative concerns as the dread of a change in leadership and fear of the spread of anarchy. American diplomats, by contrast, were motivated by far more noble ideals. The desire for national greatness forced America to expand into Louisiana and Florida. American expansion was justified because it led inevitably to the expansion of republican principles. Proud—even arrogant—the De Forest oration accurately reflected the chauvinistic tenor of the time.[24]

If his views on diplomacy and American mission won the applause of faculty and students, Andrew's attitude toward slavery earned disapproval. White welcomed Professor James Hadley's argument, as applied to the Fugitive Slave Law, that one had a right to refuse to obey an unjust law. He applauded the antislavery stance of President Woolsey and the Reverend Leonard Bacon. But these men were exceptions in a faculty favoring appeasement. White had found support for his abolitionism at home; at New Haven the possibility of ostracism was very real.

Andrew's antislavery views became the major issue in his campaign for the editorship of the *Yale Literary Magazine* at the end of his junior year. He barely won the election. In fact, the victory was probably due to support from two friends opposed to abolition: Andrew's roommate, Thomas Frederick Davies, later Episcopal bishop of Michigan, and Randall Gibson, who would serve as a general in the Confederate Army and as a senator from Louisiana. Throughout his life Andrew White had the peculiar ability to maintain cordial relations with individuals of opinions vastly different from his own. On this occasion, as on others, his ability to do so furthered his ambitions.

The newly elected editor did not enlist the *Yale Literary Magazine* in the antislavery cause because of the opposition of the rest of the editorial board. Andrew accepted the verdict of his peers and confined himself to literary matters.[25]

Commencement seemed to arrive all too quickly for the class of 1853.[26] For Andrew White the college experience had been beneficial. Honors and recognition had come rather easily. In an era when the proportion of college students in the white population was less than 1 in 2,012,[27] he had

---

24. White, "The Diplomatic History of Modern Times," 1853, WMC.

25. *Autobiography*, vol. 1, p. 68.

26. This class was generally regarded as one of Yale's finest. In addition to White, Davies, and Gibson, it boasted writer Edmund Stedman, newspaper columnist George W. Smalley, and U.S. Supreme Court Justice George Shiras.

27. Morris Bishop, *A History of Cornell* (Ithaca, 1962), p. 38.

graduated with distinction from one of the nation's very best institutions. As flattering as these achievements might be, however, they did not solve the problem of vocation. Andrew still had not been "called" to a profession. He knew only that Yale had whetted his appetite for learning and therefore concluded that more education would be a fruitful prelude to a decision.

Even before graduation, Andrew received an excellent opportunity to further his education. Connecticut Governor Thomas Seymour was appointed minister to Russia in 1853 and asked Daniel Coit Gilman, White's Yale classmate, to accompany him as an unpaid attaché at the embassy. The paid staff at American embassies was pitifully inadequate; in this way Seymour would receive clerical help while providing Gilman with a place to stay in Russia as well as letters of introduction to the best people in Europe. At Gilman's urging, Seymour extended the same invitation to White, who promptly accepted.[28]

As the venerable home of knowledge and culture, Europe was a promising arena for a young man in search of an education and a career. Andrew would not be confined to one university, nor would his arrangement with Seymour restrict him to Russia. Moreover, as the De Forest oration indicates, young White had specialized in diplomatic relations. Now the opportunity had arrived to test his learning by personal observation. George W. Smalley noted his friend's pride in his new "career":

I cannot doubt that you already arrogate to yourself that distinguished title [diplomatist] and are beginning to fancy yourself arbitrator between Russia and Turkey with dim visions of a Principality bestowed in consideration of your services by the grateful and obliged Nicholas Tsar of all the Russians. . . . I trust you will have the kindness to communicate in your reply the exact title by which you are to be addressed, that I may not be wanting in proper respect to your public character.[29]

Seymour and his two young attachés journeyed first to London and then to Paris. Impressed by France, White informed Seymour that he had decided to remain there for a time. The opportunity to travel and learn the French language clearly outweighed the prospect of a bleak winter in Russia. Andrew argued that familiarity with French, the language spoken by Russian officials, would prove to be of great value to the minister when he joined him in the Russian capital. Seymour readily agreed, and when his party departed, White was on his own in the City of Lights.[30]

28. ADW to CDW, April 5, 1855, WMC.
29. Smalley to ADW, December 20, 1853, WMC.
30. ADW to CDW, March 30, 1854, WMC.

In France, as in England, White oscillated between a genuine respect for the accomplishments of aristocracy and a stubborn defense of the republican American way. He was awed by the grandeur of a French cathedral: "I regret to give mere cold outlines of things which impress me so deeply." At the same time, however, the voice of the American was heard: "In the midst of such pomp one appreciates simplicity." White had come to France expecting to despise Emperor Louis Napoleon. Yet constant improvements in the streets, buildings, and sewers of Paris, all attributable to the benevolent Louis, challenged his preconception. Napoleon's very name nevertheless was a reminder that he was no democrat. Wavering between paternalism and republicanism, White soon settled on a convenient explanation. France, at least at present, was not fit to be a republic. Until its people were educated and trained to rule themselves, the present system of government was the best possible. The tensions between aristocratic grandeur and republican simplicity, between efficiency and democracy, were common to the American mind, especially when it confronted European tradition and autocracy. White's wealth in combination with his republican training made him particularly susceptible to such contradictory tendencies, and his sojourn in the Old World marked the beginning of a lifelong effort to reconcile them.[31]

White had not neglected his study of French while traveling, and by November 1854 he felt confident that he could serve Governor Seymour as an interpreter. In that month, after a long and wearying journey, he arrived at St. Petersburg, "one of the most beautiful cities the world has ever seen." Delighted to see his young friend once again, Seymour took pains to show him the city and people. "Governor Seymour is like a brother to me," White told his own brother, with much reason to be grateful to the minister.[32]

Outside the walls of the embassy there were many opportunities for a young man in search of an education. The capital, dotted with monuments, squares, and palaces, was immense. There was little to surpass the awesome dignity of the court, and White awaited presentation to the tsar with some consternation—and probably more than a little bit of pride: "It is a terrible ordeal especially when one goes through it in black clothes. But no matter. I suppose that is my destiny."[33]

The rationalization of efficiency with which White partly excused the government of Napoleon clearly did not apply to Russia. In fact, White

31. ADW to CDW, February 9, 1854; June 29, 1854; August 3, 1854, all in WMC.

32. *Autobiography*, vol. 1, p. 71; ADW to HKW, November 15, 1854, WMC.

33. ADW to Daniel Coit Gilman, November 19, 1854; ADW to CDW, November 16, 1854; Diary, May 28–June 9, 1855, all in WMC.

found virtually nothing praiseworthy in the Russian system. Responsibility for every activity in St. Petersburg rested on woefully incapable government officials. Russian paternalism had rendered the people so incapable of action that a man stricken with apoplexy lay in the street until notice was given at the nearest police station. If the Russian system immobilized the people, it also encouraged mass corruption. White disdainfully noted the number of people one had to bribe in order to obtain a passport. His condemnation of Russia was unqualified: "There is no government so thoroughly barbarous. There is no parallel example in all history of a young nation with a polite society so degraded, a people so crushed, an official system so unscrupulous, unless it will be found in the early Asiatic monarchies."[34]

That the government was then straining itself to meet the emergency of the Crimean War in no way mollified White's indictment. Rather, the war brought into bold relief the worst features of the Russian system. Censors exercised total discretion in circulating news from the Crimea. In fact, because he feared the censor and did not want to compromise the position of Minister Seymour, White's letters did not reveal his sympathy for the Allies. Once out of the country, however, he sought to reverse "the absurd sympathy for Russia in the present war" and consented to his parents' request to have his letters, which described the great suffering caused by the war, published in the Syracuse and Buffalo press. Defeat would not enlighten government in Russia, but White hoped it would shake officialdom out of its complacency and the peasantry out of its stoic passivity. He gave thanks for the kind treatment he had received in St. Petersburg, but prayed for the defeat of "the government the most utterly detestable and the civilization the worst ever imagined."[35]

Without waiting for the conclusion of the Crimean War, White—eager to acquaint himself with German education—left Russia in the summer of 1855. By the middle of the nineteenth century, the German university system was reputedly the best in the world. Close contact between professor and student, as well as the heady atmosphere of *Lernfreiheit* and *Lehrfreiheit*, exhilarated the large influx of American students used to rote memorization even in the best American colleges. University professors had honored places in German society. Making the connection between education and public service explicit, Gustav Droysen taught that the

34. ADW to CDW, February 8/January 26, 1855; Diary, June 14, 1855; ADW to Gilman, November 5, 1855, all in WMC.
35. ADW to CDW, June 19 and November 4, 1855, WMC.

historian's job was to change public opinion, to "set it right."[36] White chose to attend the University of Berlin because of its particularly strong emphasis on history. The Berlin faculty included August Böckh in ancient history, Leopold von Ranke in the Middle Ages, and Friedrich von Raumer in modern history. The scholarly life was most congenial to White. He described his working day to Gilman: "I work pretty well and dig at the grammar, study over ancient history with two lexicons, a great collection of historical tables, an ancient atlas, beside text and reference books sprawled out around me looking scholarly to a degree hitherto unknown in my personal history."[37]

Only Ranke disappointed the young scholar. White did not doubt that the substance of the "great gun's" lectures was good, but pronounced the manner of delivery "comically atrocious." Ranke spent most of the hour "sprawled out in his chair looking upwards and talking to himself, now quickly, now slowly, now loud, now soft, grinning and scowling and not seeming to be aware of the presence of anybody."[38] Genius, however, could always be excused. Even when poorly executed, the lecture system pioneered in Germany was far superior to the American system, which forced professors to spend most of their time listening to students regurgitate textbook lessons. In America, he wrote his mother, "the course of studies is incomplete—in England it is absurd . . . the school is more splendid in England and the scholarship more splendid in Germany."[39]

In his cluttered room in Berlin, filled with some of the seven hundred books accumulated during two years in Europe, Andrew White announced his intention of becoming a professional scholar and teacher. Historical studies were his indispensable apprenticeship: "Rise or fall it will be their studies and their fruits and if I ever write anything worth people's reading it will be based on them and if I ever teach . . . it will be by means of these researches which I am now beginning." After two years abroad, the traveler in search of a career was almost ready to return home.[40]

White spent several more months in Europe, traveling through France, Switzerland, and Italy, but his thoughts focused inevitably on his projected career. He sketched his hopes for the future to Gilman and college

36. Jurgen Herbst, *The German Historical School in American Scholarship* (Ithaca, 1965), pp. 113, 164.
37. ADW to Gilman, November 5, 1855, WMC.
38. Diary, October 30, 1855, WMC.
39. ADW to CDW, November 4, 1855, WMC.
40. ADW to CDW, July 3, 185?; July 5, 1855; March 1, 1855, all in WMC.

roommate Fred Davies: "There is one thing which I covet greatly, a residence in America in which to study, to meet men who have studied and to teach." Would a professorship in a small college satisfy this want? White was too ambitious, too proud of the learning he had acquired to accept such obscurity. He answered his own question with a contemptuous "*anybody* can have that." Determined to start at the top, White hoped to become the first professor of history at Yale and asked his friends for their support in establishing a chair for him similar to the one in Greek language and literature endowed for Theodore Dwight Woolsey.

White recognized that an immediate opening at Yale, especially for a young man without any scholarly reputation, was unlikely. He was prepared to wait, he declared, on a "snug farm" where he could study and write. After a few years—White thought that it might be five—he would publish a major work that would force the Yale faculty to welcome his triumphant return. The course, then, was irrevocably charted; scholarly fame would come sooner or later. Even if he were rejected at Yale, he would "live to take high places."[41]

Gilman and Davies heartily approved of their friend's plan and promised to do what little they could to help, but Horace White was mortified by his son's projected career as scholar-farmer. The elder White thought Andrew's course self-indulgent and a waste of his knowledge. Heartily approving of his son's condemnation of slavery, Horace thought the time ripe for him to enter politics and join the struggle for change: "It is a glorious time now for an educated man to take a stand in politics—take the stump—address Frémont clubs."[42]

Horace White's strictures struck a responsive chord. Farming was a ludicrous alternative that Andrew had probably proposed because it did not smack of crass materialism; he quickly abandoned the scheme. Letter after letter assured his parents that he was eager to begin useful work: "It pained me greatly during the past year to be doing nothing or seeming to do nothing." He cautioned his parents not to expect too much from him—at least not immediately. Andrew knew that success was uncertain in his chosen field, yet Horace and Clara were proud that he embraced the career of the scholar-teacher because "there is at least great chance to do some good and combat some error."[43]

There was one factor that infused the search for a career with a bit more urgency. Andrew planned to marry Mary Outwater, daughter of a promi-

41. ADW to Gilman, November 5 and December 5, 1855; Thomas Frederick Davies to ADW, December 8, 1855, all in WMC.
42. HW to ADW, September 18, 1856, WMC.
43. ADW to CDW, June 4, 1856, and July 23, 1857, WMC.

nent Syracuse merchant, whom he had known all his life. He thought of her often while abroad, and despite his father's opinion that he should wait four or five years until he was more established, White decided to marry shortly after his return to America. "My happiness is wholly in your hands," Mary wrote him. "You must decide the future for us both."[44] As he looked across the ocean, White realized that his days as a carefree and sometimes solitary bachelor were over. Convinced of his maturity, determined to plan his life soberly, he thought that he had reconciled himself to a life of ordinary achievement. Yet the dreams persisted; White's ambition could not be suppressed. White asked his mother to inform his brother that he still "remain[ed] five feet six or six feet five (I forgot which), as at my departure."[45] With the education he had received and his aspirations for the future, the diminutive young scholar must have thought it quite possible to be counted among the giants.

44. Mary Outwater to ADW, n.d., WMC.
45. ADW to CDW, July 19, 1855, WMC.

Chapter 2   *The Abolitionist Professor*

Hoping to win a position at Yale, White was a frequent visitor in New Haven in 1856. Any graduate who stayed out of trouble for three years and paid a fee was entitled to a master's degree; White proudly accepted one from Yale.[1] He used the occasion to cement contacts at his alma mater. Gilman reported to his friend that an appointment in the near future was likely. White's name was mentioned prominently in connection with a professorship that encompassed the history and criticism of architecture and fine arts. Although his dream was to be Yale's first professor of history, he would gladly have accepted any position in New Haven.[2]

Within months, however, White's hopes for success were shattered. The Yale Corporation, composed almost entirely of orthodox Congregationalists, thought his religious convictions not sufficiently settled. They were willing to accept an Episcopalian but knew that he had refused to endorse the Thirty-nine Articles. The suspicion persisted that White was a Parkerite, which made him akin to an infidel in the eyes of New Haven's graybeards. The board refused to make him a member of the Yale faculty.[3]

The problem of vocation, which had been so close to a solution, thus surfaced again. Soon, however, a resilient determination and the hand of fate combined to return him to his projected course. In his autobiography, White claimed that his career was determined by a remark made by President Francis Wayland of Brown University at the Yale commencement of 1856. Wayland urged graduates to settle in the West and make it a beneficial force in the nation's affairs. With these words as inspiration, White moved to secure a position at the University of Michigan.

In fact, White's familiarity with that university predated his contact with Wayland. Henry Frieze, one of his traveling companions in Europe and professor of Latin at the University of Michigan, had enthusiastically

---

1. Mark Beach, "Andrew D. White as Ex-President: The Plight of a Retired Reformer," *American Quarterly* 17 (Summer 1965): 244.

2. Daniel Coit Gilman to ADW, March 26 and June 20, 1856, WMC.

3. ADW to CDW, July 23, 1857; Thomas Frederick Davies to ADW, September 8, 1863, both in WMC.

described the western university, then under the leadership of President Henry P. Tappan. With the Yale portals closed to him, White contacted Frieze, who recommended him to Tappan. The position to be filled was the professorship of history and rhetoric. Turned down by his alma mater, White had found the type of position he desired.[4]

Apprenticeship under Tappan in the "egalitarian" West did not temper White's elitist assumptions about education. Enthusiastic about the idea of founding a university organized on the German model, he agreed with Michigan's president that higher learning should not emphasize "practical skills." Ezra Cornell would help convince him otherwise, but for the time being White hoped that the university would promote learning for its own sake. Although he advocated the inclusion of women and blacks, White did not seem to care very much that his "ideal" university would attract only the middle and upper classes.

Educated in Germany, Henry Tappan was one of the leading educational theorists in the country. His book, *University Education*, was an indispensable manual for university reformers, and White found much of its contents similar to his own thoughts on the subject. A true university, Tappan argued, like the German institution, provided libraries, facilities, and professors in all branches of human learning. A true university, "where the bauble of an academic diploma is forgotten," concerned itself only with lofty scholarship; it did not accommodate itself to the needs or wishes of the multitude by teaching "practical skills." Years after his removal as president, Tappan's response to a proposed school of dentistry at Michigan revealed his concept of a university education: "They might as well have a department for making wooden legs and glass eyes; for if dentistry is connected to some extent with anatomy and physiology so also is the art of supplying defunct limbs and eyes. The bringing together of a multitude, the use of epithets, and conferring of degrees, the making of scientific show and noise enters still largely in the American idea of a University." A Platonic philosopher by profession, Tappan defined the ideal university as a center of study and scholarship.[5]

If White agreed with Tappan's definition of a university, he embraced even more enthusiastically the president's insistence that the university should renounce all sectarian partialities while acknowledging Christi-

4. *Autobiography*, vol. 1, p. 257; Diary, December 2, 1855; Henry Frieze to ADW, August 10, 1857; ADW to Henry P. Tappan, September 11, 1857; ADW to Gilman, September 12, 1857, all in WMC.

5. Henry P. Tappan, *University Education* (New York, 1851), pp. 5–24, 43, 50, 64, 66, 68; Henry Frieze, *A Memorial Discourse on the Life and Services of Henry Philip Tappan* (Ann Arbor, 1882); Tappan to Edward Payson Evans, December 18, 1880, Evans MSS, Cornell University.

Henry Tappan, president of the University of Michigan

anity to be the only true religion and the Bible of divine inspiration. Scripture reading and prayer should constitute a daily public service conducted by professors in the presence of students. Yet freedom of conscience must prevail. Consequently, no religious profession or statement of creed would be required for admission. Tappan also opposed the creation of a faculty of theology. One faculty could not possibly represent all theological views and interests equally. The university could not be the home of unfettered study and scholarship unless and until it was emancipated from sectarian control.[6]

The student's freedom of choice extended to his course of study. Tappan tempered his belief that American students deserved a greater voice in their curricular choices by warning that the college student was the youthful product of the woefully inadequate American elementary school, not the mature graduate of a German gymnasium. Consequently, he urged that once the student chose the field of study he desired, he should, with one or two exceptions, be required to take precisely those classes taken by every other student who elected that discipline. Thus a student could pursue his own interests while the faculty ensured his competence in his chosen field.[7]

Tappan's lucid exposition of the true university had won him the presidency of the University of Michigan, in which the president shared responsibility for university policy with the Board of Regents and the Michigan state legislature. Recognizing that the success of his experiment depended on the goodwill of the legislature, and therefore of the people, Tappan brought the university to them by lecturing around the state twice a week. He called on the faculty to do the same. Thus White, who accepted many speaking engagements, explained to Gilman: "We have to bring the institution in contact with the *people* and make it influence the state."[8] Ironically, the preservation of an institution that scoffed at practical skills depended on mass support. In any event, this policy proved successful—at least for a time. In a few years, White predicted, the University of Michigan would be counted in the front rank of American universities.[9]

White's exuberance and modern teaching methods soon earned him a reputation as one of the most popular and respected instructors at Michigan. While in Europe he had discovered the virtues of the lecture system. His lectures, Charles Kendall Adams (then a student, later White's re-

6. Tappan, *University Education*, pp. 94–98.
7. Ibid., p. 74; *Autobiography*, vol. 1, p. 276.
8. ADW to Gilman, February 27, 1859, WMC.
9. ADW to CDW, January 10, 1858, WMC.

placement at Michigan and as president of Cornell) recalled, combined instruction and inspiration, sending "a sort of historical glow through all the veins and arteries of the University." Another student remembered that White "could teach history as though the great men he told about were his neighbors and the events that rocked the world had happened in his sight." To help his students follow the lectures, White distributed a syllabus— one of the first in the country in connection with historical lectures. Finally, his emphasis on modern European history, in an era when most formal teaching ended with the fall of Rome, was revolutionary. White's methods quickly attracted many of the university's best students, some of whom took his courses in addition to their regular load.[10]

Through his emphasis on great men and great deeds in history, White hoped to teach his students to honor work, not words. Since the university was the training ground for the future leaders of the nation, he constantly focused upon lessons of history that would "influence for good young men who are hereafter to be strong in the nation." Intent on supplying a principled elite to guide America in the coming decades, White scorned the historian's pose of moral neutrality.[11]

The training of students for enlightened public service necessitated activities outside the classroom, and White found time for them despite the added concerns of an enlarged family.[12] He believed that an aesthetic atmosphere was conducive to study and scholarship. Disturbed by the flat, almost barren Ann Arbor campus, he contributed his own labor and money to plant trees and bushes to adorn it.[13] Aware that atmosphere alone might not be enough to deter students from a wayward path, White assembled students at his house once a fortnight for readings from the works of eminent historians and travelers. White invited attractive young women from the best families of the city to these meetings, with the dual hope of providing an uplifting education for females and of ensuring that the university's undergraduates interacted with the most "wholesome"

10. Ruth Bordin, *Andrew Dickson White: Teacher of History* (Ann Arbor, 1958); Charles Perry, *Henry Philip Tappan: Philosopher and University President* (Ann Arbor, 1933), p. 246; ADW to CDW, November 19, 1857, WMC; *Autobiography*, vol. 1, p. 262.

11. ADW to Gilman, October 17, 1859, and ADW to the Reverend Hickock, October 27, 1862, WMC.

12. Mary gave birth to a daughter and a son during the years at Ann Arbor. On the birth of daughter Clara in 1858, the proud father wrote to Gilman: "I care nothing for you. I care nothing for Yale College. I care nothing for the prospects of the colored race nor for the University of Michigan. . . . For you must know my old friend that on Sunday evening I was presented with a daughter who weighs nine pounds (9 lb)!" (ADW to Gilman, July 13, 1858, WMC).

13. ADW to C. K. Adams, November 2, 1876, WMC; *Autobiography*, vol. 1, pp. 282–83; Perry, *Henry Philip Tappan*, p. 235.

portion of Ann Arbor's female population. White also helped his students establish a fraternity. A member of Sigma Phi while at Geneva, he thought such an organization could bolster student self-discipline. In the classroom and outside of it, White hoped to create a polite, genteel, aesthetic atmosphere conducive to the emergence of enlightened leaders.[14]

Despite White's activities, however, bitter opposition to Tappan's ideal university was apparent. Many in Ann Arbor had long resented the president's imperial personality and elitist philosophy. His eastern accent and his insistence on the title chancellor grated against the egalitarian self-image of the westerners. Tappan's opponents merely murmured when he drank wine in a state noted for temperance agitation; but when a University of Michigan student died in a drinking incident, the "Kanzler" became a convenient symbol of lax morality. Opponents began openly to criticize Tappan's nondenominationalism as irreligion, charging that he was not fit to lead the state university.[15]

Such opposition had existed throughout Tappan's tenure without greatly hindering his reform efforts. About the time of White's arrival in Ann Arbor, however, state legislators began to review more closely the budget requests of this unpopular educator. Politicians, eager to trim expenses and curry favor with the churches and temperance groups, found Tappan an easy target. His educational philosophy now seemed to smack of Prussian autocracy; Tappan's hiring of a professor without the permission of the legislature made him a would-be dictator. Prominent legislators attacked Tappan in the public press and stalled the funding of new programs.

Tappan's response confirmed the worst suspicions of his critics while alienating many of his supporters in the university: he appealed to the legislature to grant autonomy to the university. White thought Tappan's frontal assault ill advised, and he opposed legislation designed to emasculate the Board of Regents. The University Senate agreed, appointing White to a committee of three to recommend an adjustment between the president and the now openly hostile regents. On February 12, 1861, the committee recommended and the senate approved the request that the board provide senate representation on its executive and library committees. At its March meeting the regents complied; the crisis seemed to have passed.[16]

The regents' concession, however, proved to be a smokescreen for more

14. *Autobiography*, vol. 1, p. 260; Speech at the Banquet of the Sigma Phi Fraternity, June 18, 1909, and ADW to Arthur Lyon Cross, July 30, 1906, WMC.
15. Perry, *Henry Philip Tappan*, pp. 274–82.
16. Ibid., pp. 318–19.

determined efforts to oust the president. Tappan, now head of the board's executive committee, charged that the regents referred all executive functions to special committees. Despite the advice of those sympathetic to him, Tappan decided to engage actively in Republican party politics, hoping to influence the composition of the next board. Defeated in this effort, he fought on virtually alone, and few were surprised when the regents secretly met in 1863 and removed him as president of the university.[17]

The dream of a genuine university as defined by Tappan long remained Andrew White's guiding star.[18] Even before Tappan was removed, White attempted to help create his own university. Horace White died in the fall of 1860, leaving his son between $200,000 and $300,000. The young professor almost immediately declared his intention to use the money to "aid in laying goodly foundations for education" and to build the greatest library the country had ever seen.[19]

For almost two years he worked on a plan for a university, relying on his own experiences as student and teacher while at the same time borrowing heavily from the Tappan model. Aware of the difficulty of persuading a state legislature to support a university, White concluded that the ideal university should be privately endowed. Unfortunately, White's inheritance was not sufficient to build, staff, and stock the institution he envisioned. In the fall of 1862, therefore, White wrote a long letter to Gerrit Smith, well-known abolitionist and philanthropist, asking the New Yorker to join him in this new undertaking.

White's plan, sketched out in rich detail, must have appealed to the reform-minded Smith. The new university would be open to all, regardless of sex or color. Such a policy was, of course, revolutionary. Among other principles upon which the school would be founded, the reversal of the current trend of mercantile morality was primary. At first glance, an appeal to a businessman to endow an institution to counter materialism appears anomalous. Yet Smith, like Horace White, saw himself as a custodian of wealth, who could transcend mere moneymaking. Wealth's greatest virtue was that it facilitated the practice of disinterested benevolence. White knew that Smith would agree that only an institution that taught truth for its own sake could counteract the vulgar tendencies in the country.

In order to implement the ideology of the liberal university, White

17. Ibid., pp. 320–24; Thomas M. Cooley to ADW, July 12, 1863, WMC.
18. For Tappan's later comments on the university, see Tappan to Evans, November 28, 1870, and December 18, 1880, Evans MSS, Cornell University.
19. ADW to Charles Tiffany, November 12, 1860, WMC.

emphasized freedom of inquiry in all areas. This meant, of course, that the university would be nonsectarian. White's experience had taught him that sectarian control invariably demanded that the faculty stretch or cut science to fit the tenets of "revealed religion." The ideal center of education, which sought to inculcate a passion for the search for truth and to form character activated by the best humanitarian principles of Christianity, would therefore be "permeated with the spirit of Christ—yet unshackled." [20]

Though impressed by White's plan to build a "worthy" American university, Gerrit Smith pleaded ill health and cited recent financial setbacks that precluded any further philanthropic endeavors.[21] Disappointed but not disillusioned, White filed the four drafts of his letter to Smith among his papers, confident that his plan would someday bear fruit.

Although higher education was always vitally important to White, the Civil War temporarily replaced it as his central concern, probably mitigating the disappointment of Gerrit Smith's cordial refusal. White's abolitionism bordered on condescension and paternalism. He, and a few others, knew what was right and would try to set their country straight. Concern for justice, in fact, often seemed more important than concern for blacks, few of whom White had ever seen except as servants. Abolition thus was an abstraction for White, and the Civil War was an acid test of his ability to inspire and lead men to fight for a principle. Blacks, like most people, needed others to help them; duty necessitated White's involvement in the war of emancipation.

Soon after his arrival at Michigan, the students recognized the radical credentials of their professor, whose "brilliant lectures on modern history swept his students into bold opinions and resolute action."[22] White refused to separate the roles of abolitionist and teacher. No graduate of an American university, he insisted, ought to receive his diploma unless he understood that slavery had debauched all the republics of the ancient world by weakening the state in war and corrupting it in peace. Slavery broke the physical strength of all citizens by leaving them idle; it broke their moral strength by making them gods over their fellows. All people, White believed, controlled their own destinies and at the same time affected the destinies of others. Hence every individual was responsible for the existence of this monstrous evil; everyone had a duty to battle for its extinction. Students flocked to hear the professor remind them of their duty. While lecturing on Louis XIV of France, White digressed: "But my

20. ADW to Gerrit Smith, September 1, 1862, WMC.
21. Smith to ADW, September 3, 1862, WMC.
22. Perry, *Henry Philip Tappan*, p. 269.

friends we are kings—we have kingdoms to build, or ruin. Each of us is *absolute* monarch over one soul and heart and mind and destiny; each of us is a *limited* monarch over hosts of souls and hearts and minds about us. . . . The difference between Louis' realm and each of our realms is to the Infinite eye—infinitely small."[23] Ironically, White condemned slavery because it bred paternalism, rhapsodized about individual autonomy, and reminded students of their duty as educated men to lead the crusade against the peculiar institution.

White's utterances on slavery provoked complaints by angry Ann Arbor residents. Wendell Phillips, Frederick Douglass, and other abolitionist "incendiaries" lectured at the university at White's request, further polarizing an already divided community. On several occasions, enraged citizens requested that the Board of Regents remove him because of his abolitionist views. Unruffled by the tempest growing around him, White continued his lectures as before.[24]

With the firing on Fort Sumter, of course, the criticism of Professor White faded into distant memory while frantic preparations for the war effort began. As expected, White took a leading role in readying his students for the struggle. He joined with Tappan in advising the class of 1861 not to enlist until after graduation, but he immediately organized and drilled scores of eager students. Day after day the exuberant undergraduates paraded outside the door of White's home, singing as they marched. Each day Professor White appeared at his window with a few words of exhortation: "This is a conflict between twenty-two million and ten million, between freedom and slavery, between God and the devil! In such a contest you cannot fail."[25]

White expected university students to lead the army as its officers and thus directed his energies to preparing the students while finding volunteers to serve under them. Ignoring signs of failing health, White supervised minute aspects of the formation of Michigan's fighting units. He hired agents to buy flannels in Detroit. He wrote handbills and helped secure speakers and drillmasters. Constantly prodding his students, he stove to stir them to greater achievements.[26]

As White lectured about individual duty, his thoughts turned to his own responsibility. Did not conscience and logic require that he lead a company of volunteers into battle? White wrestled with the problem and

23. "Glimpses of Universal History," 1859, and "Louis XIV," WMC.
24. B. M. Cutcheon to W. H. Beadle, October 21, 1902, and ADW to Moses Coit Tyler, August 17, 1872, WMC.
25. Perry, *Henry Philip Tappan*, p. 272; Cutcheon to Beadle, October 21, 1902, WMC.
26. ADW to Gilman, April 23, 1861, WMC.

emerged with a rationalization. As teacher, organizer, exhorter, he served an invaluable function in Ann Arbor. "You will say I ought to go myself to the war," he told Gilman, "perhaps I may, but whether I do or not—there will always so long as this war lasts—be one strong man in each company from this town to represent me." [27]

Satisfied that his students represented him in the army, White soon found himself in need of more concrete representation. By the late summer of 1862, the Union's need for troops outstripped the number of volunteers. White feared that he would be drafted. Greatly agitated, he consulted Michigan's Professor Thomas M. Cooley, a leading expert on the United States Constitution and later chief justice of the state supreme court. Cooley did not know whether his colleague would be subject to the draft. "If you chance to be drafted," he reassured him, "I will see that a substitute is provided as you request." Still anxious, White wrote again several days later and received the same response. White convinced himself that the Union would benefit most if he continued and redoubled his efforts while sending an otherwise idle citizen to the front. [28]

Rationalization, however elaborate, did not completely erase the guilt of a man so insistent on individual responsibility. Absolute monarch over his own destiny, he had chosen limited participation in the most noble struggle of his era. White's autobiographical analysis of his role in the war indicates that he viewed his actions with something less than pride. As preparations for war began in earnest, he recalled, "my friends all about me were volunteering, and I also volunteered, but was rejected with scorn." The examining physician told the would-be soldier that he did not have the constitution to carry a musket: "Your work must be of a different sort." With no mention of doubts or substitutes, White concluded this chapter of his reminiscences by describing the contributions of his soldier-students. [29]

White sought a larger audience for his "work" than the student body at the University of Michigan. Intent on establishing a national reputation as a scholar while making converts for abolitionism and the Union cause, he began to publish soon after his return from Europe. White's first publication—in the August 1857 issue of *The New Englander*—was a lengthy review of F. C. Schlosser's *Weltgeschichte für das Deutsche Volk* and Cesar Cantu's *Histoire universelle*. The essay, a reworking of one of White's

27. Ibid.
28. Cooley to ADW, August 12 and August 18, 1862, WMC.
29. *Autobiography*, vol. 1, p. 89; Allen Davis, *Jane Addams: American Heroine* (New York, 1973). Davis notes the didactic purposes of autobiographies in the nineteenth century. White clearly intended his autobiography as inspiration for the young. Thus, unpleasant or unflattering experiences served no useful purpose in the narrative.

lectures at Michigan, defended the relevance of history. The historian must counteract the baneful influence of such "sham historians" as George Fitzhugh, who "proved" that the republic would perish if the nation as a whole did not embrace slavery.[30] As he reviewed the works of Schlosser and Cantu, White noted the agonies brought upon Sparta by its helots and the ferocity and effeminacy forced upon Rome when it substituted slaves for yeomen, thereby facilitating the easy triumph of the northern barbarians. Extravagant praise from Samuel J. May and other friends convinced White that he had made an auspicious beginning.[31]

Buoyed by his success, White decided to share some of his own research with the enlightened readership of *The New Englander*. While in Europe, he had searched for the correspondence of Thomas Jefferson. White's purpose, clearly stated in a short essay published in *Putnam's Monthly* in July 1857, was to demonstrate that Jefferson had been "the first and most earnest free-soil politician in the country," thereby forcing apologists for slavery who invoked his name to admit their folly.[32] Meanwhile, he prepared a much fuller exposition of his views, submitting the results to *The New Englander* early the next year. Almost immediately, editor William Kingsley approved.

Pleasure turned to dismay, however, when in the coming months Kingsley hesitated, delayed, and finally rejected the essay. The editorial board of the journal had overruled Kingsley's original judgment. "The Club" did not object to White's abolitionist views but was incensed at his praise of Jefferson. United by disdain for the Democratic party, the board never forgave the Sage of Monticello for his quasi-opposition to Washington. The readership of *The New Englander*, Kingsley explained, agreed: "[R]ight or wrong ninety-nine out of a hundred . . . have a very strong dislike for the man, in which I must be free to confess I share to almost any extent."[33]

Rebuffed by his old Yale mentors, White sent his essay to abolitionist Samuel J. May. May relayed the piece to Theodore Parker, and the two recommended that the *Atlantic Monthly* publish it. After several disappointing years, May, with "somewhat of the pride of a godfather," announced the acceptance of the article—evidently shorn of most of the

30. "Glimpses of Universal History," *New Englander* 15 (August 1857): 414.
31. Samuel J. May to ADW, September 20, 1857, WMC.
32. "A Short Exercise for the Fourth of July," *Putnam's Monthly* 10 (July 1857): 101. Many abolitionists carefully scrutinized the writings of the Founding Fathers for antislavery sentiments. See Eric Foner, *Free Soil, Free Labor, Free Men* (New York, 1970), pp. 75–76, 84. For the most recent interpretation of Jefferson and slavery, see David Brion Davis, *The Problem of Slavery in the Age of Revolution, 1770–1823* (Ithaca, 1975), pp. 164–84.
33. William Kingsley to ADW, February 20, 1858, WMC.

objectionable material.[34] Like May, White believed that the issue of slavery was paramount; so he willingly toned down the somewhat tangential praise to facilitate acceptance of his article.

With the publication of "Jefferson and Slavery," White found a friendly forum for his abolitionist ideas in the *Atlantic*, publishing two additional articles there in 1862. "The Development and Overthrow of the Russian Serf System" made virtually no references to the Civil War but was clearly intended as an antislavery tract. The article appeared two months after President Lincoln's preliminary issuance of the Emancipation Proclamation in September, addressing itself to the issues presented by that document through an analogy to Alexander II's proclamation freeing the serfs in 1861. Serfdom degraded and brutalized the serfs. The system was even worse for the masters, who presided over a stagnating country: "Farms are untilled, enterprise deadened, invention crippled, education neglected; life is of little value; labor is the badge of servility,—laziness the very badge and passport of gentility." Despite opposition from an unenlightened aristocracy, Alexander wisely realized the only way to liberate his country was to free the serfs. White found evidence everywhere that the experiment was a success.[35]

The relevance of Alexander's action to America needed no explicit statement. If backward Russia could liberate its serfs, could America, the champion of equality, refuse to free its slaves? But what of charges that freed slaves would debilitate the economy of the nation by refusing to work? Similar attitudes, White demonstrated, had greeted Alexander's proclamation. White insisted that freedom and a true stake in society provided the best inducements to work. If America hoped to strengthen the principles of republicanism, equality, and free enterprize, it had to abolish slavery—the one blight on the democratic experiment.

In "The Statesmanship of Richelieu," White approached the problem of slavery even more indirectly. He lauded the great cardinal's efforts to bring absolutism to France because by doing so Richelieu had reduced the power of the master caste. Richelieu, he went on, should have struck a blow at the serf system itself; he should not have worked by intrigue or so underestimated the sanctity of human life. White judged all men in history by their contribution to the extinction of serfdom and slavery. The fair question to ask of a historical subject then was: "Did he commit the fewest and smallest wrongs possible in beating back those many and great wrongs?" Given the unenlightened nature of sixteenth-century France,

34. May to ADW, November 2, 1858, WMC.
35. "The Development and Overthrow of the Russian Serf System," *Atlantic Monthly* 10 (November 1862): 538–52.

White saw in Cardinal Richelieu "a steady, growing force, which could only be a force for right."[36] White's emphasis on individuals rather than social forces in history underscores his attitude that such enlightened men as Richelieu and Alexander II could effect great change. The power of a cadre of educated men, he seemed to imply, would be limitless.

As White redoubled his efforts to publish, teach, and train his students for military and political leadership, his health—always delicate—began to deteriorate. His father's death in 1860 added the cares of business to an already frantic schedule. Even more upsetting was the illness of his wife, Mary, who almost perished along with their new son, Frederick, after the boy's birth in December 1859. Mother mended rapidly but Fred's condition remained uncertain. During the early 1860s, White feared that he had fatal heart disease himself. He urged Mary to use his money to aid Yale and the University of Michigan if he died.[37]

White's preparations for death were premature. The doctors diagnosed his malady as a form of dyspepsia and urged a prolonged period of rest in Europe. Twice White tried to leave the country, but he could not bring himself to abandon the war-torn nation. Finally, while traveling on a Hudson River steamer, he chanced to meet Thurlow Weed. The wily old Whig, now a Republican kingmaker, urged him to go to Europe in an attempt to prevent England's intervention in the Civil War on the side of the South. White could combine recuperation with diplomatic work essential to the Union.[38]

Weed's ominous assessment of the situation was confirmed by several months' exposure to English attitudes.[39] The delicate relations between the Union and England prompted White to warn his brother that since war was certainly possible, government bonds constituted an unwise investment. Recognizing that intervention by the British meant the probable dissolution of the Union, White vigorously presented his brief for neutrality to scores of prominent secessionist Englishmen. "I think that in some quarters I have done some good," he announced to his mother.[40]

36. "The Statesmanship of Richelieu," *Atlantic Monthly* 9 (May 1862): 611–24.

37. "The Founding of Cornell" (n.d.); ADW to Gilman, September 24, 1860; ADW to Mary White, October 26, 1860, all in WMC. White's advice to his wife was quite specific. He hoped Clara, two years old at the time, would marry "a good earnest man whom she loves and who loves her." White preferred a college professor or professional man, or, best of all, a good man living in the country. He knew Mary would be sought by many but hoped that she would not remarry. "It is hard to think of my own Mary bestowing her love on another. . . . But you must decide for yourself. I will not bind you."

38. "Founding of Cornell."

39. For White's preparations for his trip, see May to J. J. Taylor, November 14, 1862; ADW to Gilman, November 1, 1862; ADW to Fields, November 10, 1862, all in WMC.

40. ADW to HKW, April 6, 1863, and ADW to CDW, December 2, 1862, WMC.

Mary Outwater White, Andrew D. White's first wife

Intent on reaching greater numbers of Englishmen, White printed a pamphlet in response to William Howard Russell's recently published book, *My Diary North and South*. Russell, American correspondent for *The Times* of London, traveled throughout the United States in 1861 and 1862 to observe the military on both sides. Russell noted political paralysis in the North, tempered only by "some feeble twitching of the limbs at Washington." By contrast, he found a vigorous South utterly convinced of the righteousness of its cause and fully competent to vindicate it. Written by an announced opponent of slavery, Russell's detailed two-volume work, constantly predicting that the Union as it was could never be restored, further imperiled relations between the Union and England.[41]

White's published response discredited Russell's book by pointing to factual errors throughout it. More important, White asserted that while the North felt kinship with Britain, the South's hatred for England had never subsided precisely because England had so steadfastly opposed slavery. White insisted that the South had revolted for no other reason than to perpetuate the enslavement of four million blacks. Consequently, the United States had every reason to expect British cooperation: "Among all the nations, England and the United States freed from slavery are the two which ought to stand together. Between their institutions, their literatures, their beliefs, their heresies, are such links as bind no other countries." White called on the English (whose humanitarianism had motivated them to support abolition in the Empire) to endorse a similar crusade in America.[42]

The threat of intervention by England was probably never so great as White imagined it.[43] Nevertheless, as he prepared to depart for home in 1863, White felt a sense of personal accomplishment. Almost every week he received letters from Michigan boys who, he convinced himself, represented him at the front. While they fought, White fought also, and his response to Russell was widely praised. Although the outcome of the Civil War remained in doubt, White was certain that as educator, historian, and perhaps diplomat, he had answered the call of duty.

41. William Howard Russell, *My Diary North and South*, 2 vols. (London, 1863).
42. ADW to CDW, June 18, 1863, WMC; *A Letter to William Howard Russell, LLD., on Passages in His "Diary North and South"* (London, 1963), pp. 1–37.
43. Martin Duberman, *Charles Francis Adams, 1807–1886* (Boston, 1961).

Chapter 3 *New York State Senator*

White returned to the United States prepared to resume his duties as professor of history at the University of Michigan but was surprised to find an entirely new career open to him. A struggle for the Republican nomination for the New York State Senate developed in his district in Onondoga County; and White, a fresh new face, with wealth and a degree of notoriety because of the recent publication of his letter to Russell, emerged as a compromise candidate. The office, which did not necessitate the abandonment of his position at Michigan (the legislative session was only three months long), seemed all the more attractive because it was completely unsolicited. White scorned party managers, insisting that politicians be unencumbered by personal or partisan obligations. With little hesitation, then, he accepted the proffered nomination. Despite a speaking style that reminded voters of "one of them scientific purfessors lecturin," White easily carried the heavily Republican district.[1]

During White's tenure in the New York Senate, he demonstrated his conviction that education was the key to the future of recently emancipated blacks as well as to the solution of most of society's problems. Though fearful of government paternalism, especially in the form of land distribution, White was willing to allow the state and federal governments an active role in education, perhaps because the former activity leveled down, while the latter theoretically leveled up. Education would make all other reforms and virtually all other government activity unnecessary. Without it, political rights could not be effectively exercised, and economic advantage could prove only temporary; with it, the vote became meaningful and economic mobility a near certainty. Like most Radical Republicans, White did not understand that without some degree of economic security, blacks could not afford to educate themselves or their children. Thus the senator's efforts to upgrade education for free blacks in New York achieved disappointing results.

Only provisions for universal public education, White insisted, guaran-

1. *Autobiography*, vol. 1, pp. 99, 149.

teed political and civil rights. He called on the federal government to use money accumulated from the sale of public lands to subsidize schools throughout the country. White's argument for the fund was simple and compelling. To have an uneducated lower class, he warned northerners, "is to place a powder magazine beneath your habitations."[2]

If White was willing to grant blacks full political and civil rights (he supported black suffrage and an end to the $250 property qualification for blacks in the state),[3] he shared the reluctance of many Radical Republicans to help them attain an independent economic status. The argument for "forty acres and a mule" was compelling, he admitted, for without them the black sea of slavery would be exchanged for the red sea of pauperism. But this astute perception did not translate into support for land confiscation and redistribution, as proposed by Thaddeus Stevens, George Julian, and a few other Radical Republican leaders. Confiscation was such an obvious attack on property rights, as Kenneth Stampp has pointed out, that few middle-class Radical Republicans supported it.[4] White had no quarrel with the free enterprise system, viewing private ownership of property as its essential underpinning. It is difficult to imagine him supporting a policy that could so easily have served as a precedent for an attack on his own extensive holdings. He articulated his opposition to confiscation on other grounds, however. First of all, he argued, confiscation would result in a bloodbath in the South. In spite of his vehement declarations against conciliation, White, hardly a revolutionary, hoped another holocaust could be avoided and was willing to sacrifice land confiscation and the destruction of the planter-master class on the altar of peace. He consoled himself with the belief that education would better solve the problem by training blacks for jobs that would result in economic independence. Without education, blacks would squander any material inheritance; with education—the engine of progress—they would neither want nor need the largess of a paternalistic government.[5]

White again used the historical essay to win wide public support for his approach to Reconstruction. In 1866 he published "The Most Bitter Foe of Nations and the Way to Its Permanent Overthrow," his Phi Beta Kappa Society address at Yale. Without mentioning Reconstruction or the United States, White traced the history of Spain, Italy, Poland, France,

2. Notes for a Speech in Cleveland, n.d., WMC.
3. Speech in the State Senate, 1866, WMC; *Albany Argus*, March 7, 1867. Ironically, White's opponents invoked the name of Jefferson, who had asserted that blacks were biologically inferior to whites in *Notes on Virginia*. See James Mohr, *The Radical Republicans in New York during Reconstruction* (Ithaca, 1973), p. 46.
4. Kenneth Stampp, *The Era of Reconstruction* (New York, 1965), p. 130.
5. Notes for a Speech in Cleveland.

and England in an attempt to show that the institution most noxious to liberty was an aristocracy founded on traditions of oppression. Aristocrats substituted love for one's order for love of country; the exercise of power over their subject class fostered a hubris that lifted them above ordinary morality. If aristocracy (White scarcely needed to remind his audience that his argument applied to the southern plantation owners) was not destroyed, liberty could never be secure.

How, then, could the power of the master class be broken? In France, Louis XI, Richelieu, and Mazarin had opposed the aristocracy with only limited success because they failed to provide guarantees for the lower classes, the necessary bulwark against a resurgent master class. White endorsed land redistribution for France, arguing that an enfranchised peasantry possessing confiscated land would have immeasurably strengthened French society. Since he did not mention the United States in his essay, White did not have to explain his inconsistency in regard to confiscation. Self-interest was a compelling enough reason for opposing redistribution of land in the United States; but White could have defended his inconsistency on less selfish grounds, since the land in question in France was owned primarily by the Catholic church. The church had exploited the peasants who worked the land for centuries, but more important, the issue of the confiscation of *private* property was not so clearly at stake as in America. Even so, White remained so uncomfortable with this solution (even on foreign soil) that he did not reiterate it in summarizing the measures necessary to ensure liberty.

The oppressive class, White concluded, must be destroyed "at no matter what outlay of blood and treasure." The people must erect barriers against the return of aristocracy by guaranteeing civil rights in full and political rights, "at least in germ," to the subject class.[6] Characteristically, White's innate conservatism belied his often radical rhetoric. Not only did he retreat on the matter of land confiscation; he backed away from full guarantees of political rights. As the years passed, White shed even his rhetorical militance, arguing in his autobiography that Henry Clay's plan of purchasing slave children as they were born and setting them free was "infinitely better than the violent solutions proposed to us."[7] Sympathetic to the plight of the black yet increasingly fearful of violence, instability, and change, White, like so many Radical Republicans, was usually as unwilling as the statesmen he criticized to crystallize rhetoric and promises into legislation. Not surprisingly, his interest in Reconstruction ebbed rather quickly.

6. *The Most Bitter Foe of Nations and the Way to Its Permanent Overthrow* (New Haven, 1866).
7. *Autobiography*, vol. 1, p. 55.

As the New York legislature debated black suffrage, White's apparently radical position again proved to be moderate. He argued eloquently for black suffrage, attributing Negroes' apparent inferiority to legally enforced intellectual deprivation that barred them "from every incentive to mental exertion, barbarized and brutalized [as they were] by oppression of every sort." Despite this seemingly unequivocal position, however, the senator did not endorse the enfranchisement of all blacks. Manhood suffrage should be color-blind, he argued, but it should be granted only upon successful completion of a reasonable educational test, such as the ability to read the constitutions of the state and of the United States.[8] The enfranchisement of blacks, then, would be conferred in theory, but the realization of full political rights would be a deferred commitment.

In the Senate, however, White struggled to fulfill that commitment quickly by providing quality education for Negroes. He agreed with Samuel May's shrewd observation that separate schools were a "perpetual imputation of fault, unworthiness or inferiority which must tend to discourage."[9] As chairman of the Senate Committee on Literature,[10] responsible for all educational legislation, White believed that he was in a unique position to deal a fatal blow to the separate and unequal educational facilities provided by the state.

When the state's school laws were being codified, however, White was unsuccessful in an attempt to remove a clause permitting local districts to segregate schools.[11] Undaunted, he shifted to a piecemeal approach, and in 1864 his committee supported a bill to integrate the high school in Troy. Disgruntled members of the committee presented a scathing minority report that called for separate but equal facilities. Contact in schools, they indicated, led inevitably to social contact—racial mixing. The minority, many of whom had opposed White's attempt to revise the state code, asked why Troy should be subjected to this dangerous experiment when the rest of the state retained segregation.[12]

Put on the defensive by the minority attack, White spent the bulk of his time on the Senate floor attempting to refute the charge of racial amalgamation. Association of the races in the South, he reminded his colleagues, did not lead to intermarriage, nor did integrated high schools in Boston or

8. *The Constitutional Convention: Delegates at Large. Responsibility to Small Districts Impartial Manhood Suffrage* (Albany, 1867).

9. Samuel J. May to ADW, March 11, 1864, WMC.

10. *Senate Documents, 1864* (Albany, 1864) 1, no. 10; *Senate Documents, 1865* (Albany, 1865) 1, no. 21; *Senate Documents, 1866* (Albany, 1866) 1; no. 6; *Senate Documents, 1867* (Albany, 1867) 1, no. 7.

11. Mohr, *Radical Republicans*, p. 206.

12. *Albany Argus*, March 31, 1864.

New Haven. White's response indicates the success of the minority in beclouding the issue. Positive reasons for integrated schools, as for most measures to aid blacks, had to be ignored in the scramble to allay the fears of New Yorkers. The Troy bill was killed.[13]

The overwhelming difficulties of reform compelled White to change tactics again, this time arguing for a statewide free school bill. Education would be paid for by a state property tax rather than by local rate bills that assessed parents of schoolchildren, thus encouraging the poor to remove children from school. Such a general fund would equalize educational opportunity by rescuing impoverished communities hitherto neglectful of their school systems. Thus, even if education remained separate, it would approach equality. White may also have seen that the state government, with control of the funds for education, could in the long run insist on integrated schools. White's championing of a free school bill was a necessary first step in integration of the public schools.[14]

The senator, of course, did not spend all of his time on Reconstruction and the public schools. He responded to the normal demands on a politician—the dispensation of patronage and participation in party affairs.[15] His belief that the Republican party had saved the Union and was needed to protect it was unshakable; ambition for higher political office, moreover, necessitated active support of the state ticket. An effective campaigner, popular in his own district, with an increasingly wide reputation as a historian and scholar, White soon found that his endorsement was valuable to aspirants for the party's nomination.[16] Among the contenders for the GOP nomination for U.S. senator in 1867, White favored *Harper's Weekly* editor George William Curtis. Recognizing that he had little chance of winning, the noted civil service reformer withdrew. When the legislative caucus convened, White moved into the camp of Roscoe Conkling of Utica. Conkling, who had not yet made his reputation as the premier spoilsman of the day, shared White's view on Reconstruction and conservative fiscal policies. White seconded Conkling's nomination with a rousing speech that sounded the keynote of the victorious Republican campaign.[17] Conkling found the support of the scholar–civil service reformer useful for many years and proved solicitous to his requests. White, too, found the relationship beneficial. He continued to recommend appoint-

13. *Albany Argus*, March 31, 1864; *Senate Journal, 1864* (Albany, 1864), p. 508.
14. *Albany Argus*, April 10, 1867; ADW to Daniel Coit Gilman, October 19, 1871, WMC.
15. ADW to Henry Hagerman, October 24, 1866; ADW to Abraham Lincoln, April 4, 1861; Farley King to ADW, April 5, 1865, all in WMC.
16. ADW to Burt Wilder, October 22, 1867, WMC.
17. David Jordan, *Roscoe Conkling of New York* (Ithaca, 1971), p. 88; *Albany Argus*, January 12, 1867; *Autobiography*, vol. 1, pp. 135–36; Noah Davis to ADW, January 15, 1867, WMC.

ments and ask for aid long after Conkling's preference for the spoils system became abundantly manifest, salving his conscience by exhorting him to support civil service reform.[18]

While White moved toward an alliance with this symbol of the spoils system, he fought the system of political appointments that had debilitated the New York City Board of Health. Frequent cholera epidemics in New York resulted in the creation of a Citizen's Association Council of Hygiene in 1863. Appalled by the ineptitude of the Health Department, the council petitioned the state legislature to reconstitute the board and remove it from the control of Tammany politicians. Vigorous opposition by Health Department city inspector Francis I. Boole, a Tammany appointee who chose health inspectors in each ward, succeeded in tabling a resolution to place the board under state rather than municipal control, but the Senate appointed a three-man committee to investigate the situation in 1865.[19]

As a member of the committee, White heard extensive testimony that confirmed the worst charges of the Council of Hygiene. Health wardens admitted utter ignorance of medicine and hygienic practice. One official, when asked why he refused to examine a supposed case of smallpox, responded: "For the same reason that you would not go into the room. I didn't want to catch the disease myself." The astonished committee had little reason to question the testimony of William Thoms, a physician employed by the Council of Hygiene, that outbreaks of typhus fever and smallpox were common occurrences in New York.[20]

If the committee easily affirmed the existence of deplorable health conditions, it had even less difficulty in locating the source of the problem. Boole himself was utterly unqualified to be city inspector. He used the Board of Health as a vehicle for the dispensation of Tammany patronage.[21] Impressed by the necessity for a nonpolitical board of health and for educated, qualified health officials, the committee recommended the crea-

18. Conkling to ADW, January 31, 1872 and March 26, 1874; ADW to Conkling, January 4, 1871, all in WMC. White broke with Conkling in 1887, a year before the latter's death. In an interview White claimed that he had told Conkling many times that his patronage policies would increase his enemies, who would ultimately crush him. Conkling responded angrily and a quarrel ensued (Jordan, *Roscoe Conkling*, pp. 424–25).

19. Roy Lubove, *The Progressives and the Slums* (Pittsburgh, 1962), pp. 12–23.

20. James Richardson, "Mayor Fernando Wood and the New York Police Force, 1855–1857," *New-York Historical Society Quarterly* 50 (Winter 1966): 5–20; Mohr, *Radical Republicans*, p. 46. Mohr views the reform struggle in this period—"reconstruction at home"—as an attempt by radicals to consolidate electoral gains made during the war through a program of "progressive" government activity. Thus he deemphasizes the urban–rural struggle and the paternalistic impulse, both of which motivated such men as White before as well as after the Civil War.

21. *Autobiography*, vol. 1, pp. 109–110; *Senate Documents, 1865* 2, no. 38: 456, 536–38.

tion of a new board comprised of police commissioners, physicians appointed by the governor, and the health officer of the Port of New York.[22]

Without discounting the sincerity of the participants, we can understand the struggle for a new board of health only by viewing it within the context of the conflict between Republican, rural upstate New York and the Tammany-controlled city. The insistence of White and others on a nonpolitical board obscured a desire to transfer power from New York City to the state legislature. Such desires manifested themselves frequently in the middle nineteenth century in the Empire State, most notably in the almost-successful attempt in 1857 to invest the power of appointment of New York City policemen in Albany. White himself had supported a state-controlled board of fire commissioners in 1865.[23] Although he lived in the growing city of Syracuse, White identified himself as a rural representative. In a lengthy speech supporting the health bill, he cited the rampant corruption discovered by the committee in the awarding of contracts. This, he sanctimoniously claimed, "is not the rural method." The handmaiden of such corruption, the senator continued, pointing disapprovingly to the number of Irish on the present board of health, was partisan political appointment. The lesson for the legislature was clear. If virtue was to be restored to New York City, power must be wrested from corrupt Tammany politicians and ignorant, incompetent immigrants.[24]

The committee made its proposal to the Senate rather late in the 1865 session, and although it passed in the upper chamber, sufficient opposition surfaced in the Assembly to defer action until the following year. A severe cholera epidemic in the intervening summer and fall underlined the necessity for action. When the legislature reconvened, White asked for speedy action in the face of imminent danger. The legislature passed the Metropolitan Board of Health Bill, which White thought his greatest accomplishment while in the New York State Senate.[25]

Concern about corruption and immigration directed Senator White's attention to the growth of crime in the state. White thought that the American system of justice, too concerned with protecting the rights of the accused, neglected the rights of the victim. He proposed a bill that would make evidence on the character of professional criminals, heretofore judged irrelevant to the case at hand, admissible in court. The evidence

22. *Senate Documents, 1865* 2, no. 38: 475.
23. Lubove, *Progressives and the Slums*, p. 25.
24. Speech in the State Senate, n.d., WMC.
25. *Albany Argus*, February 1 and 16, 1866; ADW to Gilman, October 19, 1871, WMC. The board succeeded in saving the city from a severe epidemic in 1866. See Charles Rosenberg, *The Cholera Years* (Chicago, 1962), pp. 182–212.

would be privately submitted to the judges and would not be introduced without their consent. In cases where the evidence was not absolutely convincing, this additional information might tip the scales in favor of conviction. White's bill was referred to the Judiciary Committee, chaired by Judge Charles Folger, who bottled it in the committee. Undaunted, White took the floor to request that the bill bypass the committee. Despite Folger's apoplectic objections, the Senate debated and passed the measure. Although the proposal died in the Assembly, White's concern about "laxity in the administration of the criminal law" lasted throughout his active life.[26]

Popular, articulate, hard-working, with increasingly well-established political connections, the young senator seemed guaranteed a long and distinguished political career until an encounter with the oldest member of the Senate tipped the wheel of fortune in a new direction. Ezra Cornell, a stern-faced Quaker who resembled popular representations of Uncle Sam, had made a fortune for himself and the Western Union Telegraph Company by perfecting the system of stringing telegraph lines from pole to pole aboveground. Although mountainous wealth made little difference in Cornell's personal style—he journeyed on foot to meet with business associates hundreds of miles away—it gave him long-sought opportunities for public philanthropy.[27] On the first day of the 1864 session, Cornell introduced a bill, referred to White's Committee on Literature, to incorporate a public library in his hometown of Ithaca. Impressed by his colleague's munificence in funding the library, White was also struck by the provision for the Board of Trustees. Cornell named political opponents as well as friends to the board, and he refused to adhere to any religious tests, choosing Catholics as well as Protestants of various denominations.[28] White acted quickly on Cornell's proposal, which soon became law.

Shortly thereafter, an opportunity for the two men to work together to further the cause of education presented itself. In 1862 Congress had passed the Morrill Land Grant Act, which provided salable land in the West for each state that would use the revenue to establish an endowment for at least one college "which would emphasize agriculture and the mechanic arts." In 1863, New York, beneficiary of the princely grant of 989,920 acres, appropriated the returns from this land scrip to the People's College of Havana (now Montour Falls), provided that within three years

---

26. *Autobiography*, vol. 1, pp. 137–39; James M. Whiton, "Andrew D. White: Educator and Statesman," *Outlook* 80 (May 13, 1905):135.
   27. Philip Dorf, *The Builder: A Biography of Ezra Cornell* (New York, 1952); Alonzo Cornell, *True and Firm: Biography of Ezra Cornell* (New York, 1884).
   28. *Autobiography*, vol. 1, pp. 294–95.

it have accommodations for 250 students, ten competent professors in agriculture and the mechanic arts, a farm of 200 acres, and workshops for technical education.[29] When White and Cornell took their seats in the Senate early in 1864, the People's College, whose chief sponsor and benefactor was State Senator Charles Cook, had not yet complied with the terms of the grant.

Fearful that the state would default on its obligations as outlined by the Morrill Act and the legislature, Cornell joined in a move to divide the endowment between the empty Havana insitution and the New York State Agricultural College at Ovid. A bill to this effect was drawn up and referred jointly to White's committee and the Committee on Agriculture, headed by none other than Ezra Cornell. White, who accepted Henry Tappan's observation that diffusion of educational resources by scattering them in "feeble streams through a thousand channels" cheapens even more what was cheap enough already, opposed any attempt to divide the fund.

Gradually White's reasoning and a combination of circumstances converted Cornell to the principle of concentrating all of the resources of the grant in one institution. Evidence mounted that the People's College would fail to fulfill its obligations. Cook, who had promised to donate his farm to the institution, refused to relinquish the mortgage he held on it. More disturbing, small colleges, hearing that Cornell favored dividing the grant, descended upon Albany to demand a share of the money. Cook and the president of the People's College, the Reverend Amos Brown, seconded White's remarks about the dangers of diffusion. Whatever was done, Cook wrote to White, the fund should not be divided. Not a single state, he noted, had been guilty of that folly. If Cook could be accused of trying to secure the entire fund for his college, Amos Brown had to be regarded as a more impartial witness. Brown resigned his position in the summer of 1864 and began a correspondence with Cornell begging him not to support a division of the fund.[30] Although still not entirely convinced, Cornell was now clearly more aware of the pitfalls of diffusion.[31]

Meanwhile, White continued to fight "like a terrier against those who would tear that noble donation into bits," while resisting overtures from the enemy. Amos Brown informed him that Cook had thought of White as the next president of the People's College. Henry Randall, chairman of the

29. Daniel C. Gilman, "The Cornell University," *Nation* 1 (July 6, 1865): 45; George Rainsford, *Congress and Higher Education in the Nineteenth Century* (Knoxville, Tenn.; 1972), pp. 85–97; Morris Bishop, *A History of Cornell* (Ithaca, 1962), pp. 58–59.

30. Brown may also have had an ulterior motive: a desire to be appointed president of the new institution.

31. Charles Cook to ADW, February 24, 1864, WMC; Amos Brown to ECS, December 10, 1864, Ezra Cornell MSS, Cornell University; *Autobiography*, vol. 1, pp. 294–98.

Ezra Cornell

Presidential Search Committee, converted rumor into fact by announcing: "I would be in favor of Andrew D. White, if he would accept." Incapacitated by a stroke, eager to leave the university as a permanent monument to himself, yet "servant and not master of his money," Charles Cook may well have concluded that White's appointment as president would save his institution. White's investigations, however, revealed the chaos in Havana, and convinced him that the grant must not be divided or given to the People's College.[32]

Randall asked White to aid in the search for a replacement for Brown, if he would not accept the position himself, and the senator made inquiries to Daniel Coit Gilman. Although unable to suggest anyone, Gilman requested a conference to talk about scientific and industrial education. The two friends met and discussed the possibilities of combining arts and industrial sciences on an equal basis in a single university. The provisions of the Morrill Act necessitated such a union if a great university was to emerge from the land grant. Before his visit with Gilman, White remembered much later, probably giving too much credit to his friend, "the subject had never attracted me. Indeed, during my Senior year in college I regarded the studies of my contemporaries in the Sheffield Scientific School with a sort of contempt—with wonder that human beings possessed of immortal souls should waste their time in work with blow pipes and test tubes." Tappan's experience taught White that a state university needed public support. He evidently concluded that programs in agriculture and mechanic arts would guarantee legislative favor. A marriage between the arts and industrial sciences, he now asserted, was possible and desirable.[33]

Perhaps aware of White's new-found sympathy for industrial training, certainly impressed by his colleague's arguments for one strong institution, Cornell suggested a compromise. The fund would remain divided, but Cornell would add $300,000 of his own money to the resources of the State Agricultural College if it relocated from Ovid to Ithaca. White submitted a counterproposal: If Cornell would agree to ask for the whole grant and add $300,000 to it, White would support him. Cornell concurred and the two began to prepare a bill to establish a university in Ithaca.[34]

32. ADW to Gilman, March 5, 1864; Brown to ADW, August 15, 1864; Henry Randall to ADW, September 12, 1864, all in WMC; *Senate Documents, 1865* 2, nos. 39, 45.
33. Laurence Veysey, *The Emergence of the American University* (Chicago, 1965), p. 159; ADW to Randall, September 14, 1864; Randall to ADW, September 25, 1864; ADW to Gilman, November 14, 1864; ADW to Mrs. Gilman, May 3, 1909, all in WMC.
34. *Autobiography*, vol. 1, pp. 298–299.

Every sign seemed to indicate relatively easy passage of the Cornell bill as new and powerful allies announced their support. Horace Greeley swung the powerful *New York Tribune* behind Cornell's university. Answering rumors that Greeley had deserted them, Cornell assured his son: "Greeley was with us and *is with us*. If the People's College don't move soon it must get out of the way and let us pass." When the People's College finally moved, it succeeded only in weakening its position. In January 1865 Cook's allies introduced a bill to exempt the institution from the conditions imposed upon it in 1863. No argument, Cornell exulted, better demonstrated their weakness. The time for action had arrived; on February 7, White introduced an "act to establish Cornell University."[35]

The struggle to pass the Cornell bill proved much more difficult than White and Cornell had anticipated. A combination of Cook's friends and a strong lobby of small denominational colleges, resentful of the assertion of nonsectarianism in the proposed university charter besieged their representatives with requests to defeat the measure.[36] White and Cornell, with editorial help from Greeley, Erastus Brooks's *New York Express*, and Manton Marble's *New York World*, began to cajole their colleagues. When appeals to reason and altruism failed, they promised support for other legislation in return for the passage of the Cornell bill. Because Ezra Cornell was uncomfortable with logrolling, the major burden of the struggle fell to White. Charles Folger, for example, was favorable to Cornell but opposed the bill in its early stages because the State Agricultural College was located in his district. White won his vote by promising to support a bill to establish an insane asylum on the site of the virtually empty college. With Folger's capitulation, the Senate approved the Cornell bill in mid-March, although it appended an amendment that gave the People's College three additional months to comply with the 1864 act of the legislature—hardly enough time, White thought in assenting to the measure, to threaten the birth of Cornell University.[37]

If the struggle in the Senate was troublesome, the course of the bill in the Assembly was nightmarish. Friends of the People's College reneged on a promise to withdraw opposition in the lower house if their institution was given a three-month reprieve. Genesee College, a tiny Methodist school near Rochester, demanded $25,000 as the price of acquiescence to the new

35. Ibid., EC to AC, January 25, 1965, Cornell MSS.
36. Mohr, *Radical Republicans*, pp. 162–63; Carl Becker, *Cornell University: Founders and the Founding* (Ithaca, 1944), pp. 94–96; Bishop, *History of Cornell*, pp. 66–68; *Autobiography*, vol. 1, p. 300.
37. *Autobiography*, vol. 1, pp. 332–34; *Albany Argus*, March 1, 10, 11, and 17, 1865; *Senate Journal, 1865*, p. 438.

university. Cornell, increasingly disturbed at the difficulty of bestowing philanthropy upon the state, refused to pay extortion.[38] White and Henry Lord, the bill's manager in the Assembly, begged him to change his mind, and finally prevailed upon the old man to agree, although he insisted that a provision for the $25,000 grant, ostensibly for the Department of Agricultural Chemistry (appropriately nicknamed the Captain Kidd Professorship), appear in the Cornell bill. Lamenting that New York "never had a more corrupt assembly than the one in session," the fastidious Cornell insisted that the university bill have "no stains beyond what appears on its face."[39] After several more problems were surmounted, Cornell University was born.

Because the People's College had been granted a three-month reprieve, White and Cornell spent more than a few anxious moments praying that their creation would not be stillborn. Rumors circulated that Cook would save the college, but Amos Brown reassured Cornell that they were unfounded. "Mr. Cook has disclosed that he has given his last cent to the People's College," he reported in late April. When rumors persisted through the summer, Brown repeated his message. By July the New York State Regents had decided that if the trustees of the People's College failed to deposit $185,000 by the twenty-seventh of the month, Cornell University could commence operations. On the twenty-ninth the news arrived: no notice of deposit had been received—"the time has passed."[40]

With Cornell University a fait accompli, White turned once more to consideration of his own future. Mary White urged her husband not to stand for reelection to the Senate in 1865, but to recommence his scholarly career. Although he enjoyed the rough-and-tumble of politics, White agreed that he was better able to serve the public from the historian's pulpit by preaching on prominent public issues than from the politician's soap box by invoking history to sway votes. Nevertheless, he overruled his wife because of the pressing need for legislative protection for the fledgling Cornell University. "That is the only consideration which tempts me," he informed Gilman.[41] Several months later, he returned to the Senate for a second term.

Ezra Cornell's dependence on his young colleague increased in the months following passage of the Cornell bill. He asked White to draw up

38. *Autobiography*, vol. 1, p. 303. Cornell upped his contribution for a new university to $500,000 when he decided to found it in Ithaca.

39. EC to AC; April 23, 1865; EC to W. A. Woodward, March 20, 1865, both in Cornell MSS.

40. Brown to EC, April 26 and July 19, 1865; S. B. Woolworth to EC, July 28, 1865, all in Cornell MSS; *Albany Argus*, July 8, 1865.

41. ADW to Gilman, May 15, 1865, WMC.

the plans for the new university and to supervise the design and construction of its buildings. White volunteered to help conduct the search for a president. He suggested John Andrew, former governor of Massachusetts, who had recently declined the presidency of Amherst College. If Andrew declined, perhaps Martin Anderson, president of the University of Rochester, could be persuaded to come to Ithaca. White's letter of inquiry to his former Michigan colleague Thomas Cooley brought a response that he did not relay to Cornell. The new president, Cooley thought, should be a live man, not entirely without aspiration, a man of progressive ideas and familiarity with other institutions, a man with knowledge of the world as well as books. Cooley knew of just such a man: "Unless he has fully made up his mind to seek another course . . . the man for President of Cornell University is Andrew D. White."[42]

Undoubtedly flattered by Cooley's suggestion, White received a letter from Yale's Noah Porter that seemed perhaps more inviting. A professional position at Yale—once, and perhaps still, White's cherished dream—had opened up. Porter asked White to become "the Director, President, manager or what you may call it of an art school," as well as professor of the history of art.[43] White responded immediately, requesting a meeting with Porter, while conveying some sense of the conflicting emotions within him:

It seems a realization of some of the best among my old dreams. But what a wall to be broken through to get at the good work you suggest! Business and family ties and plans for improvement and schemes for enjoyment here have become knit into quite a firm barrier.

Yet an association with you in all pursuits . . . has to me a very great attraction. New Haven seemed Paradise the other day, and this is rather a prosy, dusty part of Creation.[44]

While White hesitated, Cornell acted to formalize his colleague's connection with Cornell University. He begged White to decline the Yale position, promising that if he elected to remain at Ithaca he would "stand as one of the founders of the Institution, and will occupy a commanding and influential position." This rather unsubtle hint soon became an offer of the presidency of Cornell University. The trustees unanimously elected him and Ezra Cornell begged him to accept. Allowing himself to be persuaded, White recognized that the amount of labor required was

42. ADW to EC, October 5, 1865, WMC; Waterman T. Hewett, *Cornell University: A History*, 4 vols. (New York, 1905), vol. 1, pp. 126–27; T. M. Cooley to ADW, September 20, 1865, WMC.
43. Noah Porter to ADW, July 7, 1866, WMC.
44. ADW to Porter, July 10, 1866, WMC.

staggering. The post required full-time attention, necessitating withdrawal from active politics and the postponement of scholarly projects. White's interests as a politician had centered on education as the reform of reforms; thus his new position seemed particularly appropriate. "Goodbye pen and ink and literary leisure," declared White to old friend Moses Coit Tyler as he embarked upon the planning of Cornell University.[45]

45. EC to ADW, August 15, 1866; ADW to Gilman, November 30, 1866; George W. Curtis to ADW, November 23, 1866; Porter to ADW, December 10, 1866; White to Moses Coit Tyler, October 23, 1868, all in WMC; Charles Folger to Cornell, November 27, 1866, Cornell MSS; *Autobiography*, vol. 1, pp. 334–36.

Part II

AN EDUCATIONAL REFORMER

Andrew D. White was a dominant figure in American higher education in the nineteenth century. The voluminous praise and vituperation directed at him testify to his central position in university reform. He emerged as one of the earliest and most vocal champions of non-denominationalism, coeducation, equality of all students, elective choice, and laissez faire in student discipline. The twentieth-century university in large measure conformed to his blueprint of the 1860s and 1870s. Yet White was never acknowledged as *the* preeminent educator of the period, in part because of his impatience with administrative detail and his political ambitions. Unlike Charles Eliot, who served for forty uninterrupted years as Harvard's president, White punctuated his twenty-year tenure with frequent leaves of absence. More important, White often proved willing to retreat temporarily from the reform goals he had set early in his administration. Anxious to promote harmony within the university community and to retain support from the legislature and from society at large, White refused to outpace public opinion. Consequently, he usually modified his principles in the face of opposition, justifying his actions by assuring himself that the Cornell Idea would triumph in the long run. White's educational ideas have indeed become commonplace in the twentieth century, but it is doubtful that his compromises facilitated their adoption.

White did not dwell upon the theme of religious freedom in his preliminary plan for Cornell, probably because he did not want to provide ammunition for the growing number of critics of the "radical" institution. In his inaugural address, however, the president pledged that he would not allow mere sectarian concerns to dictate Cornell policy. Although he battled sectarian critics for the rest of his life, White occasionally acted to mollify more orthodox trustees. He had insisted that the university serve as a haven for non-Christian and nonbelieving scholars and students, but he constantly emphasized the Christian character of Cornell and made attendance at chapel compulsory. He consciously sought faculty representatives of every denomination in an effort to silence potential opponents. While declaring that the religious affiliations of prospective professors were irrelevant, White quietly assembled a balanced faculty.

Two incidents during his presidency illustrate White's reluctance to support faculty members whose religious views displeased the trustees. Felix Adler, a prominent Jewish scholar of comparative religion, implied that Christianity was merely a sect when viewed from a world perspective. He cast doubt on Christian miracles by observing that other religions had similar legends. Several New York newspapers called upon Christian parents to boycott Cornell, and the trustees asked White to dismiss Adler. The president responded with a defense of the professor but significantly pointed to Adler's Christian education rather than insisting on the sanctity of freedom of inquiry. Soon after his remarks were published, White agreed to a trustee proposal to drop Adler from the university.

Even more troubling to White's conscience than the dismissal of Adler was the removal of William Channing Russel, professor of history, who served as acting president during White's diplomatic excursions. Russel's religious views were too unorthodox for trustee Henry Sage. During White's tenure as minister to Germany, the trustees demanded that Russel sever all connections with the university. White wrote a letter resigning his presidency; at the last moment, however, he changed his mind, did not send the letter, and returned to Cornell without criticizing the trustee action. White had decided that his resignation might end freedom of thought in religion at Cornell, whereas if he remained he could perhaps achieve his aim in the future. Ironically White, Russel, and Sage were all liberal Christians who professed acceptance of nondenominationalism. The orthodox did not have a monopoly on intolerance, and White unwittingly helped to demonstrate the validity of Felix Adler's charge that sectarianism was rampant at Cornell.

If White faced strong opposition to his religious goals for the university, he received trustee approval of his efforts to ensure the equality of all students, regardless of sex or subject interest. Students in science, agriculture, and the mechanic arts were looked down on in contemporary institutions, but White joined Ezra Cornell in insisting that no course of study be afforded special status. Cornell, moreover, was among the first universities in the United States to institute coeducation. White, Cornell, and Henry Sage agreed that the mixing of the sexes at the university level was practical and desirable.

Although coeducation was achieved virtually without a struggle, White's promise that all students would be treated equally did not become a reality during his presidency. Henry Sage believed that the university had an obligation to monitor the activities of female students. He insisted that they be forced to live in dormitories and be subject to a series of regulations enforced by an ever present matron. The women, pointing to White's belief, as expressed in his preliminary sketch of educational policy, that students should discipline themselves, petitioned for the same privileges as those accorded men. White was sympathetic and admitted that *in theory* they were entitled to more freedom; but public opinion, he asserted (certainly mindful of Sage's prodding), would not allow such concessions *at present*. Although the women found that other coeducational universities were far more liberal in matters of student discipline, White refused to yield. At the end of his administration, equality of students remained a deferred commitment.

While Cornell's women failed to win equality, the university's men battled with White about student discipline. The president had listed laissez faire in discipline as one of the unique features of Cornell but had simultaneously instituted compulsory military training. Students marched, drilled, arose, and went to bed at specified hours, and wore uniforms. They chafed under the watchful eye of the military officer, Major J. H. Whittlesey, who also supervised dormitory life. White did not perceive the inconsistency between his call for student self-discipline and the military regimen that he imposed. Student agitation, however, succeeded in overthrowing the harsher aspects of Whittlesey's rule. Almost in spite of himself, White came closer to his own educational theory.

In choice of subjects, White similarly failed to follow his own logic to its ultimate destination. He argued that a seventeen-year-old who was expected to choose a profession was capable of selecting the subjects in which he was interested. Thus one might have expected White to advocate free election of all subjects, as did Harvard's president, Charles W. Eliot. In fact, fearful of charges that free election would make students dilettantes, White allowed them only to choose among several course options. Once the student selected a course—a scientific course, for example—he *had* to complete four years of prescribed subjects. All students who elected the scientific course (or any other course) took precisely the same subjects. White's elective system gave the student far less latitude than Eliot's; but for the rest of his life, the Cornell president took credit for introducing the elective system in the United States.

White's administration at Cornell, in sum, did not always live up to the bold promises set out in the blueprint for the university. White was a hesitant reformer whose desire to prevent conflict restrained his actions, if not his rhetoric. Ironically, his contribution to education perhaps lay as much in what he promised he would do and what he said he was doing as in his actual accomplishments. Universities throughout the nation copied the Cornell Idea, and often surpassed it in practice. Despite his own lapses and inconsistencies, White was a central figure in the emergence of the American university.

Chapter 4   *Architect of a University*

"The surest pledge of long remembrance among men," Charles W. Eliot believed, "is to build one's self into a university."[1] Even before officially appointing White to the presidency of his institution, Ezra Cornell invited him to be its architect by asking him to serve on the Committee on Buildings and to frame the educational principles of Cornell University. White's experience at Michigan had proved the value of a healthy, aesthetic physical setting to mental and moral development. A strong believer in "everything which tends to throw a charm about our prosaic American life, and to banish Philistinism from Universities," he recommended that university buildings be tasteful, substantial, and architecturally correct. Conscious of Mr. Cornell's Quaker antipathy to ostentation and unnecessary expense, White warned against extravagance. Still convinced of the necessity of mitigating "anything like a dry, hard, factory tone" at the university, he sought to counteract Ezra Cornell's spartan practicality by paying for chimes, statuary, pictures, and landscape gardening with his own funds.[2]

If Ezra Cornell's preference for simplicity and utility tempered White's plans to provide an inspiring physical setting, White's preference for the English university quadrangle system preempted a bold approach to the physical plan of Cornell. Frederick Law Olmsted, hired by White as a consultant to the Building Committee, pointed out that quadrangles closed off the possibility of growth and flexibility. Predicting that in a century the quadrangle would be "simply another monument of shortsightedness, inconsideration and complacency," Olmsted begged the committee not to begin its innovative university by tying it to "formality and straightlacing." Olmsted recommended a "more free, picturesque and

1. Theodore T. Munger, "A Significant Biography," *Atlantic Monthly* 96 (October 1905): 561.
2. Report of the Committee on Buildings, March 14, 1866; ADW to Daniel Coit Gilman, July 12, 1890; ADW to Henry Sage, November 2, 1895, all in WMC.

convenient" plan to anticipate growth of the university to ten times the building accommodation originally provided.[3] White politely disagreed, and Olmsted's proposal had to wait for the more sympathetic ear of Leland Stanford.

White's attitude toward the physical plan of Cornell foreshadowed his role in the overall planning of the university. Although he hoped "to build himself into a university," he often had to cater to the wishes of the founder. Moreover, even when acquainted with departures from tradition he hesitated, although he often adopted some aspect of an innovation. He sought a close relationship between the university and the surrounding community. If the university, a state-supported institution, was to thrive, it would have to retain public support. Thus White's bold rhetorical claims for the university were often balanced by practices designed to demonstrate that Cornell University had not abandoned discipline or Christianity. White's master plan was a guide for the future; his political instincts told him that compromise was the best guarantee of institutional prosperity. He gave little thought to disparities between theory and practice and convinced himself and others that Cornell provided an unambiguous model to universities throughout the country.

The *Report on Organization*, presented to the trustees in 1866, outlined White's blueprint for Cornell University. A close examination of it, supplemented by some of the president's early policies, elucidates his educational philosophy. The need for reform in higher education was, he thought, abundantly clear. College had lost its appeal for both the trusted leaders of society and a majority of the people at large; therefore most young men of energy and ability neglected higher education. Even as White issued his report, Frederick A. Barnard amassed the statistics validating his hypothesis. Of the males in America between the ages of eighteen and twenty, 1 out of every 67 went to college in 1840, 1 out of 71 in 1860, and only 1 out of 79 in 1869. Between 1840 and 1869 the population increased by more than 21 million, while student enrollment increased by only slightly more than 4,000. Barnard also documented the decreasing status of college-trained men, finding that their numbers in government positions had actually decreased. To reverse this alarming trend, university reformers agreed, higher education had to serve the needs of society better.[4]

---

3. Frederick Law Olmsted to ADW, June 13, 1867, WMC.
4. *Report of the Committee on Organization* (Albany, 1867), p. 4; Gordon Milne, *George William Curtis and the Genteel Tradition* (Bloomington, Ind., 1956), p. 238; Karl G. Peterson, "Andrew D. White's Educational Principles: Their Sources, Development, Consequences," Ed.D. thesis, Stanford University, 1949, pp. 20, 191.

The Morrill Act, of course, provided one solution to this problem by allocating funds for practical training in agriculture and industrial arts. Chancellor Tappan must have been stunned to find his former lieutenant proudly announcing instruction in agriculture, mechanic arts, and mining and civil engineering as leading functions of Cornell University. The university, moreover, insisted that students who enrolled in these courses were the peers of those enrolled in the traditional classical course. White so vehemently demanded equality that the trustees had to overrule his recommendation that the university grant only one degree for all students. Derided elsewhere as "inferior" students, agriculturalists and industrialists were welcome at Cornell.[5]

Treated as equals and taught the most advanced techniques in their fields, Cornell graduates, White predicted, would take leading roles in their communities. His parents' insistence on duty and Tappan's notion of a trained elite left an indelible mark; White, for all his egalitarian rhetoric, steadfastly maintained his belief in a hierarchical society, hoping the educated would share their knowledge with the ignorant.[6]

If agriculturalists and industrialists hoped to gain influence, they would have to learn more than plowing and tooling. Respect, White thought, generally came to cultured men. Thus he insisted on giving all students liberal arts training.[7]

White's conviction that agricultural education could not be separated from the liberal arts buttressed his argument that the Morrill Land Grant Act did not apply only to industrial arts. As the Morrill Act did not specifically exclude "other scientific and classical studies," White interpreted it as virtual carte blanche to create an institution "to meet the new needs of our land and time."[8] The bill setting up Cornell University's corporation provided even more definitively for the liberal arts.[9] The leading object of the corporation was the teaching of agriculture and the mechanic arts in order to promote the liberal and practical education of the industrial classes. White added a crucial section to the bill that vastly increased the university's mandate: "But such other branches of science and knowledge may be embraced in the plan of instruction and investiga-

5. *Report on Organization*, p. 3; ADW to Andrew Carnegie, December 29, 1906, WMC; *Autobiography*, vol. 1, p. 390.
6. ADW to Lewis H. Morgan, October 22, 1858, WMC.
7. *Education in Political Science* (Baltimore, 1879), p. 38; *Address on Agricultural Education* (Albany, 1869), pp. 34, 46, 48.
8. Carl Becker, *Cornell University: Founders and the Founding* (Ithaca, 1944), p. 34; ADW to Justin Morrill, August 25, 1873, Morrill MSS, Library of Congress.
9. Morrill shared White's view of his bill. See George Rainsford, *Congress and Higher Education in the Nineteenth Century* (Knoxville, Tenn., 1972), p. 102.

tion pertaining to the university as the trustees may deem useful and proper."[10] The *Report on Organization* thus found ample legal precedent to justify Ezra Cornell's dictum: "I would found a university where any person can receive instruction in any subject."

Having dealt with the practical branches of the university, White moved to the more familiar ground of the classical curriculum. His aim was the same as it had been for students in the special sciences—to train the future leaders of the nation. America eagerly sought guidance from the educated: "No people in the world so quickly recognize a man who can stimulate valuable thought; no country is so open to the influence of facts cogently presented."[11] White recognized that the society might not immediately reward Cornell's graduates with political offices but hoped that an ever increasing army of the enlightened would eventually make its influence felt.[12]

In opening their university to all branches of learning, Cornell and White realized they would attract many students who could not afford the expense of higher education. Cornell therefore suggested that the university hire students as manual laborers, working to improve the campus. The manual labor principle, in fact, governed the older man's view of the university, and he proposed to employ students in the manufacturing of cheap chairs and shoes. Able to dissuade Cornell from this particular venture, White still felt obliged to make his bow to manual labor in the *Report on Organization*. Labor, he advised, should be available but not obligatory. Never comfortable with the scheme, he added a note of caution: "If any such number of students as we expect, enter the University, we could not provide labor for all of them."

Seemingly oblivious of such practical problems, Ezra Cornell wrote a letter to the *New York Tribune* on April 10, 1868, promising "that no person who earnestly desires to be thoroughly educated will find difficulty in becoming so by his own exertions at the Cornell University." A flood of letters swept across the desk of the president, including requests from harried parents of mischievous twelve- and thirteen-year-olds eager to educate (and perhaps punish) their children without incurring any expense. Politely but resolutely the beleaguered White replied that the university was not a home for wayward boys, insisting that Ezra Cornell's invitation did not extend to illiterates and preadolescents. The founder's

10. *Senate Journal, 1865* (Albany, 1865), p. 857.
11. Address at the Fiftieth Anniversary of Cortland Academy, 1870, and Report on the Instruction in Social and Political Science, n.d., both in WMC.
12. *Education in Political Science*, p. 34; ADW to C. K. Adams, March 4, 1879, WMC; *Report on Organization*, p. 7.

prediction that any student could divide the day between work and study proved an embarrassment to the president, who forced himself to remind the trustees early in 1869 that the educational preeminence of the university should not suffer because of the self-supporting feature. Manual labor remained the policy during those first years, although its success was limited. Labor was inefficient and of uncertain supply. At the end of the university's first year, the manager of Cascadilla dining hall, noting that half his crockery had been destroyed, called for an end to student labor. By the spring of 1869, the *Cornell Era* reported that only a handful of students worked. In deference to Cornell, White defended manual labor, but when the founder died in 1874, he quietly shelved it.[13]

One feature of the manual labor scheme—the provision of physical exercise—struck White favorably. The popular image of the frail, sickly pedant contributed to the disdain of many Americans for university graduates. "As long as highly educated men are dyspeptics," White claimed, "so long will they be deprived of their supremacy in society by uneducated eupeptics." To remedy this tendency, White recommended the construction of a gymnasium and baseball fields and the immediate hiring of an instructor in gymnastics. Physical fitness was so important that he proposed a university statute that would judge failure in physical culture as severely as want of progress in mental culture—either kind would subject the delinquent to deprivation of university privileges.[14]

If the Cornell student had no choice in physical education, he had some freedom in charting his mental development. Most American colleges had one prescribed course of studies, the classical course. Defenders of this system pointed out that experienced educators were better qualified than adolescents to decide on a curriculum fostering mental discipline. Moreover, free choice destroyed the fellowship that prevailed when students in the same class shared all of the same subjects. Free choice meant the introduction of laxity and caprice in higher education.[15]

Unimpressed by the arguments of the traditionalists, White committed Cornell University to a degree of free election of courses. If a seventeen-year-old must choose a profession, he argued, why might he not also select two or three subjects? White thought it fallacious to assume that "because a student is not a perfect judge regarding his complete wants, therefore he is

13. *Report on Organization*, p. 38; The Beginning of Sibley College at Cornell, June 1915, WMC; *Autobiography*, vol. 1, pp. 344–45; Waterman T. Hewett, *Cornell University: A History* (New York, 1905), vol. 1, pp. 248–50; President's Report, February 1869, WMC; Morris Bishop, *A History of Cornell* (Ithaca, 1962), pp. 86, 127.

14. *Report on Organization*, pp. 39–40.

15. Laurence Veysey, *The Emergence of the American University* (Chicago, 1965), pp. 36–40.

no judge at all." Cornell University, whose wide variety of course offerings and broad spectrum of students made a single course requirement for all virtually impossible anyway, opted for a more flexible curriculum.[16]

Although opposed to the orthodox defense of the status quo, White agreed that most students were not capable of constructing an entire course of studies on their own. Consequently, he borrowed the group system used by Tappan, which gave students a choice among several courses of study, each made up of subjects in which they were obliged to participate once they selected that particular course. If students received complete freedom of choice, White feared they might get degrees "for the study of music, the French drama, and similar dilettante branches." Most students, however, were competent to choose among courses of study carefully arranged by experienced educators.[17]

Despite White's attempt to steer a middle course between the traditionalists and the advocates of free election, the traditionalists bitterly attacked the "group system" as the opening wedge inevitably leading to the destruction of a balanced curriculum.[18] Classical languages—long a symbol to advocates of mental discipline in education—had been shunted aside, they charged. White decried any attempt to discourage the study of Latin and Greek but pointed to the folly of forcing upon professors a mass of students who "while reciting in Greek are thinking of German."[19] To the charge that knowledge should be subordinate to discipline, White responded that as a rule the attempt to give mental discipline by studies that the mind did not desire was fruitless. White branded as a fallacy the idea that only mental discipline promoted precision of the mind. Discipline came through studies that were loved, not through those that were loathed. Even more disturbing and more difficult to answer were assaults on the Cornell plan of free election and the equality of courses. The *Hamilton Literary Magazine* spoke for many critics when it charged that a Cornell degree meant nothing because a student "may have graduated in anything from a mongrel classical course to a course which treats of the ablest manner of utilizing manures."[20]

16. *Report on Organization*, p. 9; *Rochester Democrat and Chronicle*, March 25, 1885.

17. *Cornell Sun*, March 12, 1885; *Report on Organization*, p. 9.

18. For Cornell's offerings see *Report on Organization*, p. 5; The Cornell University: First General Announcement, 1868, WMC; Hugh Hawkins, *Between Harvard and America: The Educational Leadership of Charles W. Eliot* (New York, 1972), p. 84.

19. *New York Tribune*, March 20, 1868.

20. Bishop, *History of Cornell*, pp. 74–75; Peterson, "Andrew D. White's Educational Principles," p. 153; Walter P. Rogers, "Andrew D. White and the Transition Period in American Higher Education," Ph.D. thesis, Cornell University, 1934, p. 44.

Despite his best efforts, White's "group system" was regarded as license rather than limited freedom, especially after Charles W. Eliot confirmed the worst fears of critics by introducing radical freedom of choice at Harvard in the 1870s and 1880s. Although Cornell did not abandon its more structured system for free electives until 1896, the two institutions became linked in the public mind as advocates of the new order.[21] Only a few insiders recognized the far more limited nature of White's reform.[22] Alexander Winchell, professor at Michigan and Vanderbilt, declared to White: "On the subject of Liberty of Choice in Studies, I am prepared to endorse your conservative conclusions."[23] Winchell's more accurate assessment, however, was buried under an avalanche of criticism from defenders of the status quo, who labeled all attempts at change as equally pernicious.

A similarly moderate policy on student discipline parallels White's stance on electives. He thought universities had hindered the development of students by regulating virtually every aspect of their lives through an immense number of college rules. The *Report on Organization* recommended a far different system: "The system of university freedom of government by which laws are few but speedily executed and the University is regarded as neither a reform school nor an asylum is preferred." The report also abandoned the requirement that professors act *in loco parentis*, spying on and policing students. To ensure that faculty members would be regarded as "a body of friends," White recommended that the trustees provide an extra stipend to Cornell's teachers to be used to increase social contact with students.[24]

The new policy of laissez faire in student affairs, providing a wholesome atmosphere conducive to study rather than teaching through threat of punishment and a rigorous regimen, extended to minute aspects of university planning. White selected chairs for the recitation rooms with this aim in mind, commissioning Burt Wilder, professor of comparative anatomy and natural history, to study the problem. The "easier and more comfortable the seat," Wilder reported, probably confirming White's expectations, "the closer is the attention and the more rapid the progress of the pupil."[25]

It was soon apparent, however, that White did not intend to leave

21. Hawkins, *Between Harvard and America*, pp. 94, 96; Veysey, *Emergence of the American University*, p. 118.
22. In later years White himself, resentful of Eliot's preeminent position in higher education, took credit for the elective system.
23. Winchell to ADW, April 2, 1867, WMC.
24. *Report on Organization*, pp. 21–22, 37.
25. Wilder to ADW, March 15, 1868, WMC.

students entirely to their own devices. The charter of the Morrill Act, written in the midst of the Civil War, *recommended* military drill, but White *required* participation by every student at Cornell and appealed to the secretary of war to detail an officer of the United States Army to supervise military activities. Major J. H. Whittlesey was installed as professor of military science. When Congress considered repealing the law authorizing military officers to serve in universities with military departments, White protested and helped to defeat the proposal. Military training, White thought, took "slouchy, careless" university men and made them stand straight. Educated men, knowledgeable in military tactics, provided society's strongest defense against civil commotions. Of all the dangers to American democracy, the most fatal was "to have its educated men in various professions so educated that, in any civil commotion, they must cower in corners, and relinquish the control of armed forces to communists and demagogues." [26] By providing the means to protect society against disorder, White hoped to demonstrate that the university was indispensable to the community.

Greatly concerned about the role of university men in future civil disorders, seemingly oblivious of the inconsistency between military training and student self-discipline, White granted Whittlesey an enormous role in student affairs. In 1868 he wrote a resolution, approved by the Board of Trustees, that was antithetical to the goals of laissez faire:

Resolved: That the organization of the students of the University who may reside in the university buildings for discipline, police and administration shall be placed on a military basis under the immediate direction of the Professor of Military Science who shall be recognized as the Military Commandant of the students.

That the Military Commandant shall enforce the necessary regulations which may from time to time be established by university authority to insure good order at quarters and in the messhalls, with precision and regularity of attendance upon stated duties; and that all regulations so established shall be of binding obligations upon the students under such sanctions as the President with the advice of the Faculty may determine. [27]

Whittlesey imposed a stern routine upon student life. Students in the dormitories arose at five A.M. from April through September; they were permitted the luxury of an additional half hour of sleep in the winter

26. *Autobiography*, vol. 1, pp. 387–88; ADW to Editor of *Army and Navy Journal*, December 26, 1906, WMC; ADW to James A. Garfield, January 17, 1871, James A. Garfield MSS, Library of Congress; Rush Welter, *Popular Education and Democratic Thought in America* (New York and London, 1962), p. 155.

27. Quoted in William Zimmerman, "Andrew White and the Role of the University Concerning Student Life," Ph.D. thesis, Cornell University, 1959, p. 95.

months. They marched to meals and ate at assigned seats in the mess hall.[28]

Student grumbling, much to the dismay of Whittlesey and White, forced the university to abandon the harsher features of military discipline. The head of stewards at Cascadilla dormitory threatened to resign if his department remained under the major's authority, and a gradual contraction of Whittlesey's power began. The military uniform, made compulsory at the opening of the university, drew many complaints. The requirement quickly dwindled to only a compulsory military cap, yet the *Cornell Era* reported that "many still groan under the yoke." On May 26, 1871, the *Era* triumphantly printed an announcement by President White: "On account of the prevalence of extremely warm weather, the rule requiring the ordinary wearing of the University Cap, except at Military Drill, is suspended until further notice." Further notice never came. The great cap controversy was a great symbolic victory for the students, who gradually pressured the university to abandon forced marches and assigned seats at meals.[29]

Despite the complaints of students (and often their parents), White refused to make military drill optional.[30] As late as January 1873, the president insisted that all students "be required to make such proficiency in Military Tactics as to be able to organize and drill a company, and to command a battalion." For the first time, however, White stipulated that a two-thirds vote of the faculty could exempt a student from this requirement. This clause was the beginning of a slow retreat that ended in voluntary military training and discipline at Cornell.[31]

White believed that the rhetoric of the *Report on Organization* was compatible with the establishment in practice of quasi-military discipline. Military training aimed less at disciplining students than at readying them to deal effectively with social disturbances. As Major Whittlesey reported virtually no outbreaks of student violence in the early years of the university, White concluded that his policies were generally accepted. Reporting

28. Ibid., pp. 96–97; J. H. Whittlesey to ADW, June 30, 1869, and C. Bayne to ADW, May 20, 1870, WMC.

29. Zimmerman, "Andrew White and the Role of the University," pp. 96–98; *Cornell Era*, September 23, 1870, and May 26, 1871.

30. One parent protested that the General Announcement was silent on the subject of required drill: "The plan of applying military rule regulations to the management of affairs in ordinary civil life (as schools) must ever prove very unpopular with the great mass; and in my judgment is wholly at variance with the taste, habits and feelings of a Free People. Forced into the ranks, compelled day by day when suffering from ill health to undergo military drill . . . and that in an institution where there can be freedom of choice . . . is it to be wondered at that the young man was displeased" (M. M. Baldwin to ADW, November 7, 1868, WMC).

31. Peterson, "Andrew D. White's Educational Principles," pp. 255–56.

on his system of discipline to the trustees following the spring 1869 term, White modestly announced: "Considering the number of students the result has exceeded our expectations."[32]

White steadfastly insisted that Cornell be nonsectarian. On this issue he had the unequivocal support of the founder. Ezra Cornell had been expelled from membership in the Society of Friends because he married a non-Quaker. Thereafter he refused, his son remembered, "to recognize the right of any church organization to place themselves between him and the Divine Master, and attempt to exclude him from the right of worship." Cornell welcomed White's proposal to incorporate the principle of nonsectarianism in the Cornell University charter, which declared that no professor or officer of the university should be chosen with reference to any religious or political views and that a majority of the trustees must never be of any one religious sect.[33]

Denominationalist opponents, however, proved more difficult to convince. They charged that students deprived of denominational guidance might begin to view religious indifference as a proper mode of thought. In his inaugural address in 1868, White countered that the greatest deists and atheists, Voltaire, Gibbon, and Diderot, had been, without exception, educated where sectarian tests were rigid. White's boundless faith in the power of truth convinced him that the most lasting religious convictions emerged from the crucible of doubt and the free exchange of ideas.[34]

White reminded the orthodox that nonsectarianism did not imply irreligion. Common schools throughout the nation operated on the principle that religion and denominationalism were separable; the Constitution demanded such a division. Could Cornell University, funded in part by federal money, defy the doctrine separating church and state?[35]

At every opportunity, White publicized the religious character of Cornell University. Religion, he believed, was an "absolute, pressing and increasing need." At Cornell, worship was central, "a dome over all the studies. It has not been secularized, or pushed into a corner." The university chapel and the Cornell University Christian Association, which benefited from the president's pecuniary aid, were visible monuments to the university's commitment to religious principles.[36] The university, of

32. President's Report, June 1869, WMC.
33. Alonzo Cornell, *True and Firm: Biography of Ezra Cornell* (New York, 1884), p. 276; Frank Hiscock to Andrew Carnegie, April 26, 1906, WMC.
34. Veysey, *Emergence of the American University*, pp. 21–56; Peterson, "Andrew D. White's Educational Principles," p. 220.
35. Hawkins, *Between Harvard and America*, p. 125; Inaugural Address at the Opening of Cornell, 1868, WMC.
36. *Cornell Sun*, December 11, 1905; *Cornell Era*, September 29, 1869.

course, did more than build religious edifices. The first Cornell register announced a policy of obligatory chapel attendance except for those "specially excused for due cause shown to the Faculty." Above all, White placed his institution squarely beneath the Christian umbrella: "Cornell is governed by a body of Christian Trustees, conducted by Christian professors and is a Christian Institution. Its inauguration was commenced with simple Christian worship and *no* public exercise has been begun without that great comprehensive petition given by the Founder of Christianity himself, the Lord's prayer." Always insistent that the essence of Christianity was the simple message of Christ rather than finely spun theology, White sought religious training at Cornell that would remind students "that all men are brothers united in a common destiny." Sincere conviction here coincided with political expediency; White knew that the legislature might support a nonsectarian university, but was certain that no aid would be forthcoming to a non-Christian institution.[37]

White devoted little space to nondenominationalism in the *Report on Organization*, probably because the subject was controversial and perhaps because he sought to convince critics that the Cornell charter—not its president—dictated university policy. Recognizing the strength of the sectarians, White sought representation on the faculty for all major denominational groups—a violation of the spirit, if not the letter, of the charter. An exchange with George C. Caldwell, professor of agricultural chemistry at Cornell, revealed the president's fear that an omission of a denomination would arouse opposition. He asked Caldwell, who had evidently recommended an appointment in his department, to suggest instead a Methodist or a Baptist. Caldwell complied, withdrawing his initial choice. Similarly, in 1870, White explained the appointment of a Methodist minister as assistant professor of languages: "For while I would not take a less valuable man to please any denomination, yet it is fortunate when superior ability and favorable denominational connection are united." Faculty members noted the incongruity of White's approach, which sometimes resulted in the appointment of nondenominationalists on the very fringes of Christianity and at others sought orthodox sectarians.[38]

Cornell University, then, provided a home for men with pronounced sectarian loyalties and for those with none at all. Sectarian balance super-

---

37. Bishop, *History of Cornell*, p. 141; "Cornell University: What It Has Done, What It Is Doing, and What It Hopes to Do," January 27, 1873, WMC; *Cornell Era*, September 29, 1869.
38. Caldwell to ADW, December 26, 1867; ADW to William C. Russel, July 11, 1870; D. Willard Fiske to ADW, August 20, 1870, all in WMC.

seded sectarian homogeneity, but White's ringing declarations on hiring did not reflect this concession: "It makes no earthly difference what [an applicant's] political or religious views are. He may be a combination of a High Tory and a Buddhist, a Communist and Comptist. . . ."[39] White was more concerned about his potential critics than he cared to admit. Although the university might shield one or two infidels, it presumably would not countenance more than token representation by the ungodly, no matter what their academic credentials. Cornell's economy was not entirely free; but White celebrated partial victory, confident that he had weakened the forces that hindered free investigation.

If denominationalists forced the appointment of a few of their number to the Cornell faculty, White nevertheless assured himself that, given the limitations of time and money, he had put together the best faculty possible. Low faculty salaries and the prospect of a dreary, long winter in Ithaca made it unlikely that White could successfully lure the most prominent professors to Cornell. Undaunted, he decided to attract eminent scholars by offering them nonresident professorships, allowing them to deliver one course of lectures a year (of whatever length they chose), thus enriching the entire university community: "In fact, the lecturer 'shakes the bush' and the regular resident instructor 'catches the bird.' The outside and eminent lecturer, coming fresh from the world at large, gives the whole community a new stimulus by which both resident professors and students are strengthened and encouraged."[40] Taking advantage of his extensive contacts, White persuaded zoologist Louis Agassiz, poet James Russell Lowell (both at Harvard), and eminent man of letters George William Curtis to visit Ithaca as Cornell's first nonresident professors. Ithaca hotels overflowed with visitors willing to pay the fifty cents a lecture necessary to hear their favorites. White's triumph was complete when Harvard adopted the Cornell system in 1869.[41]

If the seemingly effortless success of the nonresident lecture system was in reality the product of persuasion and cajoling of reluctant scholars,[42] the establishment of a resident faculty was more visibly the result of tireless recruiting labor. Letters of introduction and public petitions of support were the usual means by which an applicant petitioned for appointment. White recognized that such testimonials failed to convey an accurate

39. ADW to Mrs. E. P. Evans, June 26, 1875, WMC.
40. ADW to Carnegie, February 14, 1911, Andrew Carnegie MSS, Library of Congress.
41. *Report on Organization*, pp. 16–18.
42. Curtis, for example, had constantly to be flattered and persuaded. Burdened with work, he sought to slip out of his commitment: "Is it necessary that my lectures should be given this year? Do we all begin at once? I ask with perturbation for I am staggered at the prospect of being ready in the spring" (Curtis to ADW, September 16, 1868, WMC).

assessment of the candidate: "No man of recent experience can doubt that an immense array of petitions could be obtained for the rebuilding of the Tower of Babel . . . [or] attesting the fitness of the most knavish contractor to build it."[43] White sought confidential statements from acknowledged authorities in each field. The university, content with nonresident professors as its "big names," sought to build a faculty of scholars still in the process of making a reputation. A staff was slowly assembled, many of whom gave long and distinguished service to the university: Eli Blake in physics; James Crafts, general chemistry; George C. Caldwell, agricultural chemistry; Evan Evans, mathematics; William Channing Russel, modern languages; Burt Wilder, natural history. With understandable pride, White received the complimentary assurance of Professor Chandler, head of Columbia College School of Science, that no other faculty in the United States had been brought together with so much care.[44]

Because White insisted that academic ability was not the only criterion for employment, personal contact with prospective faculty became even more necessary. General good culture and "manliness" were essential qualities in teachers charged with making men as well as scholars. The university, the *Report on Organization* declared, "must have men who are what we would have our sons be." In private as well as in public, White stressed the same qualifications for professors. "Like you," he told Russel, "I prize thorough-breds and gentlemen." White sought men who could inspire the students and simultaneously bind the university and the community at large. A cultured, charming faculty would facilitate recognition of the university's preeminent role in society.[45]

Having recruited a faculty of ability and culture, White still had to define its responsibilities. His experience had dramatized the dangers of a powerless faculty, unable to temper the excesses of the president or to head off a clash with the legislature. Therefore he decided to give professors a greater role in university planning. Regular faculty meetings would be held to discuss policy. Matters of discipline and the conferring of degrees would be decided by ballot. The president still retained primary responsibility for university administration, but frequent discussions and the solicitation of advice helped to ensure cooperation.[46]

In only one area of faculty–administration relations—term of office—

43. *Report on Organization*, p. 23.
44. Report of the Committee on Appointment of Faculty, September 26, 1867; Louis Agassiz to ADW, July 30, 1867; ADW to Joseph Harris, October 22, 1867, all in WMC.
45. *Report on Organization*, pp. 20–22; ADW to Russel, August 18, 1870, and ADW to E. P. Evans, February 28, 1868, WMC.
46. President's Report, June 18, 1884, WMC; *Report on Organization*, pp. 24–25; ADW to Seth Low, March 1, 1895, WMC.

did White refuse to make a recommendation. Should professors be given a fixed term or an indefinite term? If teachers were granted indefinite terms, the removal of incompetents would be difficult, if not impossible. Fixed terms, on the other hand, invariably resulted in faculty cabals to achieve or block reelection. Committed to the goals of faculty excellence and university harmony, White was unable to decide on the lesser of two evils. In essence, Cornell had no policy other than a general agreement to remove faculty only for good and sufficient cause. Among gentlemen, White probably concluded, greater assurances were unncessary.[47]

Teachers and students, White recognized, however capable and earnest, could scarcely embark upon the road to knowledge with inadequate provisions for their educational nourishment. Inadequate facilities, he wrote to Cornell, tended to discourage students: "[S]ecuring a body of Professors does not begin to worry me as much as securing a sufficient number of carpenters." The first essential and immediate need was a library, both an edifice and books, without which the faculty "will be frequently plodding in old circles, and stumbling into old errors." An ample library also attracted able men to a faculty and brought scholars from all over the globe to enrich an institution.[48]

To secure the best available books, as well as the most modern laboratory equipment and demonstration models, White traveled to Europe in 1868. His book purchases included the famous Bopp library, which, along with the Charles Anthon collection, gave the university sufficient resources for classical studies. White accumulated physical and chemical apparatus, the Rau models of plows from Hohenheim, and various models of machine movements, spending in all more than $60,000. White again and again begged Cornell for more money, often promising matching contributions of his own. How could he pass up a model of an Arabian horse that could be taken apart by veterinary students, or models for anatomy courses from which students could learn more in an hour than from a textbook in a month?[49]

Equipment purchases alone made the trip to Europe a success, but White engineered two coups there that brought great publicity to the university. After much searching, the president settled upon James Law of Belfast as Cornell's professor of veterinary science. Although Law was still a young man, his books and articles had already earned him a substantial

---

47. *Report on Organization*, p. 25.
48. ADW to EC, August 11, 1868, WMC; *Report on Organization*, p. 33; ADW to C. K. Adams, June 5, 1889, WMC.
49. *Autobiography*, vol. 1, pp. 338, 360–61; ADW to EC; April 27 and June 19, 1868, and ADW to R. H. Thurston, December 14, 1897, all in WMC.

reputation. Personally, he was "just the man" White wanted for the university. Surprisingly, Law accepted White's salary offer of $2,250. "Be careful," White twitted Ezra Cornell, "or it will be noised abroad that I am the *practical man* of the concern."[50]

If the acquisition of Law elicited Cornell's applause, White's announcement that he had persuaded Goldwin Smith, professor of history at Oxford, to come to Ithaca as a nonresident professor brought an ovation from the university community. Smith, a distinguished expert on English constitutional history and a figure of some note in English politics, had earned the affection of many Americans with his pro-Union stance during the Civil War. The recent suicide of his father and disillusionment with the English political scene made Smith amenable to White's suggestion that he visit the United States. Well aware of the publicity value of his appointment, White advised Ezra Cornell to telegraph the news at once to the Associated Press.[51]

Before Cornell University opened its doors, then, President White had provided it with equipment, an able staff, and pedagogical guidelines. Hoping that Cornell University would remain unfettered by precedents, Daniel Coit Gilman had predicted in 1865 that "the shade of Homer may hover with indignation over the modern Ithaca—but it will be in vain."[52] Gilman was both right and wrong. Cornell and its president, motivated by expediency, innate conservatism, and a genuine desire to improve relations between the university and the community, stopped short of a clean break with tradition. But, paradoxically, because White's rhetoric banished the ghost of tradition, the university became a rallying point for reformers far more willing than he to depart radically from the past.

50. ADW to EC; July 3, 1868, WMC.
51. Ibid.
52. Daniel Coit Gilman, "The Cornell University," *Nation* 1 (July 6, 1865), pp. 44–45.

Chapter 5

Launching the University

The early years of Cornell University, during which much-heralded (and much-criticized) experiments in agricultural education, nonsectarianism, and coeducation were inaugurated, illustrate White's accomplishments and limitations as an educational innovator. Recognizing that the legislature and the public viewed Cornell as "radical," White insisted that traditional values were not threatened. Nonsectarianism did not subvert Christianity; coeducation did not deter women from assuming their traditional role as mothers. The university was under siege from a host of enemies, and White was willing to compromise to ensure its survival. He was a gradualist, willing to bend (even when important principles were concerned) when convinced that bending would in the long run advance his educational goals.

When frustrating delays in the construction of buildings and faculty recruitment threatened the realization of White's dream, he redoubled his efforts to open the university in the fall of 1868. Deferral of the inaugural would inevitably disillusion prospective students and the general public, he believed, and might doom Cornell University to the fate of the People's College. On October 7, 1868, the long-awaited inauguration day arrived. A host of state luminaries assembled to wish the land grant college well, but Governor Reuben E. Fenton's conspicuous absence provided a vivid reminder that the conflict accompanying the establishment of Cornell had not subsided. Apparently bowing to denominational pressure, Fenton quietly slipped out of Ithaca before the festivities began.[1]

Months of feverish activity and the excitement of the occasion prostrated both White and Cornell, who had to be carried up the hill in order to attend the ceremonies. Each was determined, however, to deliver his inaugural address. Ezra Cornell repeated his oft-expressed wish that the university bearing his name provide a home for all students desiring education in any field of learning. To take the lead in this great experiment, he proudly announced, the trustees selected "a gentleman and a schollar

1. *New York World*, October 17, 1868; *Autobiography*, vol. 1, p. 340.

[sic], who though young in years, we present to day for inauguration with entire confidence that 'the right man is in the right place.'" [2]

White took his turn at the podium. In an address that the *New York World* called "a bold knocking at the doors of settled rules," the president announced Cornell's aim: "A deliverance from old ideas under which education has been groaning." The university, seeking to develop the individual and to benefit society, would strive to eliminate the influence of those "for whom Greed is God and Moneybags his prophet." White rededicated himself to the principles of equality and nonsectarianism. The president promised to remain uninfluenced, "either in the way of imitation or antagonism, by other educational institutions or ideas." Fatigued from months of unceasing labor, overcome with emotion at the accolades bestowed upon him, White was unable to complete his prepared speech. His voice faltered, and with a few extemporaneous remarks he completed his first presidential address. [3]

Numerous signs indicated that the university was well launched. Its entering class of 418 students was the largest to date in the history of higher education in the United States. Most state universities counted themselves fortunate if their first class numbered more than fifty. [4] If enrollment was more than ample, facilities were at least adequate. White pointed to large new lecture rooms where 250 young men eagerly absorbed the latest scientific knowledge. [5] He was confident, moreover, that the trustees would finance the steady expansion of the university. [6]

Even before the inauguration, however, the president faced a problem that would persist through much of his administration. Realizing the importance of agriculture to the land grant college, White carefully selected a professor of agriculture. His choice was Joseph Harris. After releasing Harris's name to the press, White discovered to his embarrassment that the prospective new faculty member had second thoughts about accepting the appointment. Hopeful that Harris would change his mind, the president continued to pressure him throughout the fall of 1868. "Students are asking when the course in Agriculture is to begin and expressing surprise at the absence of the professor." [7]

2. Inaugural Address of Ezra Cornell, October 7, 1868, WMC.

3. *Inaugural Address of Andrew D. White* (Ithaca, 1868); Philip Dorf, *The Builder: A Biography of Ezra Cornell* (New York, 1952), p. 349; Morris Bishop, *A History of Cornell* (Ithaca, 1962), p. 89; *Autobiography*, vol. 1, pp. 340–43.

4. Allan Nevins, *The State Universities and Democracy* (Urbana, Ill., 1962), p. 41.

5. ADW to Dr. Leslie, April 29, 1869, Daniel Coit Gilman MSS, Johns Hopkins University.

6. ADW to Frederick Law Olmsted, April 22, 1873, Olmsted MSS, Library of Congress.

7. ADW to Joseph Harris, February 24, August 27, and October 20, 1868, WMC.

The comedy of errors in the agriculture department did not cease with Joseph Harris's final refusal to move to Ithaca. The search for a replacement proved unsuccessful until 1872, when White hired Henry McCandless from Glasnevin. McCandless insisted on bringing with him costly equipment that was useless in the United States. More disturbing, however, were the white gloves he never removed, a symbol of his disdain for practical farm labor. Never comfortable amidst the crudities of life in Ithaca, the fastidious McCandless resigned his position in 1873 and moved to Canada.[8]

Distressed by the difficulty of finding a competent professor of agriculture, White was even more disturbed by the paucity of students enrolled in the agricultural course. Of Cornell's 388 pupils in 1869, one farmer calculated, 323 pursued studies usually taught in colleges, 2 studied military science, 33 agriculture, and 30 the mechanic arts. "How Agriculture is benefitted!" he sarcastically observed. Three years later, enrollment in agriculture had actually dropped. Only 14 of the 592 Cornell students, registrar William D. Wilson reported, had chosen the agricultural course. Cornell University received $900,000 under the grant of 1862, noted the influential *Nation* in 1873, and gave as a dividend two agricultural graduates a year.[9]

Although White persisted in his efforts to strengthen the department, he concluded that ultimate success was largely beyond his control. As long as a farmer with a little bit of capital could go west and secure an abundant harvest by "gently tickling the rich virgin prairies," the principles of scientific agriculture remained superfluous and students difficult to recruit. The simple fact was, White repeatedly argued, "that when farmers educate their sons, they do not educate them to be farmers." The time was not far off, however, when the frontier would be closed and Americans would be forced to substitute ingenuity and training for haphazard wastefulness. People would go on "skimming the lands in the older states and then running on to new ones," he wrote to Justin Morrill with acute perception. "But of course in a generation or two that must stop . . . and then agricultural colleges will take the place which they ought to hold." If the agricultural graduate was, at present, compelled to find employment in some other field or else compete with unskilled labor, his skills would become indispensable to the farmer in the near future. The closing of the

8. Isaac Roberts, *Autobiography of a Farm Boy* (Ithaca, 1946), p. 116; *Autobiography*, vol. 1, pp. 367–70.

9. Farmer's Rights to Lyman, July 27, 1869, and William D. Wilson to ADW, February 10, 1872, WMC; Walter Rogers, *Andrew D. White and the Modern University* (Ithaca, 1942), p. 121.

frontier and the provision for education in scientific agriculture, then, could mean the restoration of rural virtue in America.[10]

If the promise of future success consoled White, it did not assuage the need for immediate action to silence critics. In 1870 he recommended and the trustees adopted a proposal that no student receive a degree in any regular course in the university without having heard a course of lectures and passed an examination in general agriculture. To satisfy farmer-critics, White was willing to limit students' curricular choices.[11]

To attract students to the agricultural course, the president announced in 1874 that tuition would be free for all students in agriculture and recommended that the trustees provide free rooms as well. In the same year, White found an outstanding professor for the fledgling department, Isaac P. Roberts of Iowa College. Roberts introduced a standard of excellence that was to win wide recognition throughout the state. He insisted on taking meticulous inventories, kept farm accounts from each subdivision, and in a short time doubled the average yield secured by his predecessors. Roberts lectured throughout the state in an effort to improve relations between farmers and the university. The basis for a successful department had been established.[12]

Harried by attacks from agriculturalists throughout the state, White was simultaneously stunned by an even more ominous threat to the university. In 1872 the *Rochester Democrat* charged that Ezra Cornell had dreamed up the university scheme as a means of acquiring the 900,000 acres granted to New York State. "Nothing remains now," a despondent White wrote, "but the proof that we are murderers wh[ich] I confidently expect." The charge, he concluded, was all the more incredible because Ezra Cornell was "absolutely the most unselfish man I ever saw."[13]

The following year the charges were renewed, and to a nation rocked by the scandals of the Grant administration, almost any accusation seemed credible. In mid-May 1873, Jeremiah McGuire, representing the district that included the People's College in the New York Assembly, accused Ezra Cornell of land-grabbing. Confident that he could defend himself personally, Cornell supported the call for an investigation of the univer-

10. Roberts, *Autobiography*, p. 142; President's Report, June 18, 1884, and ADW to Justin Morrill, December 10, 1873, WMC; *Scientific and Industrial Education in the United States* (New York, 1874), p. 10.

11. Walter Rogers, "Andrew D. White and the Transition Period in American Higher Education," Ph.D. thesis, Cornell University, 1934, p. 69.

12. "Cornell University: What It Has Done, What It Is Doing, and What It Hopes to Do," January 27, 1873; President's Report to the Board of Trustees, July 1, 1874; William C. Russel to ADW, November 18, 1877, all in WMC.

13. ADW to Moses Coit Tyler, September 4, 1872, WMC.

sity's land grant. White's reaction to the imbroglio was characteristic. He recoiled initially and succumbed to deep depression. "This is enough to disgust one with human nature," he confided to his diary. "I can almost say 'stretch me no longer.'" White's faith in the cause of the university, however, sustained him. He assembled the faculty and students on May 16 and, in a speech widely reported in the press, treated them to a spirited defense of the founder. The president remembered that Cornell had quietly donated $500,000 for the good of higher education in the state. Was this man really a thief? White recognized that his own fate was inextricably linked to the university and its benefactor: "If he is to be disgraced, I shall feel it an honor to be disgraced with him."[14]

White decided to use the committee investigation to silence critics of the university as well as proponents of the land-grab theory. He called on Governor John A. Dix and the legislature to increase the mandate of the investigators to examine every facet of Cornell University. A three-man committee headed by Horatio Seymour ultimately exonerated Ezra Cornell of all charges against him.[15]

White's unflinching public support of Ezra Cornell belied the president's growing private disenchantment with the founder. From the outset the two men had disagreed on fiscal policy. Hoping to build a major university immediately, White urged Cornell to sell all the land scrip, but the old man refused, confident that the land would soon be worth far more than its present value. As was his habit, White yielded to Cornell's judgment, while grumbling that his own view was wiser. By 1870 the situation had deteriorated. The faculty's petition for salary increases was denied by the parsimonious Board of Trustees despite a claim that $1,900 of the $2,000 salary went to room and board alone. Noting six faculty resignations, a student informed White with stunning logic: "If the faculty all resign I suppose I shall be compelled to go elsewhere."[16]

Fearful that the existence of the university was in jeopardy, White resorted to the threat of resignation, a tactic he would use again and again to wring concessions from Cornell and the board. He evidenced interest in the nomination for a seat in Congress. White's political ambition was genuine, but his loyalty to the university was usually paramount. The president needed assurances that he was indispensable to Cornell and that his policies—so carefully thought out over decades—guided the univer-

14. Bishop, *History of Cornell*, p. 186; The Founding of Cornell, Summer 1877?, WMC; Diary, May 13, 1873, WMC; Speech before the Faculty and Students, May 16, 1873, WMC; *New York Times*, May 23, 1873.
15. New York State Senate Resolution, May 17, 1873, WMC.
16. ADW to EC, November 9, 1867; Homer Sprague to ADW, February 9, 1869; Russel to ADW, February 16, 1869; Frank Barnard to ADW, July 10, 1870, all in WMC.

sity. "I may stumble in minor matters," he told Cornell, "in things of detail [but] I see as clearly what we want for the future as if it were mapped out before me. . . . I *know* that in the main lines of planning I am right." Threatened resignation offered a perfect opportunity to force colleagues to bestow on him the accolades that seemed so necessary to his inner contentment.[17]

The possibility of a congressional seat elicited numerous requests from the faculty that he decline for the good of the university. "Don't go and get nominated for Congress, please," language professor Willard Fiske begged White, reminding him that public identification with a political party would "be a hard blow for the University" and would probably lead to a legislative investigation. An appeal to the president's commitment to the university rarely failed to move him, and he deferred his political plans.[18]

Still determined to force Cornell and the trustees to sell the land scrip, White renewed his threat to resign in a letter to the founder's son Alonzo. The fiscal policies of the board, he insisted, were fatal to the institution: "We are in debt—over one hundred thousand dollars. . . . We are forced to stop short with what we have—with no chance to develop. . . ." White's tactic did not result in disposal of the land scrip or a dramatic increase in faculty salaries, but the trustees wiped out the debt and further expansion of the university again seemed possible.[19]

Even more disturbing than Ezra Cornell's niggling fiscal policies was his neglect of university affairs. White reproached Cornell for his consuming interest in railroad building, informing him that at best a few miles of inferior track would be added to the "thousand on thousand of miles already existing in the United States."[20] White's indictment of Cornell was not justified. The old man's unwillingness to spend stemmed not from financial conservatism but from a conviction that the land scrip would yield a huge endowment in the near future—if only the trustees would be patient. Moreover, Cornell's interest in railroads did not mean disenchantment with the university. Knowing that he had few years left, Cornell pursued business opportunities, hoping to provide a rich bequest for his family and his university.[21]

To close friends, the president voiced his disillusionment, exacerbated by the financial difficulties that the university was experiencing as a result

17. Willard Fiske to ADW, August 19, 1870, and ADW to Ezra Cornell, December 5, 1872, WMC.
18. Fiske to ADW, August 19, 1870, WMC.
19. ADW to AC, October 25, 1870, WMC.
20. ADW to EC, April 27, 1874, WMC.
21. Adverse business conditions prevented Cornell from realizing his aim, and at his death in 1874 his resources were rather meager.

Daniel Coit Gilman, White's Yale classmate, later president of Johns Hopkins University

of the Panic of 1873.[22] He presented Gilman with a list of Cornell's accomplishments, claiming: "The foundations are laid but the superstructure is still to be built." Pleading ill health and the desire to devote himself full-time to scholarship, White asked Gilman to succeed him as president. But he revealed to Russel the real source of his frustration. Although White had sacrificed comfort, political prospects, literary ambition, and health for the institution, Ezra Cornell received the world's reknown. What did the president have to show for his labors? "Not a building bears my name—not a Professorship—not a department—not a scholarship." [23]

The desire for public recognition was a motivating force throughout White's career; he could bear to die, he once remarked, but not to be forgotten. A natural aristocrat, he found it difficult to defer to others, especially in university affairs, in which he was an acknowledged expert. A man of wealth, White refused to look upon himself as a mere hireling of the trustees. Cornell University was, after all, the creature of his imagination, born a decade before he met Ezra Cornell. Because Horace White had not left enough money to endow a university of which Andrew White could be the single architect, White had to watch from the wings while the limelight shone on a man whose claim to fame was that he had designed telegraph poles.[24]

The despair precipitated by threats to the university and the lack of public applause proved remarkably temporary. Initially quick to see dire implications in every setback, White compensated by developing his faith that even the most vexing difficulty would be corrected in the future. With age, White's fits of distemper, always short and seldom aired publicly, diminished. White cushioned disappointments with his belief that history would justify him and secure his rightful place in public esteem. The alternative, given his intense ambition, was probably physical and mental breakdown. White's optimism did not provide complete contentment. Throughout his life he suffered from severe headaches. Frequent vacations during periods of stress were essential. Nevertheless, White's public pose reflected confidence in the future as he became less and less willing to reveal doubts to friends or even to himself.

Even more troublesome to White than the chaotic department of agriculture and the university's financial woes were the persistent critics of

22. See also ADW to EC, December 5, 1872, Cornell MSS, Cornell University.
23. ADW to Gilman, September 22, 1873, and ADW to Russel, December 24, 1873, WMC.
24. ADW to C. J. Esty, August 24, 1886, WMC.

the institution's religious policies. At his inauguration the president had invited conflict by assaulting the sectarian spirit as the worst foe of enlarged university education.[25] Even at present, he added a year later, well-meaning gentlemen were in terror lest some new interpretation upset God's truth. White insisted that the eternal verities were not so weak that they had to be perpetually coddled.[26] Moreover, prayers at sectarian colleges were dogmatic or ceremonial, not educative, and the "thin music and feeble choir" left most students "utterly listless or worse." White reiterated his pledge of freedom of inquiry at Cornell, while promising a Christian but nonsectarian university and chapel.[27]

The pledge of a Christian institution failed to mollify those who feared that the pose of neutrality among denominations would inevitably lead to religious indifference and atheism. The job of a university faculty, Noah Porter of Yale believed, was to guide students through the treacherous shoals of interpretation. Porter attacked the theories disastrous to Christianity that received impartial hearings at Cornell. The Yale Congregationalist insisted that every educated man "must either accept or reject the ill-disguised materialism of Huxley, . . . the evolutionism of Herbert Spencer, with its demonstrated impossibility of positive theism. . . . In history every man must take or reject the atheistic fatalism of Buckle."[28]

Others, some of whom were friends of the university, echoed Porter's argument that whatever the intention, nonsectarianism eroded Christianity. John Stanton Gould, prominent agriculturalist, urged White at the very least not to abandon the title of professor of Christian ethics. Abolishing the chair, Gould asserted, was disastrous, since, as White agreed, morality was founded on the teachings of Christ.[29] A Presbyterian clergyman had articulated a similar view: "Our complaint is not that you are irreligious or atheistical—nobody supposed that you are either—but that you do not teach the dogmas of historical Christianity. As long as you hold your present position the pulpit never will be satisfied."[30]

Most sectarian opponents of Cornell preferred categorical labels of "atheism" and "infidelity" to sophisticated judgments about the unfortunate tendencies of nonsectarianism. Small denominational colleges, White reported to Moses Coit Tyler, "fairly shrieked" against the university. White assured himself that no one listened to these hysterical assertions: "We have been charged with almost everything—from Atheism to

25. Quoted in Rogers, *Andrew D. White and the Modern University*, p. 73.
26. *Address on Agricultural Education* (Albany, 1869), p. 36.
27. Bishop, *History of Cornell*, pp. 190–91.
28. Quoted in Rogers, "Andrew D. White and the Transition Period," p. 134.
29. Gould to ADW, July 29, 1868, WMC.
30. Quoted in Russel to ADW, October 31, 1880, WMC.

pocket-picking but the people after all don't quite believe the charges judging from the size of the entering class—the largest ever known to any American college or university."[31]

Although White attempted to convince himself of the ineffectualness of his critics, he repeatedly emphasized Cornell's Christian foundation. Between 1869 and 1876 he defended nonsectarianism before such diverse organizations as the Free Religious Association in Cambridge, Massachusetts, the YMCA in Utica, the North Presbyterian Church in Buffalo, and the universities of Michigan and Illinois.[32] The president reminded his audiences that the terms of the charter required nonsectarianism, but he added forcefully that the university was a Christian institution. Working days and public exercises all began with prayer. White admitted that students were expected but not forced to attend chapel services. He hoped, he said, "to attract young men to chapel, and not to drive them into it." The president somewhat disingenuously added another reason for the failure to make services obligatory: the chapel was simply not large enough to accommodate all the students.[33]

Many friends of the university regarded the president's responses to hysterical critics as unwise. Willard Fiske reported to White in 1869 that the university was flooded with applicants, seemingly oblivious of the controversy swirling around them. Under these circumstances, he asked, "wouldn't it be as well to let the Clerics rave unanswered? . . . If we plunge into a morass of words there is no saying who may get mired in the end."[34] White's own similar reasoning had not stayed his passion, so it was inevitable that he would also ignore Fiske's advice. For decades the president continued to respond to every charge of atheism, finally prompting the editor of the *Troy Daily Times* in 1898 to refuse to print his reply to Methodist attacks. Cornell was too solid to be injured by such critics, he informed White, and he urged him not to dignify "this Lilliputian attack" with a serious answer. White's letter was like "using a triphammer to mash a midget."[35] Deprived of his coveted place at Yale by New Haven's Congregationalists, White could not be convinced that a strenuous campaign against sectarianism was unnecessary.

In 1872 inadequate facilities for worship at Cornell prompted lumberman Henry Sage, the most influential member of the Board of Trustees

31. ADW to Tyler, August 2, 1869, WMC.
32. Donald E. Williams, "Andrew D. White: Spokesman for the Free University," *Quarterly Journal of Speech* 47 (April 1961): 137.
33. Sage Chapel was not completed until 1875.
34. Quoted in Horatio White, *Willard Fiske: Life and Correspondence* (New York, 1925), p. 404.
35. Charles Francis to ADW, July 11, 1898, WMC.

next to Ezra Cornell, to offer to build a spacious university chapel. A devoted communicant of Henry Ward Beecher's Plymouth Congregational Church in Brooklyn, Sage sought to make religion central at Cornell. He hoped that Sage Chapel would firmly establish Cornell as a Protestant institution, and that a permanent university preacher would supply the religious direction sacrificed by White's refusal to grant preferred status to any sect.[36]

White was delighted at the prospect of a Christian house of worship at Cornell but rejected the concept of a permanent minister, which, like the establishment of a professor of Christian ethics, would violate the nonsectarian principle. The matter came to a head in the fall of 1872, when Sage's son, Dean, offered to donate $30,000 for a permanent chaplain to be chosen from White's own Protestant Episcopal church. The president carefully informed young Sage that giving Episcopalians sole control of the pulpit was inconsistent with the charter; a permanent minister of one sect would arouse the hostility of the others.[37]

Having rejected Dean Sage's proposal, White suggested that the donation be used to bring a variety of preachers to the chapel for two-week assignments during the university year. Thus, he argued, all denominations would be represented and student interest thereby maintained. Not completely convinced, Sage sought reassurance that the preaching of the various denominationalists would not muddle the minds of students. White suggested that the invitation form could clarify the university's desire to present the great fundamental doctrines of Christianity rather than mere points of sectarian difference. He failed to note that sects emerged from conflicts over what constituted the essence of Christianity, that mere points of difference to him were matters of moment to sectarians. An advocate of Christian union himself, White seemed to be welcoming to Sage Chapel only extreme latitudinarian ministers. His insistence on a nonsectarian but Christian university, then, was an attempt to transfer his own religious philosophy to Cornell. Dean Sage acquiesced to the president's suggestion, however, and Cornell University opened its pulpit to representatives of all denominations.[38]

Sage Chapel conformed in every respect to White's hope for a university house of worship.[39] Good music, an attractive edifice, and a succession of stimulating sermons kept students awake and interested. To ensure an

---

36. ADW to Henry Sage, September 1872, WMC.
37. ADW to Dean Sage, September 26, 1872, WMC.
38. ADW to Dean Sage, September 26, 1872, WMC.
39. For Henry Sage's view of a rotating ministry, see ADW to Henry Sage, September 1872; Russel to ADW, March 19, 1874; Diary, June 12, 1875, all in WMC.

audience for its ministers and to answer those who pointed to Cornell's "paganism," the university now required all undergraduates to attend college prayers six mornings in the week at 8:15 A.M. and one service in chapel on Sundays, unless parents or guardians requested attendance elsewhere. The music, the building, and the quality of the preaching, Professor Tracy Peck reported in 1882, made attendance at chapel "much more popular—or at any rate much less unpopular." White, too, attended services regularly, and enjoyed them. Invitations were sent almost exclusively to broad-church Christian ministers, but the president certainly accepted Professor Horatio White's defense of this policy: " . . . if those who sit in darkness sometimes complain that the preachers lay less stress on doctrine and more on deed, and that the men who are invited to come are evidently too often the shakiest in their respective denominations the answer seems to be that they are not exceptions, but simply show the drift." Confident that "evolution" pointed toward one religion for the world, President White did not hesitate to hasten the coming of the millenium.[40]

The success of White's system of rotating ministers frustrated Henry Sage's plan for a permanent university preacher. Unaccustomed to having his wishes ignored, Sage fumed at White and in 1880 sounded out the Reverend Thomas Slicer about coming to Ithaca when the right moment arrived. "White will remain wedded to the present plan, which is his," Sage predicted, but he added that the president always adopted plans not his own when a majority of the Board of Trustees differed with him. The right moment to replace Cornell's rotating pulpit never arrived, and the enmity between White and Sage—brought close to the surface in the 1870s—was to erupt tragically in the next decade.[41]

While White advanced the cause of nonsectarianism in Sage Chapel, he attempted to broaden the religious perspective of the university by appointing Felix Adler to a professorship at Cornell. Adler, who had founded the Ethical Culture Society, was in White's opinion the most eloquent man in New York, and he was pleased when a group of wealthy Jews in that city endowed a chair in oriental history and literature in 1874 for the express purpose of bringing the scholar to Cornell. Adler's appointment, the *Cornell Era* editorialized, exemplified a university untrammeled by the bonds of sectarianism.[42]

Within months, however, a chorus of complaints indicated that Adler

40. ADW to Charles Dudley Warner, December 14, 1875; Horatio White to ADW, January 4, 1880; Tracy Peck to ADW, May 22, 1882, all in WMC.
41. Henry Sage to Slicer, December 8, 1880, Sage MSS, Cornell University.
42. *Cornell Sun*, May 14, 1890; *Cornell Era*, April 24, 1874.

had not laid aside his "peculiar religious beliefs." Announced as a lecturer on Hebrew literature, Adler lectured on religion only. An expert in comparative religion, Adler attempted to convince students that certain Christian concepts were present in other religions, and he pointed to the similarity of statements supposedly made by Jesus and Buddha. "We have no more right," Russel told President White, "to teach antichristian than we do to teach Christian doctrine."[43] White's assessment of Cornell's religious policy was somewhat different. Always insistent that the inculcation of Christian principles was essential to the university, he differed with his critics only in his definition of the essence of Christianity. At the same time, however, belief in unfettered freedom of inquiry forced him cautiously to yield a place to antichristian instructors, assuring himself that truth would ultimately prevail in the free marketplace of ideas. Criticized from all sides for keeping Christian and antichristian in unstable equilibrium, White chose to tolerate the heretical Adler.

By 1877 the New York press increased its criticism of Adler, who had set up "a new church or mosque or synagogue or josh-house or something of that sort" in New York City. The *New York Witness* and *New York World* warned Christian parents not to send their children to Cornell University.[44] Vacationing in Italy at the time, White responded with an open letter to the alumni and undergraduates defending the Jewish scholar. Denominational critics, he claimed, had ignored Cornell's chapel, organ, and Christian Association, but had responded with fear to the exaggerated threat of Professor Adler. White pointed out that, although Adler was of Jewish parentage, "he was a graduate of one of our most renowned Christian colleges, and had been blessed with all the safeguards against error which an institution noted for its orthodoxy could throw around him."[45] White's defense of Adler was ingenious and not entirely honest. In defending the nonsectarian principle he argued that the most orthodox institutions had produced the greatest heretics; Adler's defense required a different conclusion. The president, who might have made Adler's case a plea for the unhindered pursuit of truth, chose instead to make dubious claims for Adler amid repeated assertions of Cornell's Christian character.

Satisfied that he had proved the university had not erred in hiring Adler, White made no objection to the trustees' plan to get rid of him. To save face the trustees announced that in the future, gifts of money to endow a chair

43. Rogers, *Andrew D. White and the Modern University*, p. 76; Russel to ADW, May 19, 1874, WMC.
44. Fiske to ADW, January 4, 1879, WMC.
45. *Cornell Era*, May 4, 1877; Letter to the Alumni and Undergraduates, April 5, 1877, WMC.

that was to be filled by a stipulated individual would be refused. Issued as a general policy statement, the directive also terminated Adler's connection with Cornell. The president had bowed to community pressure, in grim contrast to the *Era*'s bold and idealistic pronouncements greeting Adler's appointment.[46]

Eased out of the university, Felix Adler had the last word about White's religious policy. In a long letter to Russel, he commented on the difficulties of maintaining a rigorously nonsectarian but Christian university that claimed also to be open to all paths of truth:

I cannot help regretting deeply the efforts of so distinguished a man as President White to establish the "Christian character" of his University. It seems to me that when he used the word Christian he means thereby "moral" in the best sense. But it is precisely this identification of the highest morality with so distinctively a sectarian system as the Christian that is peculiarly grating to the sensibilities of those who are not Christians and who do not desire to be classed as such. After all is not Cornell University our University? Is it not a State institution?[47]

To a comparative religionist like Adler, Christianity was surely as much a sect as Methodism was to White; therefore, the president's own reasoning could be used to argue against his efforts to establish Cornell's Christian character.

Amid the storms that rocked Cornell's early years, the university expanded steadily, if not always in pace with the president's hopes. Student enrollment and facilities grew, and White persuaded the trustees to broaden the university's course offerings. In 1871 he offered to donate his architecture library, one of the largest in the United States, to the university if it founded a department and hired a professor. The trustees agreed, and so Cornell University boasted the second department of architecture in existence in the United States.[48] By offering to pay the first year's expenses out of his own pocket, the president also persuaded the trustees to establish a department of electrical engineering, the first of its kind in the world.[49]

Although the president had to cajole and sometimes coerce reluctant trustees to bring Cornell close to his ideal, the university's most publicized reform for once generated a consensus of enthusiasm among Ezra Cornell, Henry Sage, and White. The founder's interest in education for women

46. Fiske to ADW, May 18, 1877, WMC.
47. Adler to Russel, April 22, 1885, WMC.
48. *Autobiography*, vol. 1, p. 375; President's Report, June 21, 1871, WMC. M.I.T. established a department of architecture several years earlier.
49. *Autobiography*, vol. 1, p. 375; Hugh Hawkins, *Between Harvard and America: The Educational Leadership of Charles W. Eliot* (New York, 1972), p. 214.

surfaced even before the university opened its doors. In 1866 he advised
Henry Wells not to build a women's college in Aurora but instead to
endow the Wells Female Department of Cornell University "and thus aid
us to engraft female education upon what I trust will become the highest
educational institution in America." Wells refused, and the disappointed
Cornell, wishing to preserve a record of his attitude toward coeducation,
wrote thus to his granddaughter, asking that she save his letter: "I want to
have girls educated in the university, as well as boys, so that they may have
the same opportunity to become wise and useful to society that the boys
have."[50]

Reluctant to add to the university's difficulties immediately, Cornell
nevertheless left the door open for coeducation in his inaugural address.
The founder hoped that the institution would prove beneficial "to the poor
young men and the poor young women of our country." In 1869 Lucy
Washburn applied for admission to the university, but Cornell rejected her
application, pointing to insufficient funding for separate accommodations
for women. Although he hoped one day to see 1,000 young women
educated at his university, Cornell suggested that Miss Washburn apply to
Vassar.[51]

White was as eager as the founder to introduce coeducation to Cornell.[52]
When writing the charter for state scholarships, he used the term "persons" instead of "young men," thus eliminating a roadblock to future
reform. At the completion of the president's inaugural address, which
urged the adoption of coeducation, Henry Sage had promised his aid
when the time was ripe. Still wary of attracting criticism for yet another
innovation, White moved cautiously, proposing a meeting of the faculties
of Michigan and Cornell to discuss the admission of women. "If we move
together," he told Tyler, "we can move the country."[53]

Meanwhile, pressure for the immediate adoption of coeducation
mounted. Catherine Beecher and Susan B. Anthony spoke in Ithaca on

50. EC to Henry Wells, April 9, 1866, and EC to Eunice Cornell, February 17, 1867,
Cornell mss.

51. Quoted in Alonzo Cornell, *True and Firm: Biography of Ezra Cornell* (New York, 1884),
p. 199; EC to Washburn, February 16, 1869; Washburn to EC, March 2, 1869; C. Cailiff to
EC, October 26 and December 18, 1868; EC to Mary Ann Cornell, January 17, 1869, all in
Cornell mss.

52. Oberlin in 1837 and the University of Iowa in 1856 had already adopted coeducation.
By 1870, Washington, Michigan, and Wisconsin were admitting females (William Zimmer-
man, "Andrew White and the Role of the University Concerning Student Life," Ph.D. thesis,
Cornell University, 1959, p. 104).

53. Bishop, *History of Cornell*, pp. 88–89; and ADW to W. T. Hewett, October 11, 1895;
ADW to Francis Finch, December 6, 1897; and ADW to Tyler, November 30, 1868, all in
WMC.

women's rights and the education of women in March 1869, provoking Cornell to deny that women had been refused admission to the university. Consequently, when Jennie Spencer, a graduate of Cortland Academy, applied to the university in 1870, she was admitted. Spencer declined to live in the men's Cascadilla Dormitory and resided in town. After one semester she left Cornell; the trek up the hill to campus had impaired her health.[54]

Spencer's departure convinced Henry Sage that the time to act had arrived, and he offered $250,000 to construct a building on campus to house women students. Though clearly in favor of the proposal, White asked that the trustees appoint an investigative committee. Sage and Ezra Cornell were with him, but the president feared opposition from other trustees and from staunch opponents of female education on the faculty, such as Goldwin Smith and Willard Fiske. Moreover, serious opposition developed among the student body. Students at Cornell, the *Era* editorialized, refused to have "their course cut down and embellished with music, embroidery and the like, aping the mild doses given at female boarding schools, as they are already clamoring to have it done at Michigan University. . . . If there are ladies who wish to come here now and take regular studies and endure the hardships with us, let them come. We have too high an estimate of their effeminate qualities to believe there are many."[55]

White assured opponents that higher education would neither de-feminize women nor alter their role in society. The deterioration of the health of young women was White's greatest fear. Consequently, though the investigative committee, which White headed, recommended coeducation, it advised that "stimulus, in the way of competitive prizes, should not be brought to bear, to any considerable extent, on the young women." The university should establish hygiene classes and insist that female students take a certain amount of exercise each day. Should any ladies show signs of declining health, the university should insist that they give up their studies temporarily or permanently. The committee members traveled throughout the nation observing coeducation and concluded that these cautionary measures would succeed in preserving the health of their delicate charges.[56]

54. *Cornell Era*, March 27, 1869; Bishop, *History of Cornell*, p. 145; ADW to Hewett, October 11, 1895, and ADW to Finch, December 6, 1897, WMC.

55. President's Report, June 21, 1871, WMC; *Cornell Era*, May 18, 1870.

56. *Report in Behalf of a Majority of the Committee on Mr. Sage's Proposal to Endow a College for Women* (Ithaca, 1872), p. 24; ADW to E. G. O'Connor, January 24, 1884, WMC. Many feared that university study disturbed the periodical nature of women: "It is not what she studies that harms her but her studying it when nature demands all her force especially her

Henry W. Sage, longtime chairman of Cornell's Board of Trustees

The committee believed that the major duties of a woman were maternal. White insisted that only a comparatively small minority of young women, those animated by love of learning, would (or ought to) take advantage of university privileges. He also argued, however, that higher education would help women to develop logical thought processes, which could be transferred to their sons. "From Mary Stuart at the Castle of Amboise to the last good woman who had shrieked against science," he asserted, ". . . the fetichisms and superstitions of this world are bolstered up mainly by women." By disciplining women's passionate nature, the university would help develop superior mothers.[57]

Finally, coeducation was desirable because of its beneficial effect on young men. Women possessed dignity, refinement, modesty, and delicacy in far greater measure than men. White and Sage observed at Oberlin that the presence of women made men more moral and less inclined to smoke and drink. The difference between a university lecture room to which only men were admitted and one that admitted both sexes, the president analogized, was "the difference between the smoking car and the back of it."[58]

Careful observation convinced White and the committee that coeducation presented few unresolvable difficulties. Academies and high schools in New York and other states mixed the sexes, and virtually all their principals testified that coeducation worked and would work in a university. The committee declared that by living in quarters apart from men, with their activities supervised by a matron, females would be freer from danger than they might be outside the college. Most female students at the universities, the committee was careful to note, married and became devoted wives and mothers. Laying to rest the "legitimate" causes of fear, the committee recommended that Sage's proposal be accepted.[59]

The arguments in support of coeducation confirmed women's traditional roles as refined, delicate, moral mothers and wives, and stressed their beneficial influence on male students; they did not stress equality between the sexes and the opening of new avenues of opportunity for women. White and the committee probably agreed with Charles W. Eliot's observation that higher education did not provide women an opportunity to contribute to society "comparable with that of the healthy wife

nerve force for the periodical function peculiar to her organization. Her weakness, some call it! Thereby arraigning the Almighty and accusing him of imperfection!" (A. W. Connor to ADW, February 23, 1883, WMC).

57. ADW to E. G. O'Connor, January 24, 1885, WMC; *Report . . . on Mr. Sage's Proposal*, p. 36; *Autobiography*, vol. 2, p. 89.

58. *Report . . . on Mr. Sage's Proposal*, p. 14; ADW to Carnegie, December 29, 1906, WMC.

59. *Report . . . on Mr. Sage's Proposal*, pp. 7, 15, 20.

and mother who bears and brings up from four to eight children." While Eliot therefore denounced coeducation and earned White's eternal enmity by acidly observing that the method might be justifiable "in a community which cannot afford anything better," [60] Cornellians embraced this opportunity to train future mothers to rear cultivated sons. The primary goal of coeducation, as they saw it, was to benefit *man*kind.

Coeducation proved an instantaneous success at Cornell.[61] The health of the weaker sex, who presented fewer excuses for absences than men, was excellent. The president attributed the absence of discipline problems at the university to the female presence. Even the *Cornell Era*, originally hostile, pronounced the experiment a success. The *Era* needlessly feared, it admitted, "the effects of women's smiles on certain of our professors, and trembled for the probable result, when conditioned women should tearfully entreat them to relent from their stern decision." [62] Although surprised that more women did not apply to Cornell, White never doubted that coeducation would be commonplace within a generation.

Although Cornell University prided itself on equal treatment for all students, regulations for women differed from those of men—one reason, perhaps, for the dearth of female applicants. White adhered to his promise to institute no special course of instruction for Sage College, thus ensuring equal access to all subjects for both sexes. In matters of discipline, however, the president deferred to Henry Sage's request that "if we erred at all, it had better be on the side of safety." Sage turned aside White's pleas for freedom of conduct and persuaded him to hire a matron for Sage College: "All that you say of the liberty given by parents to their daughters is true *and right*—But they know their daughters better than we can and are better informed than we can be of the places they visit and the persons they go and come with. . . . But students in the college are *in our* charge." Matron Kinney, Sage assured White in 1879, used her authority wisely and the "few wholesome" rules established by her won the hearty acquiescence of students.[63]

Sage College's residents did not prove to be as amenable to regulation as Henry Sage thought and Andrew White hoped. In 1881 they presented their own candidate for employment at the college, "an innocent boy 19

---

60. Charles W. Eliot, *A Late Harvest* (Boston, 1924), p. 68; *Cornell Sun*, April 10, 1883. Eliot attacked coeducation as "unwise, dangerous and impracticable" in May 1873, the month in which the cornerstone of Sage College was laid.

61. Thirty-seven women and 484 men attended Cornell in 1874 (Bishop, *History of Cornell*, p. 149).

62. ADW to Editor (paper unknown), February, 1874, WMC; *Cornell Era*, September 19, 1873; Thomas W. Higginson to ADW, January 10, 1876, and President's Report, 1875, WMC.

63. Leonard Bacon to ADW, May 16, 1872; Sage to ADW, December 17, 1875; Sage to ADW, October 15, 1879, all in WMC.

years of age," Russel noted in horror, "whose mind is weak, and whose body is not said to be unnatural. . . . As between dynamite, married men and innocent boys to be stored at the Sage, I should prefer dynamite."[64] Thwarted in this and other attempts to influence the administration of Sage by an increasingly less sympathetic president, the Cornell women wrote to other colleges in 1884, hoping to find workable alternatives to the strict policies prevailing in their dormitory. When Syracuse, Minnesota, and Michigan informed them that women lived off campus in places of their own choosing, their conduct subject to the same rules that applied to men, Sage's residents insisted on the right to come and go as they pleased twenty-four hours a day and that men be allowed free access to the dormitory. White diplomatically allowed them these rights *in theory* but pointed to public opinion as an insurmountable obstacle that prevented him from granting them in fact. He was not willing to grant concessions to women, however justified, if such action prompted criticism that endangered coeducation. The president allowed the women advisory power in the management of the college but refused to rescind the order making residence at Sage compulsory. Although insistent in his autobiography that the difficulties were gradually overcome, White failed to satisfy the students. In 1885 a petition submitted by the women to the trustees was ignored, perhaps because the president resigned at that meeting. Equality of the sexes was not achieved during White's tenure at Cornell, but the adoption of coeducation there helped to open the doors of other universities throughout the country to women.[65]

White's driving ambition left him little time to spend with his family. Even before he assumed the presidency, his busy schedule often kept him apart from Mary and the children, Clara, Fred, and Ruth.[66] Unfortunately, constant work and lack of adequate housing forced White during the early years at Cornell to live in the barracks on University Hill while his family remained in Syracuse. Although the president made the journey, treacherous in winter, on weekends, his solitary life and neglect of family duties aggravated the depression that sometimes intruded on his thoughts. "This is a dog's life," he complained to Russel.

I stand annoyed at my own forebearance sometimes. Nothing but my faith in our enterprise and hope that it is to be the beginning of great good to the country can

64. Russel to ADW, December 19, 1881, WMC.
65. Zimmerman, "Andrew White and the Role of the University," pp. 124–26; *Autobiography*, vol. 1, pp. 401–402. See also Charlotte Conable, *Women at Cornell* (Ithaca, 1977), esp. pp. 98–109.
66. ADW to CDW, October 20, 1868, WMC.

Frederick White,
Andrew D. White's son

carry me through this torment. No one knows half of it. No family. No home. No chance at the reputation I have most coveted. No cessation of duties which have always been the most irksome—no opportunity to indulge my fancy in travel and limited residence abroad—rebuffs—the cold shoulder—unsuccessful pleading and unheeded begging!—and such very green pastures in the other direction.[67]

Eager to reunite his family, White decided to build a lavish home on the Cornell campus to be used by him during his lifetime and then donated for the use of future university presidents. By 1874 the house was ready for occupancy and the White family finally settled in Ithaca.

White's hope that his children, especially his son, would make outstanding contributions to society resulted in enormous disappointment at young Frederick's errant ways. A frail boy, Fred found the pressure of his father's demands unbearable and repeatedly ran away from home. In exchange for a promise not to send his son to the Allen School in West Newton, Massachusetts, White extracted a lengthy pledge from Fred. In a formal

67. ADW to Russel, December 27, 1870, WMC.

agreement, written in White's hand and signed by both parties, Fred promised to attend any other school or schools, to accept such "government and instruction as may be provided," and to prepare diligently for entrance to Cornell University. Fred also agreed to

exert myself constantly, steadily and systematically to refrain from . . . all conduct and habits that are not those of a gentleman and especially that when in and about the house in which I live I will be civil, deferential, quiet and refrain from all conduct complained of by others of the family—that I will have no quarrels or troubles with any member of the family but will be steady polite to them and I will conduct myself in a manly way in every respect.

I pledge that I will rise at seven o'clock except when excused for special reasons and will study faithfully and energetically for at least half an hour before breakfast.

I pledge myself that I will go to church without objection or complaint once every Sunday unless especially excused for some sufficient causes and that I will not seek to be excused or ask to be excused save in case of serious illness.

I pledge myself that I will use every exertion and endeavor to make this year one of hard study, work and self-restraint preparatory to entering college and adopting a Profession in Life.

I pledge myself that I will without remonstrance or complaint give every day at least one hour and a half out of school hours closely to study—and this study hour shall be a fixed and determined hour.

I pledge myself that I will if required give two hours a day to such labor or exercise as may be required of me in making good the . . . expenditures made during the past month for my education.

I pledge myself to abstain from every injurious habit—from all bad language and ungentlemanly conduct and study and work faithfully and conduct myself a gentleman throughout the entire year.[68]

Perhaps seeking to compensate for the lack of attention given to Fred during his formative years, certainly expecting the boy to drive himself unmercifully, White imposed on his sixteen-year-old son (whose life of unceasing torment was to end tragically) a treatment that stands in grim contrast to his liberal pronouncements on student discipline.

68. Pledge of Fred White, September 28, 1875, WMC.

Chapter 6   *The Absentee President*

The often vexing details of administrative work and President White's desire for distinction outside academia left him eager for temporary escapes from university affairs, and he found them in politics and diplomacy. Universally regarded as an intellectual above reproach, he lent respectability to the Grant administration while retaining close ties with reform, "good government" Republicans. White often refused to take a firm stand on a controversial issue because it would imperil relations with either reformers or regulars. White's diplomatic and political activities enhanced his reputation, but this success was achieved by the sacrifice of any valid claim to disinterested statesmanship.

Early in 1871, President Grant offered White a diplomatic assignment that embroiled him in one of the most divisive episodes of the Grant administration. As soon as he took office, Grant expressed hopes of annexing Santo Domingo. The president of Santo Domingo, Buenaventura Báez, feeling threatened by insurgent forces led by José Maria Cabral and fearing an invasion from neighboring Haiti, sought the protection of the United States. Powerful groups in the United States supported Báez's overtures. Báez had granted lobbyists William Cazneau and Joseph Fabens of Massachusetts rights to one-fifth of the land they examined for mineralogical deposits. By the 1870s, the two controlled one-tenth of Santo Domingo and liberally granted stock in their company to prominent businessmen and Washington politicians.[1]

If powerful voices spoke in favor of annexation,[2] an equally strong coalition formed to oppose it. Although most Americans favored expan-

1. James Chapin, "Hamilton Fish and American Expansion," Ph.D. thesis, Cornell University, 1971, pp. 309–312; Charles Tansill, *The United States and Santo Domingo, 1798–1873* (Baltimore, 1938), pp. 344–46; U. S. Grant, *Personal Memoirs of U.S. Grant*, 2 vols. (New York, 1886), vol. 2, p. 550.
2. Tansill, *United States and Santo Domingo*, pp. 362–78, 398; Harold Schwartz, *Samuel Gridley Howe: Social Reformer* (Cambridge, Mass., 1956), p. 294; Allan Nevins, *Hamilton Fish: The Inner History of the Grant Administration* (New York, 1936), p. 315.

sion of some sort, many—Senators Charles Sumner, Carl Schurz, and perhaps even Hamilton Fish among them—hoped to generate markets for American products through protectorates or spheres of influence. They sought empire but hoped to avoid the odious reputation and burdensome responsibility that would accompany annexation. Some senators openly doubted that free institutions could survive in a tropical climate. The Santo Domingo treaty, moreover, proved an easy target for opponents of annexation. The whole scheme, critics charged, had been undertaken to fill the pockets of Cazneau, Fabens, and their associates.[3]

Charles Sumner advanced a litany of reasons for the defeat of the proposed annexation treaty in a series of influential speeches. To a paternalistic former abolitionist such as Sumner, annexation was unjust because it would impair the predominance of the colored race in the West Indies. The island, he asserted, was set apart for the colored race: "It is theirs by right of possession; by their sweat and blood mingling with the soil; by tropical position; by its burning sun and by unalterable laws of climate."[4] Sumner labeled unconstitutional Grant's ordering of warships to protect the Báez government while the treaty was pending. Accused of opposing the treaty in a fit of pique over Grant's refusal to reappoint his friend James Ashley as governor of Montana, Sumner in fact seems to have adopted a stance both reasoned and ideologically consistent.

Faced with the near certainty of defeat, Grant refused to heed Fish's advice to accept a protectorate, a proposal that probably would have been approved by the Senate. The president insisted on annexation or defeat, and on June 30, 1870, the treaty was defeated with a 28–28 vote.[5]

Determined to receive some satisfaction from the Santo Domingo affair, Grant decided to appoint a commission that would, he hoped, at least vindicate the rectitude of his policies. Intent on finding men who could not be suspected of collusion with the administration, he finally settled on Benjamin F. Wade, former Radical Republican senator from Ohio; Samuel Gridley Howe, noted philanthropist and lifelong friend of Charles Sumner; and Andrew D. White. Grant and Fish asked the trio to visit Santo Domingo on a fact-finding tour, perhaps hoping to revive the annexation treaty.[6] Denying that he had any pecuniary interest in Santo

3. They charged that Grant's aides, and perhaps the president himself, had been paid off to support annexation. See Chapin, "Hamilton Fish," pp. 330–38.
4. Tansill, *United States and Santo Domingo*, pp. 406, 432.
5. Chapin, "Hamilton Fish," p. 357.
6. Congress had authorized the commission in December 1870–January 1871 only with the understanding that "nothing in these resolutions contained shall be held, understood or

Domingo, Grant challenged the commissioners to expose him to the American people if they found any incriminating evidence.[7]

Although his views on annexation were unsettled, White enthusiastically accepted Grant's offer. The Cornell trustees refused to accept his proffered resignation and appointed Russel vice-president, temporarily in charge of university affairs. Meanwhile, White arranged for the inevitable separation from his family. The danger in Santo Domingo, he assured Mary, was no greater than that in New York City; but the advice he gave to his wife—and the new will drawn before his departure—must have counteracted his soothing words. He renewed his request that in the event of his death, Mary never remarry. "In regard to the children," he added, "you know my ideas. Let them be good rather than ambitious. I have always hoped that Freddy would become a lover of scientific matters of some sort—but in any case—as part of a thorough education—he ought to have some schooling in practical business and some in law."[8] Always a prudent man, White took steps to guarantee the continuing impact of his personality on his wife and children.

To facilitate the commission's study of Santo Domingo's resources, White had persuaded Grant to allow science students from leading American institutions to journey to the island. Unfortunately, the commission allowed itself to be influenced by "Professor" William Gabb, special agent of Fabens and Cazneau. Despite the reservations of the commission geologists, Wade, White, and Howe accepted Gabb's claims of vast mineral wealth throughout the island.[9] Even worse, they accepted the professor's assurance that the inhabitants unanimously favored annexation. The commissioners, Gabb reported to Fabens, had been easily hoodwinked: "I've manufactured a good four fifths of all the public opinion that will be formed by them and in this I consider that the Co. owes me at least three or four months extra salary."[10]

Gabb had little difficulty convincing the commissioners that annexation would be beneficial. They never doubted Báez's sincerity or patriotism; White was especially impressed by the Dominican president's elegant manners and conversation. Thoroughly convinced that Wade, Howe, and White had been converted to the cause, Báez consented to give them safe-conduct to any insurgents they wished to see. Thus, despite José Cabral's assertion that annexation was not the will of the Dominican

---

construed as committing Congress to the policy of annexing the territory of said republic of Dominica" (Tansill, *United States and Santo Domingo*, p. 436).

7. Schwartz, *Samuel Gridley Howe*, pp. 291–97; *Autobiography*, vol. 1, pp. 483, 487–88.
8. ADW to Mary White, January 15, 1871, WMC.
9. *Autobiography*, vol. 1, p. 488; Schwartz, *Samuel Gridley Howe*, p. 303.
10. Quoted in Nevins, *Hamilton Fish*, p. 498.

people, the commissioners concluded that the vast majority sought union with the United States.[11]

After two months of work, the commissioners returned to Washington at the end of March 1870 and presented Grant with a lengthy report. They had found no evidence that the president or any other public official had received pecuniary concessions from Báez. The report claimed that the island was "one of the most fertile regions on the face of the earth" and asserted that the people, whose physical, mental, and moral condition and educational potential were "much more advanced than anticipated," enthusiastically favored annexation.[12]

Surprisingly, the commissioners did not recommend annexation by the United States. Ben Wade, a steadfast advocate of manifest destiny, favored such a recommendation, as did Dr. Howe, who envisioned a grand opportunity for philanthropic work with the colored race. White, however, was still uncertain, afraid that if Santo Domingo achieved statehood, it would become a "rotten borough" manipulated by skillful politicians able to sway ignorant blacks. He hoped to avoid a clash with anti-annexationists and convinced his colleagues that Congress has requested only facts. In the face of the Senate's announced opposition to annexation, advice would be gratuitous, impertinent, and politically unwise.[13]

Whatever White's own attitude toward annexation, its chances had not improved since the defeat of the treaty in 1870. Grant used the commission report to vindicate the purity of his administration's motives. In a quiet message to Congress, Grant suggested that no action be taken at the current session beyond the printing of the report, a request with which the Senate swiftly complied.[14] While Grant thanked the commission, White congratulated himself. He had completed his mission without antagonizing Sumner[15] or Schurz; Grant was in his debt. An unknown quantity before his appointment, White managed to enhance his reputation and visibility without clearly defining his views on territorial expansion.

White's growing reputation led to increased political activities that took him away from Ithaca.[16] Tempted by the possibility of a political career,

11. *Autobiography*, vol. 1, pp. 490–93; *Cornell Era*, March 3, 1871; Cabral to Wade, Howe, and ADW, February 26, 1871, Hamilton Fish MSS, Library of Congress.

12. *Report of the Committee of Inquiry to Santo Domingo* (Washington, D.C., 1871), pp. 1–34.

13. ADW to Moses Coit Tyler, August 17, 1872; ADW to George Haynes, March 11, 1909; ADW to F. W. Holls, March 17, 1893, all in WMC.

14. David Jordan, *Roscoe Conkling of New York* (Ithaca, 1971), p. 167; Nevins, *Hamilton Fish*, pp. 498–99.

15. Howe, however, had been "slowly and painfully" led to the sad conclusion that Sumner was insane (Howe to ADW, August 8, 1872, WMC).

16. For White's friends' reactions to his diplomatic ventures, see Fabian Franklin, *The Life of Daniel Coit Gilman* (New York, 1910), p. 97, and Horatio White, *Willard Fiske: Life and Correspondence* (New York, 1925), p. 409.

White attended the New York State Republican Convention in Syracuse during the fall of 1871. He agreed to State Chairman Alonzo B. Cornell's request that he run for temporary chairman of the convention, although he insisted that anti-Grant forces be given a fair hearing.

The gathering at Syracuse promised to be a struggle between Roscoe Conkling and Reuben Fenton for control of the Republican party in the state. Although he supported Conkling, White hoped to promote harmony. Nevertheless, as Chairman Cornell received the nominations of White and Fentonite G. Hilton Scribner of Westchester for temporary chairman, pandemonium broke loose on the convention floor. For hours Cornell, his deputies, and the police tried to restore order. Finally a roll call was taken and White was elected, 95–58.[17]

White's acceptance speech, which gave the delegates the choice of faction and defeat or harmony and victory, was well received. Momentarily silenced, the Fenton delegates were outraged when White listed his appointments to the Committees on Credentials and Permanent Organization. Charging that these important committees, which decided the conflicting claims of delegates demanding seats on the convention floor, had been stacked with Conkling men, they attempted to break up the meeting. Convention business continued, however, and Roscoe Conkling emerged from Syracuse securely in control of the party machinery.[18]

Deeply hurt at the cries of "foul," White defended his conduct at Syracuse. Given only half an hour to make his appointments, he had relied on the counsel of his friends. The appointments had been fair, he insisted; Alonzo Cornell had not broken his promise to include all factions in the party. Such reasoning convinced few, however, and White contradicted himself by advancing ignorance as the rationale for his actions: "Not being professionally a politician I was unable to draw any clear line between the different shades of opinion. There was not even a list showing how members had voted at the organization."[19]

Although his experience at Syracuse had been distasteful, White refused to confine himself to the political sidelines, nor did he become disillusioned with Conkling or Grant. Begged by his friends to join the Liberal Republicans in 1872, White, though appalled at the corruption in Washington, actively supported General Grant. While none could deny that Grant had faults, his steadfast opposition to inflation and debt repudiation stood in stark contrast to the "Namby Pambyism which leads enough

17. *New York Times*, September 28, 1871; Thomas Collier Platt, *Autobiography* (New York, 1910), pp. 58–60.

18. *New York Times*, September 28 and October 27, 1871.

19. *Autobiography*, vol. 1, pp. 164–65; ADW to Editor of *New York Tribune*, October 2, 1871, WMC.

people to give up our best chances for steady progress and so to leave the land to the worst elements in the country." White diligently supported the stalwarts with whom he linked his political future.[20]

White's admiration for Grant and Conkling also stemmed from their opposition to the printing of inflationary paper money. As a state senator, he had supported an inflated currency because it had been necessary to the war effort; but at the end of the Civil War he had advocated a quick return to sound fiscal policies. In the mid-1870s, however, farmers, angry at the high cost of agricultural machinery and transportation, demanded inflation to ease payments of debts; these greenbackers posed a new threat to the nation's financial stability.

While at Michigan, White had lectured on the disastrous effects of paper money inflation on revolutionary France. His successor, Charles Kendall Adams, begged him to use this historical analogy to defeat greenbackism. White shared Adams's apprehensions and set to work revising his old lectures. In April 1876 he boasted that he had based his recently completed lecture on more original material than had ever been seen by an English or American student. Next to the Civil War, inflation constituted the greatest threat to the Union since 1788. White lamented that few public men were "fully aware of the weapons which a history of this sort may put into their hands." Eager to share the lessons of history with the nation's public men, the Cornell president asked David Wells, James Garfield, and Justin Morrill to arrange a series of lectures, preferably before men of both parties, in Washington.[21]

"Fiat Money Inflation in France" proved to be an enormously popular lecture. At Garfield's suggestion, White published it as a short book, and it was circulated widely during the 1876 campaign. Noting that every argument used by the greenbackers had also been used by the French, White's lecture summarized the various ways in which paper money had ruined the French economy—and would ruin the American: once paper was issued, specie disappeared from circulation; great quantities of money eroded the natural thrift of the French people and led to rampant speculation, a cancerous disease "more permanently injurious to a nation than war, pestilence or famine"; prices rose more rapidly than wages, leaving workers worse off than they had been before. The effect of paper inflation,

20. Henry Clews to ADW, August 20, 1872; ADW to Clews, August 21, 1872; ADW to E. P. Evans, August 17, 1872; ADW to Mrs. E. P. Evans, June 26, 1875, all in WMC; Jessica Tyler Austen, *Moses Coit Tyler* (New York, 1911), p. 79; ADW to E. P. Evans, August 13, 1885, WMC.

21. ADW to Wells, April 6, 1876, David Wells MSS, Library of Congress; ADW to Garfield, April 1, 1876, James A. Garfield MSS, Library of Congress; Garfield to ADW, April 5, 1876, and Morrill to ADW, April 5, 1876, WMC.

White concluded, was "the complete financial, moral and political pros-
tration of France."[22]

Elsewhere, White had made a very different argument. Defending
Lincoln's inflationary program in the New York State Senate in 1864,
White had addressed himself to the French experience:

What wonder that a vast issue of paper could not be redeemed in a country where
labor had been for ages the badge of servility and laziness the badge and passport of
gentility! What wonder that resources could not be developed in a country where
the rural laborer paid eleven-twelfths of his scanty earnings in tithes and taxes, and
where on one river alone there were thirty different custom houses, at each of
which a vessel had to pay toll. There is no parallel between those cases and this
republic of ours—full of energy, full of resources, attracting the labor and capital of
the world to its workshops, and feeding the world from its fields.[23]

The Civil War had engendered a temporary suspension of belief, but
White refused to grant another exemption to the laws of history. Although
the greenback threat soon subsided, a new dragon, silver coinage, rose in
its place, requiring even more vigilance. "Madness seems to have seized
our people," Garfield wrote in 1879, fearing the passage of a silver purchase bill. "I have never seen a time when the financial future of the
country looked as dark as now."[24] For White, inflation from silver was
identical to inflation from paper money, and he employed the French
analogy with certainty in the ensuing decades.

Amid the "madness" that enveloped the nation, the Republican party
was in the throes of a crisis of leadership. The corruption of the Grant
administration disillusioned all but a few. "Why is not Grant wiser and
firmer?" George William Curtis lamented. "Had we a commanding man
to whom to rally all would be well. But Blaine? Conkling?? Morton???"[25]
Just as disturbing to partisan Republicans was the emergence of Democrat
Samuel Tilden, who had shrewdly garnered the credit for breaking the
Tweed Ring of New York City. Governor Tilden's management of New
York won him praise from reformers. If Tilden received the 1876 Democratic nomination, the Republicans might very well lose the election.

White was not nearly as troubled as Curtis by the dearth of leadership in
the Republican party. Chosen a delegate at large to the GOP national
convention, he was an early supporter of Roscoe Conkling. That White
was a Conkling man—"or anybody's man but Mrs. White's"[26] —was

22. *Fiat Money Inflation in France* (New York, 1876), esp. pp. 32, 39, 49, 81.
23. ADW, *A Review of the Governor's Message* (Albany, 1864), p. 8.
24. Garfield to ADW, January 8, 1877, WMC.
25. Curtis to ADW, August 19, 1875, WMC.
26. Conkling to ADW, February 16, 1876, WMC.

incomprehensible to the Cornell president's reform-minded friends, and White never fully explained it. A number of reasons probably account for the attraction: the two men agreed on economic policies for the nation; they had formed their political alliance before Conkling's connection with the spoils system became apparent to White; and the New York senator assured Cornell's president that he would support a "practical" system of reform.[27] Conkling was personally gracious to White, sought his advice on major questions of policy, and satisfied his requests for favors.[28] A powerful figure in the Conkling-dominated Republican party in New York, White could certainly achieve prominence if the redoubtable Roscoe became the nation's president.

Conkling's haughty bearing and razor-sharp tongue, however, earned him a host of enemies in the party, and little likelihood existed that he would be the GOP standard-bearer. Reformers tried to use the slimness of Conkling's chance of election to persuade White to transfer his allegiance to reformer Benjamin Bristow.[29] Whatever his own assessment of Conkling's chances, White did not abandon his favorite.

While the presidential nomination hung in the balance, New York State Republicans sought to persuade the Cornell president to stand for elective office. Run for Congress, some suggested: "Quit the hard work at Ithaca and rest a couple of years at Washington!"[30] Others hoped that White would run for governor. T. H. Morgan promised that if White sought the gubernatorial nomination, he would join the ticket as lieutenant governor. George Barrow, pointing to a prevalent tendency to recognize men of letters in politics, thought White the only potential candidate capable of attracting Democrats and Liberal Republicans; they "could not cry 'Custom House' at you," he insisted. Even Rutherford B. Hayes, the GOP nominee for president, announced that should Andrew White become governor, he would be "more than satisfied."[31]

Although flattered, White decided not to seek political office. He was "more apathetic than is desirable"; a lengthy acrimonious campaign required too many sacrifices.[32] Like many of his patrician contemporaries,

27. For almost six years, Conkling assured White, "I have had no part whatever in Custom House appointments not even in so far as to say or write a word for a friend" (Conkling to ADW, February 16, 1876, WMC; see also ADW to Conkling, January 4, 1871, WMC).
28. Joseph Hawley to ADW, August 25, 1876, WMC.
29. John W. Hoyt to ADW, April 11, 1876, WMC.
30. Silas Smith to ADW, June 13, 1876, WMC.
31. T. H. Morgan to ADW, August 10, 1876; Frank Carpenter to ADW, August 12, 1876; George Barrow to ADW, August 16, 1876; Hayes to ADW, August 15, 1876, all in WMC.
32. ADW to Lewis Morgan, August 17, 1876, WMC.

White preferred to have office thrust upon him—Cincinnatus seemed far more noble than Caesar. Perhaps, too, the memory of the 1871 debacle remained vivid in his mind; certainly a gubernatorial campaign would expose him to vicious political assaults. Perhaps, more important, he decided that victory was not possible, either at the nominating convention or in the general election. Conkling had not been among those who had urged him to seek election; his candidate was Alonzo Cornell, against whom White hesitated to run. Moreover, the GOP nomination would probably be a pyrrhic victory; Tilden's popularity in New York was at its peak, and he would almost certainly carry the Democratic slate to victory. Whatever the reason for White's reluctance to run, his decision proved to be a wise one. After an intense struggle, Edwin D. Morgan emerged as the party's nominee and promptly suffered a crushing defeat in the November election.[33]

Although White, like Curtis, admired Tilden, Rutherford Hayes was his candidate. "Right" on inflation and civil service reform, the Ohio governor also carefully consulted such reformers as Curtis and White, who had every reason to hope for a Republican victory.[34] White's enthusiasm for the ticket grew amid Hayes's enthusiastic predictions: "Our chance of carrying every free state west of the Alleghenies seems to be good."[35]

Throughout the summer, despite the necessity of answering sectarian critics of Cornell University, White interrupted his work at Ithaca to campaign for the GOP ticket. In the early fall, however, feverish activity took its toll. He had contracted, he wryly noted, "clergyman's sore throat," a malady that impaired the swallowing apparatus but left the lungs intact.[36] Eager for an extended stay in the Old World, this time with his family, White again left Russel in charge of the university.

The White family spent most of 1877 and 1878 traveling through Europe. The trip was a welcome break for White, whose distaste for administrative work had become "invincible." Duty followed him to Europe, but it was pleasant duty. In 1878 the governor of New York appointed White honorary commissioner to the Paris Exposition, where he viewed—among other inventions—Thomas Alva Edison's phonograph. In Paris, White met prominent literary and scientific men from virtually every European country. He was elected to a convention that aimed at improving international copyright arrangements. No concrete accomplishments resulted from the conference, but White thoroughly

33. Jordan, *Roscoe Conkling*, pp. 245–47.
34. Ibid, p. 243; Hayes to ADW, October 13, 1876, WMC.
35. Hayes to ADW, October 13, 1876, WMC.
36. ADW to Mrs. Evans, February 21, 1877, WMC.

enjoyed his stay in Paris and proudly accepted the cross of the French Legion of Honor from the president of the republic.[37]

By bringing his family to Europe, White hoped in some way to atone for the neglect that attention to work had necessitated. All seemed to enjoy their vacation together until late in 1877. On December 7, 1877, Andrew Danforth White, not yet four years old, died. Somewhat disappointed with Fred, White had had great hopes for his second son. In a poignant letter he shared his sorrow with Edward Payson Evans:

Only a baby—how often have I thought that! but I find that a baby of four years takes a very firm hold on one's heart strings—and so many things remind one of him.

A strange, complex problem is this human nature; the sight of a little shoe—of a plaything—the chance rattling of a toy wagon—the prancing of the great marble horses wh[ich] used to arouse his wondering exclamation—or the seat where he once sat—how it grasps a man's throat in an instant.[38]

Improvements in communcation heightened awareness of death in the nineteenth century. White's mother constantly sent him obituaries of old acquaintances which in an earlier day might have escaped him. Even as a young man, he seemed constantly aware of death's presence and of the necessity for the living to rededicate themselves to the service of humanity. "So it goes—dying, dying, dying," he confided to his diary in 1854 at the death of a college friend, "and he is taken while so many to whom life is a hated thing are left." And two years later: "All my old friends seem to be leaving me for the outer world. For what am I reserved?"[39] White's answer to his own question was to devote himself to public service. In the face of little Andrew's death, White quickly suppressed his grief by immersing himself in his work—work certain to help further enlightenment and progress.[40]

In the 1870s, then, while remaining president of Cornell, White established himself as a figure of increasing importance in diplomatic and political circles. Of sufficient stature to merit serious consideration as secretary of state and minister to England, he had managed to avoid serious conflict with territorial expansionists and advocates of economic spheres of influence during his short tenure as Santo Domingo commis-

37. *Autobiography*, vol 1, pp. 508–527; Morris Bishop, *A History of Cornell* (Ithaca, 1962), p. 101.

38. ADW to E. P. Evans, December 9, 1877, WMC.

39. Diary, August 7, 1854, and March 18, 1856, WMC.

40. In yet another will written in 1882, White reminded Mary that there were "duties as well as rights attached even to moderate fortunes" (ADW to Mary White, August 3, 1882, WMC).

sioner. In Republican party affairs as well, he succeeded in maintaining cordial relations with virtually every faction. Conkling's use of him in 1871 indicates that he was widely respected by Fentonites, Greeleyites, anti-Grant men, and other segments of the GOP. The convention debacle did not permanently destroy that reputation. In an era when personality clashes dominated the national political arena, White hoped to advance politically by antagonizing no one.

Chapter 7   *Minister to Germany*

White's reward for his dedication to the Republican party finally came with Hayes's offer early in 1879 of the post of minister to Germany.[1] The Berlin mission obviously meant another prolonged absence from Ithaca. Anticipating his appointment, the Democratic *Albany Argus* acidly suggested that the absentee president sever his ties with Cornell: "If Mr. White should go to Germany the interests of a school . . . suggest that he should not stretch his presidency from Berlin to Ithaca. Between education and politics White should make a choice."[2] The *Argus* had a point, and White dutifully submitted his resignation to the trustees in March. Although distressed at his departure, the board unanimously refused to accept the resignation and agreed to his nomination of Russel as acting president. With his friend as caretaker of his house and his university, White promptly embarked once again for Germany.[3]

Few diplomatic assignments promised more satisfaction to White, whose admiration for the "New Germany" was virtually boundless. The high quality of German civilization, White had long thought, made its emergence under Chancellor Bismarck predictable and desirable: "No country is at heart more deeply reverent toward the Highest," White had lectured to his students; "none more earnest in the search for truth; none more sensitive to the idea of duty; none more pervaded by a deep morality; none more open to sacred enthusiasm for eternal right and justice."[4] Proud beneficiary of a German education, White thought that *Lernfreiheit* and *Lehrfreiheit* permeated every aspect of the society.

Only one facet of the German system disturbed White: German paternalism choked individualism; economic and political decisions were made for, not by, the average citizen. For all his injunctions on the necessity of a

1. White denied that his appointment had been a peace offering to Roscoe Conkling (*New York Times*, March 27, 1879).
2. *Albany Argus*, January 27, 1879.
3. Bishop, *A History of Cornell* (Ithaca, 1962), pp. 199–200.
4. "The New Germany," n.d., WMC.

strong central government, White regretted even a voluntary surrender of individualism. Despite this caveat, he predicted that the "multitude and variety and vitality of the New German civilization guarantee to it a career long and brilliant."[5]

White did not realize that Germany had entered an important period of transition that was to have a profound impact upon its relations with the United States. The surge of nationalism, fueled by the defeats of France and Austria, resulted in attempts to assert German economic and political power throughout the world. During White's term, Bismarck inaugurated a tariff war with the United States and began to embark upon united Germany's first imperialist adventure. The minister only dimly perceived that a conflict of interests between the two countries might very well be in the offing. Partly because of his myopia, the United States was slow to react to the initiatives of the New Germany.

White was at first somewhat puzzled about the exact nature of his duties. The American diplomatic corps had been in a state of confusion throughout much of its history. Committed to the principle of republican simplicity, the Department of State subsisted with a meager, poorly paid, and often careless staff. Thirteen ministers plenipotentiary, twelve ministers resident, five chargés d'affaires, and three hundred consuls constituted America's diplomatic corps. Usually selected for past political services, ministers were badly paid and housed. Like the Catholic church, John Hay quipped, the foreign service was fit only for celibates. Ministers received diplomatic privileges inferior to those of ambassadors and appointees usually drew upon their own personal fortunes to enhance their status among other resident diplomats.[6]

A large part of the minister's tasks were social, and White reveled in the opportunity to entertain Europe's leading men. He bombarded J. C. Bancroft Davis, assistant secretary of state under Grant, with questions about the proper retinue of an American minister. How difficult would it be to obtain servants, a spacious house, and handsome carriage horses? How many secretaries could be hired and who would pay them? Was it worth the trouble and expense to send furniture and pictures from home, to order sherry in England and claret in France? Could one find quality cigars in Berlin? Davis (who had himself served in Berlin) responded with an exhaustive list of the best wine merchants, shoemakers, tailors, hatters,

5. Ibid.; ADW to Richard T. Ely, July 6, 1885, WMC.
6. David Pletcher, *The Awkward Years* (Columbia, Mo., 1962), pp. 18–21. The United States refused to appoint ambassadors because of the expense of outfitting them in a style that in any case seemed inappropriate for a democracy.

carriage makers, harness makers, dealers in curtains, carpets, and proce-
lain, and fire insurance salesmen in the German capital. If White was
willing to dip into his own pocket to gain entrée into German society, the
State Department stood ready to help spend his money.[7]

As soon as he arrived in Berlin, White made haste to renew acquaintances with leading German scholars. His first duty as minister was to
present a gift of books to Rudolf von Gneist, eminent authority on Roman
law and the English constitution, in appreciation for services rendered in a
recent boundary dispute between the United States and Great Britain.
Before long, White numbered historians Ernst Curtius, Johann Gustav
Droysen, and Heinrich von Sybel among his rapidly growing circle of
friends; even the almost deaf Heinrich von Treitschke partook of the
minister's hospitality.[8] By early 1880 White had firmly established himself
in German society. He entertained "much and well" in his superbly
furnished apartment. In less than a year, the Whites had taken "diplomatic
and court circles by storm."[9]

Although much of White's time was devoted to social relations, several
areas of potential conflict between Germany and the United States demanded careful scrutiny. Having demonstrated Germany's military
strength, Bismarck was determined to bolster the industrial and agricultural self-sufficiency of the Fatherland. In 1879 the chancellor began to
build a tariff wall around Germany. German industries needed American
raw materials; consequently, low duties or no duties at all were levied
against many products. Agriculture, however, required protection, and
the 1879 tariff set high duties on American foodstuffs. The United States,
meanwhile, enacted tariff measures that discriminated against many German manufactured goods. Upon his arrival in Berlin, White had to
confront the possibility of a tariff war between Germany and the United
States.[10]

White attempted to minimize the adverse economic effect of the German tariff on the United States. Noting that tariff retaliation by other
European powers did not seem likely, he hoped his own nation would not
take precipitous action. The new tariff hindered American agriculturalists, he admitted to Secretary of State William M. Evarts, but other

7. ADW to J. C. Bancroft Davis, March 31, 1879, and Davis to ADW, April 5, 1879, WMC.
8. *Autobiography*, vol. 1, p. 558.
9. Quoted in Horatio White, *Willard Fiske: Life and Correspondence* (New York, 1925), p. 379.
10. Jeanette Keim, *Forty Years of German–American Political Relations* (Philadelphia, 1919), pp. 66–67.

foreign markets that had taken German manufactures would now be open
to the United States. An advocate of protection for the United States,
White was neither surprised nor alarmed when the nationalistic Bismarck
adopted a similar policy for Germany.[11]

In 1880 the Iron Chancellor stunned American manufacturers by banning American pork sausage and chopped pork. German imports of
butchered animals from the United States valued at 7,743,000 marks in
1880 dropped to 861,000 marks only two years later. Perhaps to forestall a
cry for tariff retaliation from American meat-packers, the German government explained that the ban resulted from numerous cases of trichinae
reported in American pork: the imperial decree was issued solely for
sanitary reasons. "I was very glad to receive this assurance," White naively
informed Evarts, "for my first fear was that this was but a new development of the chancellor's policy of protection to the agricultural interest."[12]

White's first fears were, of course, valid, but he continued to counsel
against tariff retaliation. Germany claimed that the ban was issued for
reasons of health; America must meet this argument with proof that its
pork presented no danger. The minister was pleased when the New York
Produce Exchange asked the new secretary of state, James G. Blaine, for an
investigation of meat-packing in February 1881. Blaine quickly appointed
Michael Scanlon, chief of the statistical bureau, whose report pronounced
the percentage of infected hogs in the United States smaller than anywhere
else. With the publication of Scanlon's report in April, packers (and White)
awaited the lifting of the ban.[13]

The Germans remained unconvinced by the report and continued to
insist that without microscopic inspection of meat, the danger of trichinae
was substantial. Soon to leave office, White was disappointed. The great
pork controversy demonstrated, he wrote to Blaine, the need for a
cabinet-level department of commerce. Uniform regulations for meat-
packing would aid the industry, especially large packinghouses that traded
extensively abroad. The German ban on pork was to last another decade,
while the congressional engine of reform slowly warmed to its task. On
March 3, 1891. Congress made microscopic inspection of meat compulsory; in the same year, President Harrison exempted German sugar from
United States tariffs. Evidently satisfied, Germany removed its restric-

11. ADW to Evarts, August 15, 1879, DMG.
12. Pletcher, *Awkward Years*, p. 162; Louis Snyder, "The American–German Pork Dispute, 1879–1891," *Journal of Modern History* 17 (March 1945): 19; ADW to Evarts, June 29,
1880, DMG.
13. Snyder, "American–German Pork Dispute," p. 26.

tions on American pork. Bismarck had successfully forced the United States to play by his rules.[14]

If Bismarck's ban on pork distressed American meat-packers, the chancellor's monetary policies brought silver interests near panic. Despite the apoplectic opposition of hard-money men, silverites had finally persuaded Congress to inflate the currency through limited bimetalism. The Sherman Silver Purchase Act of 1878 promised to be a boon to silver miners, who hoped that it would be followed by unlimited coinage of silver. The success of the American program was threatened by Germany's demonitization of silver in 1871. War with France vastly increased Germany's gold supplies, and Bismarck's decision to sell off the nation's silver reserves placed the 16:1 ratio of silver to gold in jeopardy. To the Hayes administration, so recently committed to bimetalism (which, it hoped, would increase trade), the German program, especially if copied by other European powers, threatened international financial stability.[15]

Secretary Evarts instructed White to attempt to persuade Bismarck to attend an international monetary conference—which would commit Europe to bimetalism. Upon arriving in Berlin, the minister was swayed by his belief in the mutuality of interest between Germany and the United States. Bismarck, he predicted, would gladly join in the conference. The chancellor had confessed that he might have erred in disposing of the nation's silver reserves so quickly. In fact, White had the "decided impression" that Bismarck had decided to retain all the silver still in the government's possession. Several days later White reported that Germany would probably reissue silver.[16]

With Bismarck seemingly amenable to compromise, White permitted an American spokesman for bimetalism to press the issue. William "Pig Iron" Kelley of Philadelphia, dean of the House of Representatives and its foremost advocate of protectionist policy and a dual monetary standard, had come to Berlin to speak with Bismarck about tariffs and silver. White brought the two together, and in a lengthy interview the chancellor appeared to favor bimetalism. Confident that a reversal in policy was imminent, Kelley ignored White's strictures and leaked details of the

14. Pletcher, *Awkward Years*, p. 169; Snyder, "American–German Pork Dispute," p. 28; ADW to Blaine, June 17, 1881, DMG.

15. ADW to Governor Culberson, September 28, 1896, WMC. For summaries of the complex issue of international bimetalism, see Richard Hofstadter, "Free Silver and the Mind of Coin Harvey" in *The Paranoid Style in American Politics* (New York, 1965), pp. 238–315; Jeanette P. Nichols, "Silver Diplomacy," *Political Science Quarterly* 48 (December 1933): 565–88.

16. ADW to Evarts, July 8 and 12, 1879, DMG.

interview to the press, spicing them with the prince's pithy remarks on fellow Germans.[17]

When news of Kelley's indiscretions reached Berlin, criticism mounted against the congressman, silver, and Americans in general. Kelley was written about in a way that in the United States would lead to pistol shooting, White's aide reported. *Montags Statt*, he continued, "is the chief offender with a signed article headed 'Who is Kelley?' It describes him in terms bordering on the libellous. The *National Zeitung* also attacks Kelley, and describes him as an Apostle of Silver whose silence would have been golden; a stump orator; a professional agitator; a 'loco-foco' politician; a journeying Amateur Diplomatist; and one of a class the plague of all other classes—American Diplomatists in particular."[18] L'affaire Kelley, White argued, had set back bimetalism and German–American relations.

The bad publicity that followed Kelley's disclosures prejudiced the mission of the State Department's official emissary on bimetalism, George Walker. Advised to maintain a low profile, Walker and the diplomatic corps were actually pleased when the press ignored him and mistook Kelley to be the official envoy of the United States. Walker preferred not to arrive in Berlin until Bismarck seemed amenable to compromise.[19]

Unfortunately, Kelley's appearance seemed to harden the chancellor's heart against silver; he steadfastly refused even to meet with Walker. Citing fatigue and the desire to avoid what would be an "academic discussion," Bismarck closed the door on bimetalism, although he promised to accept a definite proposal on a monetary conference from White. Depressed at the failure of his mission, Walker was deeply insulted by the chancellor's refusal to meet any American representative other than the minister: "I am free to confess that I shall be mortified to be turned away from his door as unworthy of the courtesy due to a public servant—to be fit into the category of baby vassals like Kelley—and then to have him show a willingness to talk with you as a more discreet and authoritative person."[20]

White's stature in Bismarck's eyes was little impaired by the controversy, and the minister must have been pleased by the State Department's decision to await a more auspicious occasion for the monetary conference. In the spring of 1881, Bismarck, without any prompting from the Ameri-

17. ADW to Bismarck, July 5, 1879, WMC; *Autobiography*, vol. 1, pp. 582–84.

18. Edward Henner to ADW, September 2, 1879, WMC.

19. C. Coleman to ADW, August 21, 1879, and ADW to Culberson, September 28, 1896, WMC.

20. ADW to Evarts, October 6, 1879, DMG; Walker to ADW, September 28, 1896, WMC.

can legation, indicated a willingness to participate in a conference only with the understanding that it be called for discussion rather than decision-making purposes. Ever hopeful, White believed that the chancellor favored bimetalism but sought further clarification before committing himself.[21]

Having recently resigned his position as minister, White felt free to reveal to Blaine his hostility to the State Department's insistence on a conference. Europeans, he informed the secretary, were jealous of American commercial success and therefore suspicious of any monetary plan proposed by the United States. The monetary question, he predicted, would be settled "not by seeming to place our Republic in the attitude of a supplicant before any European power, but by going on in the industrial and commercial path we have begun until the necessities of the European governments lead them to understand our position and to propose and urge monetary conferences more indispensable to their interests even than to ours."[22] While employed by the State Department, White had stoically supported a policy with which he fundamentally differed; released from his obligations as a public servant, he advised America to abjure the role of suitor and wait to be wooed.

The monetary conference of 1881 was a failure; European nations refused to adopt the American plan for acceptance of the dual monetary standard. As in the tariff war, the minister's efforts had ended inconclusively. To the end of his life, White blamed Germany's failure to adopt bimetalism on Kelley's pigheadedness.[23]

White's explanation of the incident reveals his basic assumptions about the nature of diplomacy and of German-American relations. Most comfortable with personal diplomacy, with understandings arrived at between gentlemen, White could not even entertain the thought that Bismarck had deceived him—that he had meant to torpedo the conference all along. Bismarck did not hesitate to use bluster or flattery, to pout or threaten resignation in order to get his way. Had he desired bimetalism, Kelley's petty indiscretions would hardly have deterred him. Nevertheless, White chose not to believe that he had been deceived.

Moreover, White's insistence that Kelley was to blame for keeping the United States and Germany at loggerheads enabled him to cling to his belief that a community of interests existed between the two countries. The tariff war indicated the increasing likelihood of economic conflict. White, however, refused to generalize beyond pork, ham, and sausage.

21. ADW to Evarts, April 19, 1881, and ADW to Blaine, March 21, 1881, DMG.
22. ADW to Blaine, June 14, 1881, DMG.
23. *Autobiography*, vol. 1, p. 585.

Similarly, by blaming the monetary impasse on Kelley, White avoided the conclusion that Germany was willing to dump its silver reserves on the market regardless of the effect on the United States.

Finally, White ignored indications that two nationalistic nations in search of empire might eventually clash. In 1878 the Pacific island of Samoa granted the United States full use of the port of Pago Pago and the right to establish a station for coal and other naval supplies. Samoa promised neither to exercise nor to authorize any jurisdiction within the port which would restrict the rights of the United States. In return, the United States promised to use its good offices to resolve any conflict between Samoa and other powers. In the following year, both Germany and Great Britain signed treaties of "friendship and commerce" with the Samoans, and the three powers suspiciously gauged the intentions of the others.[24]

In 1880 the Reichstag debated a Samoan subsidy bill, a measure considered by anti-expansionists as the first step toward an overt colonial policy. White sent two dispatches on the subject to the State Department. On May 3 he reported that the majority in the Reichstag opposed the Samoan bill because they feared the entanglements of empire. A week later White relayed news of the defeat of the subsidy bill to Evarts: "Our own government may rely upon it, I think it is certain, that any attempt to begin a colonial policy in the Pacific by the German Government, even with the Chancellor at its head, will be defeated. It is perfectly clear that the vast majority of the German nation has an unconquerable distrust of it."[25]

The State Department, then considering a tripartite agreement with Great Britain and Germany to give stability to the Samoan regime (and protect the American beachhead at Pago Pago), was relieved when White's second dispatch arrived. Given White's assurances, Evarts decided that the nation could remain aloof from formal entangling alliances without endangering its rights at Pago Pago.[26]

White's analysis of German intentions proved to be incorrect. Bismarck had been an avowed opponent of colonialism throughout much of the 1870s but had evidently changed his mind by the end of the decade. Although he made no explicit avowal of his new attitude, his position might have been gleaned from a careful examination of the press favorable

24. Clara Schieber, *The Transformation of American Sentiment toward Germany* (Boston and New York, 1923), pp. 42–43.

25. George Ryden, *The Foreign Policy of the United States in Relation to Samoa* (New Haven, Conn., 1933), pp. 253–54; ADW to Evarts, May 10, 1880, DMG.

26. Ryden, *Foreign Policy*, pp. 256–57.

to the administration. White, however, remained convinced that anti-imperialism would continue to dominate government circles. The defeat of the Samoa bill, in fact, did not deter Bismarck from increasing his influence on the island, and the succeeding decades saw Germany, the United States, and Great Britain scouring the island for genial chieftains who would consent to be installed as their puppets. In 1884 Bismarck won Reichstag approval for his colonial policy; upon his return to Germany as ambassador in 1897, White again had to confront German–American differences over Samoa.[27]

When White was appointed minister in 1879, he apparently thought that his tour of duty would be short and that he would return home at the end of President Hayes's term. The Cornell University trustees certainly thought so, but became uneasy by the summer of 1880 and requested a more formal declaration of intentions. If the president did not intend to return to Ithaca in the near future, they advised him, a search for a permanent replacement would begin immediately. Only Russel demurred from the resolution, which demanded that White relinquish one of his two careers.[28]

Stung by the remonstrance of the trustees, White quickly sent his resignation across the Atlantic. In a cagily worded note, however, he asked the trustees to wait until his return to America before naming a successor. Did this mean that White's return to the United States was imminent? If so, his resignation could be refused. If the trustees postponed action until his return, they might just as well retain him and hope that the Berlin post marked his final odyssey. Eminently satisfied with White when he was in Ithaca, the trustees permitted their resolve to weaken, and months slipped by while Russel remained uneasily at the helm.[29]

While Cornellians kept their eyes on Berlin for signs of White's early return, the minister's gaze often turned toward American politics—in part for signs of his diplomatic future. Hayes's appointments pleased White, who saw a steady increase in the number of qualified diplomats; perhaps the day was not far off when politics would be removed from foreign service.[30]

Hayes, unfortunately, decided not to stand for reelection in 1880, but the minister felt that the GOP had many candidates qualified to succeed him. Roscoe Conkling, conscious that his hold on New York patronage

27. Ibid., p. 255. For an excellent discussion of Bismarck's shifting attitude, see Mack Walker, *Germany and the Emigration, 1816–1885* (Cambridge, Mass., 1964), pp. 203–206.
28. Resolution of the Trustees of Cornell University, June 16, 1880, WMC.
29. ADW to Francis Finch, July 9, 1880, WMC.
30. James Angell to ADW, April 15, 1880, WMC.

was tenuous, advanced the candidacy of his patron, U. S. Grant. Other leading candidates included the "Plumed Knight," James G. Blaine; financial expert John Sherman of Ohio and James A. Garfield. Although he had a pronounced distaste for Blaine, White could support with enthusiasm any of the other candidates.

A coalition of the Blaine and Sherman forces foiled the third-term hopes of front-runner Grant, and in the scramble that followed, Garfield emerged as the compromise choice of the convention. Former president of Hiram College in Ohio, the intellectual of the House of Representatives, Garfield seemed to White an ideal choice. To Willard Fiske's dire predictions that the nomination of Chester Arthur as vice-president proved that the candidate had capitulated to the spoilsmen, White blithely responded: "You are in a strange fog about Garfield; pessimistic to the last—and Arthur will make a perfectly good 'Superfluous Highness.'"[31] As the campaign drew nearer to a close, the minister waxed even more enthusiastic about the future fortunes of the nation and the Republican party: "I see no reason, if Garfield be elected, to expect the revival of the Democratic Party for the next twenty years, or, indeed, for ever."[32]

With the Republican victory came the president-elect's request that White remain at his diplomatic post. The minister attempted to persuade his friends, suspicious of the new administration's steadfastness to the cause of civil service, to support Garfield. Noting that the president had always been a good classical scholar and "great devourer of books," the minister informed the ever cynical Fiske that one of Garfield's first acts after the election had been to commission White to purchase several Latin classics for his private library.[33] Certainly a president who desired to enhance the status of learning deserved support.

For a time it seemed that Garfield's literary tastes would be surpassed by his taste in diplomatic assistants. Commenting on widespread rumors that White would be chosen secretary of state, the *Cornell Daily Sun* enthusiastically listed his qualifications: "Although his literary tastes are predominant, yet he has great executive ability and is a skilled diplomat, and the peer of Alexander Hamilton, whom he resembles. His personal relations with Garfield are exceedingly intimate. Garfield believes him to be a man of brains and the chief of college presidents. This feeling, especially as to the brains, is mutual. Besides, he is rich and can entertain."[34] White did not expect to be named secretary of state, but he must have been dismayed

31. ADW to Fiske, June 19, 1880, WMC.
32. ADW to Moses Coit Tyler, October 30, 1880, WMC.
33. ADW to Fiske, November 6, 1880, WMC.
34. *Cornell Daily Sun*, January 26, 1881.

President James A. Garfield

when the president chose Blaine, Conkling's implacable enemy: more proof, Garfield's detractors insisted, that the vacillating executive owed his tenure in the White House to the most venal politicians in the Republican party.

Garfield's tenure, however, came to an abrupt halt only months after his inauguration when he was shot by the deranged office-seeker Charles Guiteau. White was deeply moved by the expressions of sympathy for the fallen president throughout Germany. The German press, however, also condemned the corrupt system of appointments that had created the atmosphere that spawned Guiteau. In a dispatch, ironically addressed to Secretary Blaine—certainly not a friend of civil service reform—White relayed the criticism, noting that the scramble for office in the United States engendered distrust of republicanism through Europe.[35]

With Garfield's death, White decided to help make him a martyr to the cause of civil service reform. In an address delivered in Germany and the United States, he portrayed the late president as a knowledgeable, thoughtful, sympathetic man, full of moral earnestness, faith, and courage. His career demonstrated that he was "right" on the foremost issues of his day: the Civil War, Reconstruction, and finance. Once he had helped to settle the questions of disunion and reunion, however, he was cruelly sacrificed "to a system of administration which is the greatest present disgrace and the greatest future danger to this republic." Garfield had helped solve all of America's problems but one: civil service reform was the responsibility of his successors.[36]

Increasing demands from the Cornell trustees, as well as the uncertainty of his relationship with President Arthur, prompted White's decision to return home in the late summer of 1881. At a farewell banquet given by Rudolf von Gneist, White conceded the English origin of the United States and its institutions (in later years he would approve of Herbert Baxter Adams's work on the Teutonic ancestry of America) but argued that England was a former parent who exercised little influence at present. The presence of numerous American students in Germany provided strong evidence that the Fatherland would be the United States' future parent. White promised to return home and inspire students with the exalted admiration and affection he felt for Germany.[37]

Upon his arrival in New York, White quickly attempted to fulfill his promise to Gneist and his guests. In a press interview he stressed the good feelings Germans had for America; in private and in public he evidenced

35. ADW to Blaine, July 11, 1881, DMG.
36. *James A. Garfield Memorial Address* (Ithaca, 1881).
37. *New York Times*, June 19, 1881.

little concern about tariff wars or imperialistic clashes. Asked about anti-Semitism in Germany, White insisted that the worst trouble was over. The Kaiser, he explained, viewed Jews as the best of his subjects and was opposed to discriminatory laws aimed at them. Bismarck had disagreed at first but finally concurred with the Kaiser's judgment.[38]

The returned minister kept his slight apprehensions about Germany from the press. He thought Bismarck's state insurance law embracing all workers would have no logical end short of socialism. While Germany's present leaders could steer the nation clear of that disastrous course, White shared the concern of Theodor Mommsen and other German intellectuals that the next generation of leaders might have to make serious concessions to quiet potential class conflict.[39]

Such speculation was certainly premature, and White contented himself with evidence of his growing reputation on both sides of the Atlantic. His successor in Berlin, Aaron A. Sargent, spoke neither German nor French and was therefore uncomfortable in German society. Moreover, his position as minister was quickly compromised by the publication of his salty dispatches concerning the prohibition of American pork. Sargent enhanced White's effectiveness in the eyes of the Germans.[40] In the United States, the press informed the nation that Arthur had narrowed his choice for secretary of state to White and former New Jersey senator Frederick T. Frelinghuysen. "Bosh!" White wrote in his diary, amid rumors that chances were in his favor, perhaps hoping to ease the pain if he were not appointed.[41] Frelinghuysen got the call, but White must have been assured that the future held many more diplomatic honors for the distinguished runner-up.

38. *New York Times*, September 11, 1881.
39. ADW to Evarts, February 21, 1881, DMG; Henry Richmond to ADW, May 1, 1890, WMC.
40. Van Nostwitz Wellwitz to ADW, June 14, 1883, WMC.
41. Diary, October 6, 1881, WMC.

Chapter 8   *Relinquishing the Reins at Cornell*

Even before White's departure for Berlin, many members of the Cornell community predicted a severe deterioration in the health of the university in the event of another prolonged absence. These fears were exacerbated by the president's insistence that William Channing Russel serve as his replacement. Russel, who was not far from his seventieth birthday in 1880, had been one of the first in America to conduct classes on the German seminar plan. His searching cross-examination of students alienated many (including Fred White) and earned him the nickname "Old Roman."[1] If Russel was direct and demanding with students in his ancient history course, he was even more blunt with faculty and trustees. "I accept the fact that literary and scientific men are eminently unreasoning beings," he informed White, " . . . and that they are always in a state of irritation about their salaries and ready to snap at anyone at any time, and that I am always handy."[2] The Old Roman might have added that he seldom lacked a frank rejoinder to complaints and criticism.

White was impressed by Russel's culture, breeding, and unflinching loyalty to the university, and thought his replacement could control his excesses. During his absences from Ithaca, therefore, White encouraged Russel to correspond frequently and to indulge (and perhaps dissipate) himself in an orgy of frankness. The acting president was only too eager to oblige and often lectured the absentee president on the difficulties of university administration. "You and Fiske," he wrote to White, "used to talk[ing] to nobody smaller than Bismarck and the Empress, may think these uncertainties small things, but I can assure you that it is easier to entertain two prime ministers than to make two assistant professors keep time."[3] On White's proposed appointment of a professor of German literature he wrote: "Now you know that I have the misfortune of not sharing your admiration for everybody from Syracuse. . . . While I recognize . . . the advantage he enjoys in your acquaintanceship with his

1. Morris Bishop, *A History of Cornell* (Ithaca, 1962), pp. 106–107.
2. Russel to ADW, March 14, 1875, WMC.
3. Russel to ADW, December 26, 1875, WMC.

father, I do not feel carried beyond my sense of dignity and justice to others."[4]

White patiently digested Russel's advice, reassured in the knowledge that at trustee and faculty meetings the acting president suppressed his own thoughts and presented the views of his superior.[5] Reserve your blunt honesty for me, he cautioned, "for a very small dose of the sort of thing your letter contains would make some of the best people I know furious."[6]

One of the "best people" White knew had been furious at Russel for almost a decade. Although liberal Christian Henry Sage did not want to transform Cornell into a sectarian university, he thought that every professor should be affiliated with some denomination. Sage viewed Russel's latitudinarianism as bordering on atheism. An ardent admirer of Henry Ward Beecher and a prominent member of his Brooklyn congregation, Sage failed to persuade the great minister to come to Ithaca for a permanent position. In 1875, after Beecher had been accused of conducting a liaison with one of his parishioners, Mrs. Theodore Tilton, Sage arranged a visit to Cornell. Less certain than Sage of Beecher's moral character, Russel objected to an offer of rooms at Sage College. White strode into the impasse and invited Sage's guest to his house. The president had admired Beecher's staunch advocacy of the abolition of slavery and, though unsure of his private moral conduct, thought him an uplifting influence on the university community. He hoped, too, that his invitation would forestall a break between Sage and Russel, but Henry Sage never forgot the discourtesy shown to his spiritual leader.[7]

Unhappiness with Russel's personality and religious views formed the nucleus of disaffection with his leadership, but objective evidence for the decline of the university also disturbed the trustees. The president had been absent continuously since 1876, and Cornell's enrollment had declined precipitously. In 1875 the entering class was 552, but by 1881 fewer than 400 freshmen appeared in Ithaca. Searching for an easy diagnosis of the university's malady, several trustees pointed to Russel's administrative shortcomings. Henry Sage had his own explanation, even more damaging to the acting president. The Board of Trustees, he informed White, was increasingly anxious about "professors acting with bodies of men pro-

4. Russel to ADW, February 19, 1880, WMC.
5. Russel to ADW, April 11, 1878, WMC.
6. Quoted in Russel to ADW, March 26, 1880, WMC.
7. Sage to ADW, May 12, 1872; Frank Carpenter to ADW, August 15, 1872; Sage to ADW, Janurary 2, 1873; ADW to Mrs. E. P. Evans, April 26, 1875; Sage to ADW, July 31, 1874; ADW to Charles E. West, June 23, 1883, all in WMC. Sage denied that the Beecher affair affected his attitude toward Russel (see Henry Sage to Dean Sage, May 12, 1881, Henry Sage MSS, Cornell University).

foundly irreligious." James Oliver, Cornell's mathematician, had been announced as a cospeaker with the "Great Infidel," Robert G. Ingersoll. Russel, a Unitarian, had associated openly with freethinkers. Only one course, Sage counseled, was open to the university: Cornell would lose "some of our most valued friends on the Board unless there can be complete harmony of action in rooting out these hindrances and the men who create them."[8]

Early in 1881, at a board meeting that was not attended by Russel, the trustees voted unanimously to ask for his resignation as acting president and professor. When the Old Roman confronted the trustees, they refused to provide reasons to justify their actions; Russel, however, quickly found an explanation. Sage had never forgotten the Beecher incident and had merely deferred his revenge, Russel announced to White. Residing in Ithaca permanently since 1880, Sage had helped to engineer a trustee scheme to mend fences with orthodox religion in White's absence. Russel believed that he had been removed as professor because in his medieval history course he spoke of the church as an institution rather than a divine establishment and cast doubt upon Constantine's vision of the cross. Russel implored White to check this attempt to reverse the trend of enlightened education synonymous with the name Cornell—and perhaps save his position as professor as well.[9]

The deteriorating situation in Ithaca prompted White to compose a strong letter of protest to the Board of Trustees. Sage answered that the executive committee would agree only to grant Russel an additional year's salary as severance pay. The board's resolve to remove Russel and several other professors, including James Oliver, remained unshaken despite White's argument that removal "based on the idea which a body of businessmen would be likely to have—that only those departments must be kept going which apparently draw large numbers of students . . . [are] not well based." The trustees, it seems, had explained the removals to White on the grounds of economy, and White chose to ignore the question of religion and met them on their terms. Despite his caution, White failed to reverse their course.[10]

8. Bishop, *History of Cornell*, p. 205; Sage to ADW, September 12, 1880, WMC; Joan Olson, "The Political Career of Andrew Dickson White," master's thesis, Cornell University, 1958, p. 89; Sage to ADW, December 29, 1880, and Sage to A. S. Barnes, April 13, 1881, Sage MSS.
9. Russel to ADW, January 4 and 16, 1881, and May 27, 1877, WMC; *Ithaca Journal*, August 8, 1882; ADW to Burt Wilder, February 4, 1913, WMC.
10. Sage to ADW, February 26, 1881; Francis Finch to ADW, January 14, 1881; ADW to Finch, February 5, 1881, all in WMC; Sage to ADW, May 12, 1881, and Sage to Russel, February 26, 1881, Sage MSS.

Spurred to more decisive action, White penned a formal resignation with a note to Sage that it was "final." White presented the university with a gift of $10,000 but otherwise severed all connection with it. But then the president's resolve failed him; he decided to send neither the resignation nor the accompanying note to Sage.[11]

Even as he was being abandoned by his friend, William Channing Russel decided to acquiesce in the trustees's demand for his resignation, citing his loyalty to the university above all else. In a document that Sage found "by turns arrogant, threatening and soft and tender as a weeping woman," Russel allowed himself a parting shot at the board's management policies: if the trustees continued to make tenure of office dependent on personal likes and dislikes, popularity with students, and ideological uniformity, originality and spirit would be driven from Cornell. Universities, he reminded the trustees, "are not business enterprises, nor are professors clerks or servants, nor have Trustees any right to look down on them, ignore their claims, or treat them summarily. . . . They must be free. No one near being a first class man will work long under a whip, nor can any professor do a University his best service while he feels in danger of losing his place in spite of success in his department and good conduct." Content with this statement of the basic tenets of academic freedom, Russel promised to end his formal connections with Cornell at the semester's end.[12]

When Russel's resignation became public, however, student protest erupted. Enraged at the violation of free thought by the board, the *Cornell Sun* challenged anyone to point to any error committed by the acting president. Claiming Andrew D. White as their ally, the *Sun* editors awaited a more satisfactory explanation of Russel's dismissal; meanwhile they branded the action "unjust, ungenerous and unkind, and the method of procedure discourteous." On April 12 the senior class petitioned the executive committee of the trustees to decline to accept Russel's resignation. A week later all of the female students but four signed yet another petition protesting Russel's removal. Shortly thereafter a mass protest meeting was held; the acting president's plight had become a cause célèbre.[13]

While the students petitioned and held protest meetings, faculty and alumni fumed and sent petitions of their own to the trustees. In a furious letter to White, William Anthony, professor of physics, outlined the

11. ADW to Sage, March 17, 1881, WMC. This letter had the notation "not sent."
12. Russel to Cornell Executive Committee, March 31, 1881, WMC; Bishop, *History of Cornell*, p. 219.
13. *Cornell Sun*, April 12, 18, and 20, 1881; ADW to Wilder, February 4, 1913, WMC.

faculty declaration: "The faculty is a body coordinate with the board, whose members are not hired servants doing the will of a master. As a body it has its own share of work to do in which the trustees have no right to interfere. Thus, the faculty should nominate its own members and initiate proceedings against them if necessary." The faculty and alumni assumed that Russel's removal as professor indicated that the trustees intended to monitor faculty opinion and remove the unorthodox; Cornell University had strayed far from its founding principles.[14]

Beleaguered by protests from students, faculty, and alumni, the Board of Trustees had also invited expressions of disapproval from outside the university's walls. The *New York Times* accepted assertions that the trustees sought to keep Cornell "within the rut of their own theological preferences." The *Times* darkly predicted that if in fact this was the reason for the Old Roman's removal, and if President White could not stem the tide, the days of the university were "numbered so far as broad and liberal education is concerned."[15]

Ironically, Russel energetically helped the trustees to quiet the furor. In a public letter to George Lincoln Burr, leader of the student protest movement, Russel expressed appreciation for the support of the student body. At the same time, however, he insisted, "with perfect truthfulness," that his departure would not injure the Department of History. "Able men could easily be found," he continued, "out of whom the spirit of Cornell could bring something better than my hurried work. . . . In the meantime, I shall always remember my part with a great deal of pleasure, and I shall hope for God's blessing on all of Cornell's classes, especially that of '81."[16]

A recognition that he was not indispensable may not have been too difficult for an educated gentleman such as Russel, but a retreat from religious controversy was the ultimate proof of the deposed professor's loyalty. Amid rumors that he had been asked to resign because he had disobeyed Sage's demand that Beecher preach at Cornell, Russel wrote to the *Sun* once again. Without mentioning that they had previously crossed swords over Beecher or that Sage resented his lack of religious convictions, Russel denied that the head of the Board of Trustees had asked him to invite Beecher. Only at this point did Russel's restraint give way to sarcasm. He had not invited the Brooklyn minister on his own initiative, he gratuitously added, because "it was not a good thing to have a gentleman of the peculiar kind of interest which attaches to Mr. Beecher preach

14. Anthony to ADW, June 1, 1881, and ADW to Willard Fiske, April 28, 1881, WMC.
15. *New York Times*, May 4, 1881.
16. *Cornell Sun*, April 15, 1881.

to our young ladies and young men."[17] The acting president emerged from the controversy with his honor intact. A known controversialist, he left the university with a plea for harmony and reconciliation; at the same time, though, he informed the despised Sage that he would not alter his views on either Beecher or freedom of thought. Russel's refusal to accept the role of martyr dampened student and faculty ardor in his behalf. As the semester drew to a close, defense of principle gave way to the practical matter of final examinations.

Unity in defense of Russel was further eroded by President White's decision to return to Cornell in the fall. At first determined to resign, he had utlimately decided not to abandon the university to the philistines. For White, the road to progress was slow and tortuous. In fact, he believed that when the course of progress was temporarily reversed, the public servant must fight from within; those who remained above the battle could never effect the outcome. Consequently, White decided to make his greatest sacrifice to Cornell: to resign his post at Berlin and return as president. Devoted though he was to Russel—"my old friend and associate"—White could not "see the work and sacrifices of these last fifteen years . . . lost or risked now." So White returned for the same reason that Russel resigned: harmony within the university was of paramount importance.[18]

In his zeal for an era of good feeling, however, White often seemed to be an apologist for the board. Charter guarantees of political and religious liberty, he insisted, had not been violated. White disagreed with the executive committee's removal of Russel, he told Fiske, but likened it to a "battle in which a friend falls at your side; you must press on nevertheless." As with Adler, White was willing to sacrifice Russel and compromise the university's guarantee of freedom of religious thought because he believed such actions best in the long run. He seemed willing to shelve the Cornell Idea to ensure the survival of Cornell.[19]

White wrote letters to alumni and faculty reassuring them that the university would not stifle religious liberty. Now attributing Russel's removal to an "incompatability of tempers," White denied that the acting president's theological views had swayed the board. John Fiske, whose unorthodoxy was at least as pronounced as Russel's, had recently been invited to give a series of lectures at Cornell. Obviously, then, no plot to bring rigid sectarianism to the university had been hatched. White reiterated his theme in an open letter to alumni and faculty: "As to the tenure of

17. *Cornell Sun*, April 14 and May 13, 1881.
18. ADW to Tyler, June 2, 1881, and Diary, May 29, 1881, WMC.
19. ADW to Fiske, April 28 and May 16, 1881, WMC.

Professorships, neither the expression of an abstract opinion regarding the power of the Trustees, nor the exceptional exercise of that power in the case referred to seems to me to give any just cause for alarm on the part of our Faculty." White did not tell the faculty that Henry Sage had begun to exercise his influence on faculty selection. Begging the president not to discuss the matter with anyone, Sage proposed a Congregationalist minister for the professorship in ancient history. The candidate was, he announced, "a gentleman and a Christian in every sense." White, who also sought only gentlemen and Christians for the faculty, must have wondered if Sage's definition of these terms coincided with his own.[20]

The dismissal of Russel helped White fulfill a cherished dream—the establishment of a professorship in American history, the first such position in the United States.[21] As the Russel controversy raged through the spring of 1881, White probably decided to make a full-time position in American history the price of his return to Ithaca.[22] He solicited faculty opinions about his old friend Moses Coit Tyler. The president's requests for advice were a mere formality; he had long ago made up his mind. Tyler "is a noble fellow," he wrote to Willard Fiske, "he has made his mark by his book; is much beloved; and certainly no one can object to him on the score of his opinions, since he is about taking orders in the Episcopal Church."[23] A scholar and a gentleman, Tyler seemed easily able to pass even Henry Sage's test of Christian orthodoxy.

At White's urging, Tyler was appointed to a chair in American history and literature. The new professor was acutely aware of the events that had brought White's plans to fruition: "I suppose the Trustees thought it wise to do this in order to shut up further talk about Russel's case, which has been so managed in the papers as to make him seem like a martyr to petty and vindictive prejudices and to make the University suffer in public esteem as a decaying institution in the hands of small local managers."[24] In

20. ADW to Tyler, June 2, 1881; ADW to Alumni and Faculty, May 10, 1881; Sage to ADW, July 19, 1881, all in WMC.

21. For White's attempts to hire a professor of American history in the 1870s, see ADW to Horatio Seymour, November 29, 1870; Edward E. Hale to ADW, June 4, 1870; George W. Curtis to ADW, June 5, 1870; Henry Bellows to ADW, June 7, 1870; Hewitt to ADW, July 19, 1870; ADW to Russel, August 18, 1870; John Stanton Gould to ADW, February 6, 1872; Russel to ADW, March 2, 1872; George W. Greene to ADW, September 17, 1872, all in WMC.

22. Russel and John Fiske had taught classes in American history. See Russel to ADW, October 10, 1880; John Fiske to Russel, February 3, 1881; Russel to ADW, September 19, 1879, all in WMC.

23. ADW to Fiske, March 29, 1881, WMC. Tyler's "book" was *A History of American Literature in Colonial Times, 1607–1765*, 2 vols. (New York, 1878).

24. Tyler to ADW, June 5, 1881, WMC.

a curious way, Russel's prediction had been correct; his departure had in fact strengthened Cornell's department of history, although it certainly had not strengthened Cornell.

Although proud of the new chair in American history, White recognized that his triumph had come at great cost, and he was determined at least to ensure the future welfare of William Channing Russel. White succeeded in securing a one-year lectureship at Brown University for the old man, but efforts to obtain a permanent position for him failed—perhaps because of Russel's advanced age. In 1883 White strongly recommended his former colleague for the presidency of the University of Nebraska. He asked the president of Brown to testify publicly that Russel was not irreligious. Russel did not receive the position, however, and spent his last years in bitter retirement, blaming Cornell trustees and faculty for his plight but remaining staunchly loyal to the university and Andrew D. White.[25]

White's guilt and embarrassment at the Russel affair are nowhere more apparent than in his autobiography, which was published twenty-five years later. The president made no mention at all of the dismissal and in a brief sketch outlined Russel's unstinting loyalty to the university. He balanced praise, however, with references to Russel's lack of "suaviter in modo" in his handling of delicate questions. Despite a conclusion that Russel's services "vastly outweighed the defects of his qualities," the damage was done; no other member of the Cornell community (including Henry Sage) received such a mixed blessing.[26]

The president's brief reminiscences of Russel's contribution to Cornell did not go unchallenged. Russel's son, who had obviously inherited his father's bluntness, reminded White that the autobiography did not contain the full story:

You had spoken of many of your colleagues at the University, but only with words of praise until you came to him. Then, mingled with a few kindly phrases, were your first words of blame. Blame for the man who gave to the University his best flood of brain and heart, and who left with all who knew him there a memory of unswerving devotion to duty and high aims. Blame for the man who stood between you and the . . . details and friction of a college administration, and so left you free to follow your political ambitions. His loyalty to you personally was as unfailing as that to the University. How have you now publicly repaid that loyalty![27]

25. E. J. Robinson to ADW, June 9, 1883, WMC; Bishop, *History of Cornell*, pp. 222–23; ADW to Wilder, February 4, 1913, WMC.
26. *Autobiography*, vol. 1, pp. 436–38.
27. S. J. Russel to ADW, January 11, 1906, WMC.

Russel's son was not the only man to lament Russel's plight. Even George Lincoln Burr, White's erstwhile secretary, protégé, researcher, and friend could not suppress a sad reference to Russel's departure: "I am not sure that you will find anywhere, any better example of modern intolerance in the field of education than the dismissal of one William Channing Russel from a Professorship in History at Cornell University . . . of which, perhaps, and of its reasons, the less said the better—till Modern History becomes Ancient."[28]

White, who hoped one day to chronicle intolerance—modern and ancient—and to strike a blow in the warfare of "humanity with unreason," must have strained to purge the incident from his memory. Silent acquiescence made him an accessory in the crime against Russel; perhaps silent and steady remorse was his punishment.

Goldwin Smith compared President White's return to Cornell in the autumn of 1881 with the appearance of Neptune in the *Aeneid*—"the storms are rebuked and all have gone to their caves again." Certainly White's presence on campus was accompanied by a decrease in trustee apprehension about declining student enrollment. General prosperity throughout the nation and the return of outward harmony at Cornell made the 1880s a boom decade for the university. In addition, White's return silenced some of the critics of Cornell's religious policies. By comparison with Russel, the president somehow seemed orthodox—at least to some. Lyman Abbott, who had been severely critical of Russel's "no-religious convictions," argued in the *Christian Union* that the university, under White's direction, was slowly recovering from a reputation of positive "irreligion." Enrollment and religion, the rocks upon which Russel had foundered, seemed now to indicate that prosperity had returned to Cornell.[29]

Beneath the apparent tranquillity, however, struggle for control of the university raged between White and Sage. The chairman of the Board of Trustees had assumed great power during the president's absence and was not about to relinquish it. The two men argued about finances, with Sage adamantly opposed to White's proposal that virtually all of the university's earnings be immediately spent on faculty and equipment. Very quickly the feud became personal. Sage censured the president's failure to intervene personally in order to prevent student mischief. White replied that he

28. Burr to ADW, January 22, 1888, WMC.
29. Bishop, *History of Cornell*, p. 233; Walter P. Rogers, "Andrew D. White and the Transition Period in American Higher Education," Ph.D. thesis, Cornell University, 1934, p. 178; *Cornell Sun*, December 11, 1882.

did not consider it his duty to risk position and life to discipline several rowdies, though he "would have done so for a more important object." The president fumed to his diary: "His remarks were simply those of a 'good businessman' as utterly blind to the realities of this case as to the beauties of a Sonata of Beethoven."[30]

Sage, who resented White's neglect of the presidency to pursue careers in politics and diplomacy, returned his rival's sentiment in kind. "The millionaire master" (as White dubbed him) heaped scorn on White's preoccupation with theory and neglect of detail and with his efforts to portray himself as the university's guiding genius. After a particularly irksome article in the *New York Sun*, Sage vented his spleen to his son: "Reporter had a long interview with White and White is duly accredited with being the author of C[ornell] U[niversity], through his suggestions to E[zra] C[ornell]—That is characteristic—Cornell is dead!" In 1884 Sage attempted unsuccessfully to secure trustee legislation to limit the powers of the president. Sage's conflict with Russel, in essence, was merely a prelude to a struggle with Andrew White.[31]

If the first two years of his return seemed unpleasant to White, the subsequent two were nightmarish. In 1883 John De Witt Warner, alumni trustee, made a sensation with a general indictment of the university. He assailed low faculty salaries, which resulted in a dearth of quality instruction; Sage's autocratic domination of the Board of Trustees; White's insistence on using precious funds to build costly, ostentatious buildings; and White's frequent absences in order to dabble in politics. Warner's review of Cornell's affairs, which was printed in 1884, rocked the university.[32]

White's first reaction to Warner's charges was despair and pessimism. He wondered whether higher education did indeed produce enlightened men: "Sad to think of the labor I have given to develop him and men like him. His aim is simply notoriety—he would be a little tin Ben Butler."[33] As was his habit, White reserved his unhappiest thoughts for his diary. On May 1, 1883, he reached the depths of depression: "Cold, dismal weather—all the worse on account of my disgusted and disheartened state at the attack of that wretched creature Warner on the university. What

---

30. ADW to Sage, October 17, 1884, and Diary, November 8, 1882. WMC.
31. Henry Sage to W. H. Sage, December 19, 1882, Sage MSS; Anita Shafer Goodstein, *Biography of a Businessman: Henry W. Sage* (Ithaca, 1962), pp. 236–37, 240.
32. Goodstein, *Biography of a Businessman*, pp. 238–39. For extensive press clippings on the Warner controversy, see Francis W. Halsey Scrapbook, Cornell University Archives; for Warner's attack on White, see Report as to the Condition of Cornell University, Made to Its Alumni, June 1883, WMC (esp. p. 6).
33. Diary, April 28, 1883, WMC.

have we done to deserve being trampled beneath the feet of such braying asses! What a depth of wisdom in the Scripture 'Cast not your pearls before swine lest they turn again and rend you!'"[34]

In little more than a week, however, White launched an aggressive counteroffensive to restore Cornell's reputation. Far from being incompetent and unworthy, the trustees, he claimed, had been unstinting in their generosity to the university. Harmony rather than discord, moreover, governed the board's meetings. The president denied that the quality of the faculty had deteriorated. Without mentioning that most of those he named were nonresident professors, he listed the illustrious men presently associated with Cornell: E. A. Freeman, John Fiske, Charles Kendall Adams, Henry Carter Adams, Richard T. Ely, Moses Coit Tyler. Few, if any, institutions boasted a more distinguished and talented faculty. Not content with a factual refutation of Warner's charges, White summoned forth the sarcasm usually reserved for his diary to ridicule the attack on Cornell. We have all been living in a dream, he informed the students. We thought "a great work has been done, a great work is doing," but "we are informed this is a wreck. But my degenerate young friends, you long to know why you are in so sad a plight. The telegraph brings an oracular answer. You 'are no longer clustering round great ideas'—unlike your critic you do not 'cluster' and you therefore deteriorate."[35]

White's strong defense helped unite the Cornell community against Warner's intemperate charges, and Warner's candidate for alumni trustee was defeated. The president was also able to use Warner's comments to extract increases in faculty salaries from the trustees. If Warner's blasts turned out to be little more than a tempest in a teapot, White had the added solace that the incident brought forth words of praise for his years of work in higher education. Charles Kendall Adams's prediction that White's place in history was secure must have pleased the president:

All over this broad land are to be found those who look back to your inspiring guidance as the beginning of higher and nobler aspirations. . . . And through them you are having an influence which nothing less than a Divine intelligence can measure. In addition to this you will have the substantial monument of the University. When we are all passed away the thoughtful scholar who visits these hills will pronounce blessings on your name.[36]

Adams's soothing words were especially valuable because they came at a time when the trustees had drawn the president into a struggle with one of

34. Diary, May 1, 1883, WMC.
35. *Boston Journal*, May 23, 1883; *Cornell Sun*, May 11, 1883.
36. Adams to ADW, May 17, 1883, WMC.

his closest friends. Willard Fiske had served the university as librarian and language professor since its inception. The cynical bachelor, chess expert, and master of scores of languages served as White's confidant. The president, consequently, was more than pleased when Fiske married Jennie McGraw, the daughter of Henry Sage's business partner; in fact, White loaned his friend the money needed to court Jennie, who had gone to Europe, and the marriage ceremony was performed in July 1880 at the American legation in Berlin. A frail woman of forty, Jennie McGraw Fiske lived little more than a year after her marriage and at her death left her husband $300,00 and Cornell University an estate valued at more than $1 million.[37]

Sage and Douglas Boardman, the executor of the will, refused to grant Fiske's request that $25,000 be set aside for the purchase of library books and periodicals for the Cornell Library, and very quickly the dispute became intensely petty and personal. Fiske told Sage that the library could not be run like a lumberyard; Boardman, who had opposed Jennie's marriage, frustrated Fiske's attempts to use the $600 his wife had on deposit in Ithaca. Fiske became livid when he learned that the state legislature (at the behest of Sage and Boardman) had removed from the university's charter the stipulation that the Cornell corporation could not hold real and personal property in an amount in excess of $3 million. The McGraw bequest would give the corporation more than $3 million. Further, as Boardman was surely well aware, New York State law did not permit a testator to leave less than half of her estate to her spouse. Thus without informing Fiske of his rights, the trustees had seized the McGraw money. Resigning his university posts in June 1883, Fiske joined in a suit with other McGraw heirs claiming that the legislature's action was ex post facto and therefore illegal; the bequest, they claimed, should revert to the rightful heirs.[38]

The Ithaca community excoriated Fiske as a moral viper, who had married a dying woman for her money, and Sage and Boardman assured White that the Fiske-McGraw suit was bound to fail. The president, who had failed to notify Fiske of the university's appeal to the legislature, now implored the trustees to compromise and grant Fiske a voice in the management of the estate. White followed Fiske to Europe and persuaded him to yield. Fiske offered to terminate his suit in return for the income from $100,000 while he lived if the principle were used to convert Jennie's house into an art gallery when he died. All of White's persuasiveness,

37. For a brief treatment of the Fiske-McGraw case, see Bishop, *History of Cornell*, pp. 224–32.
38. The Founding of Cornell, Summer 1887[?], WMC.

however, went for naught. Sage cabled the president that the executive committee refused to acquiesce in any settlement negotiated by him.[39]

The Great Will Case, which dragged through the courts for seven years and ultimately resulted in victory for Fiske and the McGraws, brought relations between White and Sage near open contempt. Sage blamed White for Fiske's actions, perhaps because White had aided his friend's courtship. The lumberman linked the imbroglio to his long-standing rivalry with White: "Our differences began long ago when Russel was deposed—The bitter fight then was—with R in the front, White in the background, all the time."[40] The passing of time only increased White's frustration and anger. Had Sage's telegram not intervened, he opined, he would have settled the suit. Likening the unyielding trustees' attitude to "burning the barn to draw the rats out," he thought the great need in executive committee meetings was "that even if a man be not worth a million his opinion may be worth something." If White found the crassness of the trustees distasteful, the knowledge that he had bowed time after time before trustee intransigence was even more galling. "Fiske is far superior to the Trustees morally," he wrote to Tyler, "and after all, his wickedness is the result of his commendable want of my own donkeyish patience—which for the sake of the University has led me to associate with men who spit in my face publicly and speak sweetly to me privately—and to bear their nauseous Pharisaism without winking." Conscious of the danger of factionalism to the university, White had too often allowed the Board of Trustees to dictate policy.[41]

Antagonism between White and the trustees over Russel and Fiske, and Warner's attack on the university, convinced White that the time to resign the presidency had arrived. Despite minor setbacks, he was confident that Cornell was "mainly in healthful condition." During the last years of his incumbency there had been solid accomplishments. The student population had increased, with the freshman class rising from 375 in 1881 to 575 in 1884. Student breaches of discipline had been quite rare. Cornell's students seemed to possess the maturity requisite for a program of self-discipline and liberty of choice among various areas of instruction.[42]

With considerable pride and emotion, White prepared his final report to the trustees in June 1885. The timing of his resignation, he wrote to Burr, was excellent:

39. Ibid.; Horatio White, *Willard Fiske: Life and Correspondence* (New York, 1925), p. 106.
40. Quoted in Goodstein, *Biography of a Businessman*, p. 240.
41. ADW to Tyler, January 28 and February 27, 1889; ADW to C. K. Adams, January 8, 1889, all in WMC.
42. President's Report, June 18, 1884; Address at the First Banquet of the Cornell Alumni Association of Western New York, Buffalo, April 13, 1884, both in WMC.

Everything in the university is in the highest state of prosperity. The number of students this year is a hundred larger than last and the quality is greatly improved by the scholarships and fellowships. Our income is much larger than at any previous time in our history and next year when the Comptroller pays us fully the income due from the State it will be larger still. The time has come when I can honorably deliver over the work to others.[43]

The president reviewed for the trustees the triumphant past, the prosperous present, and his vision of the future. Although White sought to banish recriminations from his report, Henry Sage must have recognized that the defense of Cornell's religious policy was aimed largely at him. The final report noted that attacks on nonsectarianism had resulted in greater solidarity among undergraduates and faculty and more generous contributions from Cornell's benefactors. The charter's religious strictures, the president urged, must continue to be observed. With no mention of Adler or Russel, White averred that religious truth was fully capable of taking care of itself in the university's free marketplace of ideas; it did not need a protectionist policy.[44]

This single statement of caution, however, was virtually buried under an avalanche of praise. White's final review of each department indicated that Cornell provided quality instruction and ample laboratory and other research facilities. Built on such a strong foundation, the university could expect continued growth and the maintenance of its position of leadership in higher education. The university was ready for expansion; the trustees should prepare to create "those departments which will round out our existing organization into full University proportions." Thus, departments of law and medicine should be created at once. With these additions, Cornell would be much closer to White's concept of an ideal university.[45]

White could be confident about the future because the trustees gave every indication that his counsel would continue to be influential in policy making. Nothing gave the retiring president more pleasure than the attachment of his name to the newly created College of History and Political Science. After twenty years he finally had a monument to his name. Moreover, despite Sage's opposition, White was given a place on the Board of Trustees. Perhaps the most convincing indication of continued influence was the willingness of the board to allow the president to choose

43. ADW to Burr, June 11, 1885, WMC.
44. President's Report, June 17, 1885, WMC.
45. Ibid.; *Cornell Era*, June 18, 1885. The trustees were receptive to White's suggestions. The law school opened in 1887 and a medical school affiliation was achieved in the 1890s. To White's continued disgust, however, ugly buildings began to dominate the campus. See, e.g., Diary, June 20, 1888, WMC.

his successor, former pupil Charles Kendall Adams. Thus, White proudly wrote to Gilman, his separation from the university was "rather more formal than real." The faculty had also enthusiastically requested that he continue to teach at Cornell; he had been given "every opportunity I could desire to aiding my successor in building on the foundation already laid."[46]

Despite his continued connection with the university, the retiring president broke down in his final, emotional address to the graduating class. "It is my last time in this capacity," he confessed to his diary. "How much that means! Thank God I have been able to see this prosperity and success."[47]

Public and private expressions of gratitude for White's contributions to higher education continued long after his tearful farewell to his students. White's administration, the *Sun* editorialized, "had been one of the most successful and brilliant in the history of higher education in America." "While your hand remained upon the helm," Gilman wrote, "one ship was sure to be steered between Scylla and Charybdis." George William Curtis shared Gilman's sentiments. "The tree will be great," Curtis predicted, "only as you have bent the twig." The *New York Times* similarly lauded the retiring president but added a disturbing assessment of Cornell's immediate past. If Cornell had recently fallen short "of the breadth and elevation of aim which characterized it at first," the fault lay not with White but with "the timidity which is apt to come upon the managers of established institutions." If White, who attributed trustee attitudes to philistinism rather than timidity, found cause for concern, he gave no indication; he convinced himself that the spread of the Cornell Idea was inevitable.[48]

News of the inaugural address of Charles Kendall Adams upset White, who was vacationing in Europe.[49] Adams referred to the administration of Charles W. Eliot of Harvard as being "entitled to the distinction of forming

46. *Autobiography*, vol. 2, p. 493; ADW to Daniel Coit Gilman, June 24, 1885, WMC; *A Letter of Andrew D. White Resigning the Presidency of Cornell University and the Professorship of History* (Ithaca, 1885).

47. Diary, June 18, 1885, WMC.

48. *Cornell Sun*, June 17 and September 30, 1885; Gilman to ADW, June 18, 1885, and Curtis to ADW, June 20, 1885, WMC; *New York Times*, June 17, 1885. The comments of Cornell graduate David Starr Jordan seemed to confirm White's optimism. While president of the University of Indiana, Jordan informed White that his university, though fifty years older, was "in a large measure the daughter of Cornell." On accepting the presidency of Stanford University, Jordan wrote to White: "My educational views are the lineal descendants of yours." See Jordan to ADW, December 4, 1890; March 23, 1891; and July 7, 1906, all in WMC.

49. For offers to White following his resignation, see A. B. Humphrey to ADW, September 21, 1885, and Fred Davies to ADW, November 29, 1885, WMC.

a great epoch in the development of higher education in America." The new president had evidently forgotten his old teacher's abiding hatred of Eliot.[50]

White's personal distaste for Eliot was matched by the conviction that he himself merited recognition as *the* educational innovator in America. Harvard's president, White argued, had on occasion leagued himself with the forces of reaction. An avowed opponent of coeducation, Eliot was insensitive to the needs of women. Moreover, his opposition to federal aid to higher education and to the creation of a national university demonstrated a parochial concern with Harvard. Hardly entitled to praise, Charles Eliot was a man whom "the shrewdest authorities on both sides of the Atlantic regard as a skillful manager of a cotton factory—a man who never showed any breadth of sympathy with the country at large, who cut himself off from Yale and Cornell, not to speak of other institutions, by gratuitous insults."[51]

White furiously scribbled notes in answer to Adams's address. The new president's assessment of Eliot far outshone his treatment of White. Adams had chosen not to acknowledge the "large and definite" place of Cornell in the history of American higher education. "My very existence is ignored," White commented acidly, evidently ignorant of Adams's lavish praise of his administration in his inaugural address, "no mention is made of my life's work." As if he recognized that his pique stemmed from personal frustration, White appended a feeble protest to his notes: "It is from no love of notice or notoriety that I regret this."[52] Still, setting the historical record straight would presumably restore him to a deserved place among the titans of American higher education.

In answer to the mock assertion that "maybe Adams is right," White listed the innovations he had introduced at Cornell. Disputing Adams's inference that the elective principle was invented by Eliot, White claimed that he had advocated the introduction of freedom of choice shortly after his return from Europe in 1856. After looking at the matter for twenty years, White did not understand that Eliot's position differed from his "theoretically."[53] Moreover, the Harvard president had opposed many of

50. *Cornell Sun*, November 19, 1885; ADW to Adams, April 11, 1878; ADW to Gilman, April 12, 1878, and July 24, 1907, all in WMC.

51. James F. Gluck to ADW, June 29, 1885, and ADW to Tyler, December 16, 1885, WMC.

52. Notes on President Adams' Inaugural Address at Cornell University, November 19, 1885, WMC. For Adams's praise of White and Cornell, see *Proceedings and Addresses at the Inauguration of Charles Kendall Adams* (Ithaca, 1886), esp. pp. 59–62.

53. White took no note of the fact that Eliot's elective system offered virtually unlimited choice while his own, once the student selected a course of study, offered virtually none. See chap. 4.

the reforms introduced at Cornell—equality of studies, equality of students, education of women with full privileges. In other areas he had limped along the trail blazed by White—nonsectarianism, faculty government, and discipline. So intense was White's wrath that he continually misspelled the Harvard president's name.[54] Orthography aside, however, the conclusion was inescapable: the dominant figure in the nineteenth-century American university was Andrew White.

Having proved to himself the worth of his services to education, White unburdened himself of his fears that his contemporaries had already forgotten him. In an unusually long entry in his diary, the retired president confessed that the address had plunged him into

a sort of stupor. Have I been dreaming thirty years—ever since I began working for a University—or am I dreaming now. Not the slightest recognition of the University or my work or Gilman's, and above all Mr. Cornell's name not mentioned. And this in a man who owed his start in life to me—whom I made President of Cornell University against fearful odds—defended him at cost of my health and reputation and the good will of friends—stood by him thro[ugh] the worst of attacks[55]—and now. He praises unjustly the worst enemy of all my efforts and ignores my work utterly—and solely to curry favor with Harvard University. . . . There is no other explanation. They are living and active and can do him more harm. I am supposed to be declining in health and can do him no more good. This is the hardest blow I have rec[eive]d. Yesterday my friend or I thought—today—what? Yet I was warned by many.[56]

At the height of his depression, White's faith in the future faltered; ironically Adams, who had recently assured White that his place in history was secure, had now cast doubt on the enduring importance of his life's work.

As in the past, the act of expressing his anger to his diary and the passage of time had a cathartic effect on White. His depression abated, his faith in the future restored by an act of will, White decided to write to his successor. With virtually no mention of himself, White rendered the opinion that Adams had underestimated the role of Cornell while overestimating that of Harvard. White's *Report on Organization* had predated Eliot's famous articles by two years. Cornell had been "the first to see that a university in the nineteenth century could only be developed out of the

54. Notes on President Adams' Inaugural Address, WMC.
55. Adams had been accused of plagiarism in his published work and White had staunchly defended him. See *The Presidency of Cornell University: Remarks of Andrew D. White* (Ithaca, 1885).
56. Diary, December 1, 1885, WMC.

beliefs, feelings, needs, aspirations of the nineteenth century." The former president had made certain that historians would have sufficient source material to judge his incumbency at Cornell.[57]

57. ADW to Adams, December 9 and 18, 1885, WMC. In 1893 White had a similar reaction to the inaugural address of Jacob Gould Schurman. Schurman praised White's contributions to Cornell but asserted that he had "returned to his first love—politics." Incensed, White again reviewed his major achievements in higher education (ADW to George Lincoln Burr and Ernest Huffcut, August 10, 1893, WMC).

Part III

REFORM OF ALL KINDS

During the period between 1884 and 1896, White immersed himself in politics and diplomacy. He continued to view himself as a reformer and was probably unaware of the extent to which class interests shaped his activities. White never doubted that educated men of wealth should rule; the elitist bias of his proposals for change can scarcely be overestimated. Defense of privilege was accompanied by often desperate fear that deference would soon disappear. The success of civil service reform and the defeat of William Jennings Bryan provided some comfort. But when disorder and personal tragedy struck him, he abandoned the evidence of his senses and mumbled incantations to progress. Faith in the future was White's only protection against despair. He employed it when political bosses threatened, when religion remained under siege despite his best efforts, and even when his wife died. White used the doctrine of progress to defend even his consciously reactionary attitudes. If he seemed to be defending the status quo, it was only because he *knew* what the lines of "historical evolution" were, and that the longest way round was sometimes the shortest way home.

Civil service reform was a central issue in the presidential election of 1884, and White urged Republicans to nominate a candidate who shared his commitment to meritocracy. When the delegates chose James G. Blaine, however, White refused to join many of his friends who had bolted the party. The Republican party, in his view, had kept the Union together, and he would not abandon it because one tainted candidate was the standard-bearer. The tide of reform was irresistible, White argued. Blaine could not stem it even if he tried. The candidate, moreover, was too wily to stand in the way of the inevitable: Blaine would enlist as a reformer because to do so was good politics.

White's friends did not fail to notice the incongruity of the attitude that supporting a corrupt candidate was the surest path to reform. Yet he ignored their strictures and paradoxically interpreted Cleveland's narrow victory as proof that he had made the correct decision. As the merit system was extended and as Republicans increasingly joined the reform effort, White became all the more certain that trained public servants would rid the country of corruption and bosses. Civil service reform linked to universal education was the only reform White supported. Because he was sure that they were the *only* reforms necessary to cure America's evils, White refused to support proposals for social and economic change.

When he was released from the onerous administrative duties at Cornell in 1885, White planned to write and lecture extensively on subjects of contemporary interest. The sudden death of his wife brought all of his activity to an abrupt halt. Work, his traditional remedy in times of crisis, now seemed irrelevent. Progress, achievement, fame, all seemed mean-ingless to White if Mary's soul were not immortal. White's depression lingered for months; he desperately tried to believe that he would meet his wife in heaven, and almost succeeded. With the help of Helen Magill, whom he later married, White finally regained his vigor and optimism. He expressed the same faith in progress but now there was a difference in tone. White looked to the past for solutions to problems of the present: he openly advocated literacy tests and restriction of the suffrage to propertyholders. Somehow White continued to view himself as a prophet of progress, but he found himself in the curious position of defending "revolutions that go backwards."

As he returned to public life in the years following his second marriage, White succumbed to pleas that he run for governor of New York. He accepted the support of boss Tom Platt, explaining that once elected, he could champion programs that would subvert the machine. When Platt reversed himself and torpedoed White's candidacy, White limply absolved him of all blame. As earlier in Germany, he would not admit that he had been duped.

Political visibility had at least one reward. In 1892 he was appointed minister to Russia. White's tenure was rather uneventful, but two years in the tsardom convinced him more than ever that the United States was the land of unlimited possibilities. When contrasted with the Sisyphean ob-stacles placed in the path of reformers in Russia, America's problems faded. White returned home, eager to renew his efforts to hasten the arrival of the millennium.

During his stay in Russia, White had almost brought to completion his magnum opus, a treatise designed to reconcile science and religion. He published *A History of the Warfare of Science and Theology in Christendom* in two volumes in 1895 and hoped that when the myths that had been associated with religion were cleared away, the essence of Christianity would emerge. He believed that everyone had spiritual needs that only religion could satisfy. He also recognized that religion and ethics were inextricably linked; thus an orderly society depended upon a healthy Christianity. *The Warfare of Science and Theology* aimed to show that recent findings of science left the core of religion undisturbed.

The reception given to White's work revealed that his message had been lost amid overwhelming evidence presented to demonstrate that science had destroyed myths peripheral to Christianity. Despite White's claims to the contrary, *The Warfare of Science and Theology* seemed to devour Christianity, core and all. The most effusive praise for the book, to White's dismay, came from nonbelievers. Many orthodox Christians pointed to White's criticisms of portions of the Bible and asked how *he* knew that some of the scriptures were superfluous while some were indispensable. If the Bible was in any way inaccurate, critics intoned, then ethics and religion were irreparably damaged.

White could answer his opponents only by reasserting that he had bared the essence of Christianity, and that religion, too, was in a process of evolution. He had merely charted the course of that evolution. When critics asked too insistently how he had separated the wheat from the chaff, he lapsed into silence, refusing to believe that his message could be anything but clear and convincing.

While White labored to reconcile science and theology, he was drawn into President Cleveland's attempt to settle the boundary dispute between Great Britain and Venezuela. The controversy threatened the commercial hegemony of the United States in Latin America. White, appointed by the president to help determine the boundary between the two countries, hoped to protect America's economic interests while avoiding war. Before the boundary commission had completed its work, the British agreed to accept arbitration, and the crisis passed, taking with it White's chance for international acclaim. The commissioner confidently took note, however, that an intricate impasse had been resolved peacefully.

The end of Cleveland's second term marked a scramble for the presidency by both parties. When the Democrats nominated William Jennings Byran, a frenzied White responded to a perceived threat to the political-economic order and made his conservative predilictions abundantly clear. He equated Bryan with socialism, forgot his pious pronouncements on the inevitable march of progress in America, and strained to prevent imminent disaster. With the Republican victory, the world seemed to right itself.

Sometimes, as with Bryan, crises fizzled, sometimes White had to wish them away, but he never failed to emerge with optimistic rhetoric. If his confidence was banal, the tension between optimistic faith and a tendency to fear the worst facilitated action in a world he viewed as deterministic.

Chapter 9   *Civil Service Reform and the*
                Election of 1884

During the final years of his Cornell presidency, White had become increasingly preoccupied with public service outside the university. Although Cornell faced attacks from many quarters, the president had found time to lend the weight of his name to the newly formed American Historical Association and to participate actively in the movement to reform the civil service.

The final two decades of the nineteenth century witnessed feverish organizational efforts by the major professions in the United States. Historians, whose numbers were increasing as higher education expanded, decided in 1884 to form an organization exclusively for members of their discipline. After constant prodding by Charles Kendall Adams of Michigan, Herbert Baxter Adams of Johns Hopkins, and Moses Coit Tyler of Cornell, a circular was sent to historians around the country inviting them to a Social Science Congress in the fall of 1884 "to have a hand in the organization of the American Historical Association." [1]

Seeking a man who would bring instant respectability to their nascent organization, the founders asked White to serve as their president. White gladly accepted and used his inaugural address to plead with historians to exploit the immediate usefulness of history. The historian, White informed his audience, must not be interested in isolated facts; he must employ them to drive home a particular lesson. The historian was a man of his own time who sought to illuminate the present with the light of the past. [2]

1. A Call for an American Historical Association at Saratoga, September 9, 1884, and Tyler to ADW, August 13, 1884, WMC. For the rise of the professions in the late nineteenth century, see Robert Wiebe, *The Search for Order* (New York, 1967); John Higham, *History* (Englewood Cliffs, N.J., 1965). Thomas Haskell's brilliant book *The Emergence of Professional Social Science* (Urbana, Ill., 1977), which extensively treats White's role in the AHA, appeared too late to influence the account presented here.
2. Herman Ausubel, *Historians and Their Craft: A Study of the Presidential Addresses of the A.H.A., 1884–1945* (New York, 1950), pp. 18, 148–50, 257.

Hoping to use history as a guide to action, White argued that the historian's job was to sketch the "great lines of historical evolution." Although the world had moved generally toward progress and moral uplift, White did not deny that men and societies had often stood in the way of increased freedom and prosperity. Only by identifying the good and evil in past societies could the historian aid in the perfection of "man as man, and secondly of man as a member of society." The historian was a moral teacher, intent on showing

through what cycles of birth, growth and decay various nations have passed; what laws of development may be fairly considered as ascertained, and under these what laws of religious, moral, intellectual, social and political health or disease; what developments have been good, aiding in the evolution of that which is best in man and in society; what developments have been evil, tending to the retrogression of men and society.[3]

Unfortunately, White did not recognize the possibility that historians might gauge the great lines of historical evolution differently. The AHA president complicated matters by agreeing that contemporary standards of judgment should be used. White's own work reflected the problems inherent in this approach. If present-day standards were to be used, he should have condemned Richelieu for wanton cruelty and efforts in behalf of monarchy in France. Yet White had excused the cardinal because he had helped to break the power of the serfholding aristocracy and because his alliance with the monarch had been the only available means of achieving his aim. What standards of judgment, then, was White using? Moreover, how did one go about constructing a hierarchy of evils? For White, the serfholding class was a greater evil than monarchy; presumably some of his colleagues disagreed.[4]

White's attempt to guide his fellow historians in their search for a valid "philosophical synthesis of human affairs" demonstrated the difficulty of achieving consensus among moral historians. He counseled his colleagues to avoid a synthesis based solely on quantitative statistics. White urged his listeners to assign "a proper place" to statistics but to use quantitative and qualitative evidence in combination.[5]

White's plea for an eclectic methodology seemed eminently reasonable, but it did not answer the dilemma implicit in his condemnation of quantitative statistics used in isolation. What was the historian to do if material and moral evidence conflicted? The president faced the issue squarely and

3. *On Studies in General History and the History of Civilization*, AHA Papers (New York, 1885), Vol. 1, p. 59.

4. Ausubel, *Historians and Their Craft*, p. 257.

5. *On Studies in General History*, p. 64.

urged the primacy of "moral statistics." His example, however, indicated that moral statistics (he meant literary evidence) might not always point in a single direction. Electoral college statistics, White argued, indicated a complete break between the North and the South. Moral evidence, he asserted, pointed to the opposite conclusion.[6] Clearly, those who differed with White on the success of Reconstruction could find moral evidence to buttress *their* positions. In his efforts to help historians find the road to truth, White had stumbled upon myriad paths, none of which could be identified as the main avenue of valid moral conclusion.

Despite its shortcomings, White's inaugural address was a major statement to the historical profession. Convinced that enlightened education was the handmaiden of progress, White had sought to rescue history from Rankean "objectivity." Anticipating the thrust of James Harvey Robinson's "new history" by two decades, he gave the discipline a social purpose. If White erred in expecting his colleagues to agree on any particular prescription that the past had written for the present, he did so out of an excessive faith in reason. Truth was "One"; White believed that reasonable people could find the "right" answer to most questions. Although White fails to convince the modern reader that reason is a panacea, mystically connected to morality, the connection he drew between history and social action helped to raise the discipline above mere antiquarianism.

Even as he wrote his AHA address, White was actively engaged in the civil service reform movement, which he regarded as one of the greatest crusades of his generation. White's desire to make ability rather than partisanship a prerequisite for public service was undoubtedly sincere, but participation in the civil service movement was also designed to further his political career. He attempted to establish his reform credentials while maintaining cordial relations with party regulars. When the nomination of James G. Blaine forced him to choose one side or the other, he remained loyal to the Republican party. Political ambition and principle, he felt, would best be served by refusing to bolt. Fighting from within (in politics as in the university), even if it necessitated distasteful compromises, was the best guarantee of the ultimate achievement of reform goals.

Characteristically, White decided to embark upon a program to educate the public to the need for civil service reform. In 1881 he proposed that the Civil Service Reform League grant prizes in colleges for essays on the spoils system. Reformers must prepare for the future by inculcating enlightened principles in the college generation.[7]

Not content to postpone reform, White attempted to bring the issue to

6. Ibid., pp. 65–66.
7. ADW to Charles K. Adams, May 18, 1878, and Dorman B. Eaton to ADW, November 4, 1881, WMC.

the reading public through a series of lectures and an article in the influential *North American Review*. The spoils system, he charged, destroyed the separation of powers between the legislature and the executive by making Congress dependent on the president for appointments. The president's influence, moreover, extended to state politics, thus making him a factor in local elections. If such awesome powers were not soon checked, all politicians would be subservient to him if they wished to remain in office.[8]

In addition to its impact on the political balance of power, the spoils system had disastrous effects on officeholders and applicants for jobs. Jobs were won by "plotting and trickery and luck, rather than by steady manly service." The youth of the nation had become disillusioned with public service, White observed, when they discovered that preferment was unrelated to ability. Moreover, if an able citizen happened to be given a place in government service, he would, in all likelihood, be rotated out of office as soon as he had gained sufficient experience to work effectively. Every bestowal of office, White gravely concluded, "makes ninety-nine enemies and one ingrate."[9]

Civil service reform, White argued, would increase efficiency by attracting able men to government service.[10] By choosing men on the basis of ability, new civil service regulations would encourage education at all levels. Whereas the spoils system rewarded blind partisanship, the Pendleton bill would not permit party service to be the basis of employment. By guaranteeing tenure to civil servants, the proposed act would ensure continuity in government while bringing an end to the sycophancy made necessary by the spoils system. The best violinist in the world, White reminded his audience, "cannot play a tune, if he must hold fast with both hands to the music-stand."[11]

Having demonstrated the evils of the existing system and the advantages of reform, White disposed of the argument that the spoils system benefited the nation by making provision "for those who are stranded and need help." The logical outcome of this attitude, he remarked, would be government asylums or pensions for such people. In either case, a vast army of the needy would be created and self-help would be at a discount. He warned against all indiscriminate charity: "Ill-considered office-giving,

8. *Cornell Sun*, October 16, 1882.

9. "Do the Spoils Belong to the Victor?" *North American Review*, 134 (February 1882): 115, 117; *Cornell Sun*, October 16, 1882.

10. For a contemporary assessment of the political scene, see John G. Sproat, *The Best Men: Liberal Reformers in the Gilded Age* (New York, 1968), p. 48.

11. "Do the Spoils Belong to the Victor?" pp. 113, 120, 124, 127.

ill-considered alms-giving, tends to create the paupers it has to care for." [12]

Reform, however, had not yet been passed by Congress, and while White labored in the fields of reform, he was continually beset by office seekers glancing covetously at Naboth's vineyard. Like most civil service reformers, he had to decide whether or not to aid his friends in the scramble for a place. At first blush, any participation in the system smacked of hypocrisy; yet, certainly reformers saw nothing disingenuous in such actions. Reform would not come a whit sooner if reformers withdrew all their patronage recommendations; such action would merely bring to office additional unprincipled spoilsmen. White made no conscious explanation for his continuing role in the spoils system. He continued to use his influence but sought jobs primarily for those he was convinced were highly qualified for the posts they sought. Recommending only those who deserved a position could not be construed as a betrayal of conscience. Trained in practical politics in the New York State Legislature, White knew that influence peddling greased the wheels of government; while redoubling his efforts to alter the basis of politics, he saw little harm in employing his influence in the cause of virtuous men. [13]

Having decided on the ability of an applicant, however, White did not hesitate to use the partisan language of the spoilsman. Thus, in recommending John H. Selkreg for the post of consul at Montreal, he referred to the applicant's "untiring" devotion to the Republican party as editor of the *Ithaca Daily Journal*. Selkreg's appointment, the Cornell president informed President-elect Garfield, "would be most favorably received not merely by his wide circle of personal friends, but by the great body of men active in the interest of the Republican Party throughout the State of New York." [14] Because White viewed the GOP as the repository of virtue and talent in the United States, he considered partisan activity to be a sign of intelligence; in this he differed little from spoilsmen. Yet White's testimonials to ability and party loyalty were sincere. He claimed that his only motive was to bring men of ability to government service. If spoilsmen made the same claim, White could only retort that they lied.

White's efforts were accompanied by a vigorous lobbying campaign for the Pendleton bill, which seemed finally to have an excellent chance of passing both houses of Congress in the wake of Garfield's assassination. President of the Ithaca chapter of the Civil Service Reform Association, White canvassed prominent citizens in the area, collecting money and

12. Ibid., p. 126.
13. Before recommending Cornell graduates for office, White carefully scrutinized their records. See George C. Caldwell to ADW, November 7, 1889, WMC.
14. ADW to Garfield, February 19, 1881, WMC.

exhorting voters to inundate their representatives with requests to support the Pendleton bill. Meanwhile, he redoubled efforts to persuade Republican politicians to lead the reform charge, rather than meekly defer to such Democrats as George Pendleton. "Give us such a speech as Seward used to make," he urged New York Senator Warner Miller. Miller's response more than satisfied him. Reform, Conkling's replacement in the upper house averred, was "in the direction of true business principles." Much heartened by Miller's enthusiasm, White soberly agreed with his judgment that if the Republican party did not assume the leadership of the civil service movement, future success at the polls was doubtful.[15]

If Warner Miller's allegiance to reform predated his contact with White, Frank Hiscock's apparent conversion to the movement seemed due to the ministrations of the Cornell president. Hiscock, a powerful Republican who became chairman of the House Appropriations Committee in 1883, attributed Democrat Grover Cleveland's insurmountable lead in the gubernatorial race to his reform principles. "My dear friend," the congressmen announced to White, "I think I shall have to join hands with you in the struggle to force patronage from party management." Hoping to strengthen Hiscock's resolve, White wrote several letters of encouragement and must have been pleased with the response: "I intend to support the Pendleton Bill, aggressively if necessary."[16]

Convinced that removing 80,000 to 200,000 offices from the clutches of the politicians was a necessary condition for any other meaningful reform, White was on occasion mistaken for an Independent who would support reformers regardless of party affiliation. The *New York Tribune* numbered him among the supporters of Cleveland's gubernatorial bid. "The defeat of the Republican ticket," the *Tribune* quoted White as having predicted, "will act like a thunder storm and clear the political atmosphere, after which I shall expect a general and successful rally to keep the Nation out of the hands of the Democrats." Despite such prophecies, however, White chose to support the Republican ticket, although admittedly he was not overly distraught by Cleveland's election.[17]

State politics, in any event, were brushed aside as the Pendleton bill moved toward a final vote in Congress. The reformers worked feverishly through December; White, George William Curtis, Sherman Rogers of Buffalo, and Matthew Hale of Albany called for a conference to prepare a

15. William Potts to ADW, September 18, 1882; Miller to ADW, February 1 and December 15, 1882, all in WMC.

16. Hiscock to ADW, October 20 and December 13, 1882, WMC.

17. Quoted in ADW to David Wells, October 31, 1882, and John Fitch to ADW, October 27, 1882, WMC.

plan for the reorganization of the Repulican party. The GOP must give solid support to the civil service movement or expect to lose public confidence.[18]

Finally in January 1883, large majorities in both houses of Congress passed the Pendleton Act. Although the act affected only 14,000 officials (about one-tenth of the total number of federal employees), it empowered the president to expand the number of jobs subject to the merit system. The spoils system, reformers exulted, had received a mortal blow. They congratulated one another and magnified individual responsibility for the bill's success. White's brother reported that Frank Hiscock called the measure "Andrew White's bill."[19] Warner Miller confessed to the Senate that his vote had been in obedience to the wishes of his constituents, "expressed to me in letters which I have received from several prominent citizens of New York who have carefully investigated and studied this question."[20]

Analysis of the motives of the people's representatives, however, reminded reformers that self-congratulations must yield to eternal vigilance. Sherman Rogers attributed passage of the act to the "cowardice" and not the "good will" of Congress. Presumably, without continued prodding from their constituents, congressmen would jump off the civil service bandwagon as quickly as they had scrambled upon it. Congressman R. R. Hitt, Republican of Illinois, had an equally ominous assessment: "I am sorry to say that on our side of the House a very large number of [congressmen] were disposed in a laughing sort of way, to assent to the measure as a meaningless thing, which might please the people, but which was essentially a humbug, and which they were only constrained to tolerate under the chastening recollection of last November."[21]

Continued agitation, and perhaps supplemental legislation, were necessary to give teeth to the reform bill. White wrote again and again to Hiscock, requesting information about those agencies regulated by the reform measures and asking for action in cases of alleged abuse. If congressmen had voted for the Pendleton bill in the hope of silencing civil service advocates, they had grossly miscalculated.[22]

18. Curtis to Holls, December 9, 1882, Frederick W. Holls MSS, Columbia University; ADW to Willard Fiske, December 26, 1882, and Curtis to ADW, December 29, 1882, WMC.

19. Horace K. White to ADW, January 5, 1883, WMC.

20. Quoted in Ari Hoogenboom, *Outlawing the Spoils* (Urbana, Ill., 1961), p. 240.

21. Rogers to ADW, January 18, 1883, and Hitt to ADW, January 14, 1883, WMC. Hitt had been assistant secretary of state when White was minister to Germany.

22. Frederic Frost to ADW, May 2, 1884; Hiscock to ADW, February 4, 1883, and

While some of his brethren expressed disillusionment with the tortoise-like response of the Republican party, White remained hopeful that the GOP was on the verge of an unequivocal commitment to the merit system. He toured the state, lecturing groups of Independent Republicans on the need to work within the party; the interests of the nation and of the GOP, he insisted, were the same: "First, to stimulate the demand for reform, to make it coherent, and to shape it; secondly, to show not by platforms but by works, by holding firmly to reforms already begun, and by pressing forward to new reforms, that the Republican party can meet this demand better than any other." [23] The "independence" of Republicans, then, must lead to a determined effort to imbue their party with principles; Independent Republicans were the most loyal Republicans.

White's dedication to his party was tested in May 1883 when he was appointed state civil service commissioner by Governor Cleveland. Here was an opportunity to help extend civil service principles throughout New York State. But to accept appointment from a Democrat, albeit one who seemed to be "independent," was inconsistent with White's devotion to his party. Rumors were afloat throughout 1883 that the Cornell president looked favorably upon a presidential bid by Cleveland, and White was at some pains to dissociate himself from an administration whose every act elicited his praise. With some reluctance he declined the position, citing university duties. [24]

Within a year White had reason to be pleased with his decision. The Arthur administration seemed to be making steady, if not spectacular, progress in extending the merit system. Even more important, the United States Civil Service Commission had recognized that universities provided the best pool for the recruitment of civil servants. It sent a circular to college presidents to acquaint them with "avenues of preferment and business for their students." President Arthur, who had gained his political baptism in the graft-filled rooms of the customhouse, astounded most observers with an apparent willingness to banish patronage from federal offices. [25]

Heartening reports from Washington were matched by comforting

---

January 8, 1884, all in WMC. White also urged the Senate to select its secretary, chief clerk, legislative clerk, and sergeant at arms under civil service specifications. (Miller to ADW, December 26, 1883, WMC).

23. Herbert Smith to ADW, January 6, 1883, and ADW to Independent Republicans of Brooklyn, February 12, 1883, WMC.

24. *Autobiography*, vol. 1, p. 207; Daniel Larnot to ADW, May 10, 1883; ADW to Cleveland, May 15, 1883; John J. Lewis to ADW, October 8, 1883, all in WMC.

25. W. Roulhac to ADW, January 9, 1884, WMC.

dispatches from Albany, where Republicans had seized the initiative in civil service legislation. Cleveland's split with Tammany Hall made him dependent upon reform Republicans to support reform proposals. Ultimately, he allied with assemblymen I. L. Hunt, W. T. O'Neill, and young Theodore Roosevelt. At first lukewarm in his enthusiasm for the merit system, Roosevelt soon gauged its political advantages. White congratulated the young man on his work in the Assembly and received a characteristically immodest reply: "Today we won another victory, passing the amendment to the civil service law through the lower house by a large vote. I think I shall be able to get the other reform bills for New York (in reference to the sheriff, county clerk etc.) through also." Ignoring warnings that Roosevelt was influenced more by expedience than by principle, White was convinced that he would help the Republican party purge itself of spoilsmen.[26]

The stage was thus set for the presidential election of 1884, the grandest opportunity yet to make the Republican party synonymous with civil service reform. Early in the year, Independent Republicans began to organize in preparation for the nominating convention. In hopes of enlisting White's support, the Independents assured him that they had no intention of bolting the party. "Of course we want your name," Francis Barlow reassured the reluctant White, "for we are not going to establish a 'new party' or go out of the Republican party but only to try and influence a reform nomination." George William Curtis had joined the group, Barlow announced, "and you know how cautious he is about embarking in new movements." White must have been convinced; by early March his name was listed as a member of the Republican Conference Committee.[27]

A host of candidates—Chester Arthur, James G. Blaine, George F. Edmunds, Benjamin Harrison, and Joseph Hawley—entered the presidential sweepstakes in 1884, and the possibility of a deadlock at the convention loomed large. Could White himself possibly emerge as a compromise candidate? White could perhaps discount the words of an old student as wishful thinking: "By the way a blush of promise lights the grim face of our party that your name may head our National ticket." Stories in German-American newspapers and the *Ithaca Journal* that Cornell's president was the most promising dark horse in the field could not be so easily ignored. On April 26, the *New York Times* gave added credence to the rumors by reprinting the *Ithaca Journal* story. If White was even to retain a

26. Henry Pringle, *Theodore Roosevelt: A Biography* (New York, 1931), p. 75; Roosevelt to ADW, March 19, 1884, and D. Littlejohn to ADW, March 21, 1884, WMC.

27. Barlow to ADW, February 24 and March 8, 1884, WMC.

glimmering of hope, however, he would have to continue to walk a tightrope between the Regulars and the Independents.[28]

Elected as a delegate at large to the Republican convention, White strained to find common ground between the warring factions of the party. In a front-page interview in the *New York Times*, he sought to coax the Regulars into supporting extension of the civil service. White admitted that only a minority of the party opposed the spoils system, but that group held the political balance of power in New York State—and perhaps in the nation. The reformers would brook no trickery; ordinary political ties sat very lightly with them. The specter of defeat served as an inducement to political accommodation.[29]

In assessing the Republican candidates, White again showed a desire for party harmony. Privately he thought that the nomination lay between Harrison, Hawley, and Robert Lincoln, "but I may be a thousand leagues wide of the mark." Personally, he had decided to support reform choice George F. Edmunds, although he gave the Vermont senator little chance of winning. In public, however, White found words of praise for every GOP hopeful. He was more than pleased with President Arthur: "I regard him as a perfectly safe man—one who enjoys and would retain confidence as president of the United States." The *Troy Times* therefore placed the Cornell president in Arthur's column. The delegate at large, however, refused to commit himself publicly and "had a good word to say" about Arthur's opponents; he even refused to engage in criticism of Blaine. By encouraging party unity, White may also have hoped for a deadlock and a compromise candidate; perhaps Francis Barnard was not the only man who "did not quite despair yet of your nomination."[30]

As the convention approached, White's attempts to share the bed of all factions of the party took on literal and comic overtones. He had originally taken rooms with Curtis, Barlow, Roosevelt, and Wadsworth but had decided in May to share accommodations with the Regulars. With some exasperation, Barlow lectured his reform cousin on loyalty and suggested a way out of the dilemma: "You cannot be nominated for the Presidency of the United States as a 'dark horse' except as the representative of the Independent and Reform element. So hang on to your 'regular' rooms . . . but room with us." White evidently followed Barlow's advice: he con-

28. O. F. Williams to ADW, March 6, 1884, WMC; *Deutsche Zeitung*, May 4, 1884, WMC. *New York Times*, April 26, 1884.

29. *New York Times*, April 25, 1884.

30. ADW to Willard Fiske, May 26, 1884 and ADW to Henry Sage, June 4, 1884, WMC; *Troy Times*, May 24, 1884; Barnard to ADW, May 30, 1884, WMC.

tinued to make his bed with the Regulars, even if at present he chose not to sleep in it.[31]

The Chicago convention in June was a raucous, disappointing affair. From the outset the New York delegation was badly split. White nominated Curtis as chairman and he was approved, but "ugly feeling arose," and White was defeated as a member of the Committee on Resolutions. In fact, White sadly concluded, the convention was dominated by "eminent foghorns—men of more lungs than brains." He was not surprised when the delegates nominated James G. Blaine, the Plumed Knight, whose armor showed everywhere dents of corruption. Through four ballots White had supported Edmunds, but the forces of reform had been ineffectual.[32]

Determined to salvage something from the debacle, a group of Independents attempted to extract a pledge of support for civil service principles from Blaine, and the candidate eventually committed himself "definitely, fully and publicly" to the merit system. Satisfying himself with the assurance that Blaine, "more widely beloved by his contemporaries than any other statesman since Henry Clay," had seen the reform light and repudiated his shady deals of the past, White pledged his support to the Republican ticket.[33]

While White reconciled himself to the GOP nominee, several Independent Republicans gathered under the banner of Grover Cleveland. Significantly, however, Carl Schurz was the only major professional politician to desert Blaine. Like White, Theordore Roosevelt made a quiet peace with his party. The Mugwumps, conscious of their anomalous position as men without a party, excoriated their timid former allies. Unwilling to be caught in a cross fire between Regulars and Mugwumps, hoping to preserve reform within the party, many Independents retreated in silence to the Republican trenches.

If White hoped to remain quietly in his tent during the campaign, the Mugwumps were determined to smoke him out. Rumors that the Cornell president supported Cleveland reached the press. One newspaper reported that White had decided to vote for the Democrats and hoped that the Mugwumps would soon begin organization work in New York: "So President White adds the weight of his great name to that of George

31. ADW to Barlow, April 24, 1884, and Barlow to ADW, May 4, 1884, WMC.
32. Diary, June 2, 5, and 6, 1884, WMC; "The Presidential Convention—A Blot on American Democracy," *McClure's Magazine* 39 (October 1912): 750.
33. *Autobiography*, vol. 1, pp. 208–209; *In Memoriam: Frederick William Holls* (privately printed, 1905), pp. 22–23.

William Curtis, Senator Andrew and others in favor of Governor Cleveland. The better element of the Republican party will very generally follow them."[34] A Democratic campaign circular even more mischievously printed White's assessment of Cleveland without comment under the heading, "What a Distinguished Republican Says":

I am a Republican but as to Governor Cleveland, I will say that he is possessed of remarkable courage, prudence and foresight. He is the best piece of timber in the Democratic Party. . . . The sentiment in this country is such to-day that the people will not trust the Democratic Party unless it nominates a man of sterling character and one who can command entire confidence. Governor Cleveland meets that demand. I think he can carry New York State over most men named as possible Republican candidates, and I am frank to say that he would make serious inroads in New England, as against any Republican not equally committed to reform.[35]

White's efforts to force the Republicans to select a reform candidate were returning to haunt him; the logical culmination of his remarks seemed to be support of Cleveland.

Reluctantly, White publicly clarified his position. In a widely printed letter to General D. H. Bruce of Syracuse, he affirmed his support of Blaine. Though he admitted respect for Governor Cleveland, he regarded the candidate as a "happy accident in his party—who will be as powerless against it if he favors a reform of the Civil Service in the Nation as was Senator Pendleton in Ohio." Thus voters should base their decisions on general party principle and performance rather than on the relative merits of two individuals. Without explicitly saying so, White had foreclosed the possibility of ever voting for a Democrat; virtue resided in the GOP, while the Democrats had opposed "all the healthful and statesmanlike measures of the past thirty years." In a letter to Willard Fiske, White was even more explicit: "I do not like Mr. Blaine any more than you do. . . . But questions of men are of comparatively small account." Thus White announced his support of the Republican ticket without praising Blaine; Cleveland was too much like a "Trojan horse" who would bring to power men intent on undoing the reforms of the recent past. By virtually foreclosing the possibility of supporting the Democrats, White failed to confront the Mugwump argument that threats to leave the party backed up by occasional nonsupport were the only means of forcing Regulars to advocate civil service reform.[36]

34. *Syracuse Courier*, July 1884, WMC.
35. Congressional First Ward Democratic Club Circular, WMC.
36. ADW to D. H. Bruce, July 20, 1884, WMC; *New York Times*, August 1, 1884; ADW to Fiske, August 11, 1884, WMC; Sproat, *The Best Men*, p. 132.

In a public letter to Theodore Roosevelt, White added one new element to his by then familiar argument by confronting charges that Blaine was opposed to the merit system. The belief that Blaine followed the dictates of expediency rather than conscience proved that he would be receptive to reform: "Whatever men have said of him, they have never charged him with want of shrewdness or quickness in ascertaining the current of public opinion." Thus, as long as the majority of the nation remained committed to the merit system, White sophistically concluded, James G. Blaine would be responsive to their demands.[37]

White's arguments did not go unchallenged. A new batch of "Mulligan letters," further documenting Blaine's dalliance with corruption, had forced Goldwin Smith into the arms of the opposition. "You cannot elect the man after that," the Briton claimed in an argument particularly painful to White, "without corrupting the young men in America." Willard Fiske entertained no doubts about Blaine's perfidy. Pointing to Republican efforts to purchase the Negro vote in the South, Fiske concurred in E. P. Evans's condemnation of White's view that the "Continental Liar" from Maine could be "reformed" by support and election. Finally, an anonymous note reminded White that the charge of expediency could be leveled at him as easily as at Blaine: "Your apology for supporting Blaine is so weak, and at the same time so disingenuous, that your friends can only regret that you were under the necessity of making it. Let us hope, however, that the *entente cordiale* between White, the politician, and White, the reformer, may not be disturbed."[38]

Lack of enthusiasm for Blaine, and perhaps the fear of disapprobation from friends, limited the Cornell president's campaign activities. He was, moreover, appalled by the conduct of the campaign—one of the dirtiest in American history. Pro-Blaine speakers faced hecklers shouting charges of corruption by the "Continental Liar from the State of Maine"; Cleveland speakers heard taunts about their candidate's illegitimate child: "Ma, Ma, where's my pa?" The political mudslinging disgusted White: "Where those English blackguards of the olden time hurled a spoiled egg or a dead cat at a candidate, our blackguards charge that at some time in the past–ten years or thirty years ago–the candidate violated the seventh commandment, and insinuate that he probably stewed and ate his grandmother."[39]

Despite the best efforts of reformers, the election of 1884 was not a forum for reasoned discussion of pressing issues. Consequently, White

37. *Daily Oregonian*, August 21, 1884, WMC.
38. Smith to ADW, September 27, 1884, WMC; Fiske to Evans, March 5, 1884, August 3, 1884, Edward Payson Evans MSS, Cornell University; anonymous note, 1884, WMC.
39. *Some Practical Influences of German Thought upon the United States* (Ithaca, 1884), p. 7.

declined a number of invitations to address campaign rallies. On one occasion, state chairman James Warren asked him to accompany Blaine on a tour of the state. As if to remind potential biographers that his support for the ticket was lukewarm, White wrote "Declined" at the bottom of the request, signed his name, and filed the letter among his correspondence. Nevertheless, party loyalty forced White to make some appearances at the end of the campaign, especially at rallies attended by German-Americans, with whom the former minister to Germany had great rapport. Although some thought his lack of enthusiasm might undermine his standing in the party, White was active enough to retain the support of Regulars and eager to acknowledge the support of any reform Republicans.[40]

After Blaine's defeat, the Mugwumps renewed their attacks on Independent Republicans who retained their allegiance to the GOP. Scorned in the press, White was probably even more piqued by the barbs hurled at him by embittered exile Willard Fiske. "Your adhesion to Blaine," White's old friend announced, "has firmly convinced me of the inutility of historical studies, and in founding my university that branch of research will be accordingly omitted. Instead of that I shall have a department of old Vienna porcelain, of which I brought home with me a few lovely specimens." In two sentences, Fiske had questioned the efficacy of history and higher education, the very wheels of White's carriage of progress. Had American voters not been motivated by crass ignorance and hypocritical bigotry, Fiske added, Cleveland would have won in a landslide. The "pecadillo" of the president-elect—

which had about as much to do with the question of his capacity to fill the Executive Office as with the Bhuddistic Mahajataka—must have cost him the vote of a vast mass of men who stand on the same plane of intelligence and pietism as do certain individuals with whom it is your unhappy lot to daily associate [Sage and Boardman]. . . . Your anticipation of a lively campaign in the direction of administrative reform, to follow the election of Blaine, amused me.

In education and in politics, White had chosen to align himself with the forces of darkness; Fiske's ironic arrow made a palpable hit.[41]

If Willard Fiske could be dismissed as a misanthrope, George William Curtis had to be regarded as a seasoned, intelligent observer of the political scene. No party seriously seeking reform could have chosen Blaine, whose nomination, Curtis argued, necessarily suspended party allegiances. The

40. ADW to R. Vose, October 28, 1884; James Warren to Hiscock, October 29, 1884; Warren to ADW, September 22, 1884; William Bostwick to ADW, October 8, 1884, all WMC; Ernest Huffcut to Burr, August 8, 1884, George Lincoln Burr MSS, Cornell University.
41. Fiske to ADW, September 8 and December 1, 1885, WMC.

Republican party, run largely by Boss Platt and Company, "would knife reform" as quickly as the Democrats. Only reform sentiment in the country restrained the instinctive venality of politicians. Such sentiment must be nurtured by support of candidates publicly committed to change. In the Great Barbecue of the Gilded Age, Curtis thought that the party was not very respectable.[42]

Cleveland's early activities indicated that he was more a reform stallion than a Trojan horse, and White oscillated between praise for the administration and defense of his support for Blaine. White thought that the closeness of the election benefited the nation by making Cleveland "see the necessity of being the President of the United States and not of party." The Cornell president's reasoning was somewhat unclear. The election's closeness seemed to underline the Mugwumps' argument that they held the balance of power in the country; thus White's argument could be used to justify desertion of the Republican party. Seeking to explain his adherence to Blaine while praising Cleveland and not his party was a difficult task.[43]

Forgetting the attacks of blackguards on Cleveland's "pecadillo" and Blaine's character, White decided that in no previous election had so many people voted "after a very close interrogation of their consciences."[44] The narrow election of a man White had opposed somehow demonstrated the enlightenment of the voters. In an open letter to the assemblage at a Pendleton dinner, the president of Cornell reconsecrated his abiding faith in education: "The politicians who think that 'the average American learns nothing and forgets nothing' are woefully astray. They forget that ours has become a land of schools, and that every school-house is a force on the side of Reform; and they may well remember that there are over twenty-thousand school-houses in the state of New York alone. General Jackson is dead; the schoolmaster lives."[45]

Satisfaction with the Democratic administration did not entice White into political apostasy. Midway through Cleveland's first term, White began to issue calls for Republican unity in preparation for the election of 1888. Addressing a Republican club in New York City, he blamed the Democrats for the establishment of two monstrous evils—slavery and the spoils system. Fortunately, White declared, waving the bloody shirt, the Republican party had swept away chattel slavery, but the second evil

---

42. Curtis to ADW, January 9, 1885, and May 4, 1884, WMC; Hoogenboom, *Outlawing the Spoils*, p. 85.
43. ADW to Burr, January 2, 1885; ADW to E. Levasseur, March 30, 1885; ADW to Fiske, February 14, 1885, in WMC.
44. ADW to Burr, November 17, 1884, and April 6, 1885, WMC.
45. ADW to Everett P. Wheeler, April 27, 1885, WMC.

remained. The job of awakening Republicans could not "be done by men standing outside the party; it must be done by men active within it."[46] The election of 1884, the attacks of the Mugwumps, and the success of Grover Cleveland had not shaken White's belief that the Republican party was the hope of the future, as it had been the salvation of the past. A temporary setback, a goat in the midst of sheep, or a sheep in the midst of goats should not lead one to reject communion with the Church of the Righteous.

No public man, Albert Beveridge once reminded civil service reformer William Dudley Foulke, could accomplish much as a political maverick. Most politicians were compelled, in pursuit of larger purposes, often to support men who did not merit support.[47] Historian John Sproat has employed a similar argument to rescue from the charge of hypocrisy the Independent Republicans who refused to support Cleveland in 1884. If the independence of those who bolted the GOP "insulated them from the professionalism of the party men, it also shielded the party men from liberalism and muffled the voice of reform in high political circles."[48] Involvement in the political process forced individuals to decide between insistence on complete adherence to principle immediately—which usually destroyed the reformers' effectiveness—and a long-term strategy that employed a compromise as a means to eventual victory. Once drawn into the political vortex, the reformer, as White viewed it, had to be willing to accommodate himself. The Mugwumps did not disagree. They argued, however, that accommodation to Blaine did not serve the cause of reform. An alliance with Cleveland, on the other hand, might force both parties to support civil service reform.

The debate over political tactics thus ended in a stalemate. Neither White nor the Mugwumps, however, admitted that they were also motivated by political ambition. The Mugwumps believed that Republican stalwarts denied them access to the political ladder of opportunity; White hoped to further his political career by demonstrating that a reformer could also be a regular. They all agreed that political ambition did not necessarily conflict with political principle. For White, ambition and party regularity were epithets without sting (although indeed they embarrassed him); in the long run, they facilitated enlightened self-government.[49]

Years later White had an excellent opportunity to demonstrate the

46. A Letter to the Republican Club of the City of New York, February 12, 1887, WMC.
47. John Braeman, *Albert Beveridge* (Chicago, 1971).
48. Sproat, *The Best Men*, p. 276.
49. See Gordon Wood, "The Massachusetts Mugwumps," *New England Quarterly* 33 (December 1960): 435–51; Gerald McFarland, "The New York Mugwumps of 1884: A Profile," *Political Science Quarterly* 78 (March 1963): 40–58.

efficacy of party regularity. In 1891 a group of reformers planned a personal appeal to President Harrison to extend the merit system. They decided that pleas from men whose party credentials were weak had little likelihood of success. In a letter to Charles Dudley Warner, White alluded to this belated vindication of his Republicanism: "Curtis, Schurz and the Mugwumps say that it will do no good for them to try; that the thing must be done, if done at all, by men inside the Republican party."[50]

Buoyed by the Mugwumps' admission of lack of political clout, White was overjoyed by Harrison's reaction to his reform arguments. Unmoved by the pleas of Roosevelt and Henry Cabot Lodge, the president listened intently as White indicated that he saw thousands of voters in the university switching allegiance to the Democrats because they favored the merit system. Therefore, unless Harrison took immediate action, New York State's 12,000 school districts would be transformed into Democratic fiefdoms.[51]

Harrison was evidently convinced, for within a year White gleefully reported to Fiske that civil service principles had been extended to departments in the Indian Bureau and Navy Yard.[52] Political expediency had forced Harrison's hand, but White remained convinced that only a party regular could have persuaded the president to embrace reform.

The struggle to bring civil service reform to government proved to White that diligence and patience were rewarded with steady results. By the end of the century, the merit system prevailed in most government offices; except for two Cleveland interludes, the reform had been enacted by Republicans. That the civil service movement did not immediately result in enlightened government did not dim White's ardor. The present was rapidly gaining on the future, and the American republic was surely nearing the Promised Land.

50. ADW to Warner, January 13, 1891, WMC.
51. *Autobiography*, vol. 1, pp. 224–28; Draft of Speech to President Harrison at Executive Mansion, 1891; ADW to Evans, January 12, 1891; Diary, January 16, 1891, all in WMC.
52. ADW to Fiske, March 21, 1892, WMC.

Chapter 10   A *Tragic Retirement*

In 1885, for the first time in almost thirty years, White found himself without official public responsibilities. Cleveland's victory in 1884 seemed to preclude another diplomatic venture, and a desire to allow Charles Kendall Adams free reign at Cornell prevented the retired president from actively engaging in university management. Nevertheless, as White completed his European vacation in 1886, several courses of action presented themselves. He might return to politics and seek elective office or he might complete the magnum opus that he had long thought would bring him lasting fame. Finally, he could lecture and agitate on the pressing issues that faced the United States—civil service reform, government aid for higher education, and the appalling increase in crime. At fifty-four White gave little thought to leisurely inactivity.

Offered the Republican nomination for a congressional seat from the district encompassing much of Tompkins, Seneca, Schuyler, and Chemung counties, White seriously considered resuming his political career. The district, however, was the home of Democratic boss David B. Hill and was hardly a GOP stronghold. Faced with the certainty of a strenuous campaign and the possibility of defeat, White declined to allow his name to be placed in nomination.[1]

Paradoxically, although White insisted that politics was being purified,[2] he studiously declined appointive political office.[3] In 1887 President Cleveland named him to the newly created Interstate Commerce Commission. The position, railroad magnate Henry Villard and other prominent Republicans advised him, was of tremendous importance; yet White declined. The position, he argued, demanded sacrifice of all other projects. For the present, scholarly pursuits and lectures formed his itinerary.[4]

1. Ernest Huffcut to ADW, August 10, 1886, and ADW to John Tyler, August 23, 1886, WMC.
2. ADW to E. P. Evans, November 4, 1886, WMC.
3. White ignored Warner Miller's remarks on the political infidelity of Cornell graduates. See, e.g., Miller to ADW, November 20, 1886, WMC.
4. *New York World*, February 24, 1887; Diary, February 23 and 24, 1887, WMC.

As White turned once again to his projected book, *A History of the Warfare of Science with Theology in Christendom*, he gave some time to his son Fred's personal battle with religion. A frail, intense, neurasthenic young man, Fred had imbibed his father's nonsectarianism with a vengeance and had extended it with an attack on the "hypocrisy and salacity" of orthodox Christianity:

I am morally certain that the great majority of thinking practical men of the present time regard the present degeneration of religion as unworthy of any attention and the Officers of the Church, Pope, Bishop, Priest and Minister, one and all as insincere hypocrites if not worse. What they want is money and power and—too lazy or stupid to gain either by work—they hoodwink females and children of both sexes with such phrases as immaculate lamb, incarnation, eucharist, aural confession, salvation, regeneration, try to repress all truth and progress—and so frighten the cowardly portion of mankind with their pictures of hell-fire, that they prefer to pay cash and believe impossible lies, to taking the risk of damnation.[5]

Fred's frequent illnesses frustrated his own hopes for a career. Confined to the role of manager of his father's business affairs, he directed his misanthropy toward venal ministers and gullible Christians.

Andrew White subscribed to many of his son's indictments of religion but had always refused to make a blanket condemnation of Christianity. White admonished his son for speaking like a heathen. He pressed Fred for a statement of his religious philosophy and was apparently satisfied by his son's assurance that he believed in a deity and the "wonderful" teachings of Jesus Christ.[6]

White probably objected to little more than Fred's strident tone. Religion's consolations, he asserted, presented the same difficulty found in the use of medicine: the dose had to be steadily increased to reproduce the original effect. Pressed to state his religious principles, White had clung to a belief in God, the Psalms, and the Sermon on the Mount.[7] Fred White, however, had taken his father's critique of Christianity to its logical culmination. When an avalanche of criticism greeted the publication of *The Warfare of Science with Theology* in 1895 and White was vilified as a heathen, he may very well have mused upon the "dangerous" results his religious philosophy had produced in his son.

Such thoughts, however, were for an unforeseen future; the present offered opportunities to write and to lecture on a multitude of subjects.[8]

5. Fred White to ADW, May 13, 1886, WMC.
6. Moses Coit Tyler to ADW, November 11, 1885; Fred White to ADW, April 13 and May 13, 1886; ADW to Fred White, April 29, 1886, all in WMC.
7. ADW to Mrs. E. P. Evans, February 22, 1874, WMC.
8. ADW to George Lincoln Burr, May 8, 1886, WMC; *The Message of the Nineteenth Century to the Twentieth* (New York, 1883) (this lecture, which inveighed against the greedy

White's ambitious plans for a lecture tour came to a tragic halt on June 8, 1887, when Mary White collapsed into the arms of her daughter, Clara, and died. The bereaved husband drew a cross on the date in his diary (a practice he followed every year until his death) and wrote poignantly: "The best wife that ever was. I so unworthy of her. . . . No last word. No message." In his anguish he reread his diary, hoping to recapture their happy years together. The result was always the same. "Alas! Alas! Why could I not have known that this was the last full day I was ever to have in the dear old house at Syracuse with my dearest Mary!"[9]

Beautiful music, flowers, and the atmosphere of love at the funeral momentarily soothed White's "ache," but within days he was again in a deep depression. On June 13 he awoke to "a sense of fearful loss." Letters of condolence afforded little relief. He did not even have "the heart" to attend the annual meeting of Cornell's Board of Trustees. All thoughts returned to Mary, and every morning promised only another "sad, sad day."[10]

In a desperate effort to preserve Mary's memory, White commissioned Franklin Simmons to build a monument of her and hired sculptor Moses Ezekial for a portrait. He left orders that Mary's room be left exactly as it had been when she died. As if to remind himself that he had not fully taken advantage of their years together, he returned to Syracuse to visit the places he identified with her—their homes, church, and school. At his own home in Syracuse, he remembered his "little brown thrush" descending the stairs: "Dearest Mary, if I could have but realized my happiness! and the treasure in my keeping."[11]

While White grieved, an old family friend heightened his sense of loss by describing Mary's incredible devotion to her husband. Mary had evidently found fulfillment in White's achievements; her existence had been utterly vicarious.

Your image was so before her eyes she could never see any other. She never had a thought which was not yours, first last and always. . . . in everything she did her object was as she expressed it "to climb up level to see with your eyes" and when I said "oh Mary you are as high as his heart and that is high enough for any woman"

---

tendencies of mercantile pursuits, was delivered often in the 1880s; fifty thousand copies of the address were published and distributed); John B. Alden to ADW, February 9, 1884, WMC.

9. Diary, June 8 and May 10, 1887, WMC.
10. Diary, June 11, 13, 15, and 19, 1887, WMC.
11. Diary, June 24 and July 12, 1887, WMC.

she only laughed softly and shook her head as she used to do when she made up her mind and did not want to argue.[12]

For thirty years White had had a companion who totally supported his every action. Mary had comforted him through scores of disappointments in politics and education; she had been at his side when he had been vindicated. Her loss weakened the part of White that was convinced that he had made a lasting contribution to American society. If Mary was now only dust, perhaps nothing was permanent or truly meaningful.

White "fairly staggered" through the next two years. He journeyed to Europe, but his footsteps in the Old World carried him to familiar places with poignant memories. Even public service was unattractive. Alonzo Cornell urged him to seek the vice-presidency of the United States in 1888. The widower was not interested: "Alas my Mary is gone, and how little is the value of such an honor to me if she does not share it."[13]

Gradually, inevitably, time abated the sharpest pangs of sorrow. That White returned to public life is not surprising; that he grieved for *years* (far, far longer than for his father, mother, or dead son) indicates that Mary's death profoundly shook his sense of self. As late as the spring of 1889, he confessed that his traditional remedy for depression had only partially worked its magic this time: "There is no help but in working on—tho[ugh] this does not at all keep that scene out of my frequent thoughts."[14]

Fortunately time enlisted an ally in its campaign to restore White's equilibrium. In September 1887 he met Helen Magill, daughter of the president of Swarthmore College. A classical scholar in her thirties, Helen Magill had been the first woman to be granted a Ph.D. in America.[15] She seemed the very antithesis of Mary White. Outspoken, she appeared to White to be "a noble specimen of the 'girl of the period' in the best sense."[16] Although White departed for Europe several months after their first meeting, he pursued a lengthy correspondence with his new "friend."[17]

The widower was especially interested in Helen's religious philosophy. White's rationalism gave him little comfort during his ordeal, and he detected a buoyancy in the Quakeress' belief in the supernatural. What was the difference, he asked, between superstition and faith? Helen

12. Jenny B. Lind to ADW, October 5, 1887, WMC.
13. Diary, July 7, August 23, and December 25, 1887, and January 6, 1888, WMC.
14. Diary, June 8, 1889, WMC.
15. Edward Magill, *Sixty-five Years in the Life of a Teacher, 1841–1906* (Boston and New York, 1907), p. 147; Morris Bishop, *A History of Cornell* (Ithaca, 1962), p. 335.
16. Diary, September 8, 1887, WMC.
17. Unfortunately, only Helen's letters to White have survived. These lengthy letters, however, enable one fairly easily to reconstruct his questions to her.

answered that a man who saw evil in the world yet insisted that it was governed by a good power had faith. The man who believed the world good for himself and a few others but bad for the rest was superstitious. Thus, Helen concluded, faith did not preclude sorrow, but it assured man that he would ultimately triumph.[18]

Helen believed in progress with all her heart, she assured White. Yet perfection of worldly conditions alone did not seem worth working for. Without a belief in permanent realities, no activity was worthwhile.

> And mere human progress . . . beautiful as the spirit which prompts such an expression, seems to me, practically considered, very meaningless. I hope I could take some satisfaction, if proved mortal myself, in promoting some future good in which I could have no part, but if it is going to be a good as fleeting as my own, I could, after all, take little satisfaction in contemplating such a process of adding zero to zero in the vain hope of making a sum.[19]

White was receptive to Helen's belief in the eternal significance of human beings and deeds. For a man who could bear to die but not to be forgotten, the concept of an immortal soul had undeniable appeal.

Scientific proof of the immortality of the soul was lacking, but Helen Magill's intense spirituality and White's consuming desire to be reunited with Mary threatened to overcome a lifetime of rationalistic doubt. Again and again the Quakeress wrote "to say something which would help you." Unless he could believe in the immortal souls of his loved ones, "when all that showed them is outwardly gone," she warned, "he could never hope to be truly united with them or with Him." Even Christ, because he sought to learn the very worst bitterness of human life, felt at least once the sense of doubt and separation. A future life "must be so," she told White. The moral side of life and spiritual intimations proved the existence of an afterlife, even to rationalists. If superstition was an inability to estimate the value of evidence, faith was a gift that enabled one, when evidence was in conflict, to "trust the larger hope."[20]

Although sympathetic to the "larger hope," White remained unable to believe, and he informed Helen that he neither wished for nor thought about salvation. There was, she agreed, much "cant and outwardness" connected with the word "salvation." But it was "the only personal blessing that we can unreservedly pray for without any selfishness. For what is it to be saved, but to be united with the good and true and beautiful in the Life of God."[21] Union with God and Mary, a promise that reason refused

18. Magill to ADW, September 13, 1888, WMC.
19. Magill to ADW, February 14, 1888, WMC.
20. Magill to ADW, November 28, 1887; June 22, 1888; and February 3, 1889, WMC.
21. Magill to ADW, March 2, 1888, WMC.

to give him, impelled White closer to the faith of his supernaturalist confidante.

Early in 1888, White began to flirt openly with superrationalist belief. He would not accept the ordinary theological dogmas upon such a basis, he admitted to Evans, but the possibility of an immortal soul was strengthened by the fact that such beliefs had taken strong hold of a large number of "noble minds." In fact, he noted in an obvious reference to Helen, they were especially powerful among "noble women." [22]

Deeply moved by Helen's eloquence, White found his instincts at war with his intellect. Supernatural religion seemed to offer solace, but his own studies demonstrated that the old-time religion was very often a cruel hoax. In October 1888, however, he almost yielded to the promptings of his heart. Throughout his adult life he had refused to participate in the Lord's Supper. Now, in the wake of Mary's death and Helen's advice, he was touched by an invitation to take communion. "I longed to remain," he confided to his diary, "[and] came very near doing so. Would—had I thought myself worthy. Would that my new advisor [Helen Magill] had been here." [23]

Never again would White come as close to a formal acceptance of supernatural religion as he had on that autumn day. In fact, at almost the same time that he agonized over communion, he reiterated the rationalists' religious creed: "We cannot be too careful to avoid all sectarian or even religious passions. . . . A religion that finds its realisation in righteous men and not in gush—is what our country most needs." [24]

Helen Magill realized that the "conversion" of her friend would not "stand the slightest test." Despite her efforts, she realized that White's attitude toward the universe was much the same as always, "that is, always changing." Supernaturalism had soothed White in the wake of Mary's death; it could be shelved when the ache subsided and replaced with rationalism more congenial to his training. "If there is one thing more than another which I dislike, it is inconsistency," Helen Magill told him, "and I really don't think you have a grain of consistency in your whole constitution." [25] Although she did not cease her attempts to "convert" White, Helen decided that her correspondent's only eternal truth was the persistence of change.

At some point during their lengthy correspondence, White became a suitor as well as a friend. If he found Helen's frankness a bit trying at times,

22. ADW to E. P. Evans, March 3, 1888, WMC.
23. Diary, October 7, 1888, WMC.
24. ADW to Robert Thurston, July 20, 1888, WMC.
25. Magill to ADW, March 6, 1888, WMC.

he had to admit that it was integral to her charm. Helen had eased his anguish in the months following Mary's death, and her continued presence renewed White's optimism. Consequently, he questioned his correspondent on her attitude toward domesticity. Surprisingly, she seemed amenable to accepting a traditional role. She liked housekeeping; it required head and heart. In fact, as Helen grew older, her understanding of the attitude of men who stoutly opposed the opening of careers to women increased. They were mistaken, but not wholly selfish or foolish as she had once been inclined to think.[26] She did not seem at all averse to subordinating her career as a teacher in a girl's school to that of an eminent husband.

If Helen was willing to accept White's concept of the proper role of wife and mother, she seemed incapable of curbing her sarcastic tongue. Her earnest attempts to puncture his pomposity must have enraged him. Proud of the many honors won during his career, White persisted in listing every degree Helen had achieved in each letter addressed to her. In case he had omitted a title, he added "etc. etc. etc." to his catalog. Helen was not amused: "I am a Friend, and I don't much like *vain titles* on the outside of my letters. And may I ask what 'etc. etc. etc.' means? I have not yet taken that degree—perhaps it is one which you yourself conferred upon me, in view of the length of my epistles."[27] Sarcasm had little effect on White, who continued to address his letters with ostentatious formality. Silence, however, was not an effective weapon against the doughty Friend; she comprised her own list of titles for White: "To the Hon. Mr. Andrew D. White Esqre. L.L.D., Ex-President of Cornell University, Ithaca, New York, U.S.A., Grand Tormentor of the Ex-professor of Ancient Languages of Evelyn College, Princeton, New Jersey, U.S.A. Etc. Etc. Etc."[28]

Helen's epistle succeeded only in arousing White's ire; undaunted, she twisted the needle yet one more time. She professed mock surprise that he did not like the honors she had bestowed upon him. Why, then, had he persisted in addressing her in a manner she found distasteful? Had White never heard of the golden rule? Upon reflection, she decided he had not.[29] Accustomed to a wife who saw only with his eyes, White was now confronted with an assertive, combative, autonomous woman. If he decided to wed a second time, he could expect a relationship far different from that with Mary Outwater.

26. Magill to ADW, July 26, 1888, WMC.
27. Magill to ADW, August 19, 1888, WMC.
28. Magill to ADW, November 28, 1888, WMC.
29. Magill to ADW, December 31, 1888, WMC.

White's courtship of Helen Magill was stormy; on at least one occasion the two agreed to break contact. The solitary life was utterly disagreeable to the widower, however, and on November 30, 1889, he made "perhaps the most momentous decision of his life" and asked Helen to marry him. Helen's love for her much older suitor graced almost every page of her letters, and she was obviously willing to overlook his eccentricities. White hoped that marriage presented a chance "for the happier future of us all."[30]

As the day of the wedding approached, White had lurking doubts about Helen. Her letters, he realized, revealed a disturbing "want of get-along-attiveness." A month before the wedding, he awoke after little sleep "and that little much troubled." He had dreamed of a visit to Swarthmore (which housed most of the Magill family), where he had asked the residents if Helen Magill were sane. There was, alas, no answer. When he awakened, the alarmed groom-to-be wrote two letters to his betrothed. Though momentarily reassured, White correctly suspected that his second marriage would be far less blissful than his first had been.[31]

Thrusting his trepidations aside, White made his marriage vows on September 10, 1890. In a simple ceremony, performed without a clergyman in the Quaker way, he ended three years as a widower.[32] "May Heaven bless and keep us," he exlaimed. "My dear Helen is my choice, because of her inherent loveliness, sweetness and goodness as well as her remarkable intellectual gifts."[33] White was certainly impressed with his new bride, but he reserved his "love" for Mary. He continued to commemorate the anniversary of Mary's death in his diary and made little reference to his second wife. For the remainder of his life, White really had two wives: "dearest Mary," who had brought him only happiness, and Helen, whose irrepressible assertiveness sometimes seemed to approach that of Nora, the "utterly impossible" character of Ibsen's *A Doll's House*, which White ironically read four days after his marriage.[34]

Whatever unpleasantness the future held, White realized that his courtship of Helen Magill had "made life again worth living."[35] As his depression began to ease, he could apply his usual remedy, involvement in public affairs. A cause was not difficult to find, and White renewed his enthusiastic advocacy of a plan to persuade the federal government to endow a national university in Washington, D.C.

30. Diary, July 13 and November 30, 1889, WMC.
31. Diary, August 4 and 5, 1890, WMC.
32. Fiske to Evans, September 12, 1890, Edward Payson Evans MSS, Cornell University.
33. Diary, September 10, 1890, WMC.
34. Diary, September 14, 1890, WMC.
35. Diary, December 31, 1890, WMC.

Helen Magill White, Andrew D. White's second wife

The concept of a national university was as old as the republic. George Washington had proposed it and made provisions in his will to aid in its construction, but many congressmen, jealously guarding state prerogatives, branded the scheme unconstitutional.[36] Again and again the project was revived only to be buried by arguments against federal paternalism. In the 1870s the national university movement came under the direction of John W. Hoyt, who guided its fortunes for the rest of the century. The peripatetic Hoyt eagerly enlisted the support of White and other prominent educators.[37]

The lines of battle could be easily drawn: advocates of federal aid to higher education tended to be receptive to a federally financed seat of higher learning; presidents of wealthy, privately endowed universities resented government interference in education. James McCosh, president of Princeton University, feared that colleges financed by state or federal governments would undermine private universities by offering cheap education. He demanded that his colleagues stop "asking for subsidies which others of us scorn to ask—as we work only a fair field and no favor."[38]

If McCosh could be dismissed as noisy and quarrelsome with arguments "flimsy in everything but malignity,"[39] Charles W. Eliot merited recognition as a worthy opponent. Harvard's president labeled land grant aid to colleges and a national university "symptoms of a deep-seated disease." The whole country was inoculated with the idea of government beneficence; Americans demanded federally financed canals, agricultural schools, and an inflated currency. Eager to see this "utterly unrepublican and un-American frame of the public mind" changed before it destroyed liberty, Eliot led a crusade against government aid to higher education.[40]

Always willing to cross swords with Eliot, White joined the defenders of the national university in 1874. He attacked the Harvard president's laissez faire philosophy as a reactionary indictment of all public education. Reminding his rival that even John Stuart Mill had exempted education from the laissez faire principle, White insisted that state universities—and perhaps even a national university—would not check private endow-

36. A summary of the history of the national university movement may be found in David Madsen, *The National University: Enduring Dream of the U.S.A.* (Detroit 1966).
37. Hoyt to ADW, July 21, 1874, WMC.
38. McCosh to ADW, April 8, 1874, WMC.
39. Justin Morrill to ADW, August 12, 1873, WMC.
40. Hugh Hawkins, *Between Harvard and America: The Educational Leadership of Charles W. Eliot* (New York, 1972), p. 152; Louis Corson, "University Problems as Described in the Personal Correspondence of D. C. Gilman, A. D. White, and C. W. Eliot," Ph.D. thesis, Stanford University, 1951, p. 143.

ments. A growing nation, he insisted, needed many more institutions of higher learning; private colleges such as Harvard should not shrink from competition. While the *New York Times* thought that White ignored the blighting effect of politics "on the higher education which he proposes to introduce into the arena of partisan struggle," its editors admitted that his defense of the national university gave the plan a "liveliness and audacity, as well as a respectability, which it before lacked."[41]

For over a decade the project languished while Hoyt gathered support for a massive lobbying effort in Congress. White virtually ignored the scores of letters Hoyt sent him until a year after Mary's death, when he set forth his plan for a national university in a series of essays in the *Forum* and the *North American Review*. The retired Cornell president outlined a multifaceted approach that would bring students to Washington and benefit colleges throughout the United States.

A university in Washington, D.C., White argued, was practical because it would use libraries and laboratories in the capital to good advantage. The Library of Congress was infinitely superior to many university libraries. Moreover, students of history and the social sciences would have living resources to instruct them on the workings of the political system. Was there a better place for a law student to study them than the seat of the United States Supreme Court? The nation's capital provided an ideal opportunity to initiate the young citizen into the world of scholarship and political reality.[42]

If the national university was of great benefit to the student, it would also purify the Washington atmosphere. Thoughtful inquiry would permeate the capital. Contact between men of public affairs and university men would be helpful to both: "The member from Podunk would be lifted above the mere considerations of local or even general politics, and the scholarly professor would learn more and more of the real world he is living in." Finally, the national university would help to bring the sections together by mixing young men from the North and South. When the men returned to their homes and achieved positions of prominence, they would certainly realize that common training and interests bound together all areas of the United States.[43]

White's advocacy of a research-oriented postgraduate university formed part of a larger plan for the general restructuring of higher education in America. Lesser "colleges," he argued, should become intermediate

41. Madsen, *The National University*, p. 80; *New York Times*, May 23 and August 18, 1874.
42. "A University at Washington," *Forum* 6 (February 1889): 623–25, 629, 632.
43. Ibid., p. 633; Speech before Banquet of the George Washington University, March 14, 1906, WMC.

schools like Eton and Harrow in England. The smaller colleges that survived this winnowing process should, White argued, confine themselves to undergraduate teaching. The modern world required specialization as much in education as in industry.[44] The capstone of White's system—the university—would thus be free to devote itself exclusively to well-prepared students. White suggested that universities admit students in the junior year, when they were ready to concentrate on advanced work. The national university would be one of a few real universities in the country; White had merely embellished the plan laid out by Henry P. Tappan.

Convinced that his plan would inevitably be adopted, White exhorted his readers to bring the future closer to the present. A realignment of America's educational institutions was "evidently coming by a process of evolution," but reformers should prepare the public mind for it through discussion and activity within specific colleges. The certainty of eventual success, White believed, did not absolve the individual of responsibility to "aid right reason." [45]

Despite his efforts, White failed to overtake the future. For a time it seemed that Congress was amenable; in 1896 a Senate committee held hearings on the "Establishment of the University of the United States." Hurrying to Washington to testify, White marshaled old and new arguments. Federal aid to higher education had not paralyzed individual effort, he insisted; private donations supplemented income in many state universities and continued unabated in private institutions. Conversely, White pointed to the danger of making education dependent on the whim of public-spirited philanthropists. Such policies enabled individual ideas to control the educational system. Was not the government the best guarantor of freedom of thought and inquiry?[46]

The legislators politely listened to the illustrious parade of advocates of the national university and quietly shelved the proposal. States-righters had more constituents than disinterested educators (who were themselves divided on the issue), and politicians concluded that inertia was safer than action. White labeled this setback a postponement rather than a defeat, but his efforts slackened. The persistent Hoyt, however, would be deterred only by death and persuaded White to lend his name, if not his voice, to

44. "The Future of American Universities," *North American Review* 51 (October 1890): 443–52; "The Future of the American Colleges and Universities," *School and College* 1 (February 1892): 67–68.

45. "The Future of American Universities," p. 452.

46. Hearing Before the Senate Committee on the Establishment of the University of the United States, February 10, 1896, WMC.

lobbying efforts. He had always talked of White as the first president of the University of the United States, but neither man lived to see the establishment of a national university.[47]

The national university was not the only subject that interested White in the years following Mary's death. Although he continued to view himself as a reformer, he now found himself constrained to "defend revolutions which go backward." The one-time abolitionist, for example, attended the 1890 Lake Mohonk Conference on the Negro Question but disavowed radical solutions to the freedman's dilemma. At Lake Mohonk, disagreement about whether or not blacks should be given an exclusively industrial education was more than compensated for by virtual consensus that the federal government could do little for Negroes. White's view of the Negro problem had markedly altered since his days as a radical Republican: "It cannot fail to strike us that, under slavery, with all its evils, there were some beautiful relations which no longer exist." Millions of blacks, he realized, remained mired in ignorance and poverty, but improvement now seemed far down the road. The crucial question for the future was: "How shall the evolution of a better future for the colored race be secured, while the peace and prosperity of the white race shall remain unharmed?" White had no specific suggestions for aiding blacks but advocated an educational test for suffrage. Although he recognized that the restriction would "doubtless disfranchise a large proportion of the colored population," he claimed that it was necessary for the survival of the republic. Long held in ignorance and bondage, blacks would have to realize that a deep chasm separated slavery and freedom; attempts to leap across it were fated to fail.[48]

White, then, was willing to allow the government to support universities but not to aid blacks. The government, he believed, should help those with ability to get an education; such action would ensure a steady flow of competent leaders for America. White frowned on most other reforms, including federal programs, to aid blacks. He justified turning a deaf ear on "the Negro question" by making education a panacea.

In an exposé of municipal government, White reiterated his desire to "defend revolutions which go backward." Public officials in cities won their positions by scoundrelism, he charged, and proceeded to plunder the treasuries. White attributed the wretched condition of cities to the theory that the city put "a crowd of illiterate peasants, freshly raked in from Irish

47. Hoyt to ADW, December 16, 1905, WMC.
48. Henry Bullock, *A History of Negro Education in the South* (New York, 1970), pp. 77–78; Isabel Barrows, ed., *First Lake Mohonk Conference on the Negro Question* (Boston, 1890), esp. pp. 117–21.

bogs, or Bohemian mines, or Italian robber nests," in virtual control. If the city was to survive, propertyholders had to be given political hegemony. Thus White proposed that the mayor and board of aldermen be elected at large rather than by ward, where bosses could easily manipulate their ethnic constituents. As an added safeguard, a Board of Control—elected solely by property owners—should control expenditures, subject to a two-thirds veto by the aldermen. Amid the threat of immigrants to Anglo-Saxon control of America, White was willing to invoke the well-worn doctrine of the stake in society.[49]

The connection between immigration and crime seemed obvious to White. In line with his theory of steady progress, White discovered that criminal procedure had grown more and more merciful. Given such findings, one might expect White to advocate even more humane treatment of criminals, perhaps even to suggest the abolition of capital punishment: the lines of "evolution" apparently pointed unfalteringly in one direction.[50]

In a series of impassioned articles and lectures, however, he consistently called for harsher treatment of criminals. The "slobbering anxiety" shown by "psuedo-philanthropists" for the comfort of murderers was a farce: "It was as much as if a man who finds his child bitten by a rabid dog should not cut out the affected part and cauterize it instantly, but should wash the wound with rose water and coddle the dog with a warm kennel and beefsteaks and insist on giving the cur his liberty."[51] White sarcastically noted that the lawful execution of murderers was the only means of taking life to which the average American objected. Thus juries found scores of murderers not guilty and returned them to the streets. Was it any wonder, then, that murderers ran rampant? Was it surprising that outraged citizens resorted to lynch law? Crime, White insisted, was not mere misfortune; "crime was crime" and the "criminal a criminal." Making allowances for those who "casually" fell into crime and could be rehabilitated, he pleaded for an all-out war "to exterminate" professional or habitual criminals.[52]

White had returned to public life in the years following Mary's death, but the tragedy had taken its toll. He constantly reverted to the promise of progress, but the term had even less meaning than it had earlier contained. White's conservative instincts, always present, began to govern his public utterances. The necessity for order and stability as preconditions for

49. "The Government of American Cities," *Forum* 10 (December 1890): 357–72. See also *Evolution vs. Revolution in Politics* (Madison, Wis., 1897).
50. *Autobiography*, vol. 1, pp. 495–97.
51. Crime and Penalty in the United States, WMC.
52. *Autobiography*, vol. 2, p. 77; *Instruction in Social Science* (Boston, 1890), p. 11.

change—a constant theme throughout White's life—now dwarfed his recommendations for social improvement. White's credentials as a reformer, it was now clear, extended little beyond the university and the creation of a meritocracy. While he continued to reverence progress, he seemed a more dour man: less confident, because of increased immigration and industrial unrest, in the ability of society to transform itself; less certain, in view of Mary's death, that his efforts had been worthwhile. To move forward, White now indicated, it was often necessary to move backward—a bewildering doctrine that made progress a phantom and of little help as a guide to action. Pulled backward and forward, White seemed to be settling into inertia; little more than an apologist for the status quo, he would have been confused by the suggestion that his belief in evolutionary progress, a constant in a world of flux, had been altered by changing temporal circumstances.

Chapter 11   *Gubernatorial Candidate and*
Minister to Russia

Soon after his marriage to Helen Magill, White was again tempted to run for political office. As before, friends begged him to try for a seat in Congress or the governor's chair. This time, however, professional politicians—among them Thomas Collier Platt, Conkling's successor as boss of New York's Republicans—urged him to run. In 1890, Platt offered him the GOP congressional nomination from Tompkins County, but White declined without comment.[1] A year later he was promised support for the governorship. Certain that he had maintained the principles of the statesman while supporting his party in 1884, the retired educator had to decide whether a race for governor would make him a mere politician, dependent on the support of the Platt machine.

Tentative steps to advance White's candidacy were taken, although he had not yet sanctioned them.[2] Unaware of Platt's indications of support, many observers doubted that White could convince regulars that he was a partisan Republican. The *Troy Press* argued that White's support for Blaine had been halfhearted. Party machinists, the editorial claimed, would not tolerate the nomination of a man who was more "patriot than partisan." White's self-appointed campaign manager, Frederick W. Holls, agreed that "practical politicians" hesitated to support someone they considered "almost a Mugwump" but thought that the increased chance of victory would counteract their cautious instincts. Platt was already favorably inclined, Holls reminded White, and once he received assurances that the candidate would finance his own campaign, he would certainly bring the regulars into line. Victory was at hand, Holls believed, if White would only reach out and grasp it.[3]

1. ADW to Willard Fiske, August 18, 1890, and ADW to Ellis Roberts, September 8, 1890, WMC.
2. During this period, White turned down an offer to become president of Stanford University (Andrew Humphrey to ADW, March 7, 1891, and Diary, March 19, 1891, WMC).
3. *Troy Press*, March 27, 1891; Holls to ADW, June 30, 1891, WMC.

Although interested, White refused to declare his candidacy, probably hoping that the party would offer him the nomination. Politicians actively sought office, statesmen accepted the call of duty. Throughout the summer, expressions of support greeted the undeclared candidate. The German Club of Syracuse emphatically endorsed him; the *New York Times* placed the Onondoga County German-American Association's resolution of support on page 1. If White moved quickly, Holls urged, he could capitalize on this publicity; capable of uniting regulars, reformers, dissident Democrats, and German-Americans, he seemed likely to receive the nomination.

Although he acted like a candidate,[4] White continued to flirt with his Republican suitors without giving final assent. On August 20, Platt, Henry Villard, and Holls urged him to run. The following day he expressed concern that a vigorous campaign would destroy his health and declared that he could not yet agree to become a candidate. Within a week, however, Holls found arguments that White could not resist. White's candidacy, he declared, would vindicate the wisdom of nominating intellectual leaders for political office. As an instructor of youth, could he refuse an opportunity to do more good for the state, for the university he had helped to found, for the cause of good government, and for the "idealism of the rising generations" than was possible by delivering hundreds of lectures? Holls assured him, moreover, that Platt had decided to assume financial responsibility for campaign expenses. Holls's plea could receive but one response: on August 31, White put himself "in the hands of my friends as regards the nomination."[5]

While White deliberated, the *New York Times* warned him that an alliance with Platt spelled disaster. In an editorial entitled "The Butchers Looking for a Victim," the *Times* speculated about Platt's motives for supporting an avowed proponent of civil service reform. A sound governor if elected, White would never have an opportunity to enact his reform program because Platt would ensure that he never sat in the governor's chair. The boss had evidently decided that the election of a Republican governor was impossible; hence he was looking for a respectable candidate to head the ticket and help produce Republican majorities in the legislative houses. If Platt thought a Republican could be elected governor, he would dump White: "The attempt to lure him to his certain defeat is infamous.

---

4. See, e.g., John Rohmer to ADW, August 19, 1891, WMC; *New York Times*, July 24, 1891; ADW to Horace K. White, August 26, 1891; William Bostwick to ADW, August 21, 1891; Carroll Smith to ADW, August 21, 1891, all in WMC.

5. Diary, August 20, 21, and 31, 1891, WMC; Holls to ADW, August 27, 1891, both in WMC.

The butchers ought to respect men who have come to eminence in callings other than politics. One of their own kind would serve their present needs well enough." Advising White to await a day when the party was "in cleaner and worthier hands," the *Times* suggested that he withdraw from the race.[6]

Day after day the *Times* hammered away, seeking to prevent this alliance. White was a "sacrificial lamb," the editors sighed in a first-page story on August 21. If the candidate refused to be swayed by claims of Platt's duplicity, the *Times* attempted to convince him that victory was impossible. White might receive some votes from disgruntled Democrats, but he would lose support from Republicans. He was not the kind of candidate who could attract votes from the immigrants of New York City. High character and eminent abilities placed White "so far above the plane of common politics that he is not in touch with those who run caucuses and manipulate and control conventions." Determined to protect White from Platt, the *Times* seemed willing to imply that only "practical" politicians could be elected. Thoroughly committed to reform from within, White believed that he could use Platt's support to win the election and then purge the party; he was therefore not receptive to the *Times*'s pleas.[7]

A few days before the Republican convention convened, Platt began to express doubts about White's candidacy, lending credence to the *Times*'s scenario. He informed White of his concern about the educator's religious views and his advocacy of restricted franchise. Such views, he claimed, could defeat the ticket. White offered to withdraw but the boss brushed him aside. Meanwhile Platt leaked stories to the press that dissension over White's candidacy racked the party. Platt had avoided an explicit disavowal of his candidate but had clearly removed his imprimatur from him on the eve of the convention. White's allies realized (even if he did not) that their candidate, who was utterly dependent on Platt's favor, could not now be nominated.[8]

When a political head count showed that White would garner barely 100 votes of 777, his supporters at Rochester decided to withdraw his name rather than expose it as "a football to a certain kicking." Fred White hurried to Rochester with a note from his father removing himself from the race. The promise of the early summer had turned to disappointment. Not surprisingly, Platt's new choice, J. S. Fassett, won the gubernatorial nomination. If the boss had not quite carried his lamb to the altar, he had pursued a completely successful strategy. Money had been raised for the

6. *New York Times*, August 19, 1891.
7. *New York Times*, August 21, 23, 26, and 30, 1891.
8. Diary, September 5, 1891, WMC; *New York Times*, September 5 and 6, 1891.

fall campaigns, the independent Republican press had been placed on record against the Democrats, and Platt had engineered the nomination of his preferred candidate.[9]

The defeated candidate was remarkably resilient. He had not desired the governorship, he now reported to himself and to friends: "I had dreaded the nomination for Governor rather than hoped for it." To Burr he claimed that he had entered the race only "when it was presented as a matter of duty." Fassett, a strong opponent of "Hillism," was younger and more vigorous; White thought that he was a reformer who had an excellent chance to win the election.[10]

White entertained virtually all explanations for his defeat except those that blamed Tom Platt. The educator realized that his views on religion and suffrage were not likely to win mass support. Thus reports that party regulars had convinced Platt that his candidacy would be disastrous seemed credible. Yet Platt, White repeatedly insisted, was not culpable. Platt had never attempted to exact any promises from White, perhaps because he knew that White would not betray his principles merely to win an election. White concluded that Platt had urged him to run because he was the strongest available candidate. He attributed his own poor showing to the opposition of spoilsmen; yet he refused to link his defeat to Platt—the most implacable foe of civil service reform in the state. White had remained in the party in order to facilitate the downfall of the bosses; yet the "practical politicians" had retained control. The Mugwumps had warned him that he would come to grief if he allied himself with corrupt men in the hope of ultimately overthrowing them; he had always countered that the politically fickle had little effect upon either party, and events had on occasion validated his claim. To retain his belief in the possibility of change within the two-party system, White simply rejected evidence of duplicity. The Republican nominee, he asserted, was well qualified. As the electorate received greater doses of enlightened education, good government principles would regain control of the party.[11]

Defeat did not convince White that scholars could not win elective office. In 1893 White's son contemplated a race for a seat in the New York Assembly. Working one's way up through the political ranks, White advised, was dangerous. If Fred won office, he would be "entangled with

9. George Priest to Bostwick, n.d., and J. J. McCabe to ADW, September 17, 1891, WMC.

10. Diary, September 9, 1891, and ADW to Burr, September 15, 1891, WMC.

11. *New York Times*, October 5, 1891; Mary Eaton to ADW, July 21, 1894, WMC; *Autobiography*, vol. 1, pp. 231–35; Holls to ADW, August 30, 1892, WMC. For White's opinion of Platt, see ADW to David J. Hill, March 10, 1897, and ADW to E. P. Evans, May 20, 1895, WMC.

all kinds of pledges and promises" and would probably be "turned-under" at the end of his term. White advised his son to build a reputation outside of politics. When people discovered that he did not seek a place and yet was "fit for it—they will give it to you." His belief that the American electorate would call for Cincinnatus persisted despite his defeat.[12]

Although "unperturbed" by his defeat, White sought a change of scenery and accepted Andrew Carnegie's invitation to visit California and Mexico. Far away from the New York of David B. Hill, he welcomed the lavish hospitality of the Stanfords, who sought his comments and advice on their newly launched university. White enjoyed his vacation, but he had become impatient with a career as lecturer-adviser and longed for renewal of his career as a diplomat.[13]

Discounting rumors that he would be appointed secretary of state if Blaine resigned because of ill health or that he would be nominated as Harrison's running mate if Vice-President Levi Morton retired, White preferred the tranquility of an ambassadorship. He had heard, he wrote to Frank Hiscock, now a U.S. senator, that Whitelaw Reid was about to resign as minister to France. He hoped that he would be considered for the post but also found Rome attractive. White gingerly circumvented the propriety of asking Hiscock to exercise influence in his behalf: "I do not wish to press or urge myself for the place, but should you think it best to advocate my appointment, I should regard it as a very great favor." White was disappointed when Thomas Jefferson Coolidge, a Blaine man, replaced Reid, but confessed to Holls that he had never "really expected" the Paris ministry and had "made no real efforts to obtain it."[14]

In May 1892, Hiscock reported that the minister to Russia would soon leave St. Petersburg and asked White whether he wanted to replace him. Probably remembering the forbidding Russian winters, White at first hesitated, but by July he readied himself for St. Petersburg.[15]

In the months before he was named minister to Russia, White became involved in several controversies that complicated Russo–American relations. Faced with political dissension, the tsar had exiled hundreds of people to Siberia. A group of Americans led by F. V. Garrison, son of the famed abolitionist, called attention to the plight of the dissidents. Compar-

12. Fred White to ADW, November 6, 1891, and ADW to Fred White, November 13, 1893, WMC.
13. Diary, February 12, May 6, and May 18, 1892, WMC. White cut his trip short because of Charles Kendall Adams' resignation as president of Cornell. He was the only trustee to vote not to accept the resignation.
14. Holls to ADW, March 8, 1892; ADW to Hiscock, February 1, 1892; ADW to Holls, June 10, 1892; all in WMC.
15. ADW to Hiscock, May 25, 1892, and Hiscock to ADW, July 21, 1892, WMC.

ing the Russian agitators to abolitionists, Garrison claimed that the tsar was particularly sensitive to world opinion and asked White to sign a petition of protest.[16]

With characteristic caution, the diplomat reminded Garrison that agitation might not help the oppressed. White labeled the statements of Garrison's committee "provocative"; he offered to sign a temperate petition but refused to sanction futile and hostile actions. When Garrison characterized his attitude as "cringing" and "fawning," White amplified his position. The tsar was one of the "purest" men ever to sit on the Russian throne, he insisted, but was temporarily under the sway of fanatics. Thus friends of Russia should attempt to "lure these beasts away rather than to drive or scare them away, when we know . . . [it] would be utterly impossible." White would take pleasure in acceding to Garrison's plea to "denounce wrong wherever we see it" but thought that in this matter "pleasure should yield to duty." Just as he had advised reformers to work within the Republican party, White admonished Garrison not to force the tsar into the embrace of fanatics.[17]

White's appointment in July 1892 came less than two weeks after the death of little Hilda, the first child borne by Helen Magill. The tragedy probably strengthened the diplomat's resolve to leave the country; new scenery might ease Helen's anguish while providing him a new field of activity to counteract his own sorrow. The *New York Times* was pleasantly surprised that White had accepted the Russian mission, "which can hardly be regarded as a specially important or desirable place for a man of his experience and abilities." For the minister designate, the post provided honor and the opportunity for public service; if official duties were not burdensome, he could complete his scholarly magnum opus.[18]

During White's tenure as minister, he was to demonstrate a lack of expertise in Russian affairs. His extremely negative view of Russia had not changed, nor did he communicate with liberal intellectuals in Russian universities who might have convinced him that progress was indeed possible. Even the reforms of Sergei Witte made little impression on White,[19] who was as certain that Russia would remain backward permanently as he was that the United States afforded limitless possibilities for change. Russian reactionaries could be praised because they were realists; Russian reformers were utopians, virtually by definition.

16. Garrison to ADW, June 5, 1891, WMC.
17. Garrison to ADW, June 13, 1891, and ADW to Garrison, June 26, 1891, WMC.
18. Diary, July 12, 19, and 21, 1892, and July 9 and 10, 1893, WMC; *New York Times*, July 22, 1892.
19. Perhaps because Witte spoke little French and no German or English. See Theodore von Laue, *Sergei Witte* (New York and London, 1963), p. 38.

The most important question faced by Minister White involved the lucrative fur seal industry of the Bering Sea. Russians, Canadians, and Americans based in the Komandorskie Islands, the Canadian Northwest, Alaska, and the Pribiloff Islands competed for the migrating seals. The Canadians wandered far from their home base in pursuit of the seals, killing them indiscriminately, without regard to age or sex. Fearing that this practice would exhaust the supply, the American government seized several Canadian vessels, arguing that no nation could trespass within a protective zone of at least one hundred miles around the Pribiloff Islands. The British, eager to protect their Canadian cousins and their own hunting rights, submitted the case to an international tribunal of arbitration.[20]

White worked feverishly in an attempt to persuade the Russians to make common cause with the United States. The minister sent Secretary of State John Foster the statement of Nikolai Grebnitskii, military chief of the Komandorskie Islands, which pleaded for the cessation of seal killing in the water. On land, Grebnitskii testified, males could be killed and females protected; thus the population would be regulated because seals were polygamous. Seals suckled only their own babies, so that killing a female also killed her offspring. Marauding must cease, the Russian concluded, or the species would be destroyed. Grebnitskii's statement was a major coup for White, because it flatly contradicted the position attributed to him by the British.[21]

While the minister strengthened the American case, he urged the minister of foreign affairs to maintain its policy of seizing poachers engaged in destroying seals on the high seas. He asked the Russians to accept the American doctrine of proprietorship, which asserted that the nation that owned the breeding grounds owned the resident animals. Finally, White asked the Russians to make no concessions to the British that would embarrass the United States. The Russians seemed amenable to his suggestions, White reported as the arbitration panel convened in Paris.[22]

Certain that Russia supported the American position, White awaited a favorable judgment from the tribunal. Reports from Paris that Russia was on the verge of a separate agreement with Britain on the seal question, however, disturbed the minister's equipoise. Instructed to undermine or delay the treaty, White received assurances that the Russians would do nothing until the tribunal had completed its work. He soon learned, however, that British ambassador Sir Robert Morier had concluded an agreement with the Russian foreign ministry. Eager to win British support

20. *Autobiography*, vol. 2, pp. 13–15.
21. ADW to Foster, December 12, 1892, DMR.
22. ADW to Foster, November 16, 1892, Dispatches from Ministers to Russia.

for an Anglo–Russian alliance to dismember China, Russia sanctioned the taking of seals anywhere in the Bering Sea outside a thirty-mile zone around the Russian sea islands, and agreed to pay damages for British vessels recently seized. In the face of the Russo–British understanding, American claims at Paris seemed preposterous.[23]

On August 15, the arbitration tribunal announced its verdict. In an effort to protect the seals, the panel set the zone closed to marauders at sixty miles, twice the radius agreed to by Russia. The settlement probably seemed generous to the arbitration commissioners, but it gave the Canadians and British wide latitude for effective hunting, as subsequent practice proved. The United States was required to pay an indemnity for the vessels it had seized and to refrain from future harassment of sealers. In sum, the United States was enjoined from monopolizing the Pribiloff Island seal business.[24]

Although White realized that the Russian foreign ministry's decision to placate Britain stemmed in part from designs on Asia, he attributed the action to successful personal diplomacy by Sir Robert Morier. Furnished with a spacious house, a large staff, and the rank of ambassador, Morier had acquired enormous influence during his long diplomatic tenure; he was, White flatly asserted, "a power." The Bering Sea controversy, then, was not decided by argument "but simply by the weight of social and other influence." By not providing diplomats with sufficient capital to compete with the British, the United States had lost an enormous sum of money at the Paris deliberations.[25]

As he had done when he was minister to Germany, White reduced international conflict to questions of personal influence. The Russians, he implied, would have stood with the United States if Morier had not enticed them with the glittering promise of his favor. The minister refused to consider the possibility that Russia had decided that Britain was a more worthwhile ally. Justice, he was certain, was on the side of the United States. National interest and justice did not conflict, White seemed to say; Morier's blandishments had simply blinded the Russians to both.

Although he had once expected a favorable decision from the tribunal, White ultimately denounced America's decision to seek arbitration as an "absurd mistake." Arbitration, the minister told Foster, should not be resorted to in a clear matter of right. As proof of his proposition, White

23. John W. Foster, *Diplomatic Memoirs* (Boston and New York, 1909), vol. 2, pp. 46–50; ADW to Walter Q. Gresham, March 21, 1893, and ADW to Foster, June 23, 1893, DMR; Edward H. Zabriskie, *American–Russian Rivalry in the Far East, 1895–1914* (Philadelphia, 1946), pp. 25–26.
24. Foster, *Diplomatic Memoirs*, vol. 2, p. 48; *Autobiography*, vol. 2, p. 17.
25. *Autobiography*, vol. 2, pp. 18–20; ADW to Gresham, August 4, 1893, DMR.

pointed to the disastrous decision: "here we are, with the great industry rooted out, and we expected to pay a large indemnity to those who did it, and who intend to keep on doing it if any new seals ever appear to make it worth their while." [26]

While White remonstrated with Russian officials on the Bering Sea matter, he joined efforts to ease the persecution of Jews. He had defended the rights of American Jews for years;[27] now he hoped to ameliorate conditions in Russia without antagonizing the government. Before his departure in 1892, prominent Jews had urged the minister to protest the tsar's treatment of their people. Jacob Schiff, Myer Isaacs, and others informed White that they had urged Harrison to appoint him; the minister, they implied, could now repay a political debt. Businessman-diplomat Oscar Straus was far more explicit. Straus charged that Charles Emory Smith, White's predecessor, had ignored the shameful treatment of Jews because he wanted to court the official classes in Russia. Legation secretary George Wurts, moreover, was an ardent anti-Semite, and Straus begged White to dismiss him.[28] Straus hoped that White would call attention to the plight of Jews in Russia:

The inquisition is still abroad. The persecution of the Jews in Russia equals in many respects the barbarity of the fifteenth century. . . . The extermination by the sword is humane compared to crowding and overcrowding to an appalling extent—the entire Jewish population consisting of some five to six million souls within the circumscribed limits known as the Jewish Pale, which is nothing more or less than a wholesale ghetto.

Straus asked White to bring his plan to alleviate such conditions to the tsar's attention. Straus wanted Turkey to set aside a section of the empire (not necessarily Palestine) and invite the exiles to settle there. The quid pro quo for this action was the agreement of wealthy American Jews to supply Turkey with the £32 million she owed Russia. White might be able to help by persuading the tsar of the obvious advantages of the Turkish offer.[29]

While Straus searched for a permanent solution to the Jewish question, he informed White of a campaign to assimilate Jewish immigrants to the United States. Alarmed at the enormous number of ignorant indigents descending upon America's shores, the minister was wary of suggestions

26. ADW to Goldwin Smith, December 18, 1895, WMC.
27. J.W. Henschberg to ADW, October 13, 1884; Pauline Sternberger to ADW, November 7, 1884; Cyrus Adler to ADW, December 11, 1896, all in WMC.
28. The Trustees of the Baron de Hirsch Fund to ADW, August 2, 1892, WMC; Straus to ADW, August 4, 1892, Oscar Straus MSS, Library of Congress; Diary, September 1, 1892, WMC.
29. Straus to ADW, March 12, 1891, WMC.

that he persuade the tsar to facilitate increased Jewish emigration. To help lay such fears to rest, Straus outlined plans to establish trade schools for Russian immigrants. Straus hoped to provide immigrants with desirable trades and eventually to relocate them throughout the United States. White enthusiastically endorsed the plan. If immigrants practiced useful trades, he would surely be more receptive to mass emigration to America.[30]

Although he had been well briefed on the problem, a solution to the persecution of Russian Jews eluded the minister. White's predecessors had agreed that interference by the United States would probably lead to increased harassment of Russian Jews, over whom the American government could claim no protective authority. White avoided formal protests and pursued his usual policy of friendly intercession with Russian officialdom.[31]

By 1893 the minister had become appalled at the treatment of Russian Jews. Still hesitant to confront the tsar, he drained his passion in dispatches to the State Department. Half of the world's five million Jews resided in Russia; yet despite their sobriety, self-denial, and foresight, the vast majority lived on the edge of starvation. Jews were barred from holding property in land, taking a mortgage on land, or farming land. As a rule they were debarred from discharging any public functions. The minister did not wonder that Jews avoided military service: army officials treated them brutally while providing no opportunities for promotion. Finally, the government severely limited educational opportunities for Jews. Even in regions where they were most numerous, laws limited the Jewish population in high schools to 10 percent (in Moscow and St. Petersburg only 3 percent). In essence, only Talmudic schools educated Jews.[32]

Despite White's sympathy, he had no specific recommendations about how to ameliorate conditions, nor was he certain that Washington should encourage emigration to the United States. The minister presented prominent Jews, such as Rabbi Joseph Krauskopf of Philadelphia, to Russian officials but did little to help keep alive the rabbi's suggestion that the government transfer Russian Jews from congested districts with relocation funds provided by Americans. White feared to go beyond personal expressions of concern; he was not willing to risk rupturing Russo–American relations on the Jewish issue. In fact, he questioned the motives of Ameri-

30. Straus to ADW, April 14, 1891, WMC.
31. Abstract of Matters at U.S. Legation, WMC; *Autobiography,* vol. 2, pp. 52–53.
32. ADW to Gresham, July 6, 1893, DMR.

can Jews by reporting to the secretary of state that the London-based Jewish Colonization Society paid for the emigration of skilled Jews to Argentina while encouraging untrained misfits to settle in the United States. Upon his return to the United States, White clarified his attitude toward immigration: the intelligent, self-supporting yeomanry was content to remain in Russia, while poor, illiterate, unskilled Polish Jews ("the so-called persecuted Jews") sought escape to the United States. White was not prepared to say that such immigration should be stopped but insisted on strict regulation.[33]

White's analysis of Russian Jewry received an enthusiastic reception in the United States, an indication of the desperation of Jews in search of friends among prominent policy makers. American Jews praised White's diplomatic dispatches, which were rendered in a manner "so concise and lucid, and in a spirit so entirely dispassionate, that [they] may be properly cited . . . as a statement whose authority is entirely beyond question." In 1895 his lengthiest dispatch was printed in Simon Wolfe's *The American Jew as Patriot, Soldier and Citizen.* Prominent Jews took pains to assure White that rumors that the most able Russian emigrants were sent to Argentina were false. White had not succeeded in alleviating the condition of Russian Jews and had rendered a harsh assessment of their plight on his return to the United States. Yet American Jews, just beginning to win sympathy in America, were encouraged to cultivate his friendship.[34]

While White dexterously maintained amicable relations with Jews and the Russian government, he carefully disavowed responsibility for a controversial extradition treaty between the United States and Russia. The agreement bound American authorities to return persons who had sought refuge in the United States after being convicted or accused of attempts on the life of the tsar or other members of the royal family. The Society of American Friends of American Freedom—formed by such notable reformers as Julia Ward Howe, Edwin Mead, and Francis Garrison—protested the agreement and petitioned White first to prevent its adoption, then to promote its repeal. "The Russian who strikes at the Czar," the society bellicosely intoned, "commits a crime against a person in behalf of a people. . . . This treaty is not a treaty with a people but with a class."

33. *Autobiography*, vol. 2, pp. 33–34; newspaper clipping, June 1895(?), and Straus to ADW, March 16, 1894, WMC; ADW to Gresham, February 17, 1894, DMR.

34. Straus to ADW, March 20, 1894; Lewis Abraham to ADW, October 12, 1895; Joseph Krauskopf to ADW, November 14, 1906, all in WMC. The increasing sympathy of American citizens toward Jews is detailed in Walter LaFeber, *The New Empire* (Ithaca, 1963), pp. 319–20.

Noting that the jury system was virtually unknown in Russia and that the United States had not even afforded Great Britain such extensive extradition concessions, the petitioners requested the minister's help.[35]

Clearly uncomfortable with the revolutionary rhetoric of the Friends of American Freedom, White noted that the extradition treaty had been negotiated in Washington. In fact, the minister's "only part in it" had been to introduce provisions rendering "the extradition of political offenders less easy." This time, however, White's attempt to assuage American critics while avoiding conflict with the Russian government proved more difficult. In the summer of 1894, the American press attributed his resignation as minister to the tsar's unhappiness at White's opposition to the treaty. The minister had reportedly spoken at university meetings called to denounce the agreement; rumors that he had labeled extradition "a deplorable mistake" spread in the American press. Fearing that a demand for his removal would arouse public opinion and endanger the treaty, the *Syracuse Standard* reported, the Russians had socially isolated the minister, thus forcing his resignation.[36]

White refuted the newspaper reports as "utterly without foundation." He had been treated graciously by Russian officials and had never made a speech at a university gathering in Russia. He did not want to return to America under "some official cloud" but ultimately decided that protest would merely keep the controversy alive. Discretion, he decided once again, was the better part of duty.[37]

Although White's perception of his role as a diplomat precluded public protest against conditions in Russia, his experiences with the tsarist government reinforced his conviction of its depravity. If progress seemed assured in America, it seemed impossible in Russia, where those who escaped starvation were likely to be felled by cholera. Ignorant, superstitious, self-indulgent peasants preferred oriental fatalism to sanitary pre-

35. Convention between the United States and Russia: Extradition of Criminals Proclaimed, June 5, 1893, WMC; Straus to ADW, March 17, 1893, WMC; Society of American Friends of American Freedom circular, February 23, 1893, WMC. Actually the jury system was used in Russia after 1864 in all but political cases.

36. ADW to Holls, June 7, 1893, WMC; *Syracuse Standard*, August 5, 1894. White was probably not strenuously opposed to the extradition treaty. In his autobiography he noted that many who posed as Russian martyrs comfortably carried on the business of counterfeiting banknotes in New York (*Autobiography*, vol. 2, p. 105).

37. ADW to Fred White, August 24, 1894, WMC. Discretion was, in fact, a dire necessity for White and for the State Department, which attempted to keep him informed of diplomatic developments affecting his mission. The minister's mail was often delivered to Sergei Witte because of the similarity of names in Russian. This mixup, which speaks volumes about the primitive nature of the American diplomatic corps, was a constant irritant to White. See, e.g., ADW to Foster, December 22, 1892, DMR.

cautions. Stagnation at the bottom, moreover, was matched by increasing reaction at the top. The minister thought that Alexander III was an honest man who had been turned permanently from reform by the assassination of his father. The heir apparent, Nicholas II, was even worse. Totally indifferent to his people, he refused even to admit that famine existed in his country. White saw no escape for the Russians; burdened with hopelessly ignorant masses and reactionary autocracy, Russia seemed destined to remain a backward oriental despotism.[38]

Curiously, the minister's pessimistic view of Russia precluded criticism of even the most reactionary politicians. Konstantin Pobedonostsev, Alexander III's minister most responsible for the persecution of Jews, Catholics, and Protestants, was undeniably a religious fanatic and an opponent of virtually every proposal for social, political, and economic reform. Yet White refused to blame him for Russia's backwardness. Swayed by Pobedonostsev's love of art and his "gentle smile," White did not deny that the Russian was responsible for persecution but insisted that his life furnished "a most interesting study in churchmanship, in statesmanship, and in human nature, and shows how some of the men most severely condemned by modern historians—great persecutors, inquisitors and the like—may have based their action on theories the world has little understood and may have had as little innate ferocity as their more tolerant neighbors."[39] In Russia, progress was impossible; Pobedonostsev was merely a manifestation of historical forces that could not be overcome. In a deterministic world, White found increasing difficulty allocating credit or blame: "The fact is that the longer I live the more I see that we are all miserable sinners and that those who do their best are after all but men of their time or a little beyond it and are not to be judged as harshly as I once judged them."[40]

If the stagnant Russian atmosphere warped White's acuity in judging individuals, it momentarily eroded his faith in steady progress for America. Economic unrest stemming from the depression of 1893 seemed to threaten American civilization. "I am not inclined to pessimism," the

38. ADW to Secretary of State, July 21, 1894, DMR; *Autobiography*, vol. 2, pp. 9–10, 27, 28, 102, 111. Curiously, White did not have much contact with liberal constitutionalists and historians, who might have given him more cause for optimism. Max Laserson, in *The American Impact on Russia, 1784–1917* (New York, 1950), pp. 296–301, posits that White lacked contact with these men because he did not regard such contact as part of his duties as minister. Given White's general temperament and his experience in Germany, this is probably not the case, but I can offer no alternative explanation.

39. "Constantine Pobedonostzeff," unpublished manuscript, Cornell University Archives. Konstantin Pobedonostsev expressed his own views in *Reflections of a Russian Statesman*, trans. Robert C. Long (Ann Arbor, 1965).

40. ADW to Burr, November 16, 1893, WMC.

minister wrote to Fred White, "but I see in this matter something far more serious than appears on the surface—bad as that is." White saw the beginning of class conflict in the United States, which, if unchecked, would result in anarchic destruction of republican institutions. "Having tasted the sweets of power and leisure," laborers would increase their "demands and inroads upon civilization." To avert disaster, capitalists had to adopt cooperative management in their businesses. White had never been so fearful of class war; his anxiety was no doubt heightened by the sight of Russian peasants whose ignorance seemed the only check of violence in Russia. America had no such check. With anarchists, criminals and murderers streaming into America, White was not at all sure that his country could escape Europeanization and life-and-death conflict between haves and have-nots.[41]

Strife at home, cholera in Russia, and general restlessness persuaded White to return home in the early fall of 1894. He had, in fact, remained at St. Petersburg longer than he had originally anticipated. Appointed in 1892, he had planned to remain at his post for a year and then relinquish it to the new administration. But when he sent President-elect Cleveland his resignation early in 1893, he was asked to stay on. Hoping to "exert influence on the Jewish question" while at the same time making his tenure longer than his immediate predecessor's (which gave him "a sort of pride"), White agreed. Another year, however, convinced the minister, as it had his secretary of legation,[42] that Russia's policy toward the United States was selfish and false; its breach of faith in the Bering Sea matter and its treatment of Jews branded it as an intractable nation.[43] With a deep sigh of relief, the minister left St. Petersburg on October 1, bringing with him a new daughter, Karin Androvna, born the year before.

Once he returned to the United States, White shed his somber caste with relative ease. The vast mass of intelligent Americans, he realized once again, still stood as a bulwark against anarchy; it was more likely that

41. ADW to Fred White, July 7, September 3, and September 11, 1894, and ADW to Straus, February 20, 1895, WMC. For White's remarks on the dangers of immigration, see "Walks and Talks with Tolstoy," *McClure's Magazine* 16 (April 1901): 509. White was not the only man whose view of progress was tested by Russia. See Christopher Lasch, *American Liberals and the Russian Revolution* (New York, 1962), pp. 1–10.

42. White's secretary of legation, G. Creighton Webb, was an eccentric who probably hastened the minister's departure. Generally known as "Crazy Webb," he constantly left the country without notice, denounced members of the diplomatic corps in public, and lied to his superior. The exasperated White was delighted to leave this "worst lunatic" (ADW to Fred White, June 12, 1894, WMC).

43. ADW to Holls, January 9, 1893, WMC; ADW to Henry T. Allen, December 16, 1893, Allen MSS, Library of Congress; G. Creighton Webb to Gresham, April 19, 1894, DMR.

Europe's monarchies, "save possibly Russia," would give way to democracy than that the American republic would be destroyed. "The transition from Russia to the United States," the diplomat informed Goldwin Smith, while commencing a lecture tour praising evolution over revolution,[44] "is one which of course arouses my patriotism and makes me for the time at least, a decided optimist. After one has been during two years in the thick of the worst political system into which civilized man has ever drifted, all the evils of American political and social life seem trivial and easy to be corrected."[45]

44. George Kennan reminded White that social forces had to be liberated if "natural evolution" was to proceed in Russia: "To what extent does the foot of a Chinese girl-baby evolve when it has to make its growth under the restraint of tight cramping bandages?" The bandages, Kennan asserted, must first be cut away (Kennan to ADW, March 22, 1896, WMC). White did not accept the revolutionary implications of Kennan's remark.

45. ADW to Holls, October 15, 1894; ADW to Evans, January 11, 1895; ADW to Smith, October 4, 1895, all in WMC.

Chapter 12 *The Dilemma of a Christian Rationalist*

In 1896, White published *A History of the Warfare of Science with Theology in Christendom*, a work that had consumed his scholarly passion for twenty years. White's original interest in the subject stemmed from his difficulties, while president of Cornell, with Protestant sectarian critics. At that time he began research on what he hoped would be his magnum opus—a definitive work that would demonstrate the futility of attempts by religious advocates to prohibit scientific inquiry while consolidating truths essential to Christianity. "I wish the clergy to read it," he told Burr, "and if they like to attack it, and no university on my shoulders."[1]

White's work was part of a general nineteenth-century attempt to reevaluate Christianity. Biblical higher criticism, studies in comparative mythology, and scientific investigation had cast doubt on the authenticity of Scripture.[2] In the last half of the century, Charles Darwin's *Origin of Species* became a symbolic rallying point for both defenders and opponents of the new viewpoint. At a conference held at Oxford University concerning the merits of Darwin's controversial thesis, American scientist John Draper listened to Bishop Wilberforce and Thomas Henry Huxley debate the theory of evolution and began to develop his sense of the conflict of science and religion. Draper defined science as the agreement of observations with calculations and pronounced the conflict inevitable: "A divine revelation must necessarily be intolerant of contradiction; it must repudiate all improvement in itself, and view with disdain that arising from the progressive intellectual development of man. But our opinions on every subject are continually liable to modification, from the irresistible advance of human knowledge."[3]

1. ADW to George Lincoln Burr, October 26, 1888, WMC.
2. See, e.g., Jerry Brown, *The Rise of Biblical Criticism in America, 1800–1870* (Middletown, Conn., 1969).
3. John William Draper, *History of the Conflict Between Religion and Science* (New York, 1874), p. vi.

Draper's *History of the Conflict between Religion and Science* insisted that the Bible was not divinely inspired; that mathematical law, not divine intervention, governed the universe; that belief in revelation was a product of minds weakened by prolonged fasting and mental anxiety. Draper made little effort to defend religion because he believed the Bible had been diverted from its true office—a guide to purity of life—and made the final arbiter of human knowledge.

By making science synonymous with a willingness to experiment in the face of authority, he had little difficulty in documenting the conflict. Reconciliation between science and Catholicism was impossible for Draper; his attitude toward Protestantism was much more ambivalent. If Protestantism adhered to Luther's maxim concerning the right of private interpretation of the Bible, then the conflict might be resolved. The scientist, however, had misunderstood the theologian; Luther thought that all individual examination of the Bible would lead to unanimity of agreement on church doctrine. He insisted on the infallibility of Scripture. Draper acknowledged the traditional hostility of both Catholicism and orthodox Protestantism to free inquiry. They would tolerate no science except that which they considered to be agreeable to the Scriptures.[4]

John Draper believed that his work was only the forerunner of a body of literature that would be called forth by the events of the times. He was proven correct, for publishing houses, once reluctant to print works deviating from religious orthodoxy, began to publish the latest of Huxley and John Fiske. The buying public, many of whom bowed before both the idol of progress and the image of Christ, probably preferred some sort of resolution to the conflict. Thus many authors proclaimed with Draper, virtually in an aside, that natural selection was actually the intent of the Lord. Several questions, however, remained unanswered in these works. Was the conflict between science and religion irreconcilable? What role could religion have in a world where truth was subject to continual modification? Finally, was the role of Protestantism significantly different from that of Catholicism?

White's ponderously titled two volumes addressed themselves to these questions.[5] Yet this work (which in the opinion of one historian probably did as much as any other in the United States "toward routing orthodoxy in the name of science") has been virtually ignored by historians of religion

---

4. Ibid., pp. 62, 217, 362; Donald Fleming, *John William Draper and the Religion of Science* (Philadelphia, 1950), pp. 122–35.

5. White insisted on this title rather than "Battlefields of Science," the title of numerous lectures he had given, which he believed would lead potential readers to think that it "had something to do with Krupp guns, or armor plates, or Whitehead torpedoes" (ADW to Burr, June 25, 1896, WMC).

in the Gilded Age.[6] An evaluation of the work and a survey of the criticisms made of it provide an excellent gauge of the spectrum of attitudes toward religion in this period of significant transformation.[7]

White's aim was not to defeat religion in the name of science. He was troubled by the decline of religion in the nineteenth century because he believed that religion satisfied people's inner needs while serving as a vital force for social order. While minister to Germany in 1881, White had noted that orthodox intransigence drove people from the churches. While science filtered down to the masses, the dominant party in the Lutheran church refused to recognize the discovery of new truths; Berlin churches, which could accommodate only 2 percent of the population, were unfilled. White's fear was "that the new generation finding Myth and Legend insisted upon as essential may throw the whole thing overboard together."[8] In his preface, White laid his aim before the reader, citing the danger that the flood of increased knowledge would sweep before it "not only outworn creeds and noxious dogmas, but cherished principles and ideals [and wrench out] . . . most precious religious and moral foundations of the whole social and political fabric." White wrote his *History of the Warfare of Science with Theology* "to aid—even if it be but a little—in the gradual and healthful dissolving away of this mass of unreason, that the stream of 'religion pure and undefiled' may flow on broad and clear, a blessing to humanity."[9]

White's aim, then, was clear. He hoped to affirm a rational, nonmythical religion and at the same time to preserve those religious truths (primarily ethical maxims such as love of God and neighbor) which he regarded as absolutes. Yet he also accepted unquestioningly the results of recent scientific investigation which threatened to destroy religion as a moral bulwark. Could the weapons of the enemies of religion be used to preserve it?

White began his attempt by asserting that there was no necessary conflict between science and religion. Thus his insistence on the word "warfare" rather than "conflict" in the title. The warfare had been need-

<del>6. Paul Carter, *The Spiritual Crisis of the Gilded Age* (De Kalb, Ill. 1971), p. 41. Except for this brief reference, Carter does not deal with White. Edward White (*Science and Religion in American Thought* [Stanford, Calif., 1952]) is the only historian I have found who treats White's work in more than a paragraph, yet his discussion is rather brief and not at all satisfactory.

7. Chapters of the book were serialized in *Popular Science Monthly* in the 1880s and 1890s.

8. ADW to Burr, April 5, 1889, WMC; *A History of the Warfare of Science with Theology in Christendom* (New York and London, 1896), vol. 1, p. 239.

9. Ibid., p. vi.</del>

lessly waged by narrow-minded theologians who insisted on linking hardened dogmas to scriptural texts. Through hundreds of pages, White chronicled the opposition of theologians to scientific inquiry. Echoing Draper, White noted that in two recent years more than 100,000 children had died in Great Britain and the United States of scarlet fever. Had Roger Bacon not been hindered, the means to save most of those victims would probably be at hand, as would cures for typhoid, typhus, cholera, and other diseases. "Put together all the efforts of all the atheists who have ever lived," the author concluded, "and they have not done so much harm to Christianity and the world as has been done by the narrow-minded, conscientious men who persecuted Roger Bacon, and closed the path which he gave his life to open."[10]

White sought to provide his readers with a clear distinction between theology and science. The essential difference was methodological. Johannes Kepler's work on comets, for example, was hailed by the scientific community, but not regarded as definitive. Eventually, astronomers modified Kepler by demonstrating that comets do not move in straight lines. The theological method was quite different: "As a rule, where there arises a thinker as great in theology as Kepler in science, the whole mass of his conclusions ripens into a dogma. His disciples labor not to test it, but to establish it; and while, in the Catholic Church, it becomes a dogma to be believed or disbelieved under the penalty of damnation, it becomes in the Protestant Church the basis for one more sect."[11] White championed unlimited free inquiry; it was as crucial to the ultimate survival of religion as it was to progress in science.

If the distinction between the methods of science and those of theology seemed clear at the outset, difficulties soon became apparent. The treatment of St. Augustine illustrates a recurring problem. Augustine did not use observation as a means of determining truth, and White castigated him for insisting that nothing could be accepted except on the authority of Scripture. Imagine, then, the confusion of the reader when White praised Augustine as an adherent of evolution because he accepted the development of very small animals from putrefying matter. Which side was Augustine on? White recognized that the great theologian's arguments emerged from scriptual exigency rather than the scientific method. Augustine had to explain how all the animals existing in the world·could have found room on Noah's modest ark. On this issue, he was on the "right side"

10. Ibid., p. 390.
11. Ibid., p. 203.

only by coincidence. White's critics would have much to say about the difficulties of separating theologians from scientists.[12]

In the hope that he had disposed of problems of definition, White began his lengthy narrative of the evolution of scientific knowledge. The pattern was always the same. The "correct" scientific approach had usually been taken by the ancient Greeks. As Christianity became more powerful, it suppressed Greek findings, substituting for them the reigning theological dogma. No one conversant with history could deny that "of all organizations in human history the Church of Rome has caused the greatest spilling of innocent blood," and scientists were not spared from torture and death.[13] Fortunately, scientists were not deterred; they continued to investigate and theorize. Theology attempted to reach a compromise with science only as its power began to wane. By this time, however, the steady march of progress could not be halted. Through twenty chapters, in such diverse areas as medicine, higher criticism, and political economy, White traced the process. In each instance, he added a vital postscript—a flat assertion that religion had benefited by the recent triumph of science.

Conscious of the previous emphasis on the Roman Catholic church as *the* enemy of science, the former Cornell president used an overwhelming number of examples of Protestant intolerance. Although he did not spare Catholics, White documented Protestant atrocities through dramatic narrative of witchcraft delusion, belief in comets as a divine signal, and opposition to vaccination: "Nothing is more unjust than to cast especial blame for all this resistance to science upon the Roman church. The Protestant church, though rarely able to be so severe, has been *more* blameworthy."[14]

The Warfare of Science repeatedly emphasized that theologians must see that their opposition to science was a serious error. Science, as White defined it, was a buttress for true religion. Religion itself was constantly evolving, always progressing. The Bible was a body of literature full of myth, legend, parable, and poem, borrowed in most instances from pagan cultures. If the essence of religion depended on the literal truth of each scriptural myth, it could not survive the endless battle that continually resulted in the survival of the fittest. One of the most dangerous myths, contrary to the teachings of science, was that of the "fall of man." White

    12. Ibid., pp. 53, 210, 212; White, "Meterology II," *Popular Science Monthly* 31 (July 1887): 374. White refused to call those on the "right side" theologians ("Comparative Mythology II," *Popular Science Monthly* 36 [March 1890], p. 600).
    13. *History of the Warfare of Science with Theology*, vol. 2, p. 31.
    14. White, "The Retreat of Theology in the Galileo Case," *Popular Science Monthly* 41 (June 1892): 153. For White's documentation of current Protestant intransigence, see ADW to Bishop McTyeire, July 15, 1878, WMC.

substituted proofs that "the tendency of man has been from his earliest epoch, and in all parts of the world, as a rule, upward." What easier task could there be than to demonstrate the increasing sophistication of implements from stone to bronze to iron to steel, or the tremendous advances in medicine and sanitation and food production? Why, then, White wondered, did religion cling to the notion of the fall of man?[15]

Critics, as we shall see, would make much of these conclusions. Was the Bible, full as it was of "the naive guesses of the world's childhood, the opening conceptions of its youth, the more fully rounded beliefs of its maturity," any longer functional? White's own answer seemed to imply that perhaps no more could be expected from religion. He admitted that not one of the books of Scripture any longer conformed to the measure of what mankind had at present reached in scientific truth. In his autobiography, published in 1905, he claimed that those myths and legends had delayed the scientific investigation of natural laws. The "revelation" of the Bible, White insisted—and his use of the word in this very limited sense infuriated many of his orthodox readers—was of the "steady striving of our race after higher conceptions, beliefs and aspirations, both in morals and religion."[16]

White's ideal religion would be free from all dogma and coercion. He claimed allegiance to the sort of church Lincoln said he would have been glad to join—a church composed of all those who loved Jesus Christ.[17] White did not take communion and participated only in those parts of the church service that represented his concept of religion. White accepted Matthew Arnold's definition of religion: "a Power in the universe, not ourselves, which makes for righteousness." The religious man was one who practiced love of his God and neighbors.

Given this view of religion, White had difficulty seeing how science constituted a threat. He had written this book, he told Burr, in the hope of giving "a fair judicial yet hardy presentation of the *truth—the truth as it is in Jesus* one might very justly say. I think the world needs it, to take the place of such gush as Newman's on one side and such scoffing as Ingersoll's on the other."[18] After all, White had devoted his long career as educator and public servant to ensuring the unfettered search for truth. As president of Cornell, White had spoken tirelessly against the tendency of sectarian colleges to insist that they had a monopoly on truth. Such an attitude could

15. *History of the Warfare of Science with Theology*, vol. 1, p. 208.
16. Ibid., vol. 1, p. 23; *Autobiography*, vol. 2, p. 433.
17. ADW to Charles Fitch, November 15, 1905, WMC; "The American Chapel at Berlin," *Outlook* 69 (December 28, 1901): 1076–78.
18. ADW to Burr, August 26, 1885, WMC.

only stay the hand of progress, and progress was the norm of the universe, the will of God. White pronounced himself in favor of all truth seeking: "God's truths must agree, whether discovered by looking within upon the soul, or without upon the world. A truth written upon the human heart to-day, in a full play of emotions or passions, cannot be at any real variance even with a truth written upon a fossil whose poor life ebbed forth millions of years ago."[19] So long at war, science and religion could enjoy a peace of mutual profit.

White's message received a wide hearing in late nineteenth-century America. While president of Cornell, he continued to teach several courses in history, and his lectures were filled with material that would be used in *The Warfare of Science*. In addition, as an educator and political figure, he was called upon to lecture throughout the country; one of his most popular and frequently presented lectures was "The Battlefield of Science." As White wrote and revised the chapters of his book, they were serialized in more than a score of articles in *Popular Science Monthly*.[20] Thus, even before the publication of the book, thousands were exposed to his views.

It is difficult to estimate the precise number of those who read *A History of the Warfare of Science with Theology in Christendom*. The first printing consisted of 3,750 copies, but numerous printings followed; and twenty-five years after the initial publication, the Cornell University library—to which White had donated the proceeds of his book—was still collecting royalties. In addition to the regular edition, White acquiesced in Appleton's proposal for a cheap edition. Finally, the book was translated into German, French, Italian, and Swedish.[21] Although hardly a best-seller, *The Warfare of Science* received wide circulation for a work of its cost, size, and scholarly content.

Another index of the impact of the book on American society may be seen in the extent, nature, and vehemence of the critical response to it. The Gilded Age has often been described as an age of innocence and optimism. But as the attack on orthodox religion mounted, many were forced to reorient themselves on a newly drawn spectrum of possible belief, to rededicate themselves on the shrine of orthodoxy, or to drift without

19. Quoted in Jurgen Herbst, *The German Historical School in American Scholarship* (Ithaca, 1965), p. 74.

20. White checked bookstalls to ensure a healthy circulation for the journal (ADW to Burr, February 28, 1896, WMC).

21. Burr to ADW, August 16, 1897; ADW to D. Appleton and Co., July 10, 1896; ADW to George W. Smalley, November 10, 1910, all in WMC; at White's death in 1918, royalties for *A History of the Warfare of Science with Theology* were $10,007.66 (Burr to E. L. Williams, January 30, 1919, Burr MSS, Cornell University.)

allegiance. If innocence in religion was not quite at an end, the endless stream of literature by Darwinists and neo-Darwinists began to administer its last rites.

Perhaps the most predictable response to *The Warfare of Science* came from Catholics and fundamentalist Protestants who defended a literal interpretation of the Bible. In a review printed in the *Chicago Tribune*, Elizabeth Reed pointed out that "the fall of man" was not a biblical expression; thus White's thirty-eight pages that "proved" the concept invalid were of limited use. At the same time, however, Reed vigorously defended the concept of original sin. "If it be true that Adam was not guilty," she asked with mock humility, "will Dr. White please furnish the name of the first transgressor?" Reed had little faith in White's use of comparative mythology as a means of proving that the Bible was not divinely inspired. The borrowing, in fact, had been from and not by the Hebrews and Christians. On and on she went, combing the text for errors of fact and scornfully concluding: "It is a matter of profound astonishment . . . that any man who claims to be a scholar is willing to take positions which careful students of history and literature know to be absolutely foreign to correct scientific conclusions." [22]

Although White had occasionally overrated and overstated his findings,[23] *The Warfare of Science* was well researched. White welcomed criticism based on the accuracy of his findings; if opponents met him upon his own ground, he was certain that victory was assured. When they did, he composed zestful replies that further demolished any attempts to read the Bible literally. "Am catching it heavily from the theologians," he wrote Edward Payson Evans with obvious relish. "You ought to see *The Churchman*'s last attack! O My!" [24] Armed with a century of biblical criticism, comparative mythology, Darwin, and other authorities, he was confident that small errors in his book would pale before the gaping errors and inconsistencies of biblical mythology.

White responded vigorously, carefully, and fully to his fundamentalist critics and was probably guilty of literary overkill. Burr suggested that his efforts were probably unnecessary. "Why bruise one's fist demolishing ruins? Let them crumble. What if the ivy *does* love and cling to them?" [25]

22. *Chicago Tribune*, July 6, 1897, p. 6. For a similar viewpoint by a Catholic scholar, see M. W. Holland to ADW, November 21, 1891, WMC.
23. See, e.g., George Philes to ADW, October 31, 1881; Burr to ADW, April 1, 1899, and June 24, 1904, all in WMC.
24. ADW to Evans, April 14, 1891, WMC.
25. Burr to ADW, September 16, 1901, WMC.

Unfortunately, not all critics were mossbacks, and White's sardonic humor and zest for battle were far less in evidence against his more formidable opponents.

In a lengthy article for the influential *North American Review*, the Reverend Walton Battershall attempted to assess the importance of *The Warfare of Science*. Granting that White's care for truth and reverence for religion were conspicuous throughout the two volumes, Battershall proceeded to analyze the definitional difficulties of the work. By conceiving theology as whatever a man or a group of men happened to think about religion, White permitted it to become embroiled with science. Under White's loose heading, he noted, marched those who were not bishops or believers in the Bible. To further complicate matters, many theologians appeared in White's book as champions of science. The list of those who associated themselves with the theory of evolution was impressive— St. Basil the Great, St. Gregory of Nyssa, St. Augustine, St. Isidore of Seville, Peter Lombard, St. Thomas Aquinas, Ralph Cudworth. Conversely, White's volumes confirmed the large pinch of truth in Huxley's observation that "extinguished scientists lie about the cradle of every science as the strangled snakes beside that of Hercules." Battershall thereby pronounced the contradistinction between religion and theology as invalid. Religion, he observed, must be defined as the science of God. As such it is outside the province of those who examine the universe. In any event, Protestantism emerged above the battle; without hierarchy or official doctrine, it had no pope to raise his hand to stay the growth of science. Thus Battershall, despite faint words of praise, seemed to conclude that the author had effected no reconcilliation.[26]

Secular critics pushed these arguments somewhat further. David Starr Jordan praised the book as "one of the great works of the century" but seemed unable to pinpoint the source of its greatness. A careful student of science and religion,[27] Jordan sensed (with Battershall) that White's list of protagonists and antagonists was inadequate. The real foe of scientific progress was, in fact, man's innate conservatism. The struggle was one of "realities against tradition and suggestion. The progress of civilization would still have been just such a struggle, had religion or theology or churches or worship never existed." Intolerance, Jordan repeated in a refrain that would become familiar to White,[28] was not confined to

26. Walton Battershall, review of *History of the Warfare of Science with Theology*, *North American Review* 165 (July 1897): 87–98.
27. See, e.g., Edward White, *Science and Religion in American Thought*, pp. 57–89.
28. See, e.g., the review by White's hand-picked successor as president of Cornell in *Forum* 22 (September 1896): 67–78. W.H. Shipman, pastor of a Methodist Episcopal church, reminded White of Tyndall's assessment of Newton's theory of light: "For a century it stood like a dam across the course of discovery" (Shipman to ADW, March 1, 1898, WMC).

religious organizations: "The same spirit that burned Servetus and Giordano Bruno, led the atheist 'liberal' mob of Paris to send to the scaffold the great chemist Lavoisier with the sneer that the public has no need of savants." Jordan implied that White had constructed an elaborate monument to the obvious. If the conflict was between tradition and new truth, then White's flailing of theologians was futile criticism of an inherent human quality; his defense of religion in this context was similarly pointless. Without saying so, Jordan reduced *The Warfare of Science* to a chorus cheering for battles already won, a chorus that chose the sides of righteousness and reaction only with the lens of hindsight.[29]

Others, however, viewed White's work as more than a wrestling match with a paper tiger. White constantly asserted that his aim was to remove those elements not essential to Christianity. He never clearly indicated what constituted that truth but hinted that it was to be found in the Sermon on the Mount and the Lord's Prayer. In a review of *The Warfare of Science*, Jacob Gould Schurman, philosopher and president of Cornell University, outlined the contemporary attitude toward truth. Knowledge, Schurman intoned, is a continuous becoming; it is never attained; it is always on the way: "Consequently the most assured dogmas of today may need modification and adaptation to the larger vision and deeper insights of tomorrow."[30] The road to relativism was strewn with tortured consciences among many men of White's generation in whom the doctrine of the absolute was not so easily excised. In most spheres, evolution was easy to accept, but one could only with difficulty conclude that it also removed ethical guidelines. Logic compelled one to view the ethics of Scripture as equivalent in value to the remainder of it, but White's desire to save religion ironically transcended logic. Reared in an age that embraced absolute laws, he could not quite accept the consequences of his own philosophy.

Contemporaries were by no means slow in identifying White's dilemma. Albert Britt, managing editor of *Public Opinion*, wondered about the social effect of substituting an unnamed First Cause for a personal God: "Are the masses of men yet sufficiently developed to determine and follow out a course of right conduct without the impelling power of a belief in, or a fear of, a personal God who rewards and punishes?" One John Shackelford wrote that White had destroyed all connections between religion and ethics for both masses and elites. If the fall of man and the atonement were cast aside, "Christ's religion goes by the boards. A religion without the

29. David Starr Jordan, review of *History of the Warfare of Science with Theology*, *Dial* 21 (September 16, 1896): 146–48.

30. Jacob Gould Schurman, review of *History of the Warfare of Science with Theology*, *Science* 4 (December 11, 1896): 879–81.

authority of God back of it is a religion without power." Still others wondered how White viewed Christ. "Humble" Baptist minister William Phillips chided White for his use of the phrase "Our Lord Jesus Christ," given his claim that Christ was not miraculously conceived, that he did not rise from the dead. "Would it not be better to say the great Nazarene, or, the Christian teacher of the world?"[31]

There is no record of White's response to this criticism, but his attitude may be discerned from his reaction to a series of letters from octogenarian Mary Eaton, who described herself as an old family friend. Eaton began with a restatement of White's aim: "If I am not mistaken the object is to prove the Christian religion a cunningly devised fable; the Bible which Christians accept a tissue of falsehoods; its Divine author a myth; his Son, that this same Bible pronounces God manifest in the flesh the greatest imposter the world has ever known; and then you inform us that it is true but in some high and mysterious sense." White, of course, had heard all this before, although perhaps not so bluntly. Mary Eaton finished her first letter with a series of questions that made her friend squirm a bit more. "What if you succeed in creating doubts in the minds of men, in taking from them all trust in the Revelation they have accepted as coming from God[?] What then? . . . What will you give us instead? A religion evolved from *human brains*, stripped of all that is Divine. An image without a soul."

White replied weakly that his aim was to provide a new basis for the Christian religion in order to strengthen it. Eaton responded by noting the hubris of a man who would take such a task upon himself. She reminded him that he had not answered her previous questions. "What, in the name of poor feeble ignorant Christians, I ask, is this new basis? No human theological foundations will be used I am sure." In letter after letter, over a period of two years, she pressed the attack, while White insisted that she misunderstood his motives. The beleagured author could take no more and asked Eaton to terminate the correspondence. He would reply no more, nor would he read her letters.[32]

This rather embarrassing exchange indicates that White had said all that he had to say about religion in *The Warfare of Science*. His vagueness about its essence was a product of confusion and, perhaps unconsciously, of a refusal to accept the unsettling implications of his own thought. If there was no deity who demanded obedience to his laws, then by what standards could human beings guide the conduct of their lives? Could the

31. Britt to ADW, January 9, 1905; Shackelford to ADW, May 23, 1909; Phillips to ADW, November 6, 1895, all in WMC.
32. Eaton to ADW, March 6, April 16, and July 21, 1894, and January 21, 1896; ADW to Eaton, January 30, 1896, all in WMC.

Sermon on the Mount be "true" in a universe whose only law was change? For the faithful, White fell short in his attempt to strengthen religion.

There were some, however, who read *The Warfare of Science* and did not frown. Lyman Abbott's *Outlook* led the way with an ecstatic review. For distinguishing between religion and dogma, Abbot ranked Dr. White's book beside the *History of Doctrine*; it belonged in every theological seminary. "The woeful error of these ages," the review concluded, "has been the merging of the interests of spiritual religion in those of intellectual theology. If *The Warfare of Science* has destroyed the body, it has been for the salvation of the spirit." Like White, Abbot feared that religion would stand against compromise with science and destroy itself; hence, those who proposed retrenchment must be applauded and encouraged.[33]

The volume of enthusiastic responses that arrived each week in the mail from the likes of Alexander Graham Bell and Lord Acton must have further buoyed the author. Andrew Carnegie agreed that the world was rapidly evolving a new and improved religion. "The Kingdom of heaven is within you. This will draw men to look within *and only at this world* and its duties, letting the future alone."[34] Mary Eaton would have wanted to know how one could know the duties of this world without gazing beyond it, but encomiums from Carnegie may have made it easier to forget her strictures.

Yet strangely, much of the praise that White received must have disturbed him deeply because it agreed with his critics about the effect of the book on Christianity. *The Nation* thought the book a significant contribution but asserted that the author's only mistake was in feeling called upon to reconcile religion and science. "It is science which is established now, and if there is to be a reconciliation, it is religious truth which must justify itself." *The Nation*'s reviewer concluded that White had not provided that justification and ridiculed his assertion that the Bible is a revelation of the ascent of man as a metaphor, which tended to confuse rather than enlighten. The remainder of the review was laudatory, but the damage had been done.[35]

That *The Warfare of Science* could be regarded simply as an assault on religion became more and more apparent.[36] Charles Watts, editor of the *Agnostics' Annual*, wrote White that dozens of letters had come to him

---

33. Anonymous review of *History of the Warfare of Science with Theology*, *Outlook* 53 (June 20, 1896): 1153.
34. Carnegie to ADW, May 6, 1896, WMC.
35. Anonymous review of *History of the Warfare of Science with Theology*, *Nation* 62 (May 28, 1896): 421–22.
36. See, e.g., Archibald Hopkins to ADW, March 27, 1897, WMC.

following the publication of *The Warfare of Science* urging him to endeavor to induce the author to write for the *Annual*. The embarrassed White declined, citing heavy pressure of work. Old friend Edward Payson Evans reported that the Truth-Seeker Company's *Catalogue of Free Thought Works* contained his book. The atheistic Evans could not resist a further reminder to White of his proximity to atheists and agnostics. "I hope you appreciate my self-sacrifice in omitting your book in my bibliography at the end of *The Christ Myth*. . . . But I remembered your position, not only as a scholar and a literary author, but as a politician." Designed as a halfway house for science and religion, *The Warfare of Science* was attracting a most unexpected and unwelcomed clientele.[37]

Even the most militant atheist of the age, Robert G. Ingersoll, declared himself pleased with White's work, and one wonders whether the author remembered that he had written the book partly to silence such scoffers as Ingersoll. Ingersoll had read the serialized chapters of the book and sensed a potential convert. He could not understand how anyone could fail to see that the church had been the principal enemy of progress. White's belief in a "Power, not ourselves, that makes for righteousness" was less congenial to Ingersoll, who could not see how people could be free or worthy of freedom until they ceased to imagine that a master exists: "The only power in the universe strong enough to make truth-seeking safe is man. . . . The Christian virtues are the slave virtues; meekness, obedience, credulity and mental non-resistance." Nevertheless, he predicted that the book would have a beneficial effect: "The tendency will be to increase intellectual hospitality—to do away with the provincialism of creed, and the egotism of ignorance."[38]

Much as White had tried to place Scripture in the perspective of evolutionary theory, another of the author's correspondents attempted to perform this task for *The Warfare of Science*. Daniel Folkman asked a number of questions troubling to a Christian seeking to reconcile science and religion. If White's work had been written fifty years later, would there be a chapter entitled "From Anthropomorphism to Atheism?" If the book were written still later, would there be a chapter called "From Religion to Ethics?"[39] In fact, these questions had been put to White even before he began to write his book. Evans believed that religion was neither

37. Fred White to ADW, February 2, 1889; Watts to ADW, March 29, 1897; Evans to ADW, February 22, 1877 and January 4, 1901, all in WMC. Evans recognized that White's political ambitions had been thwarted several times by his religious views.

38. Ingersoll to ADW, December 27, 1888, WMC; ADW to Mrs. George Kennan, March 18, 1896, Kennan MSS, Library of Congress. For White's view of Ingersoll, see Orvin Larson, *American Infidel: Robert G. Ingersoll* (New York, 1962), p. 281.

39. Folkman to ADW, December 31, 1900, WMC.

the product of divine inspiration nor priestly inventions designed to deceive people for the purpose of tyrannizing over them, but rather necessary outgrowths of the human mind. Once he had decided that religion was a mental phenomenon, he was willing to reject Christianity; in fact, such a conclusion seemed to necessitate that course. There was, for Evans, "no lawful and logical stopping place between Catholicism and infidelity. It is undoubting belief or nothing." Nor was there any point in making ethics at all dependent on religion. "To me it sounds just about as silly to hear Unitarian preachers palavering about the All-Father and saying what God likes and what He dislikes, as to hear Trinitarians separating so nicely the attributes and work of the three Persons." In 1877 Evans wrote White a long letter that served as his critique of the soon to be embarked upon project of reconciliation:

You wish to declare that scripture has nothing whatever to do with scientific facts and theories. I cannot agree with this view. Each system of religion begins with a cosmography, out of which it is developed and with which it is vitally bound up. The Christian scheme of redemption is a logical sequence of Adam's fall and if the latter be not an historical fact, the former has no raison d'etre. The dogma of the atonement is the central pillar of Christianity, the pillar whereupon the house standeth and the watchmen of Zion are wise in warning the Samsons to keep their hands off, since its fall would cause the collapse of the whole structure. But you will say you are not defending dogmatic Christianity but are standing up for the living kernal of religion. What constitutes this kernal?[40]

Andrew White refused to accept the validity of this interpretation. In the scores of letters he wrote to Evans in the fifty years of their friendship, he never addressed himself to the disagreement between them. Instead White cloaked himself in the rhetorical armor of progress and optimism. He took Evans and his wife to task for always seeing disaster in the future. Time, the great healer, would reconcile what seemed to be contradictions. Always contemptuous of "that most common and deceptive of all things," belief created by the desire to believe, White nevertheless put his faith in what was to come. The world was moving toward justice, right, and good; of that he was sure. *The Warfare of Science* might perhaps speed it just a little, but the course was irreversibly charted. Certain of his vision, White had little patience with those intent on destroying it by using the standards he himself had set. Could not one say of White's attempted reconciliation, as Evans had said of religion, that it was a necessary outgrowth of the human mind—understandable but not convincing?

Such a searching critique did not occur to White despite the prodding

40. Evans to ADW, March 25, 1874, and February 22, 1877, WMC.

of his friends. A few contemporaries, however, saw through such easy reconciliations. Judge J. B. Stallo, a contributor to *Popular Science Monthly*, had noted as early as 1873 that in a universe of perpetual change there could be no independent absolutes, "no absolute standard either of quantity or quality."[41] White would not accept such a conclusion. His humanitarianism and his concern for an ordered and orderly society compelled him to enshrine the Sermon on the Mount as an unvarying guide to conduct, equally applicable to all. The response to *The Warfare of Science*, to the author's constant chagrin, indicated that this most integral part of White's purpose was little noticed.

Henry Drummond, celebrated evolutionist and theist, eloquently asked another question that seemed to be the logical next step for those who had attempted to reconcile science and religion. "If God is only to be left to the gaps in our knowledge, where shall we be when these gaps are filled up?" Scientific progress, then, would necessitate fewer and fewer repairs by God the watchmaker. Even if those gaps were filled, Drummond continued, "is God to be found only in the disorders of the world?"[42] Andrew White had no answer to this disturbing question.

A History of the Warfare of Science with Theology in Christendom was a sanctification of reason. Like Thomas Henry Huxley, White told his readers that a belief not based on evidence was not only illogical but immoral. Hauled before the bar of reason as it was during the nineteenth century, religion gave way to ethics: the humanitarian ethics of the Andrew Whites of the world. The new ethical system, however, was not based on God's authority, and White (a religious liberal but a social conservative) would have been appalled that in helping to break "the steel chain of ideas," he had helped create an atmosphere congenial to the secularism and relativism he abhorred.[43]

41. Quoted in William Leverette, Jr., "E. L. Youmans' Crusade for Scientific Autonomy and Respectability," *American Quarterly* 1 (Spring 1965): 12–32.

42. Quoted in Carter, *Spiritual Crisis of the Gilded Age*, pp. 16–17.

43. D. H. Meyer has recently argued that Americans successfully met the challenge of nineteenth-century science because few were disposed to spell out its implications. ("American Intellectuals and the Victorian Crisis of Faith," *American Quarterly*, (December 1975). See also Eric Goldman, *Rendezvous with Destiny* (New York, 1952).

Chapter 13

The Venezuela Commission and the Election of 1896

Even before *The Warfare of Science* reached the bookstands, White was once again submerged in diplomatic activity. For many years the State Department had warily monitored a boundary dispute between Venezuela and British Guiana. The British made a series of ever widening claims, ultimately insisting on title to the strategic Orinoco River and the Yuruari region, site of the largest gold nugget (509 ounces) ever found. With each demand, the United States government came to fear that the British action, if successful, would diminish America's commercial influence in South America. As if to underscore this point, Venezuela closed all but one of the entrances to the Orinoco in October 1894; river travel facilitated trade with several countries, and the United States would suffer if Great Britain controlled the waterway.[1]

President Cleveland called for arbitration of the dispute in December 1894, and two months later Congress officially declared its opposition to the British claims in Venezuela. America's economic interests, one congressman insisted, had to be protected: if the British controlled the Orinoco, they would revolutionize "the commerce and political institutions of at least three of the South American Republics."[2] The British land grab, an increasingly jingoist press insisted, presaged an attempt to wrest hegemony in Latin America from the United States.

British activity throughout the 1890s added credence to the charges of the jingoes. In January 1895, Venezuela seized eight members of the British Guiana police force stationed on the bank of the Cuyuni River. Lord Salisbury, British prime minister, demanded reparation of £1,500,

1. I have drawn heavily on Walter LaFeber's *The New Empire* (Ithaca, 1963), pp. 242–83, for this account of the Venezuelan Boundary dispute; see also Ernest May, *Imperial Democracy* (New York, 1961), pp. 33–42.
2. Quoted in LaFeber, *New Empire*, p. 249.

adding thinly veiled threats of direct intervention if the Venezuelans failed to comply.[3]

Secretary of State Walter Q. Gresham drafted a note to Salisbury about the boundary dispute before the prime minister's ultimatum to Venezuela was delivered, but he died on May 28, 1895, before any further action could be taken. Richard Olney, Gresham's replacement, unabashedly asserted that Latin America provided a natural market for U.S. products and sent a vigorous dispatch to Salisbury in July protesting British attempts to move the frontier of Guiana farther and farther west of the line drawn by Robert Schomburgk in 1841. Venezuela, Olney reminded Salisbury, had agreed to arbitrate the dispute, but Great Britain had consistently refused. The secretary broadly interpreted the Monroe Doctrine as giving the United States virtual carte blanche to intervene in disputes "of great import to the safety and welfare of the United States."[4]

Olney's dispatch, which was secretly composed and sent to Salisbury, reached the press at about the same time that the British ultimatum was received by Venezuela. Salisbury's claim that the ultimatum was unconnected with the boundary dispute seemed absurd, especially amid rumors of military preparations in British Guiana. Recognizing the importance of foreign commerce and predicting that political capital could be reaped from the dispute, many politicians expected a vigorous affirmation of the Monroe Doctrine by Grover Cleveland.[5]

Salisbury's reply (received on December 7, 1895) flatly denied that the Monroe Doctrine applied. The United States, the prime minister acidly commented, was not entitled to insist that its interests were concerned simply because one of the disputants was situated in the Western Hemisphere. The British were not ready, moreover, to submit land long under their rule to arbitration. Would Olney agree to settle claims by Mexico to territory "which had long been comprised in the Federation" of the United States? U.S. Ambassador to Britain Thomas Bayard thought Salisbury's note "in good temper and moderate in tone," but Grover Cleveland was "mad clean through."[6]

On December 17, 1895, the president delivered a blunt reply to the British. He affirmed the applicability of the Monroe Doctrine and insisted

3. Ibid., p. 263; Nelson Blake, "Background of Cleveland's Venezuela Policy," *American Historical Review* 47 (January 1942): 259–77.

4. LaFeber, *New Empire*, pp. 257, 259–62.

5. Blake's argument (in "Background of Cleveland's Venezuela Policy") that the pressure of politicians and public opinion forced a reluctant Cleveland to act undervalues the president's deep concern for the Monroe Doctrine and foreign commerce. Cleveland's career demonstrates that he did not often violate his conscience to assuage the public clamor.

6. LaFeber, *New Empire*, pp. 265–67.

on the right of the United States to resist, "as a willful aggression upon its rights and interests," the appropriation of Venezuelan territory. Salisbury's refusal to arbitrate forced Cleveland unilaterally to appoint a commission to determine the boundary between Venezuela and British Guiana. The president hinted that if Britain failed to abide by the findings of the commission, the United States was prepared for war. Generally regarded as provocative, Cleveland's address, by announcing that the United States would not take action until the commission completed its work, actually provided Salisbury with an excellent opportunity for accommodation or strategic retreat.[7]

Soon after his address, Cleveland made five appointments to the Venezuela Boundary Commission: Justice David J. Brewer of the United States Supreme Court, who became chairman of the commission; Richard Alvey, chief justice of the Court of Appeals in the District of Columbia; Frederic Coudert, prominent attorney who had been chief counsel for the United States in the Bering Straits dispute; Daniel Coit Gilman, president of Johns Hopkins University; and Andrew Dickson White.[8] The commissioners were widely known in Europe as gentlemen of high character and thorough scholarship; Cleveland and Olney hoped to force Britain to cooperate fully by ensuring that public opinion would respect the findings of the commission.[9]

White had followed the Venezuelan dispute closely. Although convinced that the British were to blame, he dreaded the prospect of war. Cleveland's "warlike message" had been provoked by the "gross assumptions" of Great Britain, but "war would be such a calamity." The diplomat was not certain that the Monroe Doctrine had been properly invoked: "It is a great extension of the Monroe Doctrine to apply it in this case." White's reservations, however, were expressed in private. On December 27 he formally accepted membership on the commission. Three days later he completed the manuscript of *The Warfare of Science* and began to prepare for what was to be a year's preoccupation with Venezuela.[10]

After assembling in Washington, the commissioners began to recognize the immensity of the task before them. The problem was not so much legal as historical. The disputed territory, lying between the Orinoco and Essequibo rivers, had been claimed centuries before by Spain and the

7. Ibid., pp. 268–70; *Autobiography*, vol. 2, p. 118.
8. *New York World*, January 2, 1896; Roland Bainton, *George Lincoln Burr: His Life* (Ithaca, 1943), pp. 71–72.
9. Such, at least was the opinion of Brewer. See Fabian Franklin, *The Life of Daniel Coit Gilman* (New York, 1910), p. 271.
10. Diary, December 17, 18, 20, and 30, 1895, WMC; ADW to Cleveland, December 27, 1895, WMC.

Netherlands; Venezuela had inherited the Spanish claim, Great Britain that of the Dutch. Recognizing that they would have to study historical documents on two continents, the commissioners hired historians J. Franklin Jameson of Brown University and George Lincoln Burr of Cornell to investigate archives in England and Holland, reports of Roman Catholic missionaries to South America, and even a rare collection of Dutch authorities in Madison, Wisconsin. The commission compiled an atlas showing the historical development of the disputed area and published four volumes of text related to the controversy.[11]

As White plunged into the mass of material unearthed by the commission's investigators, he began to sound like an administration spokesman. In a widely reported speech before the Board of Trade and Transportation in New York, the diplomat admitted that war between the two great English-speaking nations would be calamitous. Yet, to rousing cheers, White concluded that the abandonment of international righteousness or the sacrifice of the just position of the United States constituted an even greater national disaster.[12] He was confident, nevertheless, that war could be avoided by a show of firmness, strength, and respect for international law.

Although White professed close kinship with Great Britain and claimed that there was not "a particle of jingoism" in him, a decided animus toward the English informed his attitude. He detected the same "cool, contemptuous, insulting" swagger in Salisbury's Venezuela notes as that shown by the prime minister in the Bering Sea controversy. Thus he regarded Cleveland's message, "drastic as it was, on the whole right" because it tended to produce the very effect that it was intended to produce, "i.e. as saying, Thus far shalt thou go and no further."[13] White's earlier reservations were now all but forgotten. He agreed with Cleveland and Olney that the hegemony of the United States in Latin America must be preserved.

Eager to bring the controversy to a speedy conclusion, White was ready with tentative conclusions by April 1896. Venezuela's claims, he argued, had been the same for decades; it claimed the territory from the right or south bank of the Orinoco to the left bank of the Essequibo. The English claims, by contrast, although derived from an 1814 treaty with Holland, were more vague and shifting. Nevertheless, White recognized that it was impossible to found any claims by either power in the region upon actual

11. Daniel Coit Gilman, *The Launching of a University* (New York, 1906), pp. 200–201; ADW to Fiske, March 26, 1896, and ADW to Gilman, February 3, 1896, WMC.

12. *New York Times*, January 19, 1896; *New York Press*, January 19, 1896.

13. ADW to E. L. Plumb, August 24, 1896, WMC.

local occupation, treaty stipulations, or conquest. International law, however, favored the Spanish claim inherited by Venezuela, especially as to
control of the strategic rivers: " . . . when any nation holds all the main
territory upon a river system, it has a right to control the principal channel
of that river, which brings that territory into connection with the outer
world, against any title other than one incontestably established by opposing parties." [14] Without ever mentioning the commercial interests of
the United States, White had moved to ensure Venezuela's continued
control of the strategic waterways.

   If historical investigation gave way before international law on control
of rivers, sheer practicality governed White's recommendations on a
boundary line. In 1844 Lord Aberdeen had proposed a boundary that gave
to British Guiana far less territory than Salisbury demanded a half century
later. The commissioner hoped that Salisbury could save face by accepting
a line proposed by a British official; he reminded the Venezuelans that
their objection at the time had been "rather to the manner of the offer . . .
than to the line itself." To potential British objections that the line pushed
them out of lucrative gold fields, he responded that the amount of gold
already taken had yielded a large profit. If there had been any loss at all, it
had been to Venezuela during the period of British occupancy. [15]

   The Aberdeen line, then, seemed to White a near perfect resolution of
the impasse: Britain received much of the disputed land while Venezuela
retained control of the rivers and gold fields. Just as Cleveland and Olney
had shown no interest whatever in consulting Venezuela before framing
their response to Salisbury, White decided that the South American
nation could afford to relinquish its claim to territory if it retained strategic
advantage. The hegemony of the United States in Latin America would be
undisturbed by the agreement; its prestige in the world would be enhanced because it had unilaterally imposed a settlement on the British.

   If White's suggestions were an example of realpolitik, they also seemed,
at least to George Lincoln Burr, to smack of opportunism and sophistry.
However mistaken, Burr argued, the English had as clear a warrant for
putting their extreme claims at the Orinoco as the Venezuelans for putting
theirs at the Essequibo. [16] Burr agreed that the aggressiveness of the
English demands should be referred to, but fairness dictated "that the

   14. Notes on Venezuela, n.d., and Outline, Statement of the General Questions before
the Venezuela Commission, n.d., WMC.
   15. Ibid.
   16. For White's complaints about British ignorance and lack of fair play, see *Autobiography*,
vol. 2, p. 121. For others' complaints about Britain see Henry Cabot Lodge to ADW, March
12, 1896, WMC.

extravagance and obstinacy of the Venezuelan claims should be pointed out at the same time and with equal emphasis."[17]

The boundaries suggested by White, Burr continued, were far too exact "to be either true or tactful." Like most of White's scholarship, the report was more a plea than a verdict. "I do not think you were more than half conscious of this," Burr advised his mentor, "and I fear you will resent the statement." Burr nonetheless forced himself to continue at length:

> But you will perhaps ask—you who are impatient with detail—if the conclusions are the same, what difference can it make as to the exact processes? But that dear Mr. White, if you will permit a younger scholar who loves you to suggest—and I know how gravely my own faults go to the opposite extreme—is, and always has been, the most serious defect of your work as an historian. Through wide study, with almost unerring truth, with all kindliness and freedom from bias, you have reached your own results; and then, eager to share with others, but forgetting the precise steps of your own conviction, you have cast about for arguments, and seeing them now all on one side, have too often cast good, bad and indifferent alike into the hopper.

White's approach was probably successful with people who preferred to see only one answer to a problem, but it stirred the distrust of "thoughtful men." Burr advised White to put himself in the place of the unconvinced, to reconstruct the process of discovery, meeting each difficulty with the fairness with which he met it when his own conclusions were still unformed, "but with the ripe and exact knowledge born of our completed toil."[18]

Burr's critique of White the historian was prescient and indicates that historical investigation was important to White but ultimately subordinate to political realities. White perceived that the historical claims were dubious—a claim later seconded by J. Franklin Jameson. He recognized that his role was to devise a settlement that would be acceptable to both parties without blatantly betraying history or sacrificing the interests of the United States.[19]

The commission never had the opportunity to present its recommendations because the British submitted the dispute to arbitration in November 1896. Salisbury agreed to an arbitration tribunal consisting of two Americans, two British citizens, and a Russian authority in interna-

17. Burr to ADW, April 12 and 17, 1896, WMC.
18. Burr to ADW, April 11, 1896, WMC.
19. Jameson to Venezuela Boundary Commission, June 11, 1896, WMC. Brewer took much the same attitude as that taken by Burr. "It must be borne in mind that we are not arbitrators, nor authorized to divide the territory upon a merely equitable basis, but are rather to determine a *true* divisional line—one that existed before lord Aberdeen was born" (Brewer to ADW, June 17, 1896, WMC; italics mine).

tional law. Venezuela had again not been consulted, nor were any South American countries represented on the tribunal. In any event, the work of the Boundary Commission was over. All that remained was to prepare its papers for presentation to the arbitrators. Successful diplomacy had stolen the laurels from the commissioners. Cleveland's policy, however, had been vindicated. War had been averted, and Salisbury had backed down.[20]

White's work on Cleveland's Venezuela commission did not prevent partisan political activity throughout 1896. The choice in the presidential election was clearer to White than it had even been before. William McKinley of Ohio represented progress through order and stability. The ubiquitous Frederick W. Holls thought that the Ohioan might make White his secretary of state. Holls's campaign to win the post for his friend was "under way and in full swing," and he advised White to write to McKinley. A McKinley victory would not only benefit the nation, it might win for White the post he had long coveted.[21]

Considerations of personal reward, however, were certainly not the crucial determinant of White's support of McKinley. White could not abide the Democratic party, its platform, ("socialistic and anarchistic"), or its candidate, William Jennings Bryan. He described the Democratic convention: "There was Altgeld, the anarchist backed by his bomb throwers; there was Tillman with his pitchfork, backed by battalions of wild schemers and dreamers and declaimers; and in the midst of them all a minority of eminent Democrats, who, as this motley assembly hope, can be kicked and cuffed into swallowing this foul broth just brewed."[22] The motley assembly nominated Bryan, a "mere blatherskate," and Arthur Sewall, "a crank from Maine." Bryan was a "cheap declaimer" whose reputation rested on a few "frothy harangues, in which he has shown his capacity by repeating again and again a single phrase as empty as it is blasphemous." White agreed with the *New York World* that since "lunacy" had dictated the Democratic platform, "it was fitting that hysteria should evolve the candidate."[23]

White's hysterical opposition to Bryan, who was neither an anarchist nor a socialist, underscores his commitment to the political and economic

20. LaFeber, *New Empire*, p. 276; ADW to Henry Sage, February 21, 1896, and Richard Olney to David J. Brewer, December 28, 1896, WMC.

21. Holls to ADW, June 23, 1896, WMC. In conversations with McKinley and Platt, James Russell Young had suggested White for the vice-presidency (Young to ADW, June 13, 1896, WMC).

22. *Speech of Hon. Andrew D. White on Taking the Chair at the Ratification Meeting Held at Ithaca, July 10, 1896* (Ithaca, 1896), p. 3.

23. Ibid., pp. 3, 13; Diary, July 11, 1896, WMC.

status quo. Talk of government ownership or even regulation of industries frightened him. He was willing to allow government to aid education and to protect industry, but he would brook no interference with capitalism. White had seen the baneful results of government paternalism in Europe. The Bryanites, he believed, sought to "Europeanize" America and deny its citizens their economic freedom. White was frightened enough to lay aside his belief in the inevitability of progress to oppose them.

White labeled the election "far more threatening" than the approach of the Civil War. In a widely circulated *Letter to Patriotic Democrats* White pleaded for a bipartisan coalition to defeat Bryanism and populism. The Democratic platform, he argued, advocated government ownership of many industries and was therefore the first socialist platform in American political history. White realized that free-trade Democrats would balk at supporting the protectionist McKinley. He reminded them, however, that Bryan's program would bring bankruptcy, distress, and dishonor. Were he in a similar predicament, White averred, he would certainly bolt his party. Reminding his audience that during the Civil War Democrats had placed the national interest above party concerns, White urged all patriotic citizens to unite behind William McKinley. Although some had urged him to soften his attacks on Bryan, he insisted that this was "no time for rose water." [24]

The *Letter to Patriotic Democrats* unleashed a torrent of praise and criticism. Prominent free-trade Democrat Henry Richmond of Buffalo announced his support of McKinley. Oscar Straus sent White his unequivocal endorsement of the Republican candidate. White's letter had even reached McKinley, who wrote to Holls: "Be assured that I am duly appreciative of the effective support of President White." Prominent Democrats and Republicans, then, recognized that White's efforts were having an impact on the campaign. [25]

Not all Democrats, of course, agreed with White's political analysis. A few decided to join a third party of Gold Democrats. Everett P. Wheeler thought that such action was the best way to educate voters on the necessity of a stable currency. John De Witt Warner, White's nemesis at Cornell, also supported the Gold Democrats. He admitted the force of White's charge that the Chicago convention showed signs of having been tutored "by Fagin," but argued (in an analysis somewhat similar to that

24. ADW to Mrs. David J. Hill, July 22, 1896, WMC; *New York Times*, July 16, 1896; *A Letter to Patriotic Democrats, July 14, 1896* (New York, 1896); ADW to Gilman, July 26, 1896, WMC.

25. Richmond to ADW, July 23, 1896; Straus to ADW, July 29, 1896; J. E. Clarke to ADW, July 20, 1896; A. B. Stone to ADW, July 25, 1896; Holls to ADW, July 24, 1896; all in WMC.

employed by White in 1884) that to punish the Democrats "by cherishing Fagin himself seems a novel remedy." Although Warner evidently was not sufficiently afraid of Bryan to switch to the Republicans, many sound-money Democrats agreed with White that the extraordinary threat justified temporary alliance with the GOP.[26]

Bryan's supporters strenuously attempted to refute White's letter. The *Rome Daily Sentinel* acidly editorialized that White should write another letter to Republicans telling them why they should not support Thomas Platt's New York GOP ticket. The *Rochester Herald* attacked the diplomat's efforts to blame the recent depression on free-trade Democrats: when he resorted to the methods "of unscrupulous politicians, what reason have we to attach any special value to learning and culture?"[27]

White was exasperated with the criticism of the Bryanites[28] but concluded that the unresponsiveness of the masses was temporary. He admitted that even when he had succeeded in showing large numbers of people that their interests were against the unlimited coinage of silver, they somehow retained their Democratic allegiance. Hatred of classes and sections, qualities "hardly amenable to reason," accounted for Bryan's popularity; yet White remembered the defeat of the greenback craze, "simply by right reason." Consequently, he retained "great hopes" that the populists would be thwarted.[29]

Famed sociologist Lester Frank Ward was less sanguine about the future and subtly challenged White's view of progress. Henry George's "vaporizings" and Edward Bellamy's "sugar-coated bomb," Ward mused, had helped to make socialism respectable; the Populists might succeed, bringing with them "nothing but disaster and reaction." But the defeat of Bryan, he ominously predicted, would not mean the restoration of sanity. Populism was "merely the foam from a deep current that has not ceased to flow and will not cease until it is strong enough to carry the world with it." Ward's escape from this cataclysmic vision could hardly have reassured White: when he tired of viewing men, Ward retired among flowers, rocks, and hoary fossils, drawing solace from the realization of the enormous period required to develop "even a troglodyte or a Populist."[30] Ward's views must have dismayed White; the sociologist implied that evolution would sooner or later grant the world to the socialists. If troglodytes and

---

26. Warner to ADW, July 21, 1896, WMC; *New York Times*, July 26, 1896.
27. *Rochester Herald*, July 13, 1896; *Rome Daily Sentinel*, July 16, 1896.
28. For the colorful response of individual Bryanites to White, see Charles Sanford to ADW, July 16, 1896; F. G. Franklin to ADW, September 9, 1896; S. S. Weatherby to ADW, September 12, 1896; Free Coinage to ADW, July 16, 1896, all in WMC.
29. ADW to David J. Hill, July 14, 1896, WMC.
30. Ward to ADW, July 16, 1896, WMC.

Populists required eons to develop, they were on the verge of maturity. Generally regarded as an apostle of action, Ward offered a determinist view of politics that paralyzed all who adhered to it. Paradoxically, White's optimistic determinism did not prevent him from enlisting as an active ally of the future.

The *Letter to Patriotic Democrats* proved to be the opening round of a concerted effort by White to convert wavering Democrats and to strengthen the resolve of all Republicans. He coined the term "silver slug" to oppose the epithet "gold bug" and urged Holls to persuade McKinley and Mark Hanna to circulate the phrase. Such slogans, he asserted, made people think. Before using the phrase, he had been assured by the most eminent entomologist in the country that although many bugs were useful in destroying parasites and fertilizing plants, all slugs were nuisances.[31]

In September, White's analysis of the presidential election appeared in *The Forum*. A combination of reason, threat, and vitriol, the article underlined the virtual hysteria that accompanied contemplation of a Democratic victory. He thought that the Democratic platform constituted a "virtual demand for free riot and the stoppage of the U.S. mails by any mob which can seduce a governor or scare a mayor." The "anarchists" had chosen candidates with the veneer of respectability but their ploy was transparent: they gave first place on the ticket to an "elocutionary attorney whose gifts and graces had been at the service of any corporations willing to pay the moderate fee required to secure them"; they gave second place to a banker and manager of eastern railways "who had grown rich in practicing the arts and conniving at the schemes which the convention affected to condemn."[32] White thus informed Bryan supporters (one may of course question how many of them read *The Forum*, a perennial problem for such publicists as White) that the ticket was composed of unprincipled dissemblers.

White appealed to the interests of his readers. The peasants during the French Revolution, he asserted, had had nothing to lose, while five million Americans had money in savings banks and countless others owned land. As he warmed to his task, White increasingly bared the economic assumptions that lay behind his opposition to Bryan. In times of inflation, White argued, wages never kept pace with prices. Thus free coinage of silver would injure laborers. Class conflict, moreover, was not a reality in fluid America. Capitalists produced jobs and generously engaged in numerous acts of public philanthropy. They were once workingmen themselves, he insisted, and thus sympathized with their employees.

31. ADW to Holls, July 16, 1896, WMC.
32. "Encouragements in the Present Crisis," *Forum* 22 (September 1896): 19.

If sugar-coated professions of class harmony failed to pacify the "toiling masses," White did not hesitate to sketch out the dire consequences of the election of Bryan: roughly two-thirds of the mortgages in the United States were past due; if the Democrats prevailed, many mortgages would be foreclosed before the inauguration.[33] Without explanation or apology, White leagued himself with those who possessed raw power and who were not squeamish about flexing their economic muscles to ensure continued hegemony. He evidently did not perceive that he had abandoned the rhetoric of a mutuality of interest among the classes.

White's *Forum* article evidently pleased Mark Hanna, who agreed to print and circulate "millions of copies."[34] Hanna's enthusiasm spurred further efforts, and in the final month of the campaign, White's letter to Governor Culberson of Texas (which received front-page coverage in the *New York Times* and was separately distributed as a campaign document) chided Bryan for pointing to Otto von Bismarck's support of free silver.[35] Bismarck, he informed Culberson, favored bimetalism rather than un-limited coinage of silver but was at present in search of a dupe like Bryan who would buy Germany's silver reserves. Bismarck's allusions were like the spider's invitation to the fly, White acidly observed: "Perhaps he thinks that if the American people are lavish enough to make a free gift of several hundreds of millions of dollars to the silver mine monopolists and bullion brokers of this and other countries, we can afford to let Germany have such a bagatelle as say fifty millions." If Bismarck's opinions carried so much weight, White asked, why did the Democrats fail to yield to his philoso-phy on a protective tariff?[36] The former minister to Germany, important to McKinley strategists in securing the votes of German-Americans, had blunted Bryan's attempt to associate himself with the Fatherland.

On November 3, 1896, White resolutely voted for William McKinley: "Never have I voted with a greater sense of responsibility. Quite likely it is my last vote for a Presidential candidate and in my opinion is the most important one I have ever cast."[37] The Republican victory reassured White, whose lurking fear of disaster had spurred his strenuous efforts for the ticket. He observed "great exultation of all right-thinking men" and predicted that Bryan and Altgeld had been relegated to the dustbin of

33. Ibid., pp. 23–24, 26, 27.
34. Hanna to George Lewis, October 16, 1896, WMC.
35. Both Bryan and White seemed to base their remarks on mistranslations of Bismarck's speeches. What Bismarck actually said became the subject of extended controversy. See ADW to Culberson, September 28, 1896; Robert Thiem to ADW, October 8 and 17, 1896; Jacob Bickler to ADW, October 8, 1896; ADW to Bickler, October 27, 1896, all in WMC.
36. ADW to Culberson, September 28, 1896, WMC; *New York Times*, October 3, 1896.
37. Diary, November 3, 1896, WMC.

history. While McKinley's margin was not quite as sweeping as he had wished, it was, after all, by far the largest majority that any president had ever obtained. The silver craze had probably subsided, and the election had provided business with a "simply wonderful" dose of confidence. The republic had been saved and the socialist menace banished.[38]

In an essay in *The Forum* listing "Some Practical Lessons of the Recent Campaign," White returned to his theme that education had saved the republic. The recent victory, he noted, had been "given us by the States in which education is best developed and most widely diffused." Thus "popular education, which has . . . so signally justified its existence," should be spread. If more schools were built, many more states would be added "to the grand phalanx favoring sound money and good government." A sound education, White concluded, would teach the futility of the license advocated by the anarchists and the utopianism of the socialists. Bryanism fed on ignorance, he argued, as victory made the specter of class conflict vanish from his consciousness. Having demonstrated little concern with political or economic reform during the campaign, White reasserted his belief that education was the only solution to social problems.[39]

While White's assessment of the election remained before the public, the campaign to make him secretary of state gained strength. In early December, the *Troy Daily Times* endorsed him for the post, which, Clara noted, her father considered a greater honor than the presidency of the United States.[40] Frederick Holls delivered a detailed memorandum recommending White to H. H. Kohlsaat, a wealthy backer of McKinley. Holls argued that few questioned his friend's credentials. In the experience needed, he surpassed John Sherman and William Boyd Allison. Realizing that Joseph Choate was perhaps White's most powerful rival for the post, the audacious Holls recommended that McKinley appoint this "most brilliant advocate" ambassador to England, where he would "better equip us than at any time since Seward or Charles Francis Adams served at the Court of St. James."

Having demonstrated that his candidate's abilities dictated his selection, Holls asserted that White's appointment would be politically desirable. The German vote, he argued, which had been a crucial factor in McKinley's victory, was solidly behind White. Finally, White was one of the few men in New York who was satisfactory to all factions in the state Republi-

38. Diary, November 4, 1896, and ADW to Evans, November 16, 1896, WMC.
39. "Some Practical Lessons of the Recent Campaign," *Forum* 22 (December 1896): 414–22.
40. *Troy Daily Times*, December 4, 1896; Clara White Newberry to ADW, December 14, 1895, WMC.

can party. His amicable relations with Tom Platt and the reformers would make him a popular and noncontroversial choice. Holls pointed out that superior qualifications fortuitously coincided with good politics.[41]

On January 7, 1897, Holls informed White that his letter had reached McKinley and Mark Hanna. Appointment seemed a distinct possibility, especially in view of White's highly visible service for the ticket. Hesitant to hope too strongly that his long-cherished dream would be realized, White remained "profoundly skeptical" that he would be chosen. He was distrusted in New York, he informed Holls, because he did not view patronage "as a matter of bargain, favor and pull," and party regulars would not countenance his appointment. Professing himself satisfied with an appointment as ambassador to Germany or minister to Italy, White concluded that his name was "out of the question" for secretary of state: "I am entirely content to give up all further thought concerning any official relations with the incoming administration." The rest of the communication to Holls, however, indicated that the gentleman protested too much. Though he neither expected nor coveted the post, White was "indeed conscious of a certain fitness for the position." He rehearsed his qualifications at length: he had studied history and international law intensively; he had held numerous diplomatic posts; he was familiar with virtually all foreign policy issues and intimately acquainted with men of public affairs at home and abroad; he had earned "the blessing of peace-makers in politics"; he was tenacious of fundamental principles but not a doctrinaire. White's litany of his attributes seems more like an application than a denial. He did nothing to deter Holls's efforts and certainly would not have declined an offer to serve.[42]

If White had hoped against hope, he was once again disappointed. The choice, McKinley and Hanna informed Holls, had been between White and John Sherman. Convinced that the stories of Sherman's infirmities were a plot against the old man, McKinley approved him because he would better "fill the public eye." Mark Hanna's desire to replace Sherman in the Senate was generally assumed to be perhaps a more important reason for the choice, but the result was the same. Once again White had to accept the honor of a bridesmaid, but this time a more tangible reward was in the offing. Holls had suggested that McKinley name White ambassador to Germany.[43]

41. Holls to Kohlsaat, December 1896, WMC.
42. Holls to ADW, January 7, 1897, and ADW to Holls, January 12, 1897, WMC.
43. Holls to ADW, January 25, 1897, WMC.

Part IV

WAR, PEACE, AND WAR

Convulsions, rather than steady progress, governed both international relations and White's familial affairs during the final two decades of his life. Frequent wars mocked attempts by White and others to rationalize diplomacy and ensure prolonged peace. If White could excuse the Spanish–American War as an aberration, necessitated by Spain's cruel treatment of Cuba, he found it more difficult to justify the refusal of most nations to use the Hague peace tribunal. Public opinion, he conjectured, would force politicians to arbitrate international disputes. World War I exploded even this slim hope; the conflict, all the more distressing because of Germany's violation of neutral Belgium, forced White into silence. White's anguish, which was augmented by numerous deaths among family and friends, was punctuated by only one final affirmation. He insisted, despite all the violence around him, that the world was progressing toward peace and order; good would result from the greatest evil. Months before his death, White imposed his optimistic rhetoric upon an unwilling world. Throughout his life he had regarded himself as a rational empiricist. Even as he uttered his "vague" hopes for the future world, he did not recognize that he was, in fact, an almost Jamesian neo-transcendentalist over-believer. Two contradictory strains of nineteenth-century American philosophy somehow existed in curious harmony in White's psyche: he believed that reason should govern society but adopted a suprarationalist faith (in the eventual triumph of reason) to confront an irrational world.

White, America's ambassador to Germany, applauded McKinley's efforts to avoid war with Spain. He supported the war of 1898, but his attempt to promote German–American relations actually caused a near collision between the two countries. To prevent U.S. annexation of the "mongrel" Philippines, White encouraged German territorial ambitions in the Pacific. Rebuked by the State Department, he denied that he had contributed to a conflict; yet he continued publicly to support the extension of German civilization. White's failure was underscored by America's acquisition of the Philippines in 1898. Twitted by his anti-imperialist friends and worried about the invasion of "yellow" states into Anglo-Saxon America, White insisted that the war and the pacification of the Philippines proved the altruism of the foreign policy of the United States. Despite evidence to the contrary, moreover, he was equally certain that German—American relations were excellent. Together the world's two leading civilizations would strive to raise the rest of the world to their standards.

Despite its meager accomplishments, the Hague International Peace Conference of 1899 increased White's confidence that rational discourse could replace international conflict. As head of the American delegation, White advocated a court of arbitration to which disputing nations would voluntarily submit themselves. He opposed compulsory arbitration, in part because it was impractical and would require a large army to enforce it, in part because it would force the United States to abandon the Monroe Doctrine. White convinced himself that voluntary arbitration under the aegis of a permanent tribunal constituted a giant step toward peace, and he strenuously labored to persuade the suspicious Germans to join the court.

The Hague conferees accomplished little of substance, and the treaty and the court of arbitration failed to generate much enthusiasm in the United States. Even when nation after nation ignored The Hague and engaged in war, White denied that the conference had been a merely rhetorical exercise. The Hague tribunal, he argued, served an educative function. When the masses learned that arbitration was an alternative to war, they would *force* their governments to submit disputes to the court. Arbitration would become universal, he concluded, only when public opinion backed it. Thus White's faith in the future resided in the rational good sense of an educable public. The wars of the early twentieth century failed to diminish that faith.

If White remained optimistic about the community of nations, he could derive little satisfaction from his family. Hardly a year went by without a tragedy. Daughter Clara separated from her philandering husband, became a drug addict, and died several years later. Despondent and desperately ill, son Fred took his own life. Fred's son followed his father in suicide several years later. White's sorrow was augmented by a growing recognition that he was to have no male descendants; the hope of attaining immortality through his family was slipping away. Yet the old man warded off despair. He refused to brood about events that he could not change or to entertain doubts that his neglect of his children and his frequently expressed expectations for them had been connected with their deaths. Perhaps sensing that reflections might lead to guilt, White immersed himself in work. Public service had justified slighting his family in the past; it served as a substitute for reconsidering his relationship to his dead children now by convincing him that service to a larger cause necessitated sacrifices. He believed that he would attain immortality as an educator and a statesman and did not allow himself to look back to assess the cost.

In the few years left to him, public and private disasters mounted their most serious threat to White's optimism. Continued deaths among family and friends, constant bickering with his wife, and disappointment with his youngest daughter weakened the octogenarian. World War I, however, was an even more overwhelming blow. A worldwide holocaust that made the Hague court an ironic joke was bad enough, but Germany seemed to be the aggressor. The bewildered White searched for an explanation without success. The utter disregard of Belgian neutrality by the "Huns" could be neither refuted nor condoned. Nor could White forgive German academicians for supporting the war with the argument that Prussian militarism and German education were inextricably bound. The world had gone mad, and White could not find the words to comfort either himself or the public.

White broke his public silence when the United States entered the war. Never enthusiastic about his country's participation, however, he was constantly saddened by reminders of the Germany of the past. In the midst of the military and diplomatic stalemate, White forced himself to make one final affirmation. He acknowledged "vague hopes" that this terrible war would result in a more durable peace. Out of evil must come good. White had so argued throughout his career; his evolutionary optimism dictated such a stance. He died in 1918 before the armistice was signed, yet peace would only have convinced him that the world conformed to his vision.

Chapter 14   *Ambassador to Germany*

President McKinley acted quickly to reward White for his efforts in the campaign. In April 1897, Secretary Sherman sent official notification of the sixty-five-year-old diplomat's appointment as ambassador to Germany. Holls was not certain that his friend should accept the appointment. With John Sherman's infirmities becoming more apparent every day, the State Department might need a new secretary at any time, and at least two senators had cautioned Holls that White would forfeit his claim to the position if he left the country. The diplomat, however, decided not to relinquish his ambassadorship on the dubious hope of a vacancy and enthusiastically accepted his appointment, proud that it had come "without my begging for it—and simply because the appointing power thinks me fit." [1]

White looked forward to a return to Berlin, although he knew that relations between Germany and the United States had deteriorated substantially since his last tour of duty. The Germans complained that the sugar bounty recently enacted in Washington violated the most-favored-nation treaties signed by the two countries. United States officials retorted that the ban on American pork by Germany, a policy initiated during White's tenure as minister, had constituted the opening sally in a campaign against American products. Both capitals reverberated with talk of an imminent tariff war. [2]

While the two countries vied for commercial supremacy, each scrutinized the imperialistic aims of the other. For years the Pacific islands of Samoa had been ruled jointly by the United States, Germany, and Great Britain. Each power viewed the islands as important strategic bases that might facilitate trade with China. As German activity in Kiaochow

1. Sherman to ADW, April 10, 1897, WMC; John Porter to Holls, November 12, 1897, Frederick W. Holls Papers, Columbia University; Visits to Washington, 1897–1899, incomplete typescript, Holls Papers; ADW to Fred White, March 30, 1897, WMC; *New York Times*, March 29, 1897; ADW to Willard Fiske, May 3, 1897, WMC. Holls ultimately concluded that if Sherman could hang on for another year and then leave office, White would be recalled from Berlin to replace him (Holls to ADW, November 27, 1897, WMC).
2. *Autobiography*, vol. 2, p. 134.

increased, the United States reaffirmed its determination to secure the Samoan bases.[3]

Perhaps more alarming to the State Department, the Germans had embarked on a series of adventures in South America. In 1896 Bismarck publicly labeled the Monroe Doctrine "an imprudence." Bismarck's views seemed more than bluster; on a trip to South America, White had been astonished to find that a German army engineer, with the unlikely name of Baron von Steuben, had recently completed a map-making tour of the continent, during which he had noted all stragetic areas. The Germans seemed determined to poach upon the preserve of the United States.[4]

Although he acknowledged a conflict of interest between the two countries, White expressed confidence that solutions would be reached amicably. Baron von Thielmann, Germany's ambassador to the United States, assured him that the tariff difficulties should not be taken too seriously. White needed little encouragement to arrive at a similar view. The kaiser, he argued, was the favorite of the German people. Both the imperial system and the Hohenzollerns had emerged as the "fittest" to rule Germany; White was certain that they would translate the peaceful desires of their constituents into policy. The current difficulties seemed to the new ambassador like "the case of the fly on the window-pane hiding the distant dome of St. Peters." The language of conciliation, so common to diplomats, came easily to White, who believed that the differences between the two countries were more apparent than real.[5]

Several crises demanded White's immediate attention when he arrived in Berlin in the summer of 1897. Germany had recently severed relations with Haiti when the latter country jailed Emil Luders, a ne'er-do-well of alleged German nationality. Baron Bernhard von Bülow, minister of foreign affairs, demanded that the Haitians release Luders, apologize, and pay a $30,000 indemnity within five hours. At Bülow's assurance that Germany had no intention of occupying any territory, White refused a request by the Haitian representative that the United States intervene.

3. See Ernest May, *Imperial Democracy* (New York, 1961), p. 119; Clara Schieber, *The Transformation of American Sentiment toward Germany* (Boston and New York, 1923), pp. 79–82; Jeannette Keim, *Forty Years of German–American Political Relations* (Philadelphia, 1919), p. 206.

4. Otto zu Stolberg-Wernigerode, *Germany and the United States of American during the Era of Bismarck* (Reading, Pa., 1937), p. 170; Schieber, *Transformation of American Sentiment*, pp. 177–78.

5. *New York Times*, May 23, 1897; *Autobiography*, vol. 2, pp. 243, 249; Thanksgiving Day Address, November 25, 1897, WMC. White shared his sense of optimism in a letter to E. P. Evans: "Long after we shall have disappeared matters will continue bad, but on the whole they will probably grow better, if not there will probably be an evolution out of this evil of something better" (December 22, 1897, WMC).

The ambassador advised Sherman that the Germans would regard such action as an "over officious interference with a legitimate international demand." The State Department, preoccupied with the Cuban revolution, refused to involve itself. Haiti complied with the demands and the crisis passed. As long as the Germans agreed to renounce territorial ambitions, White for one was willing to grant them increased leverage in South America.[6]

Trade differences, however, proved more difficult to reconcile. Before he left the United States, White had labored to remove the discrimination against German sugar in the Dingley Tariff. He had reminded Senators Nelson Aldrich and William Allison that a tariff war would alienate German-American voters from the Republican party. The duty, nevertheless, remained in the bill, and the ambassador had to satisfy himself with assurances that unless Germany retaliated, Congress would enact no more purely protective tariff measures.[7]

The Dingley Tariff stiffened Germany's determination to retaliate against American products. Several members of the Reichstag suggested that the ban on pork, which had been in effect for more than a decade, should be extended to all meats. White advised the State Department to refute German objections that inspection of meats in the United States was inadequate instead of adopting a "tit for tat" policy. He suggested that the U.S. Department of Agriculture investigate all reports of trichina. More important, he insisted that meat-packing houses adopt microscopic inspection; despite the initial expense, such reform would facilitate international trade.[8]

Behind White's advice to Secretary Sherman lay his conviction that the middle and lower classes in Germany wanted inexpensive beef and pork and would pressure their government to lift the ban once the meat proved to be uncontaminated. The ambassador persisted in viewing the German monarchy as a near democracy and scrutinized public opinion. When an article in the *Kreuz-Zeitung* calling for a tariff war failed to generate support, he was pleased. Counseling patience, he predicted that the impasse would soon be broken: "I have still faith in the feeling of justice which forms so strong a component in the German character, and in the gradual prevalence of a wise self-interest which will lead German officials

6. May, *Imperial Democracy*, p. 128; ADW to John Sherman, December 6, 1897, DAG.
7. ADW to Holls, April 27, 1897, and Holls to ADW, July 21, 1897, WMC; Keim, *Forty Years*, pp. 67–83.
8. ADW to Sherman, June 24, September 8, and December 27, 1897, DAG.

to pursue a course more in accordance with international fairness and comity."[9]

German officials perceived their own interests differently. Early in 1898, Germany prohibited the importation of American fresh and dried fruit, claiming that insects (the San Jose scale) on them were destroying the orchards of the Fatherland. White sent a strong note of protest but advised Sherman to take no hasty retaliatory action. The ambassador admitted that prohibition did have its lighter side: the Kaiser joked about the "apple of discord," and White remarked that the fruit that had caused all the trouble at the dawning of history was at it again. But humor did not conceal the ambassador's consternation, which mounted when an agriculturalist from Cornell's experimental station informed him that there was no evidence that the San Jose scale had ever been introduced to a new locality by infested fruit. Thus the Germans had no excuse for banning American fruit. White had been patient, probably too patient, but now even he advised the State Department that the time might be approaching "when it may be necessary to show our teeth—and plainly." He had discovered that German manufactured goods used noxious dyes; a prohibition against goods dangerous to the public health might be in order.[10]

The State Department left the form and content of the ambassador's remonstrances to his discretion. White introduced evidence that there was no danger from the San Jose scale and won substantial concessions from the German ministry. Restrictions against dried fruits and most fresh fruits were removed. Although the ban on the importation of live trees, shrubs, and plants from the United States remained, the ambassador believed that his intercession had been successful.[11]

The German ministry, however, refused to yield to pleas that the ban on meat and pork be lifted. In letters to Bülow, White demonstrated that American inspection procedures were in every way equal to those in Germany. At times, persuasion became threat; White alluded to retaliation. While he interceded with the ministry, he begged the State Department to discipline American meat-packers. They must adopt uniform microscopic inspection; they must stop their "loose talk" that trichinae in pork cannot be detected by any examination, because the Germans simply

9. ADW to Sherman, August 12 and September 8, 1897, and January 8, 1898, DAG; ADW to Holls, July 31, 1897, WMC.

10. ADW to Sherman, February 1 and 5, 1898, DAG; Diary, February 8, 1898, WMC; ADW to Daniel Coit Gilman, February 8, 1898; C. L. Watrous to ADW, February 8, 1898; M. Slingerland to ADW, February 21, 1898; Stanford Newel to ADW, March 19, 1898, all in WMC; ADW to John Hay, October 29, 1898, DAG.

11. Keim, *Forty Years*, pp. 83–85; ADW to Hay, February 27, 1899, DAG.

quoted American meat-packers to justify prohibition.[12] Within a decade, many large meat-packers, recognizing that uniform inspection laws were advantageous to trade, supported reform of their industry.[13] At the moment, though, White's arguments convinced few.

The war on American commerce continued for the remainder of the century. The ministry needed the support of the Agrarian party if its coalition was to survive. Hence it acquiesced in bans on American meat, fruit, and wood. German officials hinted broadly that a commercial agreement would bring an end to harassment, and the two countries signed a reciprocal treaty on July 10, 1900. Although Germany retained its ban on canned meats and sausages, the agreement quieted agitation on both sides.[14] White was not completely satisfied with the settlement but was hopeful that goodwill on both sides would continue to have a salutory effect.[15]

Although the projected tariff war continued to worry White, the conflict between the United States and Spain became his overriding concern. The Cuban revolution had excited the sympathy of many Americans, and increasing numbers of commercial and humanitarian groups called for intervention. In the summer of 1897, the State Department asked White, Stewart Woodford (minister to Spain), and Horace Porter (minister to France) jointly to assess pertinent developments on the continent. The trio suggested that no claims, pecuniary or otherwise, be pressed upon Spain until the tension between the two countries had eased. Porter and White emphasized the necessity of "going slow, a Fabian policy." The ambassador to Germany saw no danger of interference from the Kaiser in the conflict.[16]

White's opposition to war with Spain stemmed primarily from his racist assumptions about Cubans. Holls informed his friend in 1897 that the administration regarded war as likely but had not yet decided what to do with Cuba after the island was separated from Spain. McKinley was aware

12. ADW to Sherman, March 7 and April 7, 1898, DAG.

13. American meat-packers pushed for reforms of their industry to increase sales and push out smaller businesses. See Gabriel Kolko, *The Triumph of Conservatism* (New York, 1963), pp. 99–108.

14. The German tariff of 1902 renewed tensions between the two countries, but by then White had left office.

15. John B. Jackson to Hay, July 14, 1899; ADW to Hay, March 24 and May 23, 1900, all in DAG; Jackson to ADW, August 8, 1899, WMC. The commercial relations of the United States and Germany are discussed in Keim, *Forty Years*, pp. 64–112.

16. Diary, August 17, 1897, WMC; *Autobiography*, vol. 2, p. 161; ADW to Evans, October 7, 1898, WMC. For two views of the coming of the war, see Walter LaFeber, *The New Empire* (Ithaca, 1963), pp. 285–99, 327–51, 370–406, and Julius Pratt, *Expansionists of 1898* (Boston, 1936).

of the dangers of incorporating a "large, ignorant, priest-ridden people of an alien race and language." But the administration also predicted that independence meant anarchy "accompanied by an orgy of corruption in Cuban bonds." The economic interests of the United States, then, seemed to whisper annexation while its political interests demurred. Holls had impressed the president with a suggestion that Cuba be ceded to Mexico; but McKinley feared that after American blood had been shed, the public clamor for annexation would be overwhelming. All solutions seemed impossible or impractical and Holls solicited White's advice.[17]

The ambassador offered few solutions, but he surpassed his friend in emphasizing the danger of union between the United States and Cuba. Cuba would undoubtedly become a "rotten borough" to be manipulated by venal politicians in the United States. White later admitted that he was in favor of setting up the Cuban government "again and again, seventy times, if necessary," rather than admit Cuba as a state. He had learned in Santo Domingo that "mixed races" were utterly incompetent to govern themselves, however, and saw little hope for stability in Cuba. Amid the hopelessness of the Cuban situation, White found solace in his confidence that few would countenance statehood for the Philippines, "seven millions of mixed races, most of them of a very low type." To guarantee against *any* amalgamation, however, White proposed a constitutional amendment that would require the consent of three-fifths of all the states to admit a new state. The amendment would bar the colored races while placating antiextensionist critics of the administration.[18]

The United States did not want to annex Cuba, White told a *Tageblatt* interviewer; the administration awaited "the realization of autonomy." When the Spanish recalled General Valeriano Weyler—architect of the hated *reconcentrado* policy—late in 1897, White applauded the easing of tensions.[19]

Hopes for peace were shattered by the explosion of the battleship *Maine* in Havana Harbor early in 1898. From across the ocean, White stated his conviction—derived from talks with German naval authorities—that the explosion had taken place within the ship from the overheating of coal bunkers. White praised McKinley's attempts to avoid a conflict:

17. Holls to ADW, September 3, 1897, WMC.
18. ADW to Holls, September 14, 1897, and January 2, 1898, WMC; *New York Tribune*, April 8, 1907; *New York Sun*, April 8, 1907. In *The Black Image in the White Mind* (New York, 1971) George Fredrickson discusses the relationship between racism and anti-imperialism. White fits his category of "accommodationist" rather than "extreme racist." See esp. pp. 305–318.
19. *New York Times*, November 3, 1897.

. . . if he is successful in averting war the future historian will rank his career in this respect with that of President Washington, withstanding the powerful jingo pressure, threats, misrepresentations and abjurations of his day to prevent an untimely war with Great Britain. He will be the "Napoleon of Peace" indeed.

Of course if war must come his line will then be to wage it with the greatest determination, and in that case he will secure honorable fame in another way.[20]

Soon the ambassador recognized that war was imminent. "The whole thing is preposterous," he wrote in his diary, "and will lead to enormous troubles in the after dealing with Cuba." White had hoped that Cuba could be wrenched from Spain in some other way. But once war had been declared, he supported it vigorously, although he feared the long-term consequences.[21]

White's first task was to confirm Germany's neutrality. Bülow assured him that Germany would not interfere with either side but refused to issue an official proclamation of neutrality. Since the Franco–Prussian War, he insisted, Germany had made no such formal declarations. White was quite comfortable with personal assurances, however, and because of his excellent rapport with the foreign ministry expected to have little difficulty.[22]

Throughout the war (and after it), White took pains to convice his government of the cooperation of the Germans. He claimed that only once during the war did he find it necessary to ask the foreign ministry to overhaul a Spanish ship on the Elbe. When the ambassador furnished evidence that the ship contained contraband of war, the Germans immediately complied with his request. The German attitude during the war, he concluded, was "all that we could desire it to be."[23]

Despite White's remarks, Germany's sympathy for Spain was clear from the outset.[24] Only two newspapers, the *Frankfurter Zeitung* and the periodical *Die Nation*, avoided fervent anti-Americanism. Despite protestations of neutrality, Germany aided the Spanish whenever it could. In July 1898 the German cruiser *Irene* intervened in favor of Spain in Subig Bay in the Philippines. The foreign ministry insisted that the ship was simply "carrying away Spanish women and children in distress." The American press was convinced that the Kaiser was the secret ally of Spain,

20. ADW to Holls, March 31, 1898, WMC.
21. ADW to Sherman, February 19, 1898, DAG; ADW to Holls, March 26, 1898, WMC.
22. ADW to William Day, May 5, 1898, DAG; Diary, May 11, 1898, WMC.
23. ADW to L. A. Ault, June 23, 1915; Memorandum, February 10, 1902; ADW to Hay, February 13, 1902, all in WMC.
24. The Kaiser's attempt in 1897 to prevent the "American-British Society for International Theft and Warmongering" from snatching Cuba is discussed in May, *Imperial Democracy*, pp. 196–97.

an attitude reinforced several months later when the German steamer *Kaiserin Augusta* gave the Spanish General Augustin safe transport to Hong Kong. In the midst of war, Americans viewed these actions as anything but neutral.[25]

White was aware of the anti-American feeling in Germany, but he viewed it as not nearly so virulent as many claimed. The ambassador's dispatches emphasized the cooperativeness of the foreign ministry; his public statements stressed the historic friendship between the two countries. White convinced himself that a few malcontents had stirred up bitter feelings against the United States. In a Fourth of July address in Leipzig he predicted that good relations between the people of both countries were already beginning to surface.[26] The *Boston Post* did not agree: "The attitude of Germany does not depend upon what the people of Germany think and feel but upon how the Emperor William happens to feel at any particular moment." The *Post*'s criticisms were on target. In his zeal to reestablish good relations between the two countries, White had overemphasized the power of the masses in the German monarchical system.[27]

If the ambassador could ignore the meddling of the *Irene* and the *Kaiserin Augusta* because they had no effect on the American war effort, the activities of Admiral von Diederichs in Manila Bay proved more troublesome. Practically the entire German Asiatic fleet remained in Manila Bay, exchanging supplies with the Spanish and transporting soldiers. The arrival of more German vessels in the area finally prompted Admiral Dewey to confront Diederichs. After several meetings, German activity ceased, although Diederichs maintained that his continued presence was necessary to protect German nationals who lived on the islands.[28]

Both White and the State Department recognized that Diederichs was in the Philippines because the Kaiser hoped to take possession of the islands. In mid-June, a month before the Diederichs episode, the ambassador sent a lengthy dispatch to Washington in which he predicted that Germany might take the Philippines after the surrender of Manila. On July 9 he reported that Baron Oswald von Richthofen, acting minister of foreign affairs, had expressed interest in Samoa, the Carolines, and the Philippines. Virtually every Western nation was interested in the China

25. Schieber, *Transformation of American Sentiment*, pp. 129–32.
26. White's Leipzig address received much praise. See *New York Tribune*, July 7, 1898; *New York Times*, July 7 and 17, 1898; A. Van Vechten to ADW, October 16, 1899; J. A. Vichtery to ADW, December 3, 1899; ADW to Richard Nicholas, December 9, 1899, all in WMC; *New York Times Illustrated Magazine*, October 16, 1898.
27. Schieber, *Transformation of American Sentiment*, p. 134.
28. Keim, *Forty Years*, pp. 220–29; Von Diederichs, "A Statement of Events in Manila Bay," *Journal of the Royal United Service Institution* 59 (August 1914): 421–46.

market, and the foreign ministry recognized that Pacific possessions might give Germany an advantage.[29]

White was sympathetic to German territorial aspirations in the Pacific. He feared that American occupation of the Philippines might ultimately result in an application for statehood from "the mongrel race." Therefore he accepted America's professed disinterest in territorial expansion. German possession of the islands, moreover, seemed an excellent alternative to the chaos that would result if independence were granted. In April, White and Holls put together a plan designed to get rid of the Philippines while improving relations among the United States, Germany, and Great Britain. Holls traveled to London and hinted to Acting Foreign Minister Arthur Balfour that if the United States did not keep all of the Philippine islands, one might be offered to the Kaiser "in return for a substantial *quid pro quo* in China." The plan, Holls wrote to White, offered a "splendid opportunity . . . of using Germany's greed (about which I did not drop one indiscreet word [to Balfour]) for the purpose not only of bettering our everyday relations but also of *bringing her into line*. We would have an Anglo-Saxon Dreibund without a word on paper anywhere."[30]

Meanwhile, White encouraged Germany's interest in the Far East while advising the State Department that the United States probably could not retain any islands acquired from Spain. If America wanted Far Eastern islands, it would have to enlarge its navy at substantial cost. The ambassador had had a conversation with "an exceedingly influential personage" in the German government (whom he declined to identify at the latter's request). He had asked the official "in a jocose way" if he wanted the Ladrones and had received an affirmative reply. White asked the State Department to express sympathy with the "legitimate commercial aspirations of Germany in the Far East." In another conversation, the ambassador assured Richthofen that he favored the extension of German civilization in that area. Thus, given White's activities, it is hardly surprising to find an increasing German naval presence in Manila Bay. The ambassador was so anxious to help his government shed the "white man's burden" that he facilitated a near confrontation between Diederichs and Dewey.[31]

Secretary of State William R. Day sharply rebuked White for encouraging Germany's territorial appetite. The United States was not yet in possession of the Philippines and Carolines, he curtly informed the ambas-

29. May, *Imperial Democracy*, pp. 228–29; ADW to Day, June 18, 1898, DAG; Diary, June 18 and July 9, 1898, WMC.

30. Holls to ADW, April 17, 1898, WMC. White apparently did not realize that the United States had decided to retain at least Manila (Thomas J. McCormick, *China Market* [Chicago, 1967]).

31. ADW to Day, June 18, July 12, and July 13, 1898, DAG.

sador, and future relations depended on the treaty with Spain. Day ordered the ambassador to confine himself to his duty: "The United States has a right to expect the friendly neutrality of Germany in accordance with long established relations of the governments."[32] The secretary of state apparently expected foreign policy decisions to be made in Washington.

White defended himself by insisting that he had merely listened to Richthofen. The ambassador believed that his *personal* expressions of sympathy (and he had been careful to point out that they did not reflect official policy) did no harm.[33] Despite Day's strictures, White was unable to curb his encouragement of the Germans. In a letter ultimately printed in the *New York Tribune*, he repeated his now familiar theme: "As to any reaching out by Germany for colonial possessions or center of influence in the Far East, I have never hesitated to avow myself in favor of them. I regard every establishment of such spheres of influence by great civilizing powers . . . as a benefit to the world at large."[34] Because he continued to encourage German expansion, White's attempts to execute Day's instructions proved self-defeating. He asked Richtofen to remove the ships from Manila Bay. The minister demurred, citing the danger to German residents in the area. The ambassador stretched his instructions a bit and told Richthofen that "in general" the United States sympathized with Germany's territorial ambitions, but the time had not yet arrived for definite negotiations. White probably did not realize that his encouraging sentiments helped destroy any chance that the Germans could be induced to leave Manila Bay.[35]

White's attitude toward the Pacific islands stemmed from a profound misreading of his government's policy. The ambassador refused to believe that the United States sought any territory as a result of the war with Spain. White considered that his encouragement of Germany provided the best possible means of getting rid of territory that the United States genuinely did not want. As late as September 10, Holls reported to a credulous White that McKinley favored letting Germany have one of the Ladrones. The president was also considering giving the rest of the islands back to Spain on a promise of maintenance of order because he feared that American forces could not long endure in such an unfavorable climate.[36]

32. Day to ADW, July 16, 1898, DAG.
33. Draft of letter to Day, n.d., WMC.
34. *New York Tribune*, August 17, 1898.
35. ADW to Day, July 30, 1898, DAG. For a different view of White's accomplishments, see Wolf von Schierbrand, "Ambassador White's Work," *North American Review* 175 (November 1902): 632–41.
36. Holls to ADW, September 10, 1898, WMC.

Thus most of the evidence that he could gather indicated to White that the administration hoped to avoid territorial responsibilities.

The State Department's demand that Spain cede all of the Philippines to the United States surprised White and the Germans. As Germany debated a course of action, White began to reassess his wartime role. Now that the United States had decided to acquire territory, his encouragement of the Germans might seem unpatriotic. For the next decade, White defended himself against critics real and imagined. Early in 1899, Bülow informed White that the German consul in Manila had reported massacres by insurgents; the consul had suggested that troops be sent to protect civilians. The secretary asked the ambassador if the United States would approve such action. White replied that the danger had been exaggerated and won assurances that there would be no intervention. The United States had evidently elected to remain in the Philippines, and White abruptly ended efforts to encourage German territorial expansion.[37]

White's about-face seemed tó constitute proof of misjudgment; and in the years after his retirement in 1902, critics claimed that he had precipitated a near crisis. The retired diplomat denied that he had made any mistakes. Although his military aide had informed him that there was no longer any doubt that Admiral von Diederichs had acted "in a most *nasty* manner" in Manila and that his conduct "must surely have been by Superior incentive,"[38] White labeled the episode a misunderstanding. Diederichs's mission, he argued, was to protect German merchants from the rebel Emilio Aguinaldo, but the admiral had probably misunderstood his instructions and harassed Dewey.[39]

If the former ambassador's explanation of Diederichs's conduct was naive, his recollection of his conversations with the German foreign ministry was less than honest. White categorically denied that he had told *anybody* that the United States would be pleased if Germany took the Philippines. He claimed that only an idiot or a traitor could have advised Germany to occupy Manila. The controversy, he insisted, had been concocted by several men who sought to "smooth over" relations between the two countries at the expense of a retired old ambassador.[40] In his autobiography, White mentioned Diederichs only to say that the jingoes had fabricated "legends" about his confrontation with Dewey. "As a matter of fact," he explained, "each of the two admirals, when their relations first began in Manila, was doubtless rather stiff and on his guard

37. ADW to Hay, January 3, 1899, DAG; Diary, January 3, 1899, WMC.
38. Henry Allen to ADW, December 24, 1898, WMC.
39. *New York Sun*, April 16, 1907.
40. ADW to Melville Stone, April 18, 1907, WMC.

against the other; but these feelings soon yielded to different sentiments."[41] As he had done so often before, White reduced an international
incident to a conflict between gentlemen.

Despite his protestations, however, there is evidence that White was
aware that he had been impolitic. In 1909 he drafted a letter to one Hans
Wehberg in which he attempted to account for his popularity with Bülow.
The German secretary knew, White recalled, "that I had strong sympathy
with sundry German aspirations regarding the islands of the Pacific, that I
believed in the desirability of the development of German naval power to
counterbalance the naval power of Great Britain and that I admired
German culture as a great civilizing force in my own country and throughout the world." In rereading the draft, White must have decided that
something was amiss. He crossed out the phrase "regarding the islands of
the Pacific" and then sent the letter to Wehberg.[42] Had White recognized
that the original draft of his letter provided critics of his activities as
ambassador with too much ammunition? He had, of course, contributed
to the foreign ministry's conviction that territorial advantage could be
gained,[43] but he refused to admit that his misreading of the intentions of
the State Department fueled German ambitions to take the Philippines.

Although he had hoped the United States would not have to police the
Philippines, White accepted McKinley's argument that order had to be
restored on the islands. In 1898 he had assured his friend Elizabeth Evans
that the war had been waged "not for the conquest of territory or to aid a
few sugar manufacturers or from wild jingoism but in obedience to the
conviction that the people of Cuba have been, are, and will be under Spain
treated with frightful cruelty: that the rule of Spain has made the island a
Hell on Earth."[44] When the war ended, White extended his analysis to the
Philippines, asserting that the presence of the United States was necessary
to allow "public opinion there to have a chance to manifest itself with just
as much humanity as possible."[45] The ambassador hoped that American
involvement overseas would end quickly; he probably thought that once a
semblance of order had been restored, the United States would withdraw,
certain it had done its best. In the face of Aguinaldo's uprising, however,
optimism ebbed. White nevertheless suggested "a vague general sovereignty," which would allow the Filipinos eventually to establish their own

41. *Autobiography*, vol. 2, p. 170.
42. ADW to Wehberg, October 20 and November 8, 1909, WMC.
43. Germany bought the Caroline Islands from Spain in 1899 with the acquiescence of the
United States. White had urged Hay to approve the sale (ADW to Hay, January 24, 1899,
DAG).
44. ADW to Mrs. Evans, May 4, 1898, WMC.
45. ADW to E. P. Evans, May 13, 1899, WMC.

government. The chances of success, unfortunately, were "a thousand to one" against, and the ambassador feared that "by and by, from sheer fatigue, they will beg us to take the reins."[46]

In fact, White received information that annexation might be imminent. Herbert Squiers, a member of the United States legation in China, conveyed the sentiments of Americans living in the East to the ambassador. They were most eager, he reported, that the government retain possession of the Philippines because such action would increase American influence and trade in China. Trade was impossible, Squiers argued, "without influence and power in back of it."[47]

Meanwhile, Henry T. Allen, who had been White's military aide in Berlin and was now stationed in the Philippines, informed the ambassador that the rebels refused to surrender. They apparently did not realize, Allen wrote with unintentional irony, "that unconditioned surrender must precede any measure of self-government that may be accorded them." In 1901 Allen, now military governor of Leyte, wrote that he now realized that American ideas and ideals were "misfits" in the Philippines. The "Brownies" considered them "evidence of weakness and even cowardice." There was no doubt, Allen concluded, that a considerable military force would always be required to police the island.[48]

Allen's assessment confirmed White's worst fear, and he moved to ensure that the Philippines would never become more than a "dependency" of the United States. The ambassador wrote private letters to "persons in authority," including Assistant Secretary of State David J. Hill, urging a constitutional amendment to define the status of territories and dependencies. He proposed that a dependency be managed by a governor and council and that a territory be managed by a governor appointed in Washington and a legislature elected by the people of the territory. Thus there would be no provision for self-government in dependencies such as the Philippines. Most important, White's amendment "distinctly" declared that "no state shall be admitted from territory acquired after the year 1890, except by consent of three-fifths of the existing states." White's proposal evoked little response, but pressure for the admission of the Philippines did not mount.[49]

As the war and near collision between Germany and the United States faded into memory, White stressed the friendship between the two na-

---

46. ADW to Holls, January 19, 1899, WMC.
47. Squiers to ADW, August 9, 1898, WMC.
48. Allen to ADW, June 2, 1899, and February 12, 1901, WMC.
49. ADW to Mr. and Mrs. Evans, January 4, 1899; ADW to Holls, January 5 and 19, 1899; ADW to Hill, January 19, 1899; Holls to ADW, January 21, 1899; all in WMC.

tions. During 1899, the troublesome Samoa issue was settled. The United States retained its base at Pago Pago, while Germany received the rest of the islands. Both governments were pleased with the arrangement, which removed a potential source of conflict.[50] Relations between the two countries seemed to be improving, and the ambassador seized all opportunities to strengthen the bond of friendship. The tariff issue was scarcely noticed anymore, he asserted, and the ill feeling that arose from the Spanish–American War was all but forgotten. In May 1900 he assured visitors that relations between the two countries were never better.[51]

While he emphasized German–American friendship, the ambassador lavishly praised President McKinley. Casting aside his doubts about American policy, White exclaimed about the war: "How great seems the achievement! How petty the blemishes!" He defended the president against charges that he was an imperialist by pointing out that he had no alternative: had he left Cuba and the Philippines to anarchy or deserted them to the "tender mercies" of ambitious European nations, those who now denounced him as a tyrant would have called him a coward. White was sure that McKinley ultimately sought freedom for the islands, preparing them to make a "proper beginning." He was proud to be associated with such an enlightened administration.[52]

As long as White remained hopeful that neither the Philippines nor Cuba would be incorporated into the United States, he had no difficulty praising the policy of his government, though it would not have been his own. White defies categorization as an imperialist or an anti-imperialist. He generally opposed acquisition of territory by the United States, yet always advocated increasing spheres of influence or enlarging commercial opportunities. The ambassador's racism, more than anything else, made him cautious about America's imperialistic ventures; but once territory had been taken, he accepted what he thought was inevitable, while seeking guarantees that the gravitational pull of the United States would never result in statehood.

50. See ADW to Hay, April 7 and 19, 1899, WMC; ADW to Hay, February 20, 1899, DAG; Diary, April 3 and 6, 1899, WMC; Schieber, *Transformation of American Sentiment*, p. 82.
51. *New York Times*, April 7 and May 3, 1900.
52. "President McKinley and Peace, " *Independent* 52 (August 2, 1900): 1832–34.

Chapter 15   *The Hague Peace Conference*

If White hoped that the peace treaty with Spain would bring a relaxation of his diplomatic duties, he did not reckon with the tsar of Russia. Eager to enhance his prestige as a peacemaker and at the same time to reduce military expenses in Russia, the monarch called for an international arbitration and disarmament conference in 1899.[1] The American delegation to the conference at The Hague included Stanford Newel, minister to the Netherlands; Seth Low, former mayor of Brooklyn and presently president of Columbia University; Alfred Mahan, author of *The Influence of Sea Power upon History, 1660–1783*; and William Crozier, army ordinance expert. The secretary of the delegation was Frederick William Holls. Its president was Andrew Dickson White.[2]

U.S. opinion on the wisdom of attending the European conference was divided. Several people observed that if the delegates assented to a system of international arbitration, the United States would become entangled in every Old World dispute. America might also be forced to submit intrahemispheric disputes to an arbitration board, thus vitiating the Monroe Doctrine.[3] Despite such objections, massive support for the conference emerged. At a mass meeting at Johns Hopkins University, minister Edward Everett Hale exuberantly praised the Hague meeting. In a refrain repeated in gatherings throughout the country, Hale called for the establishment of a permanent court of arbitration, empowered to judge all questions that resisted diplomatic solutions: "The moral force of such a court, increasing with every year, would carry authority among nations, and its very existence would calm the storm of passion."[4]

Deluged by petitions from proponents and opponents of the conference, the delegates professed to take a more realistic view. Nothing would be done about disarmament, White predicted, unless the tsar unilaterally

---

1. Ernest May, *Imperial Democracy* (New York, 1961), pp. 235–36.
2. "Our Delegation to the Hague," *Review of Reviews* 19 (May 1899): 545–57.
3. Objections to the conference are rehearsed in "Possibilities at the Hague," *Nation* 68 (May 18, 1899):368.
4. *Baltimore Sun*, April 7, 1899, WMC; see also James B. Angell to ADW, July 25, 1899, WMC.

dismissed "to their peaceful avocations" a considerable number of Russian troops massed on his frontiers. "But no one expects him to do this, or anything like it." [5]

Holls had even fewer hopes for the conferences than his friend. No one expected any "great practical results," he reported, but few doubted that the United States should for political reasons play a conspicuous role in this first international peace conference. The State Department did not expect the delegates to "take the initiative in anything important," he told White. [6] The skepticism of Holls and White was more than matched by that of Alfred Mahan, who was openly opposed to arbitration and whose presence on the delegation probably reflected his desire to block "foolish" agreements. The American representatives, then, departed for the Hague convinced that they would return with few substantive accomplishments.

The instructions of the State Department to the peace commissioners underlined the limited objectives of the United States. The delegates were to support arbitration "enthusiastically" but must refuse to submit questions "involving political independence or territorial integrity." The State Department claimed that because the United States had such a small army and navy, limitation of armed forces was not applicable. Proposals to ban new firearms were deemed "impractical." The delegates, finally, were asked to support improved rules relating to wounded prisoners and to favor immunity of private property at sea. The commissioners and their superiors seemed to agree that the United States had little to gain from the conference. [7]

The proposal of British delegate Sir Julian Pauncefote to create a permanent arbitration panel quickly transformed White's view of the conference. Although he continued to oppose compulsory arbitration, the ambassador thought that the moral force of a permanent court would be a giant step toward rational alternatives to war. Few could now call the conference a "Russian trick" or a "utopian fantasy." White reported the upsurge of optimism to Secretary of State John Hay: "Many who came to scoff remained to pray, *l'appetit vient en mangeant*." He predicted that some form of arbitration would be adopted. [8]

As the American delegation settled down to work, internal dissension became apparent. Mahan opposed provisions for the immunity of private property at sea. Combatants had an obligation to do everything possible to

5. ADW to David J. Hill, April 21, 1899, and ADW to E. P. Evans, April 19, 1899, WMC.
6. Holls to ADW, April 4, 1899, WMC.
7. *Autobiography*, vol. 2, pp. 253–55.
8. ADW to George P. Fisher, May 29, 1899, and ADW to Hay, June 7, 1899, WMC.

Frederick W. Holls, White's political adviser and secretary to the American delegation at the Hague Peace Conference

weaken the adversary, he argued. White was appalled: if logically extended, such a policy would oblige nations "to go back to the marauding and atrocities of the Thirty Years' War."[9] Mahan also objected to proposals to allow neutral ships to pick up *combattants naufrages* without adequately defining their status. At the very least, he argued, the passengers should be subjected to capture. The American delegates ultimately convinced Mahan that his objections imperiled any agreement on treatment of prisoners; the usually stubborn captain agreed to drop them.[10] That Mahan intended to obstruct virtually every proposal at the conference became clear when he opposed the prohibition of asphyxiating bombs from warfare. They had not even been invented yet, he observed; besides, torpedoes promoted asphyxiation by water and were not banned. Should different methods of warfare be required on land than on the sea? Crozier agreed with his colleague but White and Holls did not. Land bombs should be outlawed, White noted, because they were directed primarily against civilians, while torpedoes were aimed at belligerents. The United States was the only country at the conference, however, that opposed the prohibition of asphyxiating bombs in war.[11]

Although the delegation debated many proposals relating to the laws and customs of war, attention focused on the establishment of a permanent arbitration tribunal. On the form of arbitration, the American delegation stood virtually united. Each delegate opposed compulsory arbitration: Mahan, Crozier, and Newel in all instances, White and Holls in most.[12] The Russian proposal provided for compulsory arbitration in the following areas: pecuniary damages caused by citizens of another country; treaties involving postal, telegraphic, and railroad services; navigation of international canals; protection of patents and literary and artistic property; conventions regarding sanitary affairs, inheritance, extradition, and mutual judicial assistance; and boundary questions that concerned purely technical, not political, questions. White agreed with his colleagues that the interest of the United States in an isthmian canal made compulsory arbitration relative to river navigation and international canals objectionable. Although inclined to accept the rest of the package, he did not seem upset when the proposal was defeated.[13]

Even the hint of an obligation to arbitrate generated protest from the

9. *Autobiography*, vol. 2, p. 317; *The First Hague Conference* (Boston, 1912), p. 114.
10. Frederick W. Holls, *The Peace Conference at the Hague* (London, 1900), pp. 505–506.
11. ADW to Hay, August 9, 1899, WMC.
12. Mahan discussed his opposition to arbitration in *Armaments and Arbitration* (New York and London, 1911), esp. pp. 10, 39, 42, 44–50.
13. ADW to Albert K. Smiley, May 24, 1905, WMC.

American delegation. Midway through the conference, the French proposed that when any two powers seemed about to drift into war, the other powers consider it a duty to remind them of the arbitration tribunal. The Americans refused to assent to this innocuous proposal, citing their traditional fear of being drawn into European conflicts. The United States was evidently willing to agree to the principle of arbitration, which White for one thought would thwart "the designs of the great international social and anarchist combinations," but it would not agree to the mildest use of the tribunal when American interests could conceivably be at stake.[14]

The attitude of the American delegation toward arbitration derived from reverence for the Monroe Doctrine. Obligatory arbitration would subject disputes in the Western Hemisphere to the judgment of European nations; none of the delegates was willing to accept any limitation on the hegemony of the United States in its own backyard. Thus, although the conference ultimately agreed upon a tribunal that would hear cases voluntarily submitted to it, the United States refused to sign without appending a reservation endorsing the Monroe Doctrine.[15] Pauncefote had asked White to withdraw the declaration: "It will be charged against you that you propose to evade your duties while using the treaty to promote your interests." White stood firm, and the United States reaped an unforeseen benefit from the conference. For the first time, an international gathering had (albeit tacitly) recognized the existence of the Monroe Doctrine.[16]

Before the agreement creating the permanent arbitration tribunal had been signed, however, its advocates had to convince the German Kaiser to give his assent. Wilhelm instructed Count Georg zu Münster-Ledenburg, head of the German delegation, to oppose arbitration in any form. As the delegate closest to the German foreign ministry, White took it upon himself to persuade Wilhelm to change his mind. Despite the vehement opposition of the other members of the American delegation—especially Low,[17] who thought this action an undue interference in German affairs—White sent Holls to Berlin with a personal letter to Bülow and the Kaiser. No "thinking man" proposed compulsory arbitration, he wrote, except in petty matters that might aid all governments. If Germany

14. *The First Hague Conference*, pp. 60, 103–107.

15. At the conclusion of the conference, Mahan and Holls engaged in an unseemly quarrel as to which of them had insisted on the Monroe Doctrine reservation. See Holls to Mahan, March 15 and 30, 1901, and Holls to Shaw, March 15, 1902, Albert Shaw MSS, New York Public Library; Holls to ADW, March 18, 1901, and Mahan to Holls, March 25, 1901, WMC; Memorandum in re Mahan and Holls, January 17, 1902, WMC.

16. *Autobiography* vol. 2, pp. 341–42.

17. Except for this action, Low seems to have assumed an inactive role at the conference. See Gerald Kurland, *Seth Low* (New York, 1971), p. 213.

objected, such provisions could be omitted. No one, White reiterated, planned to submit "questions involving the honor of any nation or of its territory or of any of those things which nations feel instinctively must be reserved for their own decision." Voluntary arbitration did not limit sovereignty, and White argued that German acquiescence would enhance Germany's world prestige. White hinted that the tribunal could untangle conflicts between Germany and the United States: Samoa, tonnage dues, the sugar bounty. Although he must have known that his government would not submit these issues to arbitration, White stated: "It is not at all unlikely that such a court would decide in your favor." The ambassador found little reason, then, for German opposition to voluntary arbitration.[18]

While the ambassador remonstrated with Bülow and the Kaiser, he enlisted the aid of Count Münster. White noted that the middle class and religious people throughout the world had been stirred by the conference; if they were disappointed, Germany's prestige would suffer. He played upon Münster's fear of socialism by repeating French Socialist Jean-Léon Jaurès's prophecy that the conference would be a failure: "You will find that the powers will concede nothing; you will come back conquered and the victory will remain to us."[19]

White's efforts seemed successful; Münster's opposition to the permanent tribunal evaporated, and he sent Philipp Zorn, the second-ranking member of the delegation, to Berlin to change the minds of the foreign ministers. Although he claimed to oppose arbitration in principle, Münster noted that German obstinacy would offend Russia, the United States, and Great Britain. The Hague court, moreover, would have neither the power nor the authority to intervene in diplomatic disputes. If Germany insisted, all provisions for obligatory arbitration would be dropped. Münster implied that his country risked nothing if it signed the arbitration treaty.[20]

Within days Germany announced that it would support the creation of the tribunal. White took much of the credit for the about-face. He did not realize that voices far more powerful than his had brought about the change. Italy and Austria-Hungary, noting that arbitration was voluntary, pressured their ally to sign the agreement. Prince Radolin, German ambassador at St. Petersburg, warned that continued opposition would cause

18. Diary, June 16, 1899, WMC; ADW to Hay, September 15, 1899, WMC; *Autobiography*, vol 2, p. 314; ADW to Baron Bernhard von Bülow, June 16, 1899, WMC.
19. Extracts from Diary Pvt. and Confidential, June 16, 1899, WMC.
20. Calvin Davis, *The United States and the First Hague Peace Conference* (Ithaca, 1962), p. 156; Diary, June 17 and 18, 1899, WMC; *Autobiography*, vol. 2, pp. 301–306.

relations with Russia to deteriorate. Bülow and Wilhelm II agreed, finally, that opposition would throw the United States into the embrace of England while participation in the tribunal might incline America toward Germany.[21]

The German decision removed the last major obstacle to agreement. On July 29, delegates assembled to sign the three conventions agreed to after months of deliberation. The United States delegation signed the first convention, which created the court of arbitration, although White noted that the agreement was subject to the declaration on the Monroe Doctrine that had been made in open session. The second convention, which related to the laws and customs of war on land, was referred to the State Department with the recommendation that it be signed. The third convention, which related to maritime warfare, was sent to Washington without recommendation, a tacit recognition of the opposition of Mahan, who favored no limitations on warfare.[22]

White's enthusiasm about the outcome of the conference stemmed from his conviction that rational discourse was the best means of preventing war. Contact and dialogue among men of goodwill, he believed, increased mutual respect and affection. If each side recognized the sincerity of the other, compromise was likely. He hoped that the moral force of public opinion would be increasingly stirred by the successful operation of the arbitration tribunal. The permanent machinery set up by the conference was invaluable because it served an educative function; it reminded people that there were alternatives to war.[23]

Only a moral public could compel arbitration; thus White justified his opposition to compulsory arbitration. It was, he thought, both impractical and ineffective. Arbitration necessitated huge national armies that were willing to unite to impose peace on warring parties. Without an educated populace, such action would be impossible; with it, unnecessary. White evidently did not entertain the thought that an international agreement for compulsory arbitration might itself serve to educate the public more profoundly than the creation of a weak tribunal. His attitude, like that of

21. Davis, *United States and the First Hague Peace Conference*, pp. 159–61. Years later White and Zorn contended for the lion's share of the credit in persuading Germany to sign the agreement. See Helen M. White to ADW, May 30, 1910; ADW to Hans Wehberg, October 20, 1909; Wehberg to ADW, September 5 and November 29, 1909; ADW to Evans, October 22, 1909; ADW to Low, September 8, 1908; ADW to Hugo Munsterberg, November 12, 1909; Munsterberg to ADW, November 16 and 23, 1909, all in WMC.
22. Holls, *Peace Conference*, p. 489. The full text of the conventions are printed in ibid., pp. 374–473. Another useful survey of the conference is James Brown Scott, *The Hague Peace Conferences of 1899 and 1907* (Baltimore, 1909), pp. 1–87.
23. ADW to Oscar Straus, October 15, 1904, WMC.

his government, allowed him to pursue the "only" path to peace without sacrificing the national interest. Thus Willard Fiske's admonition—that a "tribunal without a provision for compulsory enforcement of arbitration will be like our American compulsory school laws—a farce"—was easily dismissed by White as unrealistic. The conference, he concluded, "was one of the greatest advances ever made in the history of the modern world."[24]

White's attitude toward arbitration reflected an uncertainty about the dynamics of change. He was not certain how the "is" might become the "ought." Indeed, he scorned visionaries who thought that they could remake the world *de novo*. At the same time, however, he recognized that change was necessary and inevitable. On July 4, 1899, in the midst of the conference, White outlined his understanding of progress in a speech in commemoration of Hugo Grotius. He defended the jurist against charges that his reform did not go far enough: the spirit that permeated the era was the immoral spirit of Machiavelli; thus Grotius's system, "at the time he presented it, was the only one which could ennoble men's theories or reform their practice." Grotius, then, was praised for acting on his vision of what ought to be, although White satisfied himself that the Dutch reformer had tempered his legal code with a sense of what was possible. The lesson for the Hague conference was obvious: "May it not be that, in the not distant future, International Law, while mainly basing its doctrines upon what nations have slowly developed in practice, may also draw inspiration, more and more, from that power in the Universe not ourselves, which makes for Righteousness."[25]

The lesson, unfortunately, did not assist diplomats because it was based solely on historical hindsight and thus had no predictive value. How could one tell how much of the "ought to be" was possible in a given historical era? How could one decide when a current dogma was ready to be superseded? Thus, although it seemed to provide room for change, White's philosophy tended to be more compatible with the status quo. The "is" could always be defended as workable, while the "ought" could be condemned as foolish, utopian fancy. Traditions, White implied, should never be killed; but as they died a "natural" death, reformers should present practical alternatives.

As the Senate began consideration of the Hague treaty, a debate in

24. Diary, August 3, 1899, WMC; ADW to Oscar Straus, October 15, 1904, WMC; *New York Times*, August 20, 1899; Willard Fiske to E. P. Evans, July 10 (1899?), Edward Payson Evans MSS Cornell University; ADW to Fred White, July 10, 1899, WMC.
25. [Speech at] *The Proceedings at the Laying of a Wreath on the Tomb of Hugo Grotius* (The Hague, 1899), pp. 24–27.

several prestigious journals in the United States clarified the issues. In an
essay entitled "In the Clutch of the Harpy Powers," R. W. Johnston
lambasted the agreement as an "egregious folly" brought on by "the
hysteria of the Millennium seekers." The proposed treaty provided
Europe with the loophole necessary to destroy the Monroe Doctrine;
Ambassador White's "pleasant little explanatory speech" had little practical significance. If the treaty destroyed the Monroe Doctrine, it also
necessitated the abandonment of traditional American foreign policy. The
United States would doubtless be drawn into European conflicts; it would
be forced to "join in solidarity . . . with such enlightened political entities
as Turkey, Austria, Greece and Spain." Johnston concluded with an
urgent call for the rejection of the treaty.[26]

The delegates defended the treaty against Johnston's attack. Low argued that the conference did all that could have been done. To its credit it
left "to public opinion the vitalization of its work." Holls stoutly denied
that there had been any departure from the traditional foreign policy of the
United States. The Monroe Doctrine reservation was binding on every
nation that signed the agreement. Holls agreed that the treaty did not
guarantee peace:

> To wish even for absolute universal peace implies an approval of the present status
> of the world, or at least the possibility of thwarting any change for the better by the
> stubbornness of any one power. This would be a wrong greater even than the
> horrors of war; but peace, as the result of law and order, solemnly agreed upon by
> the civilized powers of the world—that was the real ideal and object of the
> Conference.

The tribunal, Holls reiterated, was purely voluntary; thus it did not
threaten the interests of the United States. Holls's essay was largely
defensive. He parried Johnston's assertions but could not show precisely
how the treaty might deter conflict. At times Holls seemed to call for
adoption of the treaty because it did no harm.[27]

Captain Mahan, an ardent champion of unlimited national prerogative
saw little to fear from the treaty, although he evidenced little enthusiasm
for it. In an essay in the *North American Review*, he pointed out, with an
almost audible sigh of relief, that compulsory arbitration had, at present,

26. R. M. Johnston, "In the Clutch of the Harpy Powers," *North American Review* 169
(October 1899): 448–53.

27. Seth Low, "The International Conference of Peace," *North American Review* 169
(November 1899): 625–39; Frederick W. Holls, "America at the Peace Conference," *Independent* 51 (December 28, 1899): 3470–75, and "The Results of the Peace Conference in Their
Relation to the Monroe Doctrine," *American Monthly Review of Reviews* 20 (November 1899):
560–67.

no chance of acceptance. Having put his audience at ease, Mahan might have supported Holls's recommendation that the treaty be adopted. Instead, he dwelt upon his favorite theme, the inevitability of force in the maintenance of law. Force ensured that law would be obeyed; conversely, force was often the only recourse for those whose consciences forced them to resist law. As long as conviction of conscience remained unshaken, Mahan intoned, "war is better [even] than disobedience—better than acquiescence in recognized wrong." He argued that if the dispute between the United States and Spain had been referred to arbitration, Cuba would still be ruled by the cruel, despotic monarchy.[28] Thus Mahan agreed with his colleagues that the treaty had little impact on American foreign policy. He differed with them, however, in his hopes for the future. Holls, Low, and White hoped that the Hague conference would eventually lead the masses to force their leaders to submit all disputes to arbitration; Mahan thought arbitration undesirable.

The Hague treaty failed to generate enthusiasm or opposition in the United States Senate. McKinley and Secretary of State Hay did not immediately submit it for consideration. When they did, it was accompanied by a perfunctory message of support. Cushman Davis, chairman of the Foreign Relations Committee, reported the bill favorably to the Senate, which approved each convention except for the proposals revising the laws and customs of war on land. As if to underline the purely voluntary nature of the agreement, the administration (even as McKinley initialed the treaty) refused to submit the Alaska–Canada boundary dispute to the Hague tribunal. The world had a permanent court of arbitration, but it seemed doubtful that it would attract many clients.[29]

McKinley's appointments to The Hague gave a veneer of respectability to the tribunal, but the treaty's weaknesses remained evident. Benjamin Harrison thought that his appointment was "attractive" because it was accompanied by assurances that he would "have nothing to do." Grover Cleveland refused to represent his country at The Hague, pronouncing the conference's conclusions "lame and disappointing." Frederick Holls was ecstatic when Chulalongkorn, king of Siam, appointed him to represent the tiny Asian nation at The Hague. Evidently Siam did not think the tribunal important enough to necessitate representation by one of its own subjects.[30]

28. Alfred T. Mahan, "The Peace Conference and the Moral Aspect of War," *North American Review* 169 (October 1899): 433–47.
29. Davis, *United States and the First Hague Peace Conference*, pp. 186–202; Edward Everett Hale to ADW, February 10, 1900, and Holls to ADW, March 3, 1900, WMC.
30. Davis, *United States and the First Hague Peace Conference*, pp. 203–208.

Although the world seemed to yawn as the court assembled, White's enthusiasm did not diminish. "Fear neither opposition nor detraction" had been Grotius's message to him, and he attempted to spread the message of peace through reasoned discourse. He asked Andrew Carnegie to construct a beautiful building at The Hague to house the tribunal. Such an edifice would remind the masses that the world's commitment to alternatives to war was permanent.[31] In 1902, Denmark proposed—"by a solemn act"—to refer all questions in dispute to the Hague tribunal. "The time is coming when all other nations will do so," White wrote gleefully.[32]

As White returned to his diplomatic duties in Berlin, President McKinley considered asking him to be his running mate in 1900. Theodore Roosevelt preferred to run for reelection as governor of New York, perhaps because he thought the governorship provided a better base for a 1904 presidential race. Consequently, he urged Republican leaders to draft White for the vice-presidency. Realizing that the sixty-eight-year-old ambassador did not relish strenuous work, Holls emphasized "the comparative retirement and quiet dignity of the office." Even the duties of presiding over the Senate, he pointed out, "may very easily be put upon another."[33]

If political office had once attracted White, he seemed genuinely hesitant this time to submit himself to the rigors of a campaign. Perhaps the obscurity of the vice-presidency, which Holls had attempted to make a virtue, convinced him that the office was not worth the effort. Upon receipt of Holls's letter he shot back a cable: "Prevent all action if possible until you receive my letter of today." "Profoundly skeptical" about the "whole movement," White expressed doubt that he had the health necessary to campaign. Prejudices against his nomination and election, he predicted, would be aroused by critics of *The Warfare of Science with Theology*. As always, White admitted that he would not refuse nomination if a decided "majority" of Republicans deemed it necessary. He "devoutly" hoped, however, that they would not.[34]

Despite White's discouragement, Holls loved his "country too well not to do everything in my power for your nomination." The New York lawyer, always in touch with prominent German-Americans, coordinated his friend's campaign; by June the *Philadelphia Ledger* and H. H. Kohlsaat's

31. ADW to Carnegie, June 18, 1900, Andrew Carnegie MSS, Library of Congress; William T. Stead to Holls, July 13, 1900, Frederick W. Holls MSS, Columbia University.
32. ADW to Holls, December 11, 1902, WMC.
33. *Syracuse Journal*, May 15, 1900; Holls to ADW, May 8, 1900, WMC.
34. Diary, May 18, May 19, and June 16, 1900, WMC; ADW to Holls May 19, 1900, WMC.

Chicago Times Herald had publicly endorsed his candidacy. If Roosevelt remained out of the race, White had a chance.[35]

Such hopeful signs, however, were more than matched by discouraging reports. Tom Platt refused to endorse White. On June 12, Holls reported that the Metropolitan Street Railway and other New York trusts, angered at Governor Roosevelt's Franchise Tax Law, had informed Platt that they would not contribute a nickel to the Republican party if "Teddy" were nominated for governor. Almost immediately Platt inaugurated efforts to stampede the National Convention to draft the Rough Rider as its vice-president.[36]

As Roosevelt's prospects improved, White's dimmed. His only chance had been to emerge as the only available candidate from New York. Nomination now would come only if the convention became hopelessly deadlocked. Even in that unlikely event, there was little chance that politicians would turn to White. On June 26, Holls wrote that "the intoxication of the hurrah" of the convention crowd, which had been stimulated by Platt, weakened Roosevelt's resolve; the Republicans chose a McKinley-Roosevelt slate.[37]

If White was disappointed, he hid his feelings well. He was pleased, he informed his son, that the party had obliged Roosevelt to take a place on the ticket. A Republican victory would "bury Bryanism forever," and the ambassador sent several letters of support across the Atlantic. Several of his speeches in Germany were reprinted by the Republican National Committee for distribution to German-Americans. Although the magazine *Puck* mistook Andrew White for Horace White and pictured him in a cartoon with writer Carl Schurz and editor Edwin L. Godkin, as flies caught by Bryan the spider, the ambassador's support of the Republicans was unequivocal. His modest differences with the administration over the Philippines would never impel him into the Bryan camp.[38]

McKinley needed White's support to persuade German-Americans that the two countries were not on a collision course in China. The Kaiser had

35. Holls to ADW, June 7 and 21, 1900, WMC.
36. Holls to ADW June 12, 1900, WMC.
37. Holls to ADW, June 26, 1900, WMC.
38. ADW to Holls, July 4, 1900; ADW to Fred White, July 6, 1900; ADW to Arthur von Briesen, September 24, 1900; ADW to George Tarbell, September 24, 1900; ADW to Frank Enz, September 26, 1900, all in WMC; *Ithaca Journal*, September 26, 1900; ADW to Holls, September 6, 1900; Holls to ADW, October 5, 1900; ADW to David J. Hill, November 8, 1900, all in WMC. In 1902 White defended the "retaliatory justice" of American soldiers in the Philippines: "I consider the destruction of a whole tribe of Indians or a whole island full of low class halfbreed Malays and other savages as of infinitely less account than the blotting out of a single, God-fearing, hardworking, American pioneer's family" (ADW to Roosevelt, August 15, 1902, WMC).

reacted strongly to the murder of Baron Klemens von Ketteler, German minister to China, in the summer of 1900: "I will not rest until the German flag . . . has been planted on the walls of Peking to dictate peace to the Chinese." The Germans used the violence of the Boxer Rebellion as a pretext to carve up China; a sizable military force was dispatched to Asia to ensure Chinese compliance with indemnity demands and to restore order. The American State Department feared that Germany would exact a settlement that violated the recently enunciated Open Door policy.[39] Meanwhile, reports of German atrocities in China circulated in the press. The United States demanded a negotiated settlement, while Germany maintained that punishment of the guilty should precede negotiation.[40]

Although on temporary leave in America at the time, White insisted that the Kaiser would not violate the Open Door. Alleged atrocities committed by Field Marshal General Alfred von Waldersee, whom White had known for twenty years, were "ineffably absurd." The ambassador denied reports that Wilhelm II had instructed his troops to give no quarter to the Chinese; perhaps the emperor had advised them to expect no quarter. White defended the German desire to punish the murderers of Ketteler, expected pacification but no partition of China, and applauded the extension of German civilization to Asia. German-Americans, he concluded, should expect no conflict between Germany and the United States. The recently signed reciprocal trade agreement, in fact, had cemented relations between the two countries.[41]

Although the Germans insisted for a time that they be permitted to behead the murderers of Ketteler, Secretary Hay eventually convinced them that the imperial government (with the "assistance" of the Western powers) would severely punish the criminals.[42] Although policy differences between the two countries surfaced now and again, China did not cause a breach in German–American relations, nor did it seriously diminish McKinley's popularity among German-American voters.[43]

39. White discussed his part in winning German approval of the Open Door in *Autobiography*, vol. 2, pp. 157–58, and ADW to Hay, March 24, 1900, DAG.

40. Clara Schieber, *The Transformation of American Sentiment toward Germany* (Boston and New York, 1923), pp. 97–98, 109; John B. Jackson to Secretary of State, September 25, 1900, DAG.

41. *New York Sun*, August 8, 1900; *New York Tribune*, August 8, 1900; *Syracuse Evening Telegram*, August 10, 1900; Holls to ADW, August 22 and 31, 1900, WMC.

42. Thomas J. McCormick, *China Market* (Chicago, 1967), pp. 180–81.

43. For the resolution of the conflict see Translation of Cipher Telegraphic Instruction, November 29, 1900, WMC; ADW to John Hay, January 9, 1900, and February 21, 1901, and Hay to ADW, March 21, 1901, DAG. The *New York Times*'s European edition of December 6, 1900, reported that White had criticized U.S. foreign policy as a "drag on European diplomacy" and had argued that the United States sought only commercial advantage in China. "Sounds Very Queer, If True," the page 1 headline concluded. White vehemently

The nineteenth century had ended well, with the hope of international peace stirred by the Hague conference. And the twentieth century had opened auspiciously (if indeed 1900 and not 1901 marked the beginning of the new century) with the election of McKinley. If White hoped that his remaining few years would be accompanied by peace and contentment, however, he was cruelly disappointed. The new century commenced with the premature death of the nation's president as well as of two of White's children.

The end came for William McKinley only a few months after his inauguration. The ambassador was informed by telegram that the president had been shot by an anarchist in Buffalo. Reflexively, White blamed the crime on well-intentioned defenders of radicals: "This comes from allowing every privilege to these creatures." A year after the assassination, he begged President Roosevelt to grant neither clemency nor aid to Leon Czolgosz, the assassin: "This miserable creature was living under better and more hopeful conditions than his *family* ever had known . . . he was allowed to take the Chief Magistrate of the United States by the hand and . . . [was] received by him, not merely perfunctorily, but cordially." McKinley's assassin had had the audacity to act as if society were not heading steadily on its own power toward the fulfillment of individual aspiration. White's unrelenting condemnation of Czolgosz indicates that he may have had a lurking suspicion that if progress were not agreed upon as the norm of society, radical action might be justified; but if society was gradually approaching the millennium, violent action was merely gratuitous cruelty.[44]

Although President Roosevelt asked the ambassador to remain at his post, personal crises convinced him that the time had come to leave public office. Family problems had plagued White throughout his tenure at Berlin. At first, his daughter Ruth had been the center of concern. A talented musician who seemed "impractical" to her father, Ruth for years sought permission to marry one Ervin Ferry. White believed "a hasty decision folly and madness," especially since at that time Ferry was employed by his father selling soda fountains. Engagement was therefore delayed, but when Ferry became head of the Physics Department of Purdue University, White consented to a wedding. He planned to send Ruth to Brooklyn's Pratt Institute to learn cooking and sewing but was

denied the story (ADW to Richthofen, December 6, 1900, DAG; ADW to Holls, December 10, 1900, WMC).

44. Diary, September 7, 1901; ADW to Count von Ballesstrom, September 11, 1901; ADW to Theodore Roosevelt, August 15, 1902, all in WMC. See also White's essay "Assassins and Their Apologists," *Independent* 54 (August 21, 1902): 1989–90.

persuaded that his daughter could practice at home. No school could remove Ruth's eccentricities, Fred reminded his father. With little confidence in either his daughter or Ervin Ferry, White gave Ruth away on August 21, 1900.[45]

White's hesitancy to agree to Ruth's marriage was due in part to the unhappy marital experience of his eldest daughter. At first Clara's marriage to Spencer Newberry seemed fortuitous; a talented administrator, Newberry managed the Sandusky Cement Company in Ohio, which was owned by the White family. Clara had tried to ignore Spencer's philandering, but the threat of public scandal was unbearable. Fred advised his sister to return home, using as an excuse the desire to educate her sons in an eastern school. Spencer, he informed his father, was selfish and egotistical: "Clara is a noble girl and just because she is growing old and has lost her girlish charm, Spencer wants to *marry* a younger woman. Most men would think they were well treated if their wife winked at their keeping a young girl as mistress, but *he* can't be satisfied unless he gets rid of his wife and marries a younger one. It makes me sick."[46]

White asked his son to discover whether Clara was in danger of disease, given the "performances" of her husband, but was assured that the Newberrys had not shared the same bed for more than a year. In March 1898, Clara insisted upon a separation. She would not agree to a divorce because she feared that Spencer might marry the cook. Within weeks of this declaration, the triangle was squared; the cook announced her engagement to another man, and it seemed again possible to avoid scandal. By June, however, Newberry's "performances" began again. With scandal now in the newspapers, separation became a necessity. Clara returned east and terminated her marriage.[47]

Clara, White's family physician informed him, suffered from more than mental anguish. She had at first told no one of her marital problems. Sleep became a virtual impossibility for her until Spencer had suggested "bromidia" to relax the nerves. Very quickly Clara became an addict. Her habit could be broken, Dr. Rankin insisted, but the drug had had a serious effect on the brain and nervous system. The family hired a nurse to prevent Clara from taking the drug, but Clara dismissed her. White returned home in 1901 to remonstrate with his daughter, and she promised

45. ADW to Fred White, March 11, 1895; Fred White to ADW, July 23, 1898; Fred White to ADW, September 26 and November 17, 1899; Ruth White to ADW, September 29, 1899; wedding invitation, August 21, 1900, all in WMC.
46. Fred White to ADW, January 31, 1898, WMC.
47. Fred White to ADW, February 2, February 28, March 4, March 13, and June 12, 1898, WMC. See also *Cleveland World*, June 12, 1901.

White, daughter Clara, and one of her sons

to try to break her habit. Despite occasionally encouraging reports about her mental and physical health, however, Clara remained a semi-invalid for the rest of her life.[48]

White had depended very heavily on Fred during this season of family turmoil. He had had great hopes for his son, who as a young man had been constantly ill. Fred had attended Columbia Law School in the 1880s, had been prostrated with a typhoid attack, and had returned to work too quickly in an effort to graduate with his class. He never recovered his health, nor could he overcome constant bouts of "nerves." Often he did not have the strength to write letters to his father in his own hand. Fred's melancholia increased because he knew that he had not fulfilled his father's expectations for him. Not robust enough to hold a steady job, he worked as the manager of the family's finances.[49]

48. W. E. Guerin to ADW, September 2, 1901; Ervin Ferry to ADW, September 8, 1901; George Lincoln Burr to ADW, September 9, 1901; ADW to Clara Newberry, September 30, 1901, all in WMC.

49. ADW to Burr, July 11, 1901, and Helen M. White to ADW, November 30, 1914, WMC.

Karin Androvna White, Andrew D. White's youngest daughter

Fred's frequent depressions usually elicited White's pleas that his son think positively. Fred's assurances in 1898 provoked a typical response: "I am glad to see that you have taken a leaf out of my book, and are trying to overcome the tendency to take a gloomy view of things. I regard my victory over that tendency as one of the best things I have accomplished."[50]

The will of the son, evidently, was not equal to the will of the father, and Fred's depression deepened, exacerbated by declining health. In May 1901 he wrote White that his weight had declined from 129 to 113 pounds, and that he could ingest only milk. He was trying to fight off melancholia, but

50. ADW to Fred White, September 24, 1898, WMC. In 1888 White had accompanied Fred to S. Weir Mitchell, great authority in nervous diseases (Diary, April 17, 1888, WMC).

circumstances were adverse, given Clara's problems and "fits of the blues" of his own wife, Anne. Fred despaired of ever returning to normal mental health: "This kind of thing—mental distress and worry is almost impossible to fight off, and affects the digestion which in turn reacts upon the nerves, making life seem not worth living and extinguishing hope, in spite of every effort, by comparing circumstances with those of people less fortunate, trying to look on bright sides, etc. [the remedies suggested by his father]."[51] A month later he informed his father that he felt "suicidal at times." White advised Fred to take a vacation in Europe and offered to pay the costs but was informed that his son was too sick to make the journey. Several days after he declined his father's offer, Fred wrote out a few checks, stepped into the bathroom, and shot himself in the brain.[52]

White received the news of his son's death with sadness and some guilt. "My poor unfortunate, suffering boy," he wailed to his diary. "Why could I not have been near him. Alas, alas that it should have come to this."[53] The recognition that he had not been present to help his son weighed heavily on White's mind, especially since he now had no male heirs. Although he thought of his "dear boy," he focused on "my losses—a son—an only son—and a son-in-law [Spencer Newberry], both of whom I loved deeply and the latter worse than dead."[54] In a letter to Burr, White attempted to absolve himself of any guilt for Fred's death: "In his boyhood, I was sometimes severe with him, but never since that time has he received a reproachful word from me, or indeed anything in the way of faultfinding."[55] The news that Fred's suicide had been prompted by physical distress reassured White that he had not been at fault. Fred had a constricted pylorus (the lower extremity of the stomach), an autopsy revealed, through which only liquids could pass. The constriction would probably have continued and starved him to death.[56]

White's grief was heightened by his sense that he had lost a valuable assistant. Helen Magill White frankly described her husband's state of mind in a letter to Burr:

I do not believe he will feel Fred's loss *personally* very deeply—perhaps I don't do him justice but I fear I do. Therefore when the worry consequent upon losing his

51. Fred White to ADW, May 24, 1901, WMC.
52. *Ithaca Journal*, July 9, 1901; *New York Tribune*, July 9, 1901.
53. Diary, July 11, 1901, WMC.
54. Diary, July 21, 1901, WMC.
55. ADW to Burr, July 11, 1901, WMC.
56. HKW to ADW, July 11, 1901, WMC. Clara refused to believe that this was the reason for Fred's suicide: "No man ever yet killed himself for *physical* pain, hard as the White and Bruce [Fred's in-laws] families have tried to prove it." Clara, sensitive to domestic pain, attributed her brother's death to his wife's "irritability and extravagance" (Clara White Newberry to ADW, September 2, 1901, WMC).

White at his retirement as ambassador to Germany, 1902

valuable aid has disappeared—and the first shock of self-reproach in realizing what a poor, stinted life he had is past—and he has already reacted against that better than I could have wished, I think his wonderful elasticity will bring him up.[57]

Helen knew her husband well. He had learned, as he so often told Fred, that he could will away pain and sorrow; his remedy had failed only at Mary's death and would not fail again. To comfort himself, White began work on a book about the great statesmen of world history. He had dedicated himself to public service and humanity in the abstract, and *noblesse oblige* was accompanied by personal detachment from individuals. Fred was dead, White was genuinely sorry, but (as if to demonstrate the validity of his wife's assessment) he was most conscious of his own loss: to Fred's "loyal care it has been owing that I have been able to devote myself to educational work and to official duties ahead."[58]

Fred's death strengthened White's resolve to retire. He had planned to leave public service in 1902, at the age of seventy, and now refused to be dissuaded. White's retirement prompted praise from both sides of the Atlantic. Roosevelt ranked him with Benjamin Franklin and Charles Francis Adams as a diplomat. White had taught by precept and practice; he was a perpetual example to young men of "how to avoid alike the scylla of inefficiency and the charybdis of efficiency for the wrong."[59] The Germans were equally laudatory. The Kaiser awarded White a medal bestowed upon the most deserving person of the year. "The only thing you have ever done that I do not like," he said, "is your leaving us." Politicians and intellectuals gathered at a farewell dinner at the Kaiserhof, toasted White as one of the premier scholar-diplomats of the century, and applauded the ambassador's farewell toast: "The good-will between Germany and the United States, may it ever continue and may it ever increase."[60]

The new century differed little from the old; it brought with it portents of good and evil, news of life and death. White had taught himself to roll with the punches; despite the death of McKinley and the tragedy in his family, he had great hope for twentieth-century America. Although retired from public office, he had no plans to leave public service; he would

57. H. M. White to Burr, August 6, 1901, George Lincoln Burr MSS, Cornell University.

58. ADW to Evans, November 15, 1901, WMC.

59. Theodore Roosevelt to ADW, August 5 and September 15, 1902, WMC. See also Carl Schurz to ADW, August 21, 1902, WMC.

60. For praise of White from Americans and Germans, see *New York Times*, November 8, 12, and 28, 1902; *New York Tribune*, November 7, 1902; *Washington Post*, November 12, 1902; Diary, November 27, 1902, WMC.

return to scholarship and would again teach by precept. If his son was dead, he would become immortal by adopting and training America's children, as he had done all his life. Perhaps the only way he could bear personal losses or excuse his own lack of attention to his family was by convincing himself that he was indispensable to the larger cause he served.

Always aware of his advanced age and frail health, White did not expect to live very long into the twentieth century. He hoped to complete at least his autobiography and perhaps a collective biography of several of history's greatest statesmen in "the warfare of humanity with unreason." White lived for sixteen years after his retirement as ambassador to Germany. They were years full of honors bestowed upon a venerable statesman and scholar; they were also years of sorrow, marked by the deaths of contemporaries and of children and grandchildren. Until 1917, only the death of his first wife had eroded White's normally stoic response to public and personal reversals; during World War I he was again stunned by the revelations of the atrocities committed by Germany.

Release from official duties both exhilarated and depressed White. He was delighted that he had time to write and pleased with the academic plaudits he received. Yale asked its illustrious alumnus to represent his alma mater at the tercentenary of the Bodleian Library at Oxford. The excursion ultimately netted White an honorary doctorate of civil law.[1] From Oxford, White journeyed to the University of St. Andrews in Scotland, where Andrew Carnegie was installed as lord rector. Not to be outdone by their English cousins, the Scots granted the retired diplomat a doctorate of law.[2] White also agreed to deliver the Dodge Lectures at Yale in 1903, planning to use the platform to combat lenient approaches to crime and to launch a campaign to reform the diplomatic service of the United States.[3] In addition, he consented to become a trustee of the newly founded Carnegie Institute. White attempted to persuade Andrew Carnegie to found a national university in Washington, D.C., but the steel magnate was not enticed: "Don't care two cents about future glory," he snapped.[4] White did persuade Carnegie to donate $1.5 million for a

1. White evidently campaigned to get Oxford to award him a doctorate. See ADW to Willard Fiske, October 1, 1902, WMC.
2. *Autobiography*, vol. 2, pp. 209–210.
3. ADW to Arthur T. Hadley, November 24, 1902, WMC.
4. David Madsen, *The National University: Enduring Dream of the U.S.A.* (Detroit, 1966), p.

Temple of Peace at The Hague. A concrete symbol of dedication to world peace, he hoped, might instruct the masses to demand that their rulers abandon war.[5] Accomplishments on two continents helped to convince White that his usefulness was not at an end.

Despite a schedule that might have tired a younger man, White did not escape the depression that often accompanies the termination of public office. Recurrent headaches necessitated travel to the southern climes of Italy, "sheltered from the wintry winds, with plenty of sunlight and good bracing air."[6] Helen Magill chided her husband by calling his trips "faith cures,'" but whatever the reason, they helped to refresh him. Travel provided only a temporary respite, unfortunately, and White continually fought off despair. In January 1903 he wrote in his diary: "Still depressed—trying to revise my MSS [autobiography] but under great difficulties. Am getting discouraged. Discouraged as never before in my life."[7]

White completed his manuscript, however, and later in 1903 the Century Company contracted to publish it. Originally titled "Reminiscences and Suggestions," the autobiography (published in 1905) retained its didactic purpose. The author hoped to provide young leaders with a model of behavior. He had taken "very kindly views of the world," he admitted, primarily because he believed in "holding up good things to admiration rather than scolding about bad things."[8] White recognized that to accomplish these aims and to amuse the reading public, he had to "suppress much" and dwell on "the lighter things." Perhaps because he had emphasized his intimacy with great men throughout the world, the book sold remarkably well.[9]

Buoyed by the positive reaction to his autobiography, White redoubled efforts to complete his manuscript on seven of the world's greatest statesmen. His purpose was the same: "I would present these statesmen and their work as especially worthy to be studied by those who aspire to serve

113; ADW to David J. Hill, May 20, 1903; Carnegie to ADW, April 26 and December 27, 1901; ADW to Carnegie, May 21 and June 11, 1901; John Hoyt to ADW, June 7, 1901; Memorandum to Carnegie, December 1901, all in WMC.

5. ADW to Frederick W. Holls, April 30, 1903, WMC.
6. ADW to Carnegie, November 28, 1902, Andrew Carnegie MSS, Library of Congress.
7. Diary, January 3, 1903, WMC.
8. ADW to Fiske, January 6, 1902, WMC.
9. For reviews see James Whiton, "Andrew D. White: Educator and Statesman," *Outlook* 80 May 13, 1905: 132–37; Theodore T. Munger, "A Significant Biography," *Atlantic Monthly* 96 (October 1905): 556–66; "The Autobiography of Andrew D. White: Its Excellencies and Its Defects," *Arena* 34 (July 1905): 97–106.

their country in any way." [10] *Seven Great Statesmen in the Warfare of Humanity with Unreason* (1910), fully as much as the autobiography, presented White's theory of historical development and his prescription for the social ills that plagued his country.

White's statesmen (Sarpi, Grotius, Thomasius, Turgot, Stein, Cavour, and Bismarck) were united by a steadfast belief that only evolution could accomplish change. White agreed that Grotius's laws permitting the enslavement of captured foes were deplorable. He excused such dangerous "concessions" because Grotius would have risked his entire system of jurisprudence if he had taken an uncompromising attitude. Frederick the Great's assessment of Joseph II, therefore, aptly expressed White's fear that doctrinaires were ineffectual: "He usually made the mistake of taking the second step before the first." Turgot's methods, White asserted, were identical to Grotius's. He, too, "did not believe that a new heaven and a new earth could be brought in by an illiterate mob." Consequently, the French statesman opposed immediate universal suffrage and supported education, which would gradually equip his countrymen for self-government. The terror of the French Revolution, White implied, proved that Turgot had been right. Throughout his life, White had attempted to balance the need for change with his dread of disorder. The difficulty, of course, lay in determining how much change was possible without disturbing the stability of society. Given this dilemma, it is not surprising that White repeatedly turned to history, replete with examples of gradual, nondisruptive change. White's statesmen had, after all, accomplished impressive feats. History validated White's hypothesis by allowing him to circle back upon his theme: evolutionary change could be achieved; revolutionary change, accompanied by death and destruction, was therefore less desirable than gradual change. If both methods could successfully produce results, the former was obviously preferable. [11]

Despite his best efforts, however, White did not help the reformer, whose proposals for evolutionary change met with stony silence. His treatment of Christian Thomasius, the ideal scholar-doer, is instructive. Thomasius's principles were far in advance of his time: he argued for religious toleration and higher education for women, against witchcraft persecution and sectarian control of higher education. Such attitudes were anathema in late–seventeenth-century Germany. Surprisingly, White defended the "drastic" measures taken by Thomasius: "But his was a

10. *Seven Great Statesmen in the Warfare of Humanity with Unreason* (New York, 1910), p. ix.
11. Ibid., pp. 91, 93, 98, 233, 357–58.

period when, as a rule, only drastic measures could avail. . . . When
Christian Thomasius began his work, sweet reasonableness was absurd;
mild methods futile. Only a man who could fling himself, and all that he
was, and all that he hoped to be, into the fight—who could venture
everything and continue venturing everything until the last—could really
be of use." [12]

At first glance White seems to be enunciating a revolutionary doctrine.
His use of the terms "drastic" and "fight," however, must in this instance
be taken metaphorically. Thomasius was far more a scholar than a doer.
For him, thought *was* action; thus White was willing to take rhetorical
liberties in describing his contributions. [13] The German scholar's "drastic"
action, White implied, was important despite its failure to transform
society. Thomasius had put forth ideas of "vast use to the world; germ
ideas, some of which have been obliged to wait for centuries before coming
to full bloom" in institutions and laws. White did not attempt to establish a
causal connection between Thomasius's advocacy and ultimate adoption;
he praised this fellow-educator for *having the right ideas.* [14]

More than half a century had passed since White had written his essay
on Richelieu, but the philosophical thrust remained the same. He still
believed that society had to adopt several moral imperatives necessary for
progress. Those imperatives inevitably found their advocates, whose role
was to prepare the masses to accept the change; White's elitist bias is too
blatant to overlook. Yet White was certain that reform could be imposed
only upon a society that was "ready" for it. How did one decide when it
was ready? If society, in fact, changed, then White concluded that it was
ready for change. This view could easily become the doctrine that "what
is, is right"; but White sincerely attempted to find a place for human will in
his deterministic schema. He turned to champions of causes who had been
vindicated by history, implying always that violence could not expedite
the adoption of reform. But would rational, peaceful advocacy prove more
efficacious? White believed that it would, but he had not penetrated the
internal dynamics of evolution and offered no substantive evidence for
what was, in essence, a leap of faith.

White continued to assess international developments in the pages of the

12. Ibid., pp. 160–61.
13. A contrast with Grotius may be instructive. Grotius, too, was a scholar, but he
operated within a society torn by factional strife. White was therefore inclined to believe that
"drastic" action in this context would produce actual violence.
14. *Seven Great Statesmen* is full or pronouncements congruent with White's prescriptions
for society. He praises Turgot and Grotius for assailing the sectarian influence, points to
Turgot's advocacy of education as a force for morality and good citizenship, applauds
Grotius's advocacy of internationl peace conferences.

Atlantic Monthly. The scholar-diplomat commented on current affairs in general, but the Russo–Japanese War riveted his attention on tsardom. Although he believed that common sense on both sides might have prevented the war, his sympathies lay with Japan, whose victories convinced him that he had accurately assessed the depravity of the Russian government and people. Meaningful change seemed impossible as long as Russia lacked an intelligent middle class, and White saw little evidence that one was emerging. He retained only the slenderest reed of hope: perhaps the humiliation of defeat by the Japanese would move the army to revolt and replace the tsar with "a man on horseback." Even this solution seemed implausible on reflection, given the army's obvious reverence for the tsar.[15]

As Japan decimated the Russian navy, White decided that a continuation of the war would not bring change to Russia. He advised President Roosevelt to try to persuade the combatants to submit their dispute to the Hague tribunal. White proposed the main outlines of settlement: Russia would recognize "the capture of Port Arthur as an accomplished fact, . . . redeem her old pledges to the world regarding Manchuria, make some sensible agreement regarding Korea, and possibly . . . restore to Japan the island of Saghalin." The tsar, on the other hand, would gain a new winter port on the Pacific as well as guaranteed full use of the railway and connecting facilities.[16]

In the summer of 1905, Roosevelt finally saw an opportunity and helped mediate an end to the war. White rejoiced in the Treaty of Portsmouth, which struck a blow for international arbitration even though it bypassed the Hague tribunal. Throughout the conflict, White's main interest had been reform in Russia. When war failed to produce change, he advocated peace, but each time he recognized the enormous obstacles. The tsar was incompetent, taxation was unbearable, the best young men sent off to a "useless and wicked war." Even Nicholas's creation of a parliament in 1905 did not appreciably heighten White's optimism. Mass ignorance made universal suffrage impossible, he noted, and the tsar's ignorance dimmed the Duma's chances of success. Neither the inevitability of progress nor the ability of people to change the world—doctrines that White, the "incorrigible optimist," had seen operating throughout world history—

15. "The Situation and Prospect in Russia," n.d., WMC. In a statement for the press, White attributed American sympathy for Japan to Russian acquiescence in cruelty to Armenia, its treatment of Jews, and its high-handed treatment of Finland ("Russia and U.S. in 1904," WMC).

16. ADW to Roosevelt, May 28, 1905, and clipping from Newspaper Enterprise Association, January 11, 1905, WMC.

seemed to apply to Russia.[17] The iron law of history, which smiled on the
United States, destined Russia to a downward spiral. White refused to
entertain doubts about his country, yet fear of the future often welled up in
him. Evidently Russia was a safe outlet for his pessimism: he could sneer at
the passive, ignorant masses there, the corrupt government, the feebleness
of liberal reform. White's analysis of Russia usually had a cathartic effect.
He often combined vituperative denunciations of tsardom with inflated
optimism about the United States.[18]

White closely followed developments in Russia for the remaining dozen
years of his life and usually found his predictions confirmed. Although the
Duma was a failure, he regretted the tsar's decision to dissolve it in 1906.
For the next ten years the tsar continued to live in a "fool's paradise,"
emerging occasionally to shout "Pas de concessions. Pas de concessions."[19]
Years of enumerating Russia's internal weaknesses did not prepare him for
the revolution of 1917, but he was certain that the abdication of the tsar
would result in anarchy, leaving the way open for an even more despotic
dictator. "A republic cannot be made without republicans"; Russia was
forever wedded to autocracy.[20] White did not live long enough to comment on the regime of Lenin, but he undoubtedly would have viewed it as
well adapted to Russia: a new despot provided a socialist economy that
satisfied the passive masses.[21]

If White disdained passivity in economic and political activity, he
recognized that human will was powerless in the face of death. For a man
in his seventies, death was ever present; White often wondered how
posterity would remember him. One by one his friends passed away:
Charles Kendall Adams in 1902, Frederick Holls a year later ("Am dazed
and stunned by it," White wrote in his diary. "Cannot realize that a man so
full of health, strength, ability and high purpose can have so suddenly left
us—and only 46 years old!"),[22] Willard Fiske in 1904, Gilman in 1908,

17. *New York Times*, January 24, 1905; *Boston Advertiser*, August 22, 1905. White did not
see revolution as a possibility in Russia: "It would be just as reasonable to expect wild cattle on
the plains to revolt against the cowboys as to expect the Russian peasants to revolt against the
autocracy" ("A Day with Andrew D. White at His Home in Ithaca," *Craftsman* 8 (September
1905): 733.
18. See, e.g., "A Day with Andrew D. White," pp. 714–34. For White's most sober
comments about the possibilities of change everywhere, see ADW to J. Helder, June 16,
1906, WMC.
19. ADW to Mrs. David J. Hill, July 23, 1906, and Henrick van Loon to ADW,
September 2, 1907, WMC.
20. ADW to Albert Shaw, December 29, 1917, WMC; *Cornell Sun*, March 19, 1917.
21. Russia, White argued, had been virtually socialist under the tsars. See ADW to T. F.
Crane, April 8, 1918, WMC.
22. Diary, July 24, 1903, WMC.

Elizabeth Evans in 1911.[23] White had even read his own obituary, which was printed in a Socialist paper in Italy.[24] Although the newspaper graced the death notice with a portrait of Herbert Asquith, the new British premier, White was rather pleased at the complimentary treatment that he had received. The mistake occasioned lighthearted comment, but it was undeniably macabre. Twice White had been pronounced dead (he had also been "killed" on the way to Santo Domingo). The next obituary would probably be accurate.

Before he read the exaggerated report of his demise, White gave serious thought to his epitaph. In October 1905 he wrote a lengthy summary of his career and ordered that it be placed on a monument of himself:

Here lies what was mortal of Andrew Dickson White L.L.D. (Yale and St. Andrews), L.H.D. (Columbia), Ph.D. (Jena), D.C.L. (Oxford). A friend and advisor of Ezra Cornell. One of the Founders of this University. Author of the Educational Features of its Charter,—of its Plan of Organization—of its system of Fellowships and Scholarships—of Graduate Representation in its governing body,—of the Report on the Admission of Women, and of the Provision for its Unsectarian Administration and Pulpit. He was its ardent champion against indifference, misrepresentation and opposition,—its first President and Professor of History 1865–1885 and a member of its Board of Trustees during——years.

Further reflection prompted White to pen a possible and more inclusive addition:

In his last days he said, "I would be remembered not as an Ambassador or Minister or as the occupant of any position or recipient of any distinction; but as one who aided to suggest and develop the fundamental ideas of Cornell University; to free advanced education from the trammels of routine and sectarian control, to promote studies for the ennobling of American Political and Social Life, and to establish the International Peace Tribunal of the Hague. And I would take my final rest among the friends, the students and the scenes I have loved so well."[25]

This was quite a mouthful, even for a man eager to help shape his own historical reputation. A year later, the epistle may have seemed a bit pretentious; so he decided to jettison it in favor of a simple slab of rubbed white stone with a conventional epitaph.

---

23. ADW to George Lincoln Burr, August 8, 1902; Ira Place to ADW, September 18, 1904; H.S. White to ADW, September 18, 1904; ADW to Burr, October 1, 1904; ADW to E. P. Evans, November 14, 1904; ADW to Goldwin Smith, November 22, 1904; ADW to Evans, October 31, 1905; Evans to ADW, September 13, 1911; Daniel Coit Gilman to ADW, August 20, 1907; ADW to Gilman, August 24, 1907; Theodore T. Munger to ADW, October 14, 1908, all in WMC.
24. ADW to Burr, April 27, 1908, WMC; *New York Sun*, May 9, 1908.
25. Memorandum, October 25, 1905, WMC.

The death of old men was natural, a cause for nostalgic regret. The death of his own children and grandchildren was more disheartening, but White struggled to prevent continuous family tragedies from unnerving him. Fred's death had been a source of sorrow and guilt, and White transferred his hopes for his son to his grandson, Andrew D. White II. "I rather hope for him the life of a scholar and professor," he wrote to Willard Fiske.[26] White monitored the education of "Disson"; he castigated Fred's widow for going abroad twice and interrupting the formal schooling of the fifteen-year-old.[27] The boy seemed precocious, but he was moody and withdrawn, increasingly so after the death of his father. With White's concurrence, Anne Bruce White sent her son to boarding school in California. The change of scenery, all hoped, might make Disson less morose. In February 1907 White opened a letter from the headmaster of the Thacher School and learned that his grandson had killed himself. Sherman Thacher reported that Andrew was an excellent student but was restless. On occasion he had talked of killing himself but fellow students had dissuaded him. On January 30 he had admitted to his closest friend, Cyrus Hill, that he had never been so happy but threatened suicide once again. Hill did not take him seriously, and one day later Andrew was dead. He had shot himself two or three times in the mouth and lived long enough only to mutter to Thacher: "I am a fool. I shot myself twice in the mouth—like my father—I am a fool."[28]

White's love for his grandson was inextricably tied to his desire to achieve immortality through family. He described Disson's funeral in his diary: "My poor grandson's remains were wonderfully preserved—face as natural as if in sleep and no mark of any wound visible. He had matured greatly seeming larger and finer looking than when I saw him. So departs my last representative in the direct line—and I had hoped so much from him."[29]

White had evidently never hidden his expectations from his children, and in the days after Andrew's suicide, he may have pondered his relationship to them. On February 22, Clara reassured her father: "But don't worry dear Father, Andrew Dickson's tremendous wish to die had nothing in common with wishing for the death of any one else."[30] This enigmatic statement, admittedly made by a deeply unhappy woman who was herself near death, may mean that White believed that Andrew blamed him for

26. ADW to Fiske, February 4, 1902, WMC.
27. ADW to Anne Bruce White, September 9, 1903, WMC.
28. Sherman Thacher to ADW, January 31, 1907, and memorandum of Sherman Thacher, c. February 7, 1907, WMC.
29. Diary, February 7, 1907, WMC.
30. Clara Newberry to ADW, February 22, 1907, WMC.

Fred's death. Perhaps he sought reassurance from his daughter that he had not contributed to the suicide of either Fred or Disson, but he never indicated whether her response satisfied him.

A few months later White had yet another funeral to attend. Clara Newberry had been confined to a sanitarium since her broken marriage, virtual mental breakdown, and heavy dependence on drugs.[31] She vacillated between a wish for the contentment of death and a recognition that she must cling to life. On the twentieth anniversary of her mother's death, Clara lamented that Mary had been lucky enough to die "while she was young and free from sorrow! And twenty-five years ago tomorrow I was married! And now I'm getting well and hope to see my grandchildren grow up to be a source of pride to us all."[32] The doctors assured Clara that she was recovering and prescribed rest and avoidance of mental anguish. She must try to "avoid, and not sympathize with those in trouble." Clara lacked her father's will, however, and the only way for her to escape depression was to ask the family to keep all bad news from her. Her will to live nevertheless failed her, and on September 24, 1907 (the fiftieth anniversary of his marriage to Mary Outwater), White rushed to the sanitarium just before his eldest child died.[33]

White's anguish was undoubtedly genuine, but his reaction to Clara's death was characteristically self-centered. He remembered her as the "best, kindest, sweetest of daughters. I do not think that she ever gave *me* a moment of pain by any conduct of her own. Her sorrows and indeed her martyrdom have been a great grief to *me*."[34] (Italics mine.) White, perhaps more than most parents, had defined his children primarily in relation to himself. They were the reflection of *his* hopes; their failures and their successes were a judgment upon *him*. Judgments, moreover, continued to rain upon him. If his eightieth birthday brought joy, honor, and congratulations from Kaiser Wilhelm, James Bryce, John D. Rockerfeller, and Andrew Carnegie, his eighty-first birthday was followed by the sudden death of Ruth's daughter, eleven-year-old Ursula Ferry. The reaction by now was predictable: "I ought to have done more to show her my deep and real affection for her. Alas! I cannot recall her and tell it to her now."[35]

31. The relationship between drugs and Victorian women is discussed in John Haller and Robin Haller, *The Physician and Sexuality in Victorian America* (Urbana, Ill. 1974), esp. 286, 303.
32. Clara Newberry to ADW, June 7, 1907, WMC.
33. Clara Newberry to ADW, June 30, 1907; Lillian Crozier to ADW, September 18, 1907; Ruth Ferry to ADW, September 25, 1907; ADW to Evans, October 3, 1907; Elizabeth Evans to ADW, October 16, 1907, all in WMC.
34. Diary, September 25, 1907, WMC.
35. Diary, November 10, 1913, WMC; see also White's note written on Ursula Ferry to ADW, November 7, 1913, WMC.

White at Cornell University, which he hoped would guarantee his place in history

Throughout his life, White had lamented his lack of attention to his family; death reminded him of the high price the public man paid to his loved ones.

While the dead brought White's guilt and remorse to the surface, surviving members of his family often made him sullen. Helen Magill missed few opportunities to castigate her husband: he donated books to Cornell, thus dissipating her inheritance; he refused to allow her to travel alone or visit her family; he did not allow her to go to Ruth's wedding. An intensely emotional woman, Helen was deeply hurt by White's coldness. In 1901 she confessed to Burr that while White was a "great and good man," he would be happier "if he could *really care* a little more about people, and sympathize with their joys or pains or disappointments." White remained "a puzzle" to his second wife:

He is so full of generous and noble instincts as regards the human race in general—and in certain ways as sympathetic in personal and private relations— and yet he lives so little in the lives and interests of the individual men and women that surround him. So to me he seems with all his greatness and goodness, to have always missed the best of life—for out of the heart are its issues.[36]

During the last years of White's life, the two constantly sniped at each other: Helen begged White not to put a picture of himself and Mary Outwater in Prudence Risley Hall at Cornell. There were, she implied, already enough public indications that he preferred his first wife. White had placed a portrait of Mary in every room in their house. He had cut short his honeymoon with Helen to dedicate a bust of Mary at the Cornell Library. Through the years, Helen complained, White had given her no public affection and precious little evidence of his feelings in private. She was hurt and unhappy and even more piqued by White's response, which cited his secretary's opinion of Helen's shortcomings. Helen upbraided her husband for needing assistance to "size up [his] . . . own wife." White made few references in letters or in his diary to Helen, but he must have recalled the doubts he had expressed about her before their marriage.[37]

If married life was less than blissful, the old man found little consolation in his young daughter Karin, who had been born during his ministry in Russia. Although sixty years her senior, he tried to be a good father, especially after his retirement. Every morning he arose at six and walked with Helen, Karin, or both, "generally over the highlands north of Fall Creek where the air is always very fresh and pure, then toward town,

36. Helen M. White to Burr, August 6, 1901, Burr MSS, Cornell University.
37. Helen M. White to ADW, January 15, January 18, and November 24, 1909, and April 5, 1910, WMC.

catching the trolley and going down to get the morning Rochester paper."[38] Nevertheless, Karin proved to be a disappointment to her parents. She had a keen mind, but seemed devoid of logic or feeling. "The better your argument," Helen wrote to her husband, "the more excited and stubborn she gets and her mind *grows absolutely impervious to reason*"[39] Helen blamed White, noting that his conversation was much more interesting when he was among men than when he was with his daughter. One who had exercised so much influence on the world at large, she acidly commented, should be able to exert some on his children. "But perhaps diplomacy, like charity should begin at home."[40] Such advice, when given to an eighty-year-old man, is very likely gratuitous, but Helen was certainly on target in recognizing that White did not overinvest in his daughter as he had in his son and grandson. Public service was the arena of men, he believed, despite his advocacy of coeducation. He had expected Clara and Ruth to marry and raise families, not to pursue careers; no evidence exists that his hopes for Karin were different.[41]

While she lived, White's mother had constantly reminded him of his duty to his family. He regretted his neglect of his wife and children but was always able to convince himself that public service outweighed family obligation. This view, in fact, explains his attitude toward women; dutiful wives and mothers, like Mary Outwater, kept the family intact, while freeing their husbands to serve the larger cause of humanity.[42] Nevertheless, White recognized that his family had paid a price for his neglect and for his spasmodic attempts to mold his male descendants in his own image. Each death and each family crisis prompted expressions of guilt, because White sensed that his children had too often become instruments of his own desire for immortality.

If White's family life brought him little happiness, the war in Europe forced him to question his most basic assumption—the inevitability of progress. Germany, his model of an efficient, educated society, had evidently been the aggressor. White was bewildered; he spent his final few years in the midst of a world war, fighting a private battle to preserve faith that reasonable men might peacefully construct a just society.

The outbreak of war must have surprised White. No one, he asserted, could predict the outcome of the struggle, but perhaps when the combat-

38. ADW to Fiske, August 29, 1904, WMC.
39. Helen M. White to ADW, May 28, 1915, WMC.
40. Helen M. White to ADW, August 5, and 11, 1912, WMC.
41. Karin never married.
42. In this sense Fred, incapacitated by illness, had served a woman's role. By managing the family's finances, he had freed his father for public service.

ants' resources were depleted, "some international congress, perhaps the Hague, may make some proper bases for peace." He signed a petition urging President Wilson to ask the disputants to turn to the Hague.[43]

White's natural sympathies, of course, lay with Germany, but the Kaiser's violation of Belgian neutrality disturbed him. White viewed the action as "an unpardonable sin" but searched desperately for an explanation. Americans did not know the provocation Germany suffered from France, Russia, and Great Britain. Perhaps Wilhelm had learned of agreements between them and acted to avert catastrophe to his nation. "Putting it all together, then," White decided to suspend judgment on the origin of the conflict.[44]

Reports from friends in Europe, however, brought White closer to a condemnation of Germany. Edward Sarolea, who had helped revise *The Warfare of Science*, described the German occupation of Belgium. The German troops, he wrote to White, "are murdering my little Fatherland, and making fair Belgium a perfect substitute for Hell! *Could you not utter some public protest?*" The Germans burned villages, bombarded towns, and destroyed a priceless Gothic church and a famous old university library. "The insolence, the brutality of the German soldates," Sarolea concluded, "are revolting, are fiendish." German occupation of Ghent was imminent, and Sarolea informed White that an answer to his letter would be opened and might cost the Belgian his life. Sarolea wrote to White repeatedly, documenting German atrocities. He knew that the former diplomat viewed Germany as a second fatherland: "With your old and well founded sympathies for Germany," Sarolea wrote, "your position in regard to this war must be painful."[45]

White's position was painful indeed, and the attitude of German scholars only complicated it. In 1914, several German intellectuals formally declared that the spirit of German science and Prussian militarism were complementary. "We believe," their manifesto said, "that the welfare of all European culture depends on the victory which German militarism will win."[46] For men such as White, and the hundreds who followed him to Germany, the state and the school existed in a symbiotic relationship, each autonomous in its own sphere. Government supported higher education, and the universities produced questioning men prepared to reform

43. William Short to ADW, August 24, 1914, WMC; *Cornell Sun*, August 5, 1914.
44. ADW to George Blackman, August 20, 1914, WMC; Diary, August 26, 1914, WMC.
45. Sarolea to ADW, September 1 and October 16, 1914; ADW to Mr. Johnson, February 2, 1915; ADW to Henry Van Dyke, February 2, 1915, all in WMC.
46. Quoted in Jurgen Herbst, *The German Historical School in American Scholarship* (Ithaca, 1965), p. 166.

society. Thus White had made light of the objections to a national university because he was convinced that the state attached no strings to financial
aid. Now the critics seemed to be right, and White agreed with Cornell
Professor Waterman T. Hewett that the teachings of Heinrich von
Treitschke, Clemens von Delbrück, and others had hardened the
academic conscience of Germany.[47]

Hewett urged White to speak out against Germany, but White declined
to comment publicly on the war. The violations of Belgian neutrality and
the Hague agreements, the irrefutable testimony of military execution of
hostages made a pro-German position untenable. Yet White's animus
toward England remained. The "insolence and arrogance" of Britannia
had long been directed at Germany. The Kaiser might have averted war
for a time, but he probably could not have prevented it. Remaining
neutral, White refused to allow a friend to make public his sentiments
regarding England until the "circumstances attendant upon the origin and
progress of the European conflict became untangled."[48]

White's sympathies for Germany eroded still further in 1915. In April
he confessed that he could no longer give the Germans the benefit of the
doubt: "they seem determined to trample on all the best secured rights of
nations." Ironically, signs of his former love for Germany were everywhere. His granddaughter, Helen Ferry, wrote to him in German, and old
friends begged him to counter Allied propaganda. White was simply
bewildered. When newspaper editors elicited his comments about the
war, the usually garrulous old man regretted "deeply that I can think of
nothing which I can say at present."[49]

White's hatred of England and his disillusionment with Germany resulted in a desire for America to avoid involvement in the war. Even after
the sinking of the *Lusitania*, he opposed attempts to establish the right of
United States citizens to travel on ships carrying military supplies to
belligerents because such action might draw America into the conflict.
Perhaps, he wrote to S. S. McClure, joint action of the neutral powers
could guarantee "not only the rights of neutrals but of mankind in general
in view of such ruthless violations of them as we see now *on all sides*" (italics
mine). The prospects for peace, he admitted, were grim. Americans,

47. ADW to Hewett, October 27, 1914 and Hewett to ADW, November 8, 1914, WMC.
48. ADW to Hewett, October 27, 1914; Reinhardt Rahr to Norman Hapgood, October
30, 1914; Rahr to ADW, November 19, 1914; ADW to William J. Starr, September 30, 1914,
all in WMC; Diary, January 25, 1915, WMC. White, however, asked Charles Francis Adams
to publicize Britain's "outrageous insults and injuries" to the United States. He did not despise
Germany, he admitted, as much as he despised Britain (ADW to Adams, December 30, 1914,
WMC).
49. See ADW to Ogden Reid, May 8, 1915, WMC; *New York World*, May 9, 1915.

moreover, had turned their backs on mediation. Only two Cornellians joined White in signing a petition urging President Wilson to mediate. By the end of 1915, preparedness competed with strict neutrality to dominate American policy. White advocated that the army train by building roads and working in mines. Constructive accomplishments would justify preparedness, and perhaps the military would never have to do any fighting.[50]

Pro-German groups used White's autobiography to argue that Germany had laid an embargo on arms shipments to both sides during the Spanish–American War. The United States, they argued, should adopt the same neutral policy. The old man became a pawn in this cause célèbre as pro-British and pro-German groups traded charges in the editorial pages of the *New York Times*. Robert Lansing entered the fray. White, he asserted, had searched for and found no regulations forbidding the shipment of contraband of war from German ports. The embarrassed former ambassador did not remember what he had done. The affair, which plagued White throughout 1916, embittered him against the press, the war, and the champions of both sides; everyone evidently regarded him as a liar or a man in his dotage.[51]

As 1916 ended, White hoped that the prolonged military deadlock would produce peace. The Hague machinery, so long neglected, might ultimately prove to be the world's salvation. Within months, however, the situation changed. Congress overwhelmingly favored war, he wrote in his diary on March 31, 1917, noting that Wilson still hesitated: "Something much like anarchy seems to prevail as regards public opinion." As if to underscore the berserk direction of international affairs, Russia had "gone to pieces between fanatics, corruptionists and idiotic creatures of all sorts." The revolution seemed to awaken warmongerers throughout Europe and the United States. White's archetypical example of reaction, Russia, now proclaimed itself the harbinger of change. The world had indeed gone topsy-turvy.[52]

Sympathy for Germany was treasonous in America once war was declared, but White could not easily erase a lifetime appreciation of German culture. He received constant reminders of his view of the superiority of German civilization: the best field glasses are German, his grandson wrote, and thus of course unavailable. Could White send his or

---

50. ADW to McClure, July 21, 1915; and ADW to David Starr Jordan, July 22, 1915, WMC; *Cornell Sun*, December 4, 1915; J. B. Brougham to ADW, January 20, 1916, WMC.

51. H. D. Burrill to ADW, June 1, 1915; Henry T. Allen to ADW, February 20, 1916; Heinrich Charles to ADW, February 3, 1916, all in WMC. White's account of Germany's policy during the Spanish–American War was inconclusive. See *Autobiography*, vol. 2, pp. 168–69.

52. *Cornell Sun*, December 22, 1916; Diary, March 31, 1917, WMC.

those of some Cornell professor or student? One correspondent cruelly wrote that she could not harmonize the sketch of Kaiser Wilhelm in White's autobiography "with the world's execration of him now." Cornell music professor Hollis Dann asked White whether he objected to a Schumann performance. Dann objected to playing the music of *living* German composers only. White agreed but must have noted the advanced state of antipathy to Germany which prompted the question.[53]

White's shattered hopes for German–American friendship could not be forgotten. In a long letter in 1917, he finally revealed his anguished feelings: "The two nations seemed predestined to give the other what it needed, and each to stir in the children of the other the noblest thoughts. I receive letters from time to time from old German friends but I dare not trust myself to answer them, and I am but one out of a vast body of Americans who feel toward Germany as toward a second mother country." As he dictated the letter, White looked out upon the Cornell campus and saw "long lines of splendid young men such as we have always trained to love Germany and appreciate what she has done for ourselves and for the world." Now these students grimly drilled to defend their country against the "Huns." The image was unbearable. "I dare not trust myself to think longer upon it all." These were certainly White's truest sentiments, but he still refused to make them public. The nation would not sympathize with genuine ambivalence.[54]

Amid sorrows, public and private, the eighty-five-year-old White summoned his will for one final affirmation. The war, he postulated, was an aberration that would lead to greater international cooperation, a final apocalypse that would bring about permanent peace. I "can only indulge in vague hopes," he wrote, "that all this present condition of things, involving as it is doing so distressingly the modern world, may in some way be only a dream."[55] He recognized the vagueness of his hopes, but they were all he had; giving voice to them was a dam against despair. On November 4, 1918, three days short of his eighty-sixth birthday, he died. A special organ recital at Cornell in his memory played the works of the composers he loved—Handel, Wagner, Mendelssohn, Schubert. The announcement of the performance in the White manuscript collection appears next to a circular from the American Defense Society—"Use

53. Arthur Newberry to ADW, January 6, 1918; Mabel Stillwell to ADW, November 14, 1917; Hollis Dann to ADW, April 26, 1918, all in WMC.
54. ADW to Christer Sitler, April 16, 1917, and Fabian Franklin to ADW, May 6, 1917, WMC.
55. ADW to Christer Sitler, April 16, 1917, WMC.

Nothing German." Even his death prompted reminders of the dilemma of his final years.[56]

White died before the war ended, but his affirmation in the midst of it undoubtedly expresses the sentiments he would have articulated at its close. White was not by nature a happy or confident man, but he overcame his doubts by repeating to himself that there was a grand design to a seemingly inchoate universe, that it was benevolent, and that he played a not inconsequential part in hastening the arrival of a reformed world.

56. The *New York Times*'s obituary missed the essence of White's ambivalence: "Happy long life with honor at the close" (November 5, 1918).

Bibliography

MANUSCRIPT COLLECTIONS

Henry T. Allen MSS, Library of Congress
George Lincoln Burr MSS, Cornell University
Andrew Carnegie MSS, Library of Congress
Joseph Choate MSS, Library of Congress
Roscoe Conkling Collection, New York Public Library
Thomas Frederick Davies MSS, General Theological Seminary of the Protestant
     Episcopal Church, New York
J. C. Bancroft Davis MSS, Library of Congress
Dispatches from United States Ministers to the German States and Germany,
     1879–1881, Record Group 59, General Records of the Department of State,
     National Archives
Dispatches from United States Ambassadors to Germany, 1897–1902, Record
     Group 59, General Records of the Department of State, National Archives
Dispatches from United States Ministers to Russia, 1892–1894, Record Group 59,
     General Records of the Department of State, National Archives
Edward Payson Evans MSS, Cornell University
Hamilton Fish MSS, Library of Congress
John W. Foster MSS, Library of Congress
James A. Garfield MSS, Library of Congress
Daniel Coit Gilman MSS, Johns Hopkins University
Frederick W. Holls MSS, Columbia University
George Kennan MSS, Library of Congress
Alfred T. Mahan MSS, Library of Congress
Justin Morrill MSS, Library of Congress
Levi P. Morton MSS, New York Public Library
Frederick Law Olmsted MSS, Library of Congress
Albert Shaw MSS, New York Public Library
Oscar Straus MSS, Library of Congress
David Wells MSS, Library of Congress
Andrew D. White Microfilm Collection, Cornell University. In addition to copies
     of White papers and White's diary, this collection contains copies of letters to and
     from White gathered from more than one hundred manuscript collections
     throughout the United States. The original White papers, White's diary, and
     many of the letters are in the Department of Manuscripts and University
     Archives at Cornell University Libraries.

NEWSPAPERS

Albany Argus, 1864–1867
Cornell Daily Sun
Cornell Era
New York Times

OFFICIAL PUBLICATIONS

Annual reports to the Board of Trustees of Cornell University, 1868–1885
New York State Senate Documents, 1864–1867
New York State Senate Journal, 1864–1867
Report of the Commission of Inquiry to Santo Domingo, Washington, 1871

PUBLISHED WORKS OF ANDREW D. WHITE

Address at the First Annual Banquet of the Cornell Alumni Association of Western New York. New York, 1884.
Address Delivered before the Students of Cornell University in Reply to Certain Attacks upon the Institution. Ithaca, 1884.
Address on Agricultural Education. Albany, 1869.
"The Administration and Protection." *Gunton's Magazine* 23 (October 1902): 273–89.
"The American Chapel at Berlin." *Outlook* 69 (December 28, 1901): 1076–78.
"Animal Symbolism in Ecclesiastical Architecture." *Popular Science Monthly* 50 (December 1896): 187–96.
"Assassins and Their Apologists." *Independent* 54 (August 21, 1902): 1989–90.
Autobiography of Andrew White, 2 vols. New York, 1905.
"The Cardiff Giant: The True Story of a Remarkable Deception." *Century Magazine* 64 (October 1902): 948–55.
"College Fraternities." *Forum* 2 (May 1887): 243–53.
The Constitutional Convention: Delegates at Large. Responsibilities to Small Districts. Impartial Manhood Suffrage. Albany, 1867
The Constitution and American Education. Ithaca, 1887
"The Development and Overthrow of the Russian Serf System." *Atlantic Monthly* 10 (November 1862): 538–52.
The Diplomatic Service of the United States with Some Hints toward Its Reform. Washington, 1905.
"Do the Spoils Belong to the Victor?" *North American Review* 134 (February 1882): 111–33.
"Early and Late Impressions." In *Beecher Memorial*, ed. Edward Bok. Brooklyn, N.Y., 1887
"Educational Conditions and Problems." *Educational Review* 13 (May 1897): 469–72.
Education in Political Science. Baltimore, 1879.
"Encouragements in the Present Crisis." *Forum* 22 (September 1896): 16–20.
European Schools of History and Politics. Baltimore, 1887.
Evolution versus Revolution in Politics. Madison, Wis., 1897.
Fiat Money Inflation in France. New York, 1876.

The First Hague Conference. Boston, 1912.

"First Mission to Germany, 1879–1881." *Century Magazine* 66 (August 1903): 591–604.

"The Future of the American Colleges and Universities." *School and College* 1 (February 1892): 65–73.

"The Future of American Universities." *North American Review* 51 (October 1890): 443–52.

"Glimpses of Universal History." *New Englander* 15 (August 1857): 398–427.

"The Government of American Cities." *Forum* 10 (December 1890): 357–72.

"Historical Instruction in the Course of History and Political Science at Cornell University." In *Methods of Teaching History*, ed. G. Stanley Hall. Boston, 1885.

A History of the Warfare of Science with Theology in Christendom, 2 vols. New York, 1896.

"How I Was Educated." *Forum* 2 (February 1887): 559–73.

"Impressions of the German Emperor." *Century Magazine* 69 (February 1905): 483–501.

In Memoriam: Frederick William Holls. Privately printed, 1905.

Instruction in Social Science. Boston, 1890.

James A. Garfield: Memorial Address. Ithaca, 1881.

"Jefferson and Slavery." *Atlantic Monthly* 9 (January 1862): 29–40.

A Letter of Andrew D. White Resigning the Presidency of Cornell University and the Professorship of History. Ithaca, 1885.

"Letter to the Editor." *Northern Christian Advocate.* February 24, 1870.

"Letter to the Editor: A Monument to Francis Laurent." *Nation* 87 (August 6, 1908): 114–15.

A Letter to Patriotic Democrats, July 14, 1896. New York, 1896.

A Letter to William Howard Russell, LL.D., on Passages in His "Diary North and South." London, 1863.

Memorial from Citizens of Ithaca, N.Y., to the Hon. Theodore Roosevelt, President of the United States, in the Interest of Armenian Subjects of the Turkish Government. N.p., 1906.

The Message of the Nineteenth Century to the Twentieth. New York, 1883.

The Most Bitter Foe of Nations and the Way to Its Permanent Overthrow. New Haven, 1866.

My Reminiscences of Ezra Cornell. Ithaca, 1890.

"The Need of Another University." *Forum* 6 (January 1889): 465–73.

"The Next American University." *Forum* 5 (June 1888): 371–82.

On Studies in General History and the History of Civilization. New York, 1885.

An Open Letter to the Alumni and Undergraduates of Cornell University. N.p., 1877.

"Our Monster Political Conventions." *Review of Reviews* 6 (August 1892): 99.

A Patriotic Investment. New Haven, 1903.

Political Education. Washington, 1878.

The Presidency of Cornell University: Remarks of Andrew D. White. Ithaca, 1885.

"The Presidential Convention—A Blot on American Democracy." *McClure's Magazine* 39 (October 1890): 719–20, 750.

"President McKinley and Peace." *Independent* 52 (August 2, 1900): 1832–34.

[Speech at] *The Proceedings at the Laying of a Wreath on the Tomb of Hugo Grotius.* The Hague, 1899.

"Recollections in War-Time." *Century Magazine* 69 (July 1904): 412–20.

"The Relations of the National and State Governments to Advanced Education."
  Old and New 10 (October 1874): 475–94.
Report of the Committee on Organization. Albany, 1867.
*Report in Behalf of a Majority of the Committee on Mr. Sage's Proposal to Endow a College
  for Women.* Ithaca, 1872.
"A Revelation of America to Germany." *Independent* 54 (December 4, 1902):
  2868–70.
Review of the Governor's Message. Albany, 1864.
"Russia in Wartime." *Century Magazine* 69 (August 1904): 597–602.
Samuel Pierpont Langley. Washington, 1907.
"Sanitary Science and Public Instruction." *Popular Science Monthly* 41 (June 1892):
  421–29.
Scientific and Industrial Education in the United States. New York, 1874.
Seven Great Statesmen in the Warfare of Humanity with Unreason. New York, 1910.
"A Short Exercise for the Fourth of July." *Putnam's Monthly* 10 (July 1857):
  100–107.
Some Important Questions in Higher Education. Ithaca, 1885.
Some Practical Influences of German Thought upon the United States. Ithaca, 1884.
"Some Practical Lessons of the Recent Campaign." *Forum* 22 (December 1896):
  414–22.
Speech at Semi-Centennial Celebration, Onondoga County Orphan Asylum. Syracuse,
  1895.
"Speech before the Faculty and Students." *Albany Evening Journal*, May 23, 1873.
Speech in Reply to the Toast "the President of the United States." N.p., 1898.
Speech in Senate. N.p., 1865.
Speech on Taking the Chair at the Ratification Meeting, July 10, 1896. Ithaca, 1896.
"The Statesmanship of Richelieu." *Atlantic Monthly* 9 (May 1862): 611–24.
"A University at Washington." *Forum* 6 (February 1889): 622–33.
"Walks and Talks with Tolstoy." *McClure's Magazine* 16 (April 1901): 507–518.

BOOKS

Aaron, Daniel. *Men of Good Hope.* New York, 1951.
Adams, Charles Kendall. *Proceedings and Addresses at the Inauguration of Charles
  Kendall Adams.* Ithaca, 1886.
Austen, Jessica Tyler. *Moses Coit Tyler.* New York, 1911.
Ausubel, Herman. *Historians and Their Craft: A Study of the Presidential Address of the
  A.H.A., 1884–1945.* New York, 1950.
Bainton, Roland. *George Lincoln Burr: His Life.* Ithaca, 1943.
Barrows, Isabel, ed. *First Lake Mohonk Conference on the Negro Question.* Boston,
  1890.
Becker, Carl. *Cornell University: Founders and the Founding.* Ithaca, 1944.
Berman, Milton. *John Fiske: The Evolution of a Popularizer.* Cambridge, Mass., 1961.
Billington, Ray. *Frederick Jackson Turner.* New York, 1973.
Bishop, Morris. *A History of Cornell.* Ithaca, 1962.
Bordin, Ruth. *Andrew Dickson White: Teacher of History.* Ann Arbor, 1958.
Braeman, John. *Albert J. Beveridge.* Chicago, 1971.
Brown, Jerry. *The Rise of Biblical Criticism in America, 1800–1870.* Middletown,
  Conn., 1969.

Bullock, Henry. *A History of Negro Education in the South.* New York, 1970.
Carter, Paul. *The Spiritual Crisis of the Gilded Age.* De Kalb, Ill., 1971.
Cawelti, John. *Apostles of the Self-Made Man.* Chicago, 1965.
Clive, John. *The Shaping of the Historian: Macaulay.* New York, 1973.
Cornell, Alonzo. *True and Firm: Biography of Ezra Cornell.* New York, 1884.
Davis, Calvin. *The United States and the First Hague Peace Conference.* Ithaca, 1962.
Davis, David Brion. *The Problem of Slavery in the Age of Revolution, 1770–1823.* Ithaca, 1975.
Dorf, Philip. *The Builder: A Biography of Ezra Cornell.* New York, 1952.
Draper, John. *History of the Conflict Between Religion and Science.* New York, 1874.
Duberman, Martin. *Charles Francis Adams, 1807–1886.* Boston, 1961.
Ekirch, Arthur. *The Idea of Progress in America, 1815–1860.* New York, 1944.
Eliot, Charles W. *A Late Harvest.* Boston, 1924.
Ellmann, Richard. *Golden Codgers: Biographical Speculations.* New York, 1973.
Fleming, Donald. *John William Draper and the Religion of Science.* Philadelphia, 1950.
Foner, Eric. *Free Soil, Free Labor, Free Men.* New York, 1970.
Foster, John W. *Diplomatic Memoirs,* 2 vols. Boston and New York, 1909.
Franklin, Fabian. *The Life of Daniel Coit Gilman.* New York, 1910.
Fredrickson, George. *The Black Image in the White Mind.* New York, 1971.
Frieze, Henry. *A Memorial Discourse on the Life and Services of Henry Philip Tappan.* Ann Arbor, 1882.
Gilman, Daniel Coit. *The Launching of a University.* New York, 1906.
———. *University Problems in the United States.* New York, 1898.
Goldman, Eric. *Rendezvous with Destiny.* New York, 1952.
Goodstein, Anita Shafer. *Biography of a Businessman: Henry W. Sage.* Ithaca, 1962.
Grant, U. S. *Personal Memoirs of U. S. Grant,* 2 vols. New York, 1886.
Grimes, Alan P. *The Political Liberalism of the* New York Nation, *1865–1932.* Chapel Hill, N.C., 1953.
Haller, John, and Haller, Robin. *The Physician and Sexuality in Victorian America.* Urbana, Ill., 1974.
Hammond, Charles. *About the Bible.* New York, 1900.
Hawkins, Hugh. *Between Harvard and America: The Educational Leadership of Charles W. Eliot.* New York, 1972.
Herbst, Jurgen. *The German Historical School in American Scholarship.* Ithaca, 1965.
Hewett, Waterman T. *Cornell University: A History,* 4 vols. New York, 1905.
Higham, John. *History.* Englewood Cliffs, N.J., 1965.
Himmelfarb, Gertrude. *Darwin and the Darwinian Revolution.* New York, 1962.
Hofstadter, Richard. *The Paranoid Style in American Politics.* New York, 1965.
———. *Social Darwinism in American Thought.* Philadelphia, 1944.
Holls, Frederick W. *The Peace Conference at the Hague.* London, 1900.
Hoogenboom, Ari. *Outlawing the Spoils.* Urbana, Ill., 1961.
James, Henry. *Charles W. Eliot,* 2 vols. Boston, 1930.
Jones, Howard Mumford. *Moses Coit Tyler.* Ann Arbor, 1933.
Jordan, David. *Roscoe Conkling of New York.* Ithaca, 1971.
Jordan, David Starr. *Care and Culture of Men.* San Francisco, 1896.
Keim, Jeannette. *Forty Years of German–American Political Relations.* Philadelphia, 1919.
Kolko, Gabriel. *The Triumph of Conservatism.* New York, 1963.
Kurland, Gerald. *Seth Low.* New York, 1971.

LeFeber, Walter. *The New Empire*. Ithaca, 1963.

Larson, Orvin. *American Infidel: Robert G. Ingersoll*. New York, 1962.

Laserson, Max. *The American Impact on Russia, 1784–1917*. New York, 1950.

Lincoln, Charles Z. *Messages from the Governors*. Albany, 1909.

Lubove, Roy. *The Progressives and the Slums*. Pittsburgh, 1962.

McCormick, Thomas J. *China Market*. Chicago, 1967.

McLoughlin, William. *The Meaning of Henry Ward Beecher*. New York, 1970.

Madsen, David. *The National University: Enduring Dream of the U.S.A.* Detroit, 1966.

Magill, Edward. *An Address upon the Co-Education of the Sexes*. Philadelphia, 1873.

———. *Sixty-five Years in the Life of a Teacher, 1841–1906*. Boston and New York, 1907.

Mahan, Alfred T. *Armaments and Arbitration*. New York and London, 1911.

Marchand, C. Roland. *The American Peace Movement and Social Reform, 1898–1918*. Princeton, N.J., 1972.

Marty, Martin. *Righteous Empire: The Protestant Experience in America*. New York, 1970.

Mathews, Joseph. *George W. Smalley*. Chapel Hill, N.C., 1973.

May, Ernest. *Imperial Democracy*. New York, 1961.

Meyer, D. H. *The Instructed Conscience*. Philadelphia, 1972.

Milne, Gordon. *George William Curtis and the Genteel Tradition*. Bloomington, Ind., 1956.

Mohr, James. *The Radical Republicans and Reform in New York during Reconstruction*. Ithaca, 1973.

Nevins, Allan. *Hamilton Fish: The Inner History of the Grant Administration*. New York, 1936.

———. *The State Universities and Democracy*. Urbana, Ill., 1962.

Noble, David. *The Paradox of Progressive Thought*. Minneapolis, 1958.

Perry, Charles. *Henry Philip Tappan: Philosopher and University President*. Ann Arbor, 1933.

Persons, Stow. *The Decline of American Gentility*. New York, 1973.

Platt, Thomas Collier. *Autobiography*. New York, 1910.

Pletcher, David. *The Awkward Years*. Columbia, Mo., 1962.

Pobedonostsev, Konstantin. *Reflections of a Russian Statesman*. Trans. Robert C. Long. Ann Arbor, 1965.

Pratt, Julius. *Expansionists of 1898*. Boston, 1936.

Pringle, Henry. *Theodore Roosevelt: A Biography*. New York, 1931.

Rader, Benjamin. *The Academic Mind and Reform*. Louisville, Ky., 1966.

Rainsford, George. *Congress and Higher Education in the Nineteenth Century*. Knoxville, Tenn., 1972.

Richards, Leonard. *Gentlemen of Property and Standing*. New York, 1970.

Roberts, Isaac. *Autobiography of a Farm Boy*. Ithaca, 1946.

Rosenberg, Charles. *The Cholera Years*. Chicago, 1962.

Russell, William Howard. *My Diary North and South*, 2 vols. London, 1863.

Ryden, George. *The Foreign Policy of the United States in Relation to Samoa*. New Haven, Conn., 1933.

Schieber, Clara. *The Transformation of American Sentiment toward Germany*. Boston and New York, 1923.

Schwartz, Harold. *Samuel Gridley Howe: Social Reformer*. Cambridge, Mass., 1956.

Sheehan, Donald. *This Was Publishing*. Bloomington, Ind., 1952.

Smith, Timothy. *Revivalism and Social Reform in Mid-Nineteenth Century America*. New York, 1957.

Sproat, John. *The Best Men: Liberal Reformers in the Gilded Age*. New York and London, 1968.

Stampp, Kenneth. *The Era of Reconstruction*. New York, 1965.

Starr, Kevin. *Americans and the California Dream*. New York, 1973.

Stolberg-Wernigerode, Otto zu. *Germany and the United States of America during the Era of Bismarck*. Reading, Pa., 1937.

Straus, Oscar. *Under Four Administrations*. Boston, 1922.

Tansill, Charles. *The United States and Santo Domingo, 1798–1873*. Baltimore, 1938.

Tappan, Henry P. *University Education*. New York, 1851.

Tomsich, John. *A Genteel Endeavor*. Stanford, Calif., 1971.

Trefousse, Hans. *Benjamin Franklin Wade*. New York, 1963.

Unger, Irwin. *The Greenback Era*. Princeton, N.J., 1964.

Veysey, Lawrence. *The Emergence of the American University*. Chicago, 1965.

Walker, Mack. *Germany and the Emigration, 1816–1885*. Cambridge, Mass., 1964.

Welter, Rush. *The Mind of America, 1820–1860*. New York, 1975.

———. *Popular Education and Democratic Thought in America*. New York, 1962.

White, Edward. *Science and Religion in American Thought*. Stanford, Calif., 1952.

White, Horatio. *Willard Fiske: Life and Correspondence*. New York, 1925.

Whitehead, John. *The Separation of College and State*. New Haven, Conn., 1973.

Wiebe, Robert. *The Search for Order*. New York, 1967.

Wolf, Simon. *The American Jew as Patriot, Soldier, and Citizen*. Philadelphia, 1895.

Wright, Albert Hazen. *The Background of Andrew D. White, First President of Cornell University: His Ancestry*. Ithaca, 1960.

Wyllie, Irvin. *The Self-Made Man in America*. New Brunswick, N.J., 1954.

Zabriskie, Edward H. *American–Russian Rivalry in the Far East, 1895–1914*. Philadelphia, 1946.

ARTICLES

Adams, Charles Kendall. "Mr. White's Warfare of Science with Theology." *Forum* 22 (September 1896): 65–78.

Anonymous. "Andrew D. White's Special Plea for Private Ownership of Railways." *Arena* 34 (July 1905): 79–82.

———. "The Autobiography of Andrew D. White: Its Excellencies and Its Defects." *Arena* 34 (July 1905): 97–106.

———. "A Day with Andrew D. White at His Home in Ithaca." *Craftsman* 8 (September 1905): 714–34.

———. "Our Delegation to the Hague." *Review of Reviews* 19 (May 1899): 545–57.

———. "Possibilities at the Hague." *Nation* 68 (May 18, 1899).

———. Reviews of ADW, *A History of the Warfare of Science with Theology in Christendom*, in *American Historical Review* 2 (October 1896): 107–113; *Critic* 28 (June 27, 1896): 456; *Outlook* 53 (June 20, 1896): 1153; *Popular Science Monthly* 49 (August 1896): 560–62.

Battershall, Walton. Review of ADW, *A History of the Warfare of Science with Theology in Christendom*. *North American Review* 165 (July 1897): 87–98.

Beach, Mark. "Andrew D. White as Ex-President: The Plight of a Retired Reformer." *American Quarterly* 17 (Summer 1965): 239–47.

———. "President's Eye View of the History of Higher Education." *History of Education Quarterly* 12 (Winter 1972): 575–87.

Blake, Nelson. "Background of Cleveland's Venezuela Policy." *American Historical Review* 47 (January 1942): 259–77.

Blodgett, Geoffrey. "Frederick Law Olmsted: Landscape Architecture as Conservative Reform." *Journal of American History* 62 (March 1976): 869–89.

Burr, George Lincoln. "Andrew D. White." *Nation* 107 (November 17, 1918: 577–78.

———. "Sketch of Andrew D. White." *Popular Science Monthly* 48 (February 1896): 546–56.

Edwards, E. J. "Andrew D. White:Educator and Diplomat." *Review of Reviews* 26 (December 1902): 697–701.

Gilman, Daniel C. "The Cornell University." *Nation* 1 (July 6, 1865): 44–45.

Holls, Frederick W. "America at the Peace Conference." *Independent* 51 (December 28, 1899): 3470–75.

———. "The Results of the Peace Conference in Their Relation to the Monroe Doctrine." *American Monthly Review of Reviews* 20 (November 1899): 560–67.

Howe, Daniel Walker. "American Victorianism as a Culture. *American Quarterly* 27 (December 1975): 507–32.

Hull, Charles. "Andrew D. White." *World's Work* 4 (October 1902): 2675–77.

Johnston, R. M. "In the Clutch of the Harpy Powers." *North American Review* 169 (October 1899): 448–53.

Jordan, David Starr. Review of ADW, *A History of the Warfare of Science with Theology in Christendom. Dial* (September 16, 1896): 146–48.

Leverette, William, Jr. "E. L. Youmans' Crusade for Scientific Autonomy and Respectability." *American Quarterly* 21 (Spring 1965): 12–32.

Low, Seth. "The International Conference of Peace." *North American Review* 169 (November 1899): 625–39.

McFarland, Gerald. "The New York Mugwumps of 1884: A Profile." *Political Science Quarterly* 78 (March 1963): 40–58.

Mahan, Alfred T. "The Peace Conference and the Moral Aspect of War." *North American Review* 169 (October 1899): 433–47.

Meyer, D. H. "American Intellectuals and the Victorian Crisis of Faith." *American Quarterly* 27 (December 1975): 585–603.

Munger, Theodore T. "A Significant Biography." *Atlantic Monthly* 96 (October 1905): 556–66.

Nichols, Jeannette P. "Silver Diplomacy." *Political Science Quarterly* 48 (December 1933): 565–88.

Richardson, James. "Mayor Fernando Wood and the New York Police Force, 1855–1857." *New York Historical Society Quarterly* 50 (Winter 1966): 5–20.

Schurman, Jacob Gould. Review of ADW, *A History of the Warfare of Science with Theology in Christendom. Science* 4 (December 11, 1896): 879–81.

Snyder, Louis. "The American-German Pork Dispute, 1879–1891." *Journal of Modern History* 17 (March 1945): 16–28.

Tattler. "Notes From the Capital: Andrew D. White." *Nation* 102 (January 6, 1916): 11–12.

Von Diederichs, Admiral. "A Statement of Events in Manila Bay." *Journal of the Royal United Service Institution* 59 (August 1914): 421–46.

Von Schierbrand, Wolf. "Ambassador White's Work." *North American Review* 175 (November 1902): 632–41.

Whiton, James M. "Andrew D. White: Educator and Statesman." *Outlook* 80 (May 13, 1905): 132–37.

———. Obituary of Andrew D. White. *Outlook* 120 (November 20, 1918): 449–50.

Williams, Donald E. "Andrew D. White: Spokesman for the Free University." *Quarterly Journal of Speech* 47 (April 1961): 133–42.

Wood, Gordon. "The Massachusetts Mugwumps." *New England Quarterly* 33 (December 1960): 435–51.

Youmans, E. L. "The Accusation of Atheism." *Popular Science Monthly* 11 (July 1877): 367–70.

———. "The Conflict of Ages." *Popular Science Monthly* 8 (February 1876): 493–94.

THESES

Chapin, James. "Hamilton Fish and American Expansion." Ph.D. thesis, Cornell University, 1971.

Corson, Louis. "University Problems as Described in the Personal Correspondence of D. C. Gilman, A. D. White, and C. W. Eliot." Ph.D. thesis, Stanford University, 1951.

Moress, Jane. "Andrew D. White and George Lincoln Burr: The Building of an Historical Library." B.A. honors thesis, Cornell University, 1954.

Olson, Joan. "The Political Career of Andrew Dickson White." Master's thesis, Cornell University, 1958.

Peterson, Karl G. "Andrew D. White's Educational Principles: Their Sources, Development, Consequences." Ed.D. thesis, Stanford University, 1949.

Rogers, Walter P. "Andrew D. White and the Transition Period in American Higher Education." Ph.D. thesis, Cornell University, 1934.

Zimmerman, William. "Andrew D. White and the Role of the University Concerning Student Life." Ph.D. thesis, Cornell University, 1959.

Zurer, Victor. "Andrew D. White as Minister to Germany, 1879–1881." M.A. thesis, Cornell University, 1966.

Index

Andrew D. White—Educator, Historian, Diplomat

Designed by Elizabeth Leah Anderson.

Composed by Graphic Composition, Inc., in 10 point VIP Janson,
2 points leaded, with display lines in VIP Janson.

Printed offset by Thomson-Shore, Inc.
on Warren's Olde Style 60 lb. basis.

Bound by John H. Dekker & Sons, Inc., in Joanna book cloth
and stamped in All Purpose foil.

Library of Congress Cataloging in Publication Data
(For library cataloging purposes only)

Altschuler, Glenn C
  Andrew D. White, educator, historian, diplomat.

  Bibliography: p.
  Includes index.
    1. White, Andrew Dickson, 1832–1918.   2. Diplomats—United States—Biography.
3. Historians—United States—Biography.   4. College teachers—United States—Biog-
raphy.   I. Title.
E664.W58A57   973.8'092'4 [B]   78–58065
ISBN 0–8014–1156–4